The Global Tobacco Epidemic and the Law

For Max and Zoe

The Global Tobacco Epidemic and the Law

Edited by

Andrew D. Mitchell

Professor and Australian Research Council Future Fellow, Melbourne Law School, University of Melbourne, Australia

Tania Voon

Professor, Melbourne Law School, University of Melbourne, Australia

Edward Elgar

Cheltenham, UK • Northampton, MA, USA

Published by
Edward Elgar Publishing Limited
The Lypiatts
15 Lansdown Road
Cheltenham
Glos GL50 2JA
UK

Edward Elgar Publishing, Inc.
William Pratt House
9 Dewey Court
Northampton
Massachusetts 01060
USA

A catalogue record for this book
is available from the British Library

Library of Congress Control Number: 2014932600

This book is available electronically in the ElgarOnline.com
Law Subject Collection, E-ISBN 978 1 78347 152 2

ISBN 978 1 78347 151 5

Typeset by Columns Design XML Ltd, Reading
Printed and bound in Great Britain by T.J. International Ltd, Padstow

Contents

Contributors

Neil Boister
Professor, University of Waikato, Hamilton, New Zealand

Neil Boister is a Professor of Criminal Law, International Criminal Law and Transnational Criminal Law. His principal research interest for the last 15 years has been the suppression of transnational crime through international law. Neil's PhD from the University of Nottingham under the supervision of Professor David Harris was on the international drug conventions and resulted in the publication of *Penal Aspects of the UN Drug Conventions* (The Hague: Kluwer Law International, 2001). Since then he has broadened his interests to all forms of transnational crime. His book, entitled *An Introduction to Transnational Criminal Law*, was published by Oxford University Press in September 2012. He works as a consultant for NGOs in the area of the legal regulation of transnational crime and was involved in the development of the *Protocol to Eliminate Illicit Trade in Tobacco Products*. Finally, he is the author of a number of pieces in mainstream international criminal law including *The Tokyo International Military Tribunal, A Reappraisal* (Oxford University Press, 2008) and *Documents on the Tokyo International Military Tribunal* (both together with Professor Robert Cryer of the University of Birmingham).

Oscar A Cabrera
Executive Director, O'Neill Institute for National and Global Health Law; Visiting Professor of Law at Georgetown University Law Center, Washington, DC, United States

Oscar Cabrera is the Executive Director of the O'Neill Institute for National and Global Health Law and a Visiting Professor of Law at Georgetown University Law Center. He earned his law degree in his home country of Venezuela (Universidad Católica Andrés Bello) and his Master of Laws (LLM), with concentration in Health Law and Policy, at the University of Toronto. Before starting his master's degree program, Oscar worked as an Associate at a Venezuelan law firm (d'Empaire Reyna Bermúdez). Oscar has worked on projects with the World Health Organization, the Centers for Disease Control and Prevention, and the Campaign for Tobacco-Free Kids, among other organisations. He has studied and is interested in various health-law-related fields, such as health and human rights, sexual and reproductive rights, global tobacco litigation, and health systems law and policy.

Juan Carballo
PhD Candidate, National University of Córdoba, Córdoba, Argentina

Juan Carballo is currently a PhD candidate on Law and Social Sciences at the National University of Córdoba, Argentina, with a thesis under development on non-communicable diseases regulation from a human rights perspective. Carballo was a Law Fellow at the O'Neill Institute from 2009–11. He earned his law degree in his home country of Argentina at the National University of Córdoba, and his Master of Laws (LLM) at Georgetown University Law Center, sponsored by the Fulbright Commission. He has written papers and book chapters on constitutional law, environmental law and human rights, with a focus on the right to health.

Rob Cunningham
Senior Policy Analyst, Canadian Cancer Society, Ottawa, Canada

Rob Cunningham is a Senior Policy Analyst with the Canadian Cancer Society based in Ottawa. He has worked in tobacco control since 1988. He is the author of the book, *Smoke and Mirrors: The Canadian Tobacco War* (International Development Research Centre) and has been a contributor to numerous initiatives supporting the adoption of tobacco control legislation in Canada and internationally. Rob has appeared as a lawyer in cases concerning tobacco control, including in cases before the Supreme Court of Canada. In his capacity as a representative of an NGO, Rob has also participated in negotiations for the *WHO Framework Convention on Tobacco Control*.

Mark Davison
Professor, Monash Law School, Monash University, Melbourne, Australia

Mark Davison is Professor in the Faculty of Law at Monash University, special counsel with Knightsbridge Lawyers, and a member of the Australian Government's Expert Advisory Group on Plain Packaging of Tobacco Products. He is also a member of the Intellectual Property Committee of the Law Council of Australia. Mark is the author of all three editions of Shanahan's *Australian Law of Trade Marks and Passing Off* that have been published since the 1995 trademarks legislation was passed. Additionally, he has published *The Legal Protection of Databases* and two editions of *Australian Intellectual Property Law*, both of which were published by Cambridge University Press. Mark has also authored several casebooks and editions of those casebooks dealing with intellectual property and Australian trade practices law. In addition, he has written a number of book chapters and articles relating to plain packaging of tobacco.

Katherine DeLand
Managing Director and CEO, DeLand Associates, LLC, California, United States

Katherine DeLand founded DeLand Associates in 2011 to fill a growing niche for independent, flexible, highly trained and responsive consulting, advising and project management in international law, health and public policy. She focuses on multilateral negotiations, large-scale public health project management and donor relationships, and sustainable health and development policy design and implementation. She has worked in Switzerland, Kenya, Australia and the United States for organisations as diverse as the World Health Organization, the L'Etwal Foundation, the World Bank, the US Centers for Disease Control and Prevention, and the University of Sydney. She holds degrees in law, public health and biochemistry.

Lukasz Gruszczynski
Assistant Professor, Institute of Law Studies, Polish Academy of Sciences, Warsaw, Poland

Lukasz Gruszczynski is Assistant Professor of International Law at the Institute of Law Studies, Polish Academy of Sciences. He earned his PhD from the European University Institute in Florence in 2008. During his PhD studies, Lukasz was also a visiting researcher at the University of Michigan Law School and an intern at the Legal Affairs Division of the World Trade Organization. In 2010, he published *Regulating Health and Environmental Risks under WTO Law: A Critical Analysis of the SPS Agreement* with Oxford University Press. Lukasz's current research focuses on food safety, international trade law, including technical barriers to trade, and the regulation of tobacco products. His most recent book, edited with Wouter Werner (*Deference in International Courts and Tribunals: Standard of Review and the Margin of Appreciation*), will also be published by Oxford University Press and is expected in the second half of 2014. Lukasz is a managing editor of the *Polish Yearbook of International Law* and a correspondent editor of the *European Journal of Risk Regulation*.

Peter K Henning
Law Clerk, Appellate Court of Düsseldorf, Düsseldorf, Germany

Peter Henning is a Law Clerk at the Appellate Court of Düsseldorf. He studied law at the Heinrich-Heine-University of Düsseldorf (Dipl iur) focusing on international law and litigation. He is currently working on his doctoral thesis, dealing with *Advertising Bans for Tobacco Products in International, European and German Law*, with the Chair of German and Foreign Public Law, European Law and Public International Law, Professor Dr Ralph Alexander Lorz at the Heinrich-Heine-University of Düsseldorf. During his studies and doctoral studies, he has interned inter alia with the Corporate Group of Freshfields Bruckhaus Deringer LLP in Hamburg and Düsseldorf, Germany, and the Litigation Group of Noerr LLP in Berlin, Germany. He was previously the Executive Director at the Friends of the Düsseldorf Faculty of Law, the Alumni and Network Association of the Düsseldorf Faculty of Law, Germany.

Locknie Hsu
Associate Professor, School of Law, Singapore Management University, Singapore

Locknie Hsu is an Associate Professor and former Associate Dean at the School of Law, Singapore Management University (SMU). Her specialisations are in international trade and investment law, ASEAN integration law and dispute settlement, and she has published extensively on various issues in these fields. She received her LLB degree from the National University of Singapore (NUS) and her LLM degree from Harvard University. She is an Advocate and Solicitor of the Singapore Bar and practised commercial law until she joined the Faculty of Law, NUS. In early 2007, Locknie was appointed the first Singapore Academic Coordinator of the World Trade Organization-NUS *Regional Trade Policy Course* for Asia-Pacific government officials, in which she also co-taught WTO dispute settlement with WTO officers. Since joining the SMU School of Law in 2007, she has won three teaching awards for outstanding teaching. Locknie has worked with various government agencies and international organisations, including the Singapore Mission to the United Nations in Geneva, as well as the ICC International Court of Arbitration. She has conducted training sessions on trade law and policy, trade and health regulation, dispute settlement and negotiations and has undertaken consulting work with various agencies, such as the World Bank, during Vietnam's WTO accession process.

Jonathan Liberman
Director, McCabe Centre for Law and Cancer, Melbourne, Australia

Jonathan Liberman is Director of the McCabe Centre for Law and Cancer, a joint initiative of the Cancer Council Victoria and the Union for International Cancer Control. The McCabe Centre's mission is to contribute to the effective use of the law for cancer prevention, treatment, supportive care and research. Jonathan is a lawyer with 15 years' experience in legal and policy research, advice and advocacy on issues relating to cancer control at both domestic and global levels. Pursuant to an arrangement between the Secretariat to the *WHO Framework Convention on Tobacco Control* (WHO FCTC) and the Union for International Cancer Control, the McCabe Centre performs the functions of a WHO FCTC knowledge hub on matters within the Centre's expertise, in particular legal challenges to implementation of the WHO FCTC. In this role, the McCabe Centre supports the Convention Secretariat in facilitating the exchange of information and cooperation between parties to the WHO FCTC in relation to these matters. Jonathan is a member of the Australian government's expert advisory group on plain packaging and of the Standing Committee on Tobacco of the Inter-Governmental Committee on Drugs. He is a Senior Fellow of Melbourne Law School.

Gemma Lien
Legal Corporate Secretary, Public Health England, London, United Kingdom

Gemma Lien is the Legal Corporate Secretary of Public Health England, an executive agency of the Department of Health. Her prior experience includes time as a staff lawyer with the Convention Secretariat, *WHO Framework Convention on Tobacco Control*; consultant for the Tobacco Free Initiative, World Health Organization; and illegal-drug-use trend analyst with the Merseyside Police Department (United Kingdom). She has coordinated multilateral working groups and negotiations, drafted national legislation and policy and liaised with government ministries, diplomatic missions and intergovernmental and non-governmental organisations. She holds degrees in law, public international law and international relations (LLB, LLM, MA) and a postgraduate certificate in corporate governance and business ethics (PGCert).

Tsai-yu Lin
Professor, National Taiwan University College of Law, Taipei, Taiwan

Tsai-yu Lin is Professor of Law at National Taiwan University College of Law and the Director of the Asian Center for WTO and International

Health Law and Policy (ACWH) at National Taiwan University. Tsai-yu undertook her LLM at Edinburgh University (United Kingdom) and her PhD in Law at National Chengchi University (Taiwan). She has actively published books and articles in the areas of WTO laws, international investment law and international health law. Recent publications include 'Systemic Reflection on the *EC-IT Product* Case: Establishing an "Understanding" on Maintaining the Product Coverage of the Current Information Technology Agreement in the Face of Technological Change' (*Journal of World Trade*, 2011) and 'The Forgotten Role of WHO/International Health Regulations in Trade Responses to 2009 A/H1N1 Influenza Outbreak' (*Journal of World Trade*, 2010). She is also the commissioner of the International Trade Commission, Ministry of Economic Affairs, Taiwan; a member of the Editorial Committee of the *Asian Journal of WTO & International Health Law and Policy*; and a member of the Indicative List of Governmental and Non-Governmental Panellists for resolving WTO disputes. Tsai-yu currently advises the Taiwan Government on trade and related health law and policy issues.

Chang-fa Lo
Justice of the Constitutional Court, Taipei, Taiwan

Chang-fa Lo was appointed Justice of the Constitutional Court in Taiwan in October 2011 and is a part-time Professor at the National Taiwan University. Prior to his current position, Chang-fa was Chair Professor and Lifetime Distinguished Professor at National Taiwan University (NTU), Dean of the NTU College of Law, Director of the Asian Center for WTO and International Health Law and Policy of NTU College of Law (ACWH), Director of the Center for Ethics, Law and Society in Biomedicine and Technology of NTU, Commissioner of Taiwan's Fair Trade Commission (in charge of the competition law in Taiwan), Commissioner of Taiwan's International Trade Commission, and legal advisor for Taiwan's GATT/WTO accession negotiations. In his capacity as the Director of ACWH, Chang-fa launched two English-language journals: *Asian Journal of WTO and International Health Law and Policy* and *Contemporary Asia Arbitration Journal* in 2006 and 2008 respectively. In his capacity as Dean of NTU College of Law, he also launched an English-language journal, *NTU Law Review*. Prior to his teaching career, he practised law in Taipei. He received his SJD degree from Harvard University Law School in 1989. He was appointed by the WTO as a panellist for the case *Brazil – Retreaded Tyres* in 2006 and as a member of the Permanent Group of Experts under the Agreement on Subsidies and Countervailing Measures in 2008. He is author of 12 books, editor of four books, and author of about 70 journal papers.

Andrew D Mitchell

Professor, Melbourne Law School, University of Melbourne, Melbourne, Australia

Andrew Mitchell joined the faculty at Melbourne Law School in 2006 and is currently an Australian Research Council Future Fellow, Director of the Global Economic Law Network, and Assistant Director Research at the Melbourne School of Government. In 2007, following a nomination by the Australian Government, the WTO's Dispute Settlement Body added him to the Indicative List of Governmental and Non-Governmental Panellists to hear WTO disputes. He has law degrees from Melbourne Law School, Harvard Law School and the University of Cambridge. His previous employers include the International Monetary Fund, the Organisation for Economic Co-operation and Development, Davis Polk & Wardwell, and Allens Arthur Robinson (now Allens Linklaters). Andrew also consults for the private sector and governmental and non-governmental organisations including Telstra and the World Health Organization. He has over 80 academic publications and has taught at numerous other law schools in Canada, the US and Australia.

Leonid Shmatenko

Junior Research Fellow, Teaching Assistant and Doctoral Candidate, Heinrich-Heine-University, Düsseldorf, Germany; Law Clerk, Appellate Court of Düsseldorf, Düsseldorf, Germany

Leonid Shmatenko studied law at the Heinrich-Heine-University of Düsseldorf, Germany (Dipl iur), focusing on international law and arbitration. In 2008–09 he was part of the Heinrich-Heine-University of Düsseldorf Team to the 16th Willem C Vis International Commercial Arbitration Moot, which was awarded an honourable mention for its written submissions. Currently, Leonid Shmatenko is a Junior Research Fellow, Teaching Assistant and Doctoral candidate with the Chair of German and Foreign Public Law, European Law and Public International Law of Professor Dr Ralph Alexander Lorz at the Heinrich-Heine-University of Düsseldorf, Germany. His doctoral thesis deals with investment law and investor–state arbitration in Eastern Europe. During his studies, he has interned with the International Arbitration Groups of Freshfields Bruckhaus Deringer LLP in Paris (France), Clayton Utz in Sydney (Australia) and Orrick Hölters & Elsing in Düsseldorf (Germany). His research work focuses on the market of the Commonwealth of Independent States, international arbitration, investment law and international economic law. He has recently published numerous scholarly works on international arbitration.

Deepti Singh
Legal Consultant, Public Health Foundation of India, New Delhi, India

Deepti Singh is a Legal Adviser and public health policy specialist, having worked in the area of health policy and advocacy for more than five years. She has a Master's in Laws (Human Rights) from the National Law School of India University, Bangalore, India. She is working with the Public Health Foundation of India as a Legal Consultant and works closely with the Ministry of Health on the country's national tobacco control programme. Deepti provides legal aid to the Advocacy Forum for Tobacco Control, a coalition of 65 Indian NGOs and individuals working in the area of tobacco control in India. She is a member of the District-level Monitoring Committee on Tobacco Control formulated by the Directorate of Health and Family Welfare, Government of the National Capital Territory, Delhi to facilitate the enforcement of complaints related to an advertising ban of tobacco products under the Indian *Tobacco Control Act 2003*. She is also a nominated member and acting Director of Policy and Programmes for the Indian Centre for Alcohol Studies. Deepti has presented several papers on health policies in various global health and policy conferences and participated as a legal specialist in a number of talk shows on health policies. Her major areas of interest are public health policies; consumer activism; tobacco and alcohol control policy research and analysis, litigation; and integration of tobacco and alcohol control into other health and development programmes.

Jamie Strawbridge
Former Managing Editor, Inside US Trade, Washington, DC, United States

From 2008 through July 2013, Jamie Strawbridge served as the Managing Editor of *Inside US Trade*, a Washington-based journal that provides exclusive news on US trade issues for an expert audience. In that capacity, Jamie oversaw all news stories and analyses related to legal issues arising under the World Trade Organization and US free trade agreements, as well as all issues related to the intersection of trade disciplines and tobacco control efforts. From September 2012 through July 2013, he concurrently served as Chief Editor of *Inside US–China Trade*, a separate weekly publication focused on US–China trade and investment issues. Jamie has covered trade policy issues in Washington since 2006, and his work has been featured in media outlets ranging from the *Wall Street Journal* to Comedy Central's the *Colbert Report*. He has been called upon to deliver impartial analysis of trade policy developments, including on C-SPAN's *Washington Journal* and in conferences organised by business representatives. Jamie received his undergraduate degree in English from Williams College in 2004. He is currently pursuing his Juris Doctor degree from Georgetown University.

Todd Tucker
Gates Scholar, University of Cambridge, Cambridge, United Kingdom

Todd Tucker is a writer and researcher on global governance issues. His work has been cited in the *New York Times*, on CNN, and in many other press outlets and academic publications. From 2004 through mid-July 2012, Todd directed research on trade issues for the non-profit consumer group Public Citizen, where he edited the *Eyes on Trade* blog. Before that, he wrote on Latin American issues for the Center for Economic and Policy Research. In 2012, he was awarded a Gates Scholarship for the University of Cambridge, where he is writing on international investment arbitration from a social science perspective.

Tania Voon
Professor and Associate Dean (Research), Melbourne Law School, University of Melbourne, Melbourne, Australia

Tania Voon is Professor and Associate Dean (Research) at Melbourne Law School. She is a former Legal Officer of the Appellate Body Secretariat of the World Trade Organization (WTO) and has previously practised law with Mallesons Stephen Jaques (now King & Wood Mallesons) and the Australian Government Solicitor, and taught law at Georgetown University, the University of Western Ontario, the Australian National University, Monash University, and Bond University. Tania undertook her Master of Laws at Harvard Law School and her PhD in Law at the University of Cambridge. She has published widely in the areas of public international law and international economic law. She is the author of *Cultural Products and the World Trade Organization* (Cambridge: Cambridge University Press, 2007), a member of the Editorial Board of the *Journal of International Economic Law*, and a member of the Indicative List of Governmental and Non-Governmental Panellists for resolving WTO disputes. Tania has provided expert advice and training to entities such as Telstra, the Australian Department of Foreign Affairs and Trade, the WTO, and the World Health Organization, and NGOs such as Cancer Council Victoria.

Heather Wipfli

Associate Director, USC Institute for Global Health; Assistant Professor of Preventive Medicine and International Relations, University of Southern California, Los Angeles, United States

Heather Wipfli is the Associate Director of the USC Institute for Global Health and an Assistant Professor of Preventive Medicine and International Relations at the University of Southern California (USC). Her principal research interest over the past 15 years has been the global control and prevention of non-communicable disease. Heather received her PhD from the Graduate Institute of International and Development Studies at the University of Geneva, Switzerland. Prior to joining USC she served as a technical officer at the World Health Organization in the Tobacco Free Initiative and as Project Director at the Institute for Global Tobacco Control at the Johns Hopkins Bloomberg School of Public Health. She has published extensively on global tobacco control, capacity-building in low- and middle-income countries, global policy diffusion, and innovative global health curriculum. She has a forthcoming book on the development and implementation of the *WHO Framework Convention on Tobacco Control* published by Johns Hopkins University Press.

Chuan-Feng Wu

Assistant Research Professor, Institutum Iurisprudentiae Academia Sinica, Taipei, Taiwan

Chuan-Feng Wu serves as an Assistant Research Professor at Institutum Iurisprudentiae, Academia Sinica and has a joint appointment as Assistant Professor at the Institute of Health and Welfare Policy, National Yang-Ming University. He received his JSD from the University of California, Berkeley, and LLM from Harvard Law School. In addition to degrees in law, Chuan-Feng also holds a master's degree in Health and Welfare Policy. His specialty fields of study include healthcare laws and ethics, international human rights and the right to health, and healthcare distributive justice. Chuan-Feng's recent works include 'State Responsibility for Tobacco Control: The Right to Health Perspective', 'Transnational Pharmaceutical Corporations' Legal and Moral Human Rights Responsibilities in Relation to Access to Medicines', 'Can Compulsory Health Insurance Be Justified? An Examination of Taiwan's National Health Insurance', 'An Appraisal of the Global Pharmaceutical Intellectual Property Framework from the Right to Health Perspective' (in Chinese), and 'Benefits with Boundaries: Healthcare Distribution and Medical Technology Development' (in Chinese).

Amit Yadav

Legal Consultant, Public Health Foundation of India, New Delhi, India

Amit Yadav is a registered advocate with the Bar Council of India and a member of the Delhi and Saket Bar Associations in New Delhi. He works as a Legal Consultant at the Public Health Foundation of India and as a Manager-Legal at HRIDAY (Health-Related Information Dissemination Amongst Youth). As part of his work, Amit has undertaken various advocacy and capacity-building efforts in tobacco control, including preparation of policy briefs and interaction with key policymakers, corporate leaders and parliamentarians alike. Amit guides policy research on health issues and provides legal inputs on all policy-related outcomes and activities, including preparation of policy briefs and policy recommendations based on the project results. He has a keen interest in various aspects of public health, having handled a wide range of legal research on public health laws and policies including the *WHO Framework Convention on Tobacco Control*, the *Cigarettes and Other Tobacco Products Act*, the *Right to Information Act*, the *Consumer Protection Act*, the *National Health Bill*, and the *Alternative Reproduction Treatment Bill*. Amit holds an LLM (with two Gold Medals) and an MPhil degree from the National Law School of India University, Bangalore. He has written more than 20 publications, including manuscripts, reports, monographs and abstracts on various issues related to tobacco control, public health law and other developmental issues. Amit is a member of the Institutional Review Boards of the Indian Institute of Public Health, New Delhi and the Centre for Chronic Disease Control, New Delhi.

Acknowledgments

We gratefully acknowledge the funds provided for independent research by the Australian National Preventive Health Agency (Grant ID 203MIT2011) and the Australian Research Council pursuant to the Linkage Project scheme (project number LP120200028), which assisted in various aspects of the production of this volume. We also appreciate the support provided by Melbourne Law School and the University of Melbourne.

We are especially grateful to Devon Whittle for his helpful research and editorial assistance with numerous chapters, and for similar assistance we thank Georgina Dimopoulos, Caroline Henckels, Stephen Lloyd and Shawn Rajanayagam. Thank you also to Catherine Gascoigne for assistance in the initial stages of conception of this volume, and to Thijs De Jong for compilation of the bibliography. Jessica Casben shepherded the proofs through the final stages and compiled the index, along with Mariela Maidana-Eletti.

Several chapters in this volume (Chapters 6, 7, 9, 10 and 11) developed from papers first published as part of the *Transnational Dispute Management* special issue we edited on 'Legal Issues in Tobacco Control' (volume 9, issue 5) in November 2012, available at www.transnational-dispute-management.com, and are incorporated with the kind permission of Anton Hoenson.

The opinions expressed in each chapter are those of the relevant authors and are not necessarily shared by any employer or other entity.

1. Introduction

Andrew D Mitchell and Tania Voon

Although the harms of tobacco smoking have been long known, they continue to be felt around the world. Close to 6 million deaths are attributable to tobacco smoking and second-hand smoke each year:[1]

> Tobacco kills more than tuberculosis, [HIV/AIDS] and malaria combined. In the next two decades, the annual death toll from tobacco is expected to rise to over 8 million, with more than 80% of those deaths projected to occur in low- and middle-income countries. If effective measures are not urgently taken, tobacco could, in the 21st century, kill over 1 billion people.[2]

Tobacco regulation thus forms a key part of responding to this acknowledged global epidemic.[3]

As tobacco regulation has intensified around the world, tobacco companies have used increasingly bold domestic and international legal challenges to defeat or delay stronger regulation. This volume offers a range of perspectives on these various legal challenges, exploring first the twin areas of international law that impact significantly on this field – international health law, and international trade and investment law[4] – and then the different jurisdictional backgrounds in which tobacco regulation operates. Part I of the book introduces the World Health Organization (WHO) in the context of tobacco control, including the key instruments of the *WHO Framework Convention on Tobacco Control* (WHO FCTC)[5] and the recently concluded *Protocol to Eliminate Illicit Trade in Tobacco Products*.[6] Part II addresses the implications for tobacco control of international trade law and international investment law, including under the World Trade Organization (WTO), and bilateral and regional agreements for the liberalisation of trade and investment. In Part III, the book showcases the current state of regulating tobacco in several countries and regions around the world. While not every continent could be represented, each chapter provides insights into the kinds of legal and political battles being faced locally in the pursuit of tobacco regulation. Some areas face similar challenges, while others present unique circumstances. Africa, for example, which is not covered here, has relatively low smoking rates but must now fight upward trends created by economic growth and other factors (for example by preventing take-up of smoking and increase in the number of cigarettes smoked per smoker);[7] in contrast, several of the developed countries examined in Part III have succeeded in significantly reducing smoking rates but now face the challenge of maintaining and deepening those reductions (for example through smoking cessation).

The chapters in this volume were finalised at various times in 2013, and ongoing events throughout the year demonstrated the significance of the topic to the global community. As 2013 has drawn to a close, among the most significant international issues on the tobacco control landscape are the international legal challenges continuing against Australia and Uruguay. The challenge to Uruguay's tobacco packaging and labelling requirements is brought by a Philip Morris company in Switzerland[8] under a bilateral investment treaty between Switzerland and Uruguay,[9] as discussed elsewhere.[10] The corresponding challenge to Australia's mandatory standardised tobacco packaging requirements (so-called 'plain' tobacco packaging) is brought by Philip Morris Asia Limited[11] under a bilateral investment treaty between Australia and Hong Kong.[12] In addition, several countries (five at the time of writing) have challenged these Australian laws within the World Trade Organization.[13] We have explored elsewhere these trade and investment law challenges to plain packaging as implemented in Australia.[14] The chapters in this volume provide a wealth of material for better understanding these different legal challenges against Australia and Uruguay, including through background on the obligations of Australia and Uruguay as parties to the WHO FCTC in Part I, exploration of tobacco control issues under international trade and investment law in Part II, and closer examination of plain tobacco packaging in the domestic context of Australia (Chapter 14) and the regional context of Europe (Chapter 11) in Part III.

Another key concern about tobacco control that has dominated domestic and international debate throughout 2013 arises from the *Trans-Pacific Partnership Agreement* (TPP) currently being negotiated between 12 countries, including the United States,[15] which will further liberalise trade and investment between the parties across a wide range of areas when the treaty is implemented.[16] Negotiations were expected to conclude in 2013[17] but are now likely to end in 2014.[18] If tobacco is included in the TPP along with other goods, this would likely mean that parties would accept obligations, for example, to reduce tariffs on tobacco imports, not to discriminate against imported tobacco products, and to treat foreign tobacco company investors fairly and equitably. The potential for the TPP to apply to tobacco products has therefore raised concerns among many commentators from the perspective of public health,[19] while others have pointed out that many trade agreements recognise health objectives through explicit exceptions[20] and that domestically produced tobacco is generally no less harmful than imported tobacco.[21] The United States' role in conjunction with proposals to 'carve out' tobacco from the TPP[22] is examined in detail in Chapter 10 of this volume. A separate Malaysian proposal regarding tobacco has also now been put forward.[23]

The significance of the treatment of tobacco under the final TPP treaty is heightened by the likely inclusion of investor-state dispute settlement (ISDS) in the TPP, which will allow foreign investors to bring legal challenges against TPP parties alleging violation of the investment obligations under the treaty, just as has happened in the current cases against Australia and Uruguay mentioned above. The previous Australian Government's position had been, since 2011, not to pursue ISDS where this would provide foreign investors with greater protections than domestic investors[24] – a position reflected in a leaked draft text of the investment chapter of the TPP, which showed that only Australia would not be covered by the ISDS provisions being contemplated.[25] However, the new Australian Government elected in September 2013 has returned to the previous approach of including ISDS in international investment agreements on a case-by-case basis.[26] Evidence of implementation of this approach is seen in the conclusion in late 2013 of a preferential trade and investment agreement between Australia and Korea, which includes an ISDS mechanism.[27] In connection with the TPP, Australia has stated that ISDS is now on the table.[28] Because of the threat of a tobacco industry claim against TPP parties, if tobacco is included in a treaty including ISDS, the need for appropriate public health exceptions and clarification of the scope of parties' obligations becomes all the more apparent.

As foreshadowed above, Part I of this volume addresses tobacco control in the context of the World Health Organization in order to provide an understanding of the general international health landscape in which domestic tobacco control operates. In Chapter 2, Katherine DeLand, Gemma Lien and Heather Wipfli provide an insightful history and up-to-date reflection on the global significance of the WHO FCTC, a cornerstone of international tobacco control efforts with currently 177 parties.[29] This is followed in Chapters 3 and 4 by contrasting discussions of the legal significance of the WHO FCTC and its associated implementing guidelines and protocols by Chang-fa Lo and Jonathan Liberman respectively. While Lo points to the important role played by guidelines and protocols in extending the WHO FCTC, Liberman emphasises the legally binding nature of the treaty and the significance of the guidelines in its proper interpretation under international law. Neil Boister ends Part I in Chapter 5 with a detailed examination of the rather surprising role played by the European Anti-Fraud Office in the development of the *Protocol to Eliminate Illicit Trade in Tobacco Products*.[30]

Part II of this volume contains five chapters exploring different aspects of the complex field of international trade law and international investment law as they relate to tobacco control measures. Todd Tucker begins in Chapter 6 with an elucidation of the legal challenge brought by Indonesia under the WTO dispute settlement mechanism against the United States ban on flavoured cigarettes. The WTO's Appellate Body found the United States in violation of some of its WTO obligations in that dispute – including article 2.1 of the WTO's *Agreement on Technical Barriers to Trade* (TBT Agreement)[31] – because of the discriminatory impact of the ban on imported products (specifically clove cigarettes, primarily imported from Indonesia) in comparison with 'like' domestic products (specifically menthol cigarettes, primarily produced in the United States and exempt from the ban).[32] The decision must be carefully examined in detail to be able to understand the nuances of its implications for tobacco control and public health more generally. Tucker cautions against the potential for WTO rulings to weaken domestic public interest regulation in areas such as tobacco control, where domestic politics and policy objectives must be carefully balanced. The dispute is continuing because the parties cannot agree on whether the United States has properly implemented the adverse ruling against it.[33] Specifically, rather than removing the exemption from the ban for menthol cigarettes, the United States is undertaking further investigations of the appropriateness of a ban from a health perspective, through its Food and Drug Administration.[34]

Lukasz Gruszczynski goes on in Chapter 7 to assess whether the WHO FCTC could constitute an 'international standard' for the purposes of the TBT Agreement, a question that could arise in the current WTO challenges involving Australia's plain tobacco packaging scheme. Article 2.2 of the TBT Agreement requires that WTO members' 'technical regulations' not be 'more trade-restrictive than necessary to fulfil a legitimate objective' such as 'protection of human health'. Article 2.5 states that '[w]henever a technical regulation is prepared, adopted or applied for one of the legitimate objectives explicitly mentioned' in article 2.2 'and is in accordance with relevant international standards, it shall be rebuttably presumed not to create an unnecessary obstacle to international trade'. If the WHO FCTC and its associated guidelines constitute an international standard, this would lend weight to a WTO member such as Australia responding to a challenge against a tobacco control measure under article 2.2. Article 2.2 may be particularly significant for Australia because, unlike the United States flavouring ban, plain tobacco packaging does not obviously discriminate in its effects against imported products. Gruszczynski concludes that 'there are good grounds for regarding the WHO FCTC and its guidelines as "relevant international standards" for the purpose of the TBT Agreement'.

In Chapter 8, Lin examines the implications of ISDS for tobacco control measures, concluding that the structure and operation of the ISDS system does not provide an appropriate forum for resolving challenges to such measures. Chapters 9 and 10 provide a suitable lead in to Part III of the volume, with Locknie Hsu examining tobacco control in the ten countries that make up the Association of Southeast Asian Nations, and Jamie Strawbridge addressing tobacco and trade policy under the Obama Administration in the United States. Both chapters address issues concerning international trade while focusing on challenges for tobacco control in particular regions. Both chapters include discussion of the importance of the TPP negotiations for tobacco control.

Part III of this volume provides case studies of tobacco control in particular areas of the world. Chapters 11 and 14 focus on the specific case of plain tobacco packaging, with Peter Henning and Leonid Shmatenko evaluating the potential for plain packaging in the European Union in Chapter 11, and Mark Davison explaining the failed challenge to plain packaging in Australia's highest court in Chapter 14. These chapters offer useful comparisons of one particular tobacco control measure in different geographic, legal and political contexts. Chapters 12 and 13 focus on the Americas, with masterful explications of tobacco control in Canada by Rob Cunningham and in Latin America by Oscar Cabrera and Juan Carballo. The book concludes with a focus on Asia, looking at the different circumstances faced in Taiwan and India in Chapters 15 (by Chuan-Feng Wu) and 16 (by Amit Yadav and Deepti Singh) respectively.

We hope that Part III of this volume in particular will offer lessons for other countries and regions, illustrating the difficulties that have been faced by tobacco control over the years in different places, and the solutions and steps that have been taken to overcome these difficulties. Together with the broader international law discussions in Parts I and II, the volume is intended to offer hope for the ongoing international disputes, clarifying the relevant complex areas of law and showing how they can interact effectively with domestic policy. Celebrations of the endgame for tobacco are arguably premature[35] – much more remains to be done – but the progress made to date in tobacco control can nevertheless be acknowledged and the path cleared for its continuation, despite legal hurdles.

NOTES

1. World Health Organization, 'WHO Global Report: Mortality Attributable to Tobacco' (World Health Organization, 2012) 4.
2. Ibid (citations omitted).
3. See generally, eg, World Health Organization, 'Report on the Global Tobacco Epidemic, 2013: Enforcing Bans on Tobacco Advertising, Promotion and Sponsorship' (World Health Organization, 2013).
4. See generally Benn McGrady, *Confronting the Tobacco Epidemic in a New Era of Trade and Investment Liberalization* (World Health Organization, 2012).
5. *WHO Framework Convention on Tobacco Control*, opened for signature 16 June 2003, 2302 UNTS 166 (entered into force 27 February 2005).
6. WHO FCTC Conference of the Parties, *Protocol to Eliminate Illicit Trade in Tobacco Products*, WHO Doc FCTC/COP5(1) (12 November 2012).
7. See generally Evan Blecher and Hana Ross, *Tobacco Use in Africa: Tobacco Control through Prevention* (American Cancer Society, 2013).
8. See, eg, *Philip Morris Brands Sàrl v Uruguay (Decision on Jurisdiction)* (ICSID Arbitral Tribunal, Case No ARB/10/7, 2 July 2013).
9. *Agreement between the Swiss Confederation and the Oriental Republic of Uruguay on the Reciprocal Promotion and Protection of Investments*, signed 7 October 1988, 1976 UNTS 389 (entered into force 22 April 1991).
10. Benn McGrady, 'Implications of Ongoing Trade and Investment Disputes: Philip Morris v Uruguay' in Andrew Mitchell, Tania Voon and Jonathan Liberman with Glyn Ayres (eds), *Public Health and Plain Packaging Of Cigarettes: Legal Issues* (Edward Elgar, 2012) 173.
11. See, eg, *Philip Morris Asia Ltd v Australia (Procedural Order No 7)* (Permanent Court of Arbitration, Case No 2012-12, UNCITRAL Arbitration Rules, 31 December 2012).
12. *Agreement between the Government of Hong Kong and the Government of Australia for the Promotion and Protection of Investments*, signed 15 September 1993, 1748 UNTS 385 (entered into force 15 October 1993).
13. *Australia – Certain Measures Concerning Trademarks and Other Plain Packaging Requirements Applicable to Tobacco Products and Packaging: Request for the Establishment of a Panel by Ukraine*, WTO Doc WT/DS434/11 (17 August 2012); *Australia – Certain Measures Concerning Trademarks, Geographical Indications and Other Plain Packaging Requirements Applicable to Tobacco Products and Packaging: Request for the Establishment of a Panel by Honduras*, WTO Doc WT/DS435/16 (17 October 2012); *Australia – Certain Measures Concerning Trademarks, Geographical Indications and Other Plain Packaging Requirements Applicable to Tobacco Products and Packaging: Request for the Establishment of a Panel by the Dominican Republic*, WTO Doc WT/DS441/15 (14 November 2012); *Australia – Certain Measures Concerning Trademarks, Geographical Indications and Other Plain Packaging Requirements Applicable to Tobacco Products and Packaging: Request for Consultations by Cuba*, WTO Doc WT/DS458/1 (7 May 2013); *Australia – Certain Measures Concerning Trademarks, Geographical Indications and Other*

Plain Packaging Requirements Applicable to Tobacco Products and Packaging: Request for Consultations by Indonesia, WTO Doc WT/DS467/1 (25 September 2013).

14. Tania Voon and Andrew Mitchell, 'Time to Quit? Assessing International Investment Claims Against Plain Tobacco Packaging in Australia (2011) 14(3) *Journal of International Economic Law* 515; Tania Voon and Andrew Mitchell, 'Face Off: Assessing WTO Challenges to Australia's Scheme for Plain Tobacco Packaging' (2011) 22(3) *Public Law Review* 218.

15. The countries are Australia, Brunei Darussalam, Canada, Chile, Japan, Malaysia, Mexico, New Zealand, Peru, Singapore, the United States, and Vietnam: *Statement of the Ministers and Heads of Delegation for the Trans-Pacific Partnership countries* (10 December 2013) Australian Government, Department of Foreign Affairs and Trade <http://www.dfat.gov.au/fta/tpp/131210-tpp-leadership-statement.html>.

16. See generally Tania Voon (ed), *Trade Liberalisation and International Co-operation: A Legal Analysis of the Trans-Pacific Partnership Agreement* (Edward Elgar, 2013); CL Lim, Deborah Elms and Patrick Low (eds), *The Trans-Pacific Partnership: A Quest for a Twenty-first Century Trade Agreement* (Cambridge University Press, 2012); Jane Kelsey (ed), *No Ordinary Deal: Unmasking the Trans-Pacific Partnership Free Trade Agreement* (Allen & Unwin, 2010).

17. *Trans-Pacific Partnership Leaders Statement* (8 October 2013) Australian Government, Department of Foreign Affairs and Trade <http://www.dfat.gov.au/fta/tpp/131008-tpp-leadership-statement.html>.

18. See *Statement of the Ministers*, above n 15.

19. See, eg, Jane Kelsey, 'The Trans-Pacific Partnership Agreement: A Gold-Plated Gift to the Global Tobacco Industry?' (2013) 39 *American Journal of Law & Medicine* 237; Deborah Gleeson and Sharon Friel, 'Emerging Threats to Public Health from Regional Trade Agreements' (2013) 381 *The Lancet* 1507.

20. See, eg, *General Agreement on Tariffs and Trade*, LT/UR/A-1A/1/GATT/2 (signed 30 October 1947), as incorporated in *Marrakesh Agreement Establishing the World Trade Organization*, opened for signature 15 April 1994, 1867 UNTS 3 (entered into force 1 January 1995) annex 1A (*General Agreement on Tariffs and Trade 1994*) article XX(b).

21. See, eg, Simon Lester, 'Free Trade and Tobacco: Thank You for Not Smoking (Foreign) Cigarettes' (15 August 2012) 49 *Free Trade Bulletin* 1, 4.

22. Office of the United States Trade Representative, *Fact Sheet: TPP Tobacco Proposal* (18 May 2012); Office of the United States Trade Representative, *Fact Sheet: New US Proposal on Tobacco Regulation in the Trans-Pacific Partnership* (21 August 2013).

23. 'Malaysia Poised to Table Complete Carveout from TPP for Tobacco Measures' (25 August 2013) *Inside US Trade* (online); Carey Biron, 'US, Malaysia Skirmish over Free-Trade Tobacco' (7 September 2013) *Inter Press Service* (online).

24. Australian Government, Department of Foreign Affairs and Trade, *Gillard Government Trade Policy Statement: Trading Our Way to More Jobs and Prosperity* (April 2011) 14. See also Australian Productivity Commission, *Bilateral and Regional Trade Agreements: Productivity Commission Research Report* (2010) 271–4.

25. Available at <http://www.citizenstrade.org/ctc/wp-content/uploads/2012/06/tpp investment.pdf>.

26. See, eg, Julie Bishop, *Free Trade Focus* (28 March 2013).

27. Tony Abbott and Andrew Robb, 'Australia concludes FTA negotiations with the Republic of Korea' (Joint Media Release, 5 December 2013); *Korea-Australia FTA (KAFTA) – Key Outcomes* (2013) Australian Government, Department of Foreign Affairs and Trade <http://dfat.gov.au/fta/akfta/fact-sheet-key-outcomes.pdf> 3. (The treaty text itself is unavailable to the public at the time of writing.)

28. 'Minister: Australia Open to ISDS in TPP if Other Countries Give on Tariffs' (13 December 2013) 31(49) *Inside US Trade* (online).
29. *Parties to the WHO Framework Convention on Tobacco Control* (27 November 2013) WHO FCTC <http://www.who.int/fctc/signatories_parties/en/>.
30. See above n 6.
31. *Marrakesh Agreement Establishing the World Trade Organization*, opened for signature 15 April 1994, 1867 UNTS 3 (entered into force 1 January 1995), annex 1A (*Agreement on Technical Barriers to Trade*).
32. Appellate Body Report, *United States – Measures Affecting the Production and Sale of Clove Cigarettes*, WTO Doc WT/DS406/AB/R (adopted 24 April 2012) [298(a)(v)]. See also Tania Voon, 'International Decision: *United States – Measures Affecting the Production and Sale of Clove Cigarettes*' (2012) 106(4) *American Journal of International Law* 824.
33. WTO, *United States – Measures Affecting the Production and Sale of Clove Cigarettes: Recourse to Article 22.2 of the DSU by Indonesia*, WTO Doc WT/DS406/12 (13 August 2013). See also 'US, Indonesia Clash over Cross-Retaliation in Clove Cigarette Dispute' (6 September 2013) 31(35) *Inside US Trade* (online).
34. *Menthol in Cigarettes, Tobacco Products; Request for Comments*, 78 Fed Reg 44484 (24 July 2013). See also Jamie Strawbridge, 'US Implementation of Adverse WTO Rulings: A Closer Look at the Tuna-Dolphin, COOL, and Clove Cigarettes Cases' (30 October 2013) 17(23) *ASIL Insights* (online).
35. The *International Conference on Public Health Priorities in the 21st Century: The Endgame for Tobacco* was held in New Delhi, India, from 10 to 12 September 2013, under the auspices of the Public Health Foundation of India and Health Related Information Dissemination Amongst Youth (HRIDAY).

PART I

Tobacco control in the context of the World
Health Organization

2. The WHO Framework Convention on Tobacco Control and the Tobacco Free Initiative

Katherine DeLand, Gemma Lien and Heather Wipfli

I INTRODUCTION

Tobacco use is one of the most serious public health threats facing the global population. Nearly 6 million deaths per year – one every 6 seconds – are attributable to tobacco use,[1] and one out of every ten adult deaths is tobacco-related.[2] More than 5 million of those deaths are due to direct tobacco use, while 600 000 are attributable to exposure to second-hand tobacco smoke.[3] The total number is expected to rise to 8.3 million by 2030.[4] Most tobacco-related deaths occur in low- and middle-income countries,[5] and all of them are preventable.

In 1996, recognising the critical nature of the tobacco-related health crisis, the member states of the World Health Organization (WHO) decided to take concerted action, adopting Resolution 49.17, which initiated development of a 'framework convention on tobacco control'. Under article 19 of the *Constitution of the World Health Organization* (WHO Constitution),[6] the WHO has the legal authority to develop binding treaties on health-relevant issues. Exercising this power for the first time in its history, an intergovernmental negotiating body comprising all the WHO member states was established in 1999, and the treaty – the *WHO Framework Convention on Tobacco Control* (WHO FCTC)[7] – was finalised and adopted in 2003.

As the first legally binding, coordinated global health governance response to non-communicable disease, the WHO FCTC marks a watershed in public health history. This chapter explores the development and negotiation of the WHO FCTC, as well as the core elements of the treaty's final text. Specifically, the chapter (i) identifies shifts in the global tobacco control environment in the late 1900s leading to the development and adoption of the WHO FCTC; (ii) examines the main events and processes of the WHO FCTC negotiations; and (iii) reviews the core elements of the final treaty text.

II THE GLOBALISATION OF THE TOBACCO INDUSTRY AND THE TOBACCO EPIDEMIC

The foundations of the global tobacco market were laid in the early years of the twentieth century.[8] During the first decades, the structure of the modern tobacco industry was formed and its political influence solidified. Also at this time, the tobacco industry first tested revolutionary new advertising techniques and learned the powerful influence advertising had on its business. In high-income countries, public acceptance of cigarette smoking quickly increased, and consumption began to rise. For example, between 1930 and 1940, per capita cigarette consumption in the United States doubled to 2558 per annum, and by 1939, 66 per cent of American men under the age of 40 were smokers.[9]

However, the rise in popular cigarette use was accompanied by some worrying disease trends. By 1930, the incidence of lung cancer in the United Kingdom (UK) was rising five times faster than that of all other cancers, giving the UK the highest rate of lung cancer in the world. By 1948, lung cancer had become the second most common type of cancer among British men.[10] Other countries with comparable smoking rates experienced similar trends.

Throughout the 1950s, the scientific community focused research on the link between smoking and rising cancer rates, with data implicating tobacco use to the unprecedented changes in national cancer profiles. In 1962 and 1964, respectively, the United Kingdom Royal College of Physicians and the Advisory Committee to the United States Surgeon General issued reports entitled 'Smoking and Health'. Both reports concluded that cigarette smoking was causally related to lung cancer and recommended legislative action to control its use.[11]

The release of the reports marked the peak of cigarette consumption in many Western countries and the beginning of modern tobacco control efforts. With the increased awareness of the health harms of tobacco use and the development of a solid base of evidence on which tobacco control policies are most effective, significant reductions in tobacco consumption began to be seen in many high-income countries and some developing countries. For example, in the 1960s, 50 per cent of the adult male population of the United States (US) smoked, and by 1970 nearly 75 per cent of Polish men smoked.[12] In 2003, thanks to aggressive tobacco control programmes, smoking prevalence decreased to 25 per cent and roughly 40 per cent among US and Polish men, respectively.[13] Concurrently, between 1985 and 2000, lung cancer deaths in men decreased in many European countries: the UK (down 38 per cent), Finland (down 36 per cent), the Netherlands (down 29 per cent), Luxembourg (down 24 per cent), Austria (down 23 per cent) and Ireland (down 22 per cent).[14]

However, while progress was being made in reducing tobacco consumption in Europe and the US, the concurrent increase in social, economic and political globalisation created new challenges for controlling tobacco use worldwide. Between 1970 and 1998, the tobacco industry underwent a complete transformation, becoming a fully globalised, transnational enterprise.[15] Prior to the 1980s, large tobacco companies mainly exported cigarettes from facilities in the US and Western Europe.[16] In the last few decades of the twentieth century, the bulk of tobacco production moved to low- and middle-income countries.[17]

Overall global tobacco production grew by 128 per cent between 1975 and 1998; in that same period, production in developed countries fell by 31 per cent.[18] Land in the US devoted to tobacco-growing was halved, while it almost doubled in China, Malawi and the Republic of Tanzania.[19] By 1998, four companies controlled 75 per cent of the world's cigarette market: Philip Morris, British American Tobacco, Japan Tobacco and the China National Tobacco Corporation.[20] The latter's share was almost entirely attributable to its near monopoly over the enormous Chinese market, but the others were tireless in their pursuit of worldwide sales. The major transnational tobacco companies established a presence in almost every country. By the late 1990s, each of the three largest transnational tobacco companies owned or leased manufacturing facilities in over 50 countries.[21]

Three central factors fuelled the tobacco industry's global expansion and consolidation: first, the formerly closed economies in the former Soviet Union, Eastern Europe and China were opened to international trade;[22] second, the World Bank and International Monetary Fund exerted pressure on countries to liberalise foreign investment laws and privatise state-owned tobacco companies;[23] and last, the free trade areas in Asia and Latin America saw substantial expansion.[24] By the mid-1990s, smoking prevalence rates among men in many low- and middle-income countries reached an estimated 60 per cent.[25] Where female smokers were previously uncommon, industry penetration and marketing resulted in increased prevalence, especially among young women.[26] As the tobacco industry globalised, increasing its reach and market presence, the country-level profiles of tobacco-related burden of disease grew increasingly similar, regardless of country income level.

In 1999, it was estimated that if the then-current level of consumption continued, by 2030, tobacco use would kill up to 10 million people annually, with 70 per cent of those deaths occurring in developing countries.[27] It was further forecast that if use was unchecked by 2030, tobacco would be both the leading cause of premature mortality in industrialised nations and the leading cause of avoidable death worldwide.[28]

Armed with such alarming statistics, the WHO's normative approach to tobacco control called for the health burden created by tobacco consumption to be viewed as an epidemic of a 'communicated disease', with the tobacco industry and its commercial practices as the 'vector' of that disease.[29] The WHO also recognised that the negative consequences of tobacco use were broader and more cross-cutting than the adverse impact on individual health. Tobacco also presents development and economic concerns, including the link between tobacco use and poverty, as exemplified in low-income households where it was noted that tobacco purchases diverted scarce family resources away from food and other basic needs, and that those diversions could result in malnutrition, among other problems.[30] Additionally, the evidence regarding the public health and environmental damage caused by tobacco cultivation practices was growing, suggesting that tobacco was a concern throughout the entirety of its production cycle.

It became increasingly clear to the WHO and to tobacco control advocates throughout the world that singular, country-level tobacco control efforts would not be enough to counter an unregulated global tobacco industry. The tobacco epidemic presents a range of transnational issues that require multinational cooperation and effective international action.

III PAVING THE WAY FOR THE WHO FCTC

The idea of an international treaty on tobacco control negotiated under the auspices of the WHO had been mentioned in academic writings and WHO expert committee reports as early as 1979.[31] However, until the impact of globalisation took tobacco-related disease to epidemic proportions, there was no political appetite to operationalise article 19 of the WHO Constitution. But by the early 1990s, it was clear to all that tobacco was a serious, global public health threat, with a powerful, sophisticated, well-financed industry promoting its ever-increasing use.

Effectively tackling the international threat was going to require an international approach.

The concept of a treaty on tobacco control was fully developed and crystallised through the work of two women: Ruth Roemer and Allyn Taylor. Roemer was a public health lawyer based at the University of California–Los Angeles, who had been commissioned by the WHO in the early 1980s to write a book on the use of legislation to tackle the world tobacco epidemic.[32] In the early 1990s, Roemer was impressed by an article written by Taylor, then a doctoral student in law at Columbia University, advocating that the WHO utilise its (until then) neglected constitutional powers to develop a legal framework to advance global public health.[33] Roemer contacted Taylor to suggest that such a legal framework could be used in relation to tobacco control.[34] Over the next few years, Taylor focused her dissertation work on the development of international treaty law for tobacco control, while Roemer campaigned for an international treaty at various international public health conferences and engaged with senior staff at the WHO, including Dr Neil Collishaw, coordinator of the WHO's (then quite modest) tobacco control unit, to promote the idea.[35] In 1994, at the ninth World Conference on Tobacco or Health in Paris, the team drafted, and was successful in having adopted, a resolution encouraging the development of an international framework convention on tobacco control to respond to the increasingly trans-border nature of tobacco use.[36] The resolution marked the first international forum in which the idea of a tobacco control treaty was formally endorsed.

With momentum for the treaty approach growing, in 1995, the World Health Assembly (WHA) adopted resolution WHA48.11 requesting the Director-General of the WHO to report on the feasibility of developing an international instrument on tobacco control.[37] Roemer and Taylor were commissioned to write a background paper setting out various options for developing a legal strategy for consideration by the WHA at its next session. Their paper recommended the development and implementation of a framework convention on tobacco control. The WHO Director-General produced a brief report for the WHO Executive Board summarising the key recommendations of the background paper,[38] which led to the Executive Board adopting Resolution EB97.R8, *International Framework Convention for Tobacco Control*.[39] This, in turn, paved the way for the WHA to adopt resolution WHA49.16 in May 1996, requesting the Director-General to initiate development of a framework convention on tobacco control and related protocols.[40] For the first time in the WHO's history, it was applying its power to develop international law to address a public health threat. With this momentous decision, WHO member states demonstrated their determination to alter the landscape of the tobacco epidemic, shifting power away from the industry and back to the hands of governments.

In 1998, Dr Gro Harlem Brundtland, former Prime Minister of Norway and a medical doctor, was elected WHO Director-General.[41] Brundtland was personally dedicated to the development of a tobacco control treaty and created the Tobacco Free Initiative (TFI) as one of two cabinet projects. The TFI's core work was to establish global leadership in four priority areas: (i) building and strengthening of national and regional tobacco control capacity; (ii) information management to establish a solid evidence base and develop a global surveillance and electronic information exchange system; (iii) technical and secretariat functions associated with the development of the WHO FCTC and analysis of industry actions, political mapping, and the trade and international legal aspects of tobacco control; and (iv) external liaison and advocacy, including coordinating tobacco control within the United Nations system, mobilising non-governmental organisations, and interacting with relevant private sector groupings.[42]

Brundtland's commitment to the development of an international legal framework addressing tobacco control was in part due to the advocacy of a handful of her closest advisors. Two global tobacco control leaders, Judith McKay of Hong Kong and Derek Yach of South Africa, were members of her transition team and responsible for advising her in the development of her strategic plan. They were able to take advantage of a unique moment in history to push the tobacco control treaty process forward.

With the election of its first woman Director-General, the WHO was ready for a new era. Brundtland brought strong, clear and innovative leadership, a keen interest in modernising the institution and a focus on global governance and political visibility. Additionally, political momentum for tobacco control was high following litigation against the tobacco industry in the United States that culminated in the release of over 35 million pages of previously confidential tobacco industry documents pursuant to the *Tobacco Master Settlement Agreement*.[43] These documents provided the public health community with clear evidence and detailed insight into the deception and tactics the industry had used for decades to develop, produce and market its products. The internal documentation also revealed the industry's full knowledge of how damaging tobacco use is; its purposeful, calculated use of misdirection and falsehoods to undermine the evidence of the health harms caused by tobacco use; and its willingness to increase the addictive qualities of tobacco products to keep its customer base.[44] The documents provided a strong incentive to exclude the industry from any involvement in the development of a tobacco control convention.

By this time, the scientific evidence linking tobacco use to adverse health consequences was overwhelming, and much advanced since the original reports of the 1960s by the UK Royal College of Physicians and the US Surgeon General. Furthermore, sectors other than health were taking an interest in tobacco control. The World Bank's 1999 publication, *Curbing the Epidemic: Governments and the Economics of Tobacco Control* (*Curbing the Epidemic*), provided perhaps the single most important tool used in preparing for the negotiations on the framework convention on tobacco control. The report linked tobacco to broader issues of development, examining the social and economic impact of tobacco use.[45] It further identified cost-effective tobacco control interventions that would promote health by reducing consumption, while concurrently enhancing government revenues.[46] In doing so, *Curbing the Epidemic* expanded the credible evidence base for global tobacco regulation and helped to reverse the long-standing perception that the tobacco industry was too economically beneficial to developing and tobacco-producing countries to allow for effective regulation.

In preparation for the framework convention negotiations, TFI established numerous global partnerships and initiated global multi-sectoral cooperation for tobacco control. First, it initiated a Policy Strategy Advisory Committee (PSAC) to gain policy coherence on tobacco control, solidify support for WHO activities, and expand the base of advocacy and action. The PSAC included representatives from the World Bank, the United Nations Children's Fund, the World Self-Medication Industry (representing pharmaceutical companies that produce cessation-oriented nicotine replacement therapies), the International Nongovernmental Coalition Against Tobacco, the Campaign for Tobacco Free Kids and the US Centers for Disease Control and Prevention.[47]

In addition, the WHO advocated for the establishment of a platform for United Nations (UN) interagency dialogue and cooperation on tobacco control. Accordingly, the UN Secretary-General endorsed the UN Ad Hoc Interagency Task Force on Tobacco Control (Task Force) by a resolution of the UN Economic and Social Council (ECOSOC) in 1999 to coordinate the tobacco control work being carried out by different UN agencies.[48] Chaired by the WHO and with representation from 22 UN agencies, as well as the World Bank, the International Monetary Fund and the World Trade Organization, the Task Force replaced the former UN tobacco focal point, which had been situated within the UN Conference on Trade and Development.[49] The WHO was designated as the lead agency for tobacco control coordination, and the focus of the UN debate on tobacco shifted from supply to health.

IV NEGOTIATING THE WHO FCTC

In May 1999, the WHA adopted Resolution WHA52.18, establishing an Intergovernmental Negotiating Body (INB) open to all WHO member states, in accordance with Rule 42 of its Rules of Procedure.[50] The INB was to 'draft and negotiate the proposed WHO framework convention on tobacco control and possible related protocols'.[51] To lay the groundwork for the negotiations, the WHA also established a working group, similarly open to all WHO member states, with the mandate to prepare proposed draft elements of the nascent treaty.[52] The working group met twice (in October 1999 and March 2000), successfully developing an ambitious and broad set of proposed components for the future WHO framework convention on tobacco control.[53]

In May 2000, the WHA considered the report submitted to it by the working group and called on the INB to begin negotiations on the text of the treaty.[54] At its first session, the INB accepted the working group's proposed draft elements as the base text from which to initiate negotiations.[55] With this one act, a number of potentially deal-breaking issues were resolved before formal negotiations even began.

For instance, the working group's report explicitly supported a primary focus on demand-reduction strategies, citing the World Bank's *Curbing the Epidemic* report.[56] By stressing the need for measures aimed at reducing demand for tobacco products, the political pressures surrounding questions of reducing supply were largely resolved. The questions and concerns regarding the economic impact of explicitly supply-side reduction measures were not insignificant. In the lead-up to the negotiations, some tobacco-producing countries expressed fears that they would bear the consequences of supply-reduction strategies and reduced demand for tobacco in direct employment losses and would gain few of the benefits, as their population had low smoking rates.[57] Given this, had the initial stages of the negotiations focused heavily on supply-reduction provisions, there was a substantial possibility that low- and middle-income countries would not have participated in the process or, worse, may have fought against the treaty.

Six sessions of the INB were held over the next two and a half years; over 170 states participated in one or more of the sessions. In addition, numerous inter-sessional regional negotiating meetings and technical conferences were convened to support and advance the process.[58] The intensive negotiating process increased the political profile of tobacco as a global public health concern and raised awareness among policymakers of the impact of tobacco use and the existence of effective interventions. One of the key outcomes of the negotiations, besides the treaty itself, was a broad recognition of the need for coordinated, multi-sectoral involvement for tobacco control to be successful. The expanded profile tobacco control garnered was reflected in the increasingly diverse composition of delegations to the negotiations. Whereas participation was heavily weighted toward Ministries of Health in the early sessions, by the end, many delegations included representatives from Ministries of Trade, Finance and Foreign Affairs, among others.[59]

During the negotiations, regional blocs became important political vehicles, especially for a number of low- and middle-income countries that were facing growing rates of tobacco use. Many of these countries recognised that once adopted and entered into force, the treaty would not only advance tobacco control nationally and internationally, but would also be a means to redress social injustice in public health. Regions used preparatory meetings prior to each INB session to develop common positions, which allowed groups of countries to hold substantial and occasionally formidable influence over the direction of negotiation debate. Further, by meeting between INB sessions and developing unified platforms, many regions were able to address some of the more contentious issues, including mitigating divisions between tobacco-producing countries and non-producers.[60] Acting in regional blocs also helped low-income countries, many of which had only one delegate at a given INB session, to cope with the demands of the protracted and simultaneous negotiating sessions.[61] Acting concertedly heightened the impact of developing countries' interventions and served to balance their weight against powerful-country positions.[62]

In addition to member states (and appropriate regional economic integration organisations), civil society, scientific experts and advocacy networks participated as observers throughout the negotiations, playing a key role in the development of the convention.[63] The frequency with which the negotiations were convened allowed for continuous networking and interaction among tobacco control advocates, which improved the overall coherence and strength of the messaging but also suggested that coordination and collaboration would be a great boon to these groups. The development of the Framework Convention Alliance (FCA) provided the necessary cohesion, thereby greatly enhancing the impact civil society was able to have on the negotiations. The FCA served to increase communication between non-governmental organisations (NGOs) that were already engaged and sought to systematically reach out to and support new and small NGOs, particularly in developing countries. By the end of the negotiations, the FCA comprised more than 200 NGOs from over 90 countries and had established itself as an important lobbying alliance.[64]

During negotiation sessions, to increase awareness of and expand access to information about specific issues relevant to the developing framework convention text, the WHO, member states and observers, including the FCA and other relevant entities, held lunchtime seminars and workshops on various technical aspects of the convention. Additionally, civil society developed and distributed capacity-building guides and policy recommendations to delegates, with the aim of strengthening national tobacco control programmes.[65] The technical seminars and the publication and distribution of information evolved into what former WHO Executive Director for Non-communicable Diseases and Mental Health, Dr Derek Yach, has called 'the best university of global tobacco control'.[66]

V PROVISIONS OF THE WHO FCTC

At its sixth session, in February 2003, the INB concluded its negotiations successfully and closed its work.[67] The text of the treaty was submitted to the WHA for its consideration and, in May 2003, the WHA unanimously adopted the WHO FCTC.[68] The treaty was opened for signature on 16 June 2003 and closed on 22 June 2003, with 168 signatories.[69] By November 2004, 40 countries had ratified, accepted, approved, formally confirmed or acceded to the convention (depending on the country's legal procedures),[70] and, on 27 February 2005, the WHO FCTC entered into force.[71] This short time scale makes the WHO FCTC among the fastest treaties in history to be negotiated, adopted and entered into force.[72]

The final text was a victory for those advocating for a strong, comprehensive treaty, as it includes far-reaching, important and agreed statements of principle, as well as a broad range of concrete, national tobacco control policies as its core, substantive provisions. The preamble to the WHO FCTC articulates the right of parties to the treaty to protect public health, recognises the global nature of the tobacco epidemic, notes the increase in global consumption of tobacco products, and affirms the scientific evidence of the health harms caused by tobacco use and exposure to tobacco smoke. The social, economic and environmental consequences of tobacco consumption and the need to take these into consideration are also highlighted.

The objective of the WHO FCTC, outlined in article 3, is:

> to protect present and future generations from the devastating health, social, environmental and economic consequences of tobacco consumption and exposure to tobacco smoke by providing a framework for tobacco control measures ... in order to reduce continually and substantially the prevalence of tobacco use and exposure to tobacco smoke.

One of the successes of the WHO FCTC negotiations is that the treaty contains both demand-reduction and supply-side strategies. The key substantive demand-reduction provisions are contained in articles 6–14 (see Box 2.1). These include obligations to:

- undertake comprehensive bans on tobacco advertising, promotion and sponsorship (with an exception for countries, such as the US, that deem a comprehensive ban unconstitutional);[73]
- regulate tobacco product content and disclosure of that content and related emissions;[74]
- ban misleading descriptors that imply that certain products are safer than others (eg the terms 'light' or 'mild');[75]
- include large, visible, clear, legible rotating warnings that cover at least 30 per cent of tobacco packaging, with encouragement for even larger, graphic warnings;[76] and
- adopt measures to protect people from exposure to tobacco smoke in 'indoor workplaces, public transport, indoor public places and, as appropriate, other public places'.[77]

The WHO FCTC also recognises the importance of taxation as a tobacco control policy and encourages parties to use increased taxation to discourage consumption.[78]

The core supply-reduction provisions are set out in articles 15–17 (see Box 2.1) and include reducing illicit trade in tobacco products,[79] regulating the sale of tobacco products to and by minors,[80] and promoting economically viable alternatives for tobacco growers.[81]

Novel features of the treaty include a provision addressing liability of the tobacco industry,[82] mechanisms for scientific and technical cooperation and exchange of information,[83] and recognition of civil society participation as 'essential in achieving the objective of the Convention and its protocols'.[84]

BOX 2.1 WHO FCTC DEMAND AND SUPPLY REDUCTION PROVISIONS

Articles 6–14: Demand-reduction provisions

- price and tax measures of tobacco products;
- protection from exposure to tobacco smoke in indoor and outdoor places;
- regulation of the contents and emissions of tobacco products and disclosure of these by manufacturers and importers;
- regulation of tobacco product packaging and labelling;
- health warnings and messages on tobacco products;
- education, communication, training and public awareness of tobacco control issues and the adverse effects of tobacco consumption;
- tobacco advertising, promotion and sponsorship of tobacco products;
- the promotion of cessation and treatment of tobacco dependence.

Articles 15–17: Supply-reduction provisions

- illicit trade in tobacco products, including smuggling, illicit manufacturing and counterfeiting;
- sale of tobacco products to and by minors;
- the provision of support for economically viable alternatives for tobacco workers, growers and individual sellers.

Understanding that the tobacco industry would be the single greatest barrier to successful implementation of the treaty, provisions to protect against industry interference are also included in the text. Language in the preamble clearly articulates that parties 'need to be alert to any efforts by the tobacco industry to undermine or subvert tobacco control efforts and ... need to be informed of activities of the tobacco industry that have a negative impact on tobacco efforts'.[85] Perhaps most importantly, article 5(3) of the WHO FCTC lays out an obligation that parties, in developing and implementing tobacco control policies, must 'act to protect those policies from commercial and other vested interests of the tobacco industry'.

Notably, the relationship between legitimate trade in tobacco products and tobacco consumption (perhaps the most evident trans-border issue in tobacco control) does not appear in the WHO FCTC. Throughout the negotiations, an alliance of the majority of developing countries fought to secure specific language prioritising public health and tobacco control over trade.[86] Their efforts were strongly, sometimes fiercely, supported by NGOs with a specific interest in tobacco control advocacy.[87] Although the final text includes no specific reference to prioritising health over trade, there are echoes of this discussion in the preamble, which states that parties are '[d]etermined to give priority to their right to protect public health'.[88] The considerations of trade and tobacco also resonate in article 2(2), which provides that:

> [t]he provisions of the Convention and its protocols shall in no way affect the right of Parties to enter into bilateral or multilateral agreements, including regional or subregional agreements, on issues relevant or additional to the Convention and its protocols, provided that such agreements are compatible with their obligations under the Convention and its protocols.

While such a compatibility provision is not unique to the WHO FCTC, the negotiators did consider whether or not to specifically mention trade in this context. While trade was finally not included, it is nonetheless to be expected that, consistent with the overarching approach to interpreting international legal instruments articulated in the *Vienna Convention on the Law of Treaties*,[89] the obligations under the WHO FCTC will be interpreted as being consistent with international legal trade obligations. While a full discussion of trade in the context of the WHO FCTC is outside the scope of this chapter, there is a robust literature on this topic as well as some ongoing disputes in various international trade forums that will further clarify these issues.[90]

VI GOVERNANCE OF THE WHO FCTC

The Conference of the Parties (COP) to the WHO FCTC is the governing body for the treaty. It is the primary decision-making body for treaty matters and reviews global implementation of the treaty, drives forward effective implementation of its provisions and sets the priorities and budget for the Convention Secretariat, which is housed in the WHO. The first session of the COP was held in February 2006,[91] by which time 116 countries had ratified the WHO FCTC, including many countries that were originally its strongest critics, including Japan, China and Germany.[92] The following two sessions of the COP were held in 2007 and 2008,[93] after which the COP has consistently been convened at two-year intervals,[94] in accord with its rules of procedure.[95]

Article 7 of the WHO FCTC mandates the COP to propose appropriate guidelines for the implementation of articles 8–13. Exercising its authority under article 23 of the WHO FCTC, the COP has expanded this list to include articles 5(3), 6, 14, 17 and 18.[96] The guidelines are developed by working groups, established by the COP and composed of member states expressing an interest in participating. The working groups are mandated to develop guidelines and recommendations for the implementation of a given treaty provision. The working groups submit progress reports to the COP until their work is complete, at which time they submit the finished guidelines for consideration and adoption. Box 2.2 lists the WHO FCTC articles for which guidelines have been adopted.

BOX 2.2   WHO FCTC IMPLEMENTATION GUIDELINES

Guidelines have been adopted for the following provisions:

- Article 5(3) – Protection of public health policies with respect to tobacco control from commercial and other vested interests of the tobacco industry
- Article 8 – Protection from exposure to tobacco smoke
- Articles 9 and 10 – Regulation of the contents of tobacco products and regulation of tobacco product disclosures (partial guidelines)
- Article 11 – Packaging and labelling of tobacco products
- Article 12 – Education, communication, training and public awareness
- Article 13 – Tobacco advertising, promotion and sponsorship
- Article 14 – Demand-reduction measures concerning tobacco dependence and cessation

Guidelines are expected to be adopted for other provisions,[97] including economically sustainable alternatives to tobacco-growing (articles 17–18) and price and tax measures to reduce the demand for tobacco (article 6).

While not constituting legally binding obligations on their own, the guidelines are developed through a vigorous, multilateral consultative process, are based on evidence and best practice, and are intrinsically a part of legally binding interpretation of the treaty. As evidence of the weight they carry, the WHO FCTC and its guidelines have been referred to in disputes in other contexts to help determine the scope of the obligations of parties to the WHO FCTC and the reasonable expectations for government behaviour when they become parties. This was the case, for example, in the 2012 decision by the Oslo District Court upholding the Norwegian Government's ban on point-of-sale tobacco-product advertising.[98]

In accordance with article 33, the WHO FCTC COP may adopt protocols to the WHO FCTC. In the framework convention model of treaties, protocols are separate agreements under the umbrella of the parent convention, providing a more detailed approach to the governance of a particular topic. At its first session in 2006, the COP established working groups to elaborate templates for possible protocols on illicit trade in tobacco products and cross-border advertising of tobacco products.[99] The expert groups submitted the requested templates to the COP for consideration at its second session[100] and, following discussions, the COP established an Intergovernmental Negotiating Body on a Protocol on Illicit Trade in Tobacco Products.[101] Negotiations began in 2008,[102] and the final text of the *Protocol to Eliminate Illicit Trade in Tobacco Products* (Protocol)[103] was adopted in November 2012 at the fifth session of the COP.[104] The objective of the Protocol is to eliminate all forms of illicit trade in tobacco products, in accordance with the terms of article 15 of the WHO FCTC.[105] Part III of the Protocol, 'Supply Chain Control', contains provisions regarding licensing, due diligence, tracking and tracing, record-keeping, security and preventive measures, sale by Internet, telecommunication or any other evolving technology, free zones and international transit, and duty-free sales. Other important provisions of the Protocol cover offences, seizure payments and disposal/destruction of confiscated products.[106]

VII IMPLEMENTING THE WHO FCTC

Since the entry into force of the WHO FCTC in 2005, there has been substantial positive movement in implementing its provisions globally.

By 2013, 2.3 billion people were protected by at least one demand-reduction measure fully implemented by their government, up from 1 billion in 2007.[107] Many countries have succeeded in reducing smoking prevalence dramatically over a short period of time. In Uruguay, for example, from 2005 to 2011, the prevalence of current tobacco use decreased annually by an estimated 3.3 per cent (equivalent to 23 per cent over six years), while Turkey witnessed a 13 per cent relative reduction in smoking prevalence between 2008 and 2012.[108]

Additionally, new data indicate that these reductions in demand translate directly to reductions in deaths. A study published in 2013 found that global implementation of five of the core WHO FCTC demand-reduction measures at their highest levels between 2007 and 2010 will result in 15 million fewer smokers, thereby averting 7.4 million premature deaths by 2050 (see Figure 2.1).[109]

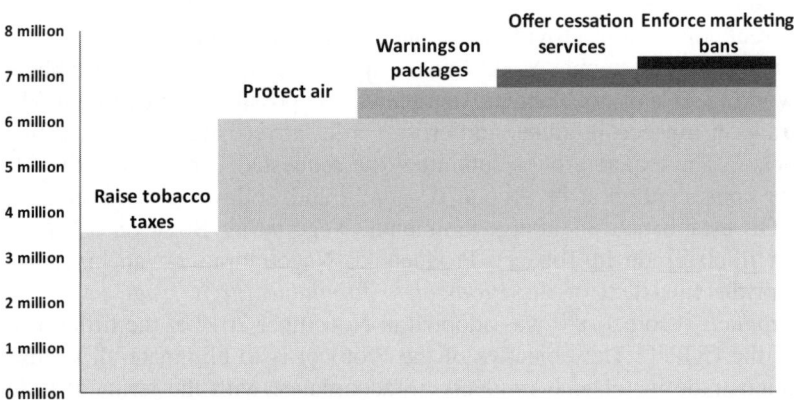

Figure 2.1   Deaths averted by 2050

As countries continue to implement the treaty to the full extent of their obligations and in accordance with political will, these trends are expected to continue.

VIII CONCLUSION

By all accounts, the WHO FCTC has been a genuine success – for the parties to the treaty, for the WHO, and for public health in general. As of the end of 2013, the WHO FCTC had 177 parties, covering more than 87 per cent of the world population.[110] Though some countries central to tobacco and tobacco control continue not to be parties (eg the US, Indonesia and Argentina), the treaty's influence can be felt in all regions of the world, as the profile of and commitment to tobacco control have steadily increased since the first steps were taken in its development. As noted in this chapter, it is not just the treaty itself, but the process of its development and implementation that has changed the tobacco control landscape. Public health advocates now see multilateralism, international law and regulation as key tools in the promotion of health. Additionally, the understanding of global health governance and health policy as necessarily multi-sectoral can be traced, at least in part, to the negotiation and implementation of the WHO FCTC. As a community, our approaches to global public health have increased substantially in sophistication, impact and profile in the past 15 years, and much of the learning that has led to those changes is attributable to the development of the WHO's first – and, to date, only – treaty.

NOTES

1. Colin Mathers and Dejan Loncar, 'Projections of Global Mortality and Burden of Disease from 2002 to 2030' (2006) 3 *PLoS Medicine* 2011, 2021; World Health Organization, 'WHO Report on the Global Tobacco Epidemic, 2008: The MPOWER Package' (World Health Organization, 2008) 14.
2. World Health Organization, 'Tobacco' (Fact Sheet No 339, July 2013) <http://www.who.int/mediacentre/factsheets/fs339/en/index.html>.
3. Mattias Öberg et al, *Global Estimate of the Burden of Disease from Second-Hand Smoke* (World Health Organization, 2010) 38.
4. Mathers and Loncar, above n 1, 2021.
5. Ibid; World Health Organization, 'WHO Report on the Global Tobacco Epidemic, 2008: The MPOWER Package' (World Health Organization, 2008) 16; World Health Organization, 'WHO Report on the Global Tobacco Epidemic, 2011: Warning about the Danger of Tobacco' (World Health Organization, 2011) 8.
6. Opened for signature 22 July 1946, 14 UNTS 185 (entered into force 7 April 1948).
7. *WHO Framework Convention on Tobacco Control*, opened for signature 16 June 2003, 2302 UNTS 166 (entered into force 27 February 2005).
8. For a detailed history of the tobacco epidemic, see Allan Brandt, *The Cigarette Century: The Rise, Fall and Deadly Persistence of the Product that Defined America* (Basic Books, 2007); Robert Proctor, *Golden Holocaust: Origins of the Cigarette Catastrophe and the Case for Abolition* (University of California Press, 2011).
9. Gene Borio, *Tobacco Timeline* (1993) <http://archive.tobacco.org/resources/history/Tobacco_History20-1.html>.
10. Ibid.
11. Royal College of Physicians, *Smoking and Health: A Report of the Royal College of Physicians on Smoking in Relation to Cancer of the Lung and Other Diseases*

(Pitman Medical Publishing Co Ltd, 1962); Advisory Committee to the Surgeon General, *Smoking and Health* (Public Health Service Publication No 1103, 1964).

12. Judith Mackay and Michael Eriksen, *The Tobacco Atlas* (World Health Organization, 1st ed, 2002) 24; Witold Zatoński, 'Democracy and Health: Tobacco Control in Poland' in Joy de Beyer and Linda Waverley Brigden (eds), *Tobacco Control Policy: Strategies, Successes and Setbacks* (World Bank and Research for International Tobacco Control, 2003) 97.

13. Omar Shafey, Suzanne Dolwick and G Emmanuel Guindon (eds), *Tobacco Control Country Profiles* (American Cancer Society, 2nd ed, 2003) 418, 317.

14. Peter Boyle et al, 'Measuring Progress against Cancer in Europe: Has the 15% Decline Targeted for 2000 Come About?' (2003) 14 *Annals of Oncology* 1312, 1317.

15. Prabhat Jha and Frank Chaloupka, *Curbing the Epidemic: Governments and the Economics of Tobacco Control* (World Bank, 1999) 14–15.

16. Mackay and Eriksen, above n 12, 50.

17. Ibid 50.

18. Rowena Jacobs et al, 'The Supply-Side Effects of Tobacco-Control Policies' in Prabhat Jha and Frank Chaloupka (eds), *Tobacco Control in Developing Countries* (Oxford University Press, 2000) 311, 314.

19. Mackay and Eriksen, above n 12, 46.

20. Marcelo Crescenti, 'The New Tobacco World' (1998) 3 *Tobacco Journal International* 51, 52.

21. Ross Hammond, 'Consolidation in the Tobacco Industry' (1998) 7 *Tobacco Control* 426, 426–428.

22. Ibid.

23. Ibid.

24. Jha and Chaloupka, *Curbing the Epidemic*, above n 15, 23.

25. CK Gajalakshmi et al, 'Global Patterns of Smoking and Smoking Attributable Mortality' in Jha and Chaloupka, *Tobacco Control*, above n 18, 9, 17.

26. Global Youth Tobacco Survey Collaborating Group, 'Differences in Worldwide Tobacco Use by Gender: Findings from the Global Youth Tobacco Survey' (2003) 73 *Journal of School Health* 207.

27. Jha and Chaloupka, *Curbing the Epidemic*, above n 15, 23.

28. Douglas Bettcher et al, 'International Law and Health, Two Approaches: The World Health Organization's Tobacco Initiative and International Drug Controls' (2000) 94 *Proceedings of the Annual Meeting of the American Society of International Law* 193, 193–4.

29. Gian Luca Burci, 'Introductory Note to WHO: Framework Convention on Tobacco Control' (2003) 42 *International Legal Materials* 515, 516.

30. Debra Efroymson et al, 'Hungry for Tobacco: An Analysis of the Economic Impact of Tobacco Consumption on the Poor in Bangladesh' (2001) 10 *Tobacco Control* 212, 216.

31. World Health Organization, 'Controlling the Smoking Epidemic: Report of the WHO Expert Committee on Smoking Control' (Technical Report Series No 636, World Health Organization, 1979).

32. Ruth Roemer, *Legislative Action to Combat the World Smoking Epidemic* (World Health Organization, 1982); Ruth Roemer, *Legislative Action to Combat the World Tobacco Epidemic* (World Health Organization, 2nd ed, 1993).

33. Allyn Lise Taylor, 'Making the World Health Organization Work: A Legal Framework for Universal Access to the Conditions for Health' (1992) 18 *American Journal of Law & Medicine* 301.

34. Ruth Roemer, Allyn Taylor and Jean Lariviere, 'Origins of the *WHO Framework Convention on Tobacco Control*' (2005) 95 *American Journal of Public Health* 936, 937.
35. World Health Organization, *History of the World Health Organization Framework Convention on Tobacco Control* (World Health Organization, 2009) 3.
36. Roemer, Taylor and Lariviere, above n 34, 937.
37. World Health Assembly, *An International Strategy for Tobacco Control*, WHA Res 48.11, 48th sess, 12th plen mtg, WHO Doc A48/1995/VR/12 (12 May 1995).
38. Director-General of the World Health Organization, 'The Feasibility of an International Instrument for Tobacco Control' (World Health Organization, WHO Executive Board Doc EB97/INF.DOC./4, 1995).
39. Executive Board of the World Health Organization, *International Framework Convention for Tobacco Control*, EB Res EB97.R8, 97th sess (23 January 1996).
40. World Health Assembly, *International Framework Convention for Tobacco Control*, WHA Res 49.17, 49th sess, 6th plen mtg (25 May 1996).
41. *Dr Gro Harlem Brundtland, Director-General*, World Health Organization <http://www.who.int/dg/brundtland/bruntland/en/index.html>.
42. World Health Assembly, *Tobacco Free Initiative: Report of the Director-General*, 52nd sess, Provisional Agenda Item 13, WHO Doc A52/7 (18 March 1999) 2.
43. National Association of Attorneys-General, *Tobacco Master Settlement Agreement* (23 November 1998) <http://www.naag.org/backpages/naag/tobacco/msa/>.
44. Norbert Hirschhorn, *Evolution of the Tobacco Industry Positions on Addiction to Nicotine* (World Health Organization, 2008) 10.
45. Prabhat Jha and Frank Chaloupka, *Curbing the Epidemic: Governments and the Economics of Tobacco Control* (World Bank, 1999) 15, 25.
46. Ibid 72–3.
47. World Health Assembly, *Tobacco Free Initiative: Report of the Director-General*, 53rd sess, Provisional Agenda Item 12.10, WHO Doc A53/13 (10 March 2000) 7.
48. United Nations Economic and Social Council, *Tobacco or Health*, ECOSOC Res 1999/56, 46th plen mtg, UN Doc E/1999/L.53 (30 July 1999).
49. United Nations Economic and Social Council, *Ad Hoc Interagency Task Force on Tobacco Control: Report of the Secretary-General*, UN Doc E/2000/21 (1 May 2000).
50. The INB was also open to 'regional economic integration organizations constituted by sovereign States, Members of WHO, to which their Member States have transferred competence over matters governed by this resolution, including the competence to enter into treaties in respect to these matters, may actively participate, in accordance with Rule 55 of the Rules of Procedure of the Health Assembly': see World Health Assembly, *Towards a WHO Framework Convention on Tobacco Control*, WHA Res 52.18, 52nd sess, 9th plen mtg, WHO Doc A52/7 (24 May 1999) [1(3)].
51. Ibid [1(1)].
52. Ibid [1(2)]. The working group was also open to regional economic integration organisations: see ibid [1(3)].
53. Intergovernmental Negotiating Body on the WHO FCTC, *Proposed Draft Elements for a WHO Framework Convention on Tobacco Control: Provisional Texts with Comments of the Working Group*, 1st sess, Provisional Agenda Item 8, WHO Doc A/FCTC/INB1/2 (26 July 2000) 1.
54. World Health Assembly, *Framework Convention on Tobacco Control*, WHA Res 53.16, 53rd sess, 8th plen mtg, WHO Doc A53/VR/8 (20 May 2000).
55. Intergovernmental Negotiating Body on the WHO FCTC, *Summary Records*, 1st sess, 5th plen mtg, WHO Doc A/FCTC/INB1/SR (26 July 2000) 48–9.
56. Intergovernmental Negotiating Body on the WHO FCTC, above n 53, 3.

57. Derek Yach et al, 'Globalization and Tobacco' in Ichiro Kawachi and Sarah Wamala (eds), *Globalization and Health* (Oxford University Press, 2006) 39, 58.

58. *Intersessional Consultations* (2013) WHO FCTC <http://www.who.int/fctc/about/whofctc_inb/consultations/en/index.html>.

59. Intergovernmental Negotiating Body on the WHO FCTC, *List of Participants*, WHO Doc A/FCTC/INB1/DIV/2/Rev.1 (18 October 2000) 1-23; Intergovernmental Negotiating Body on the WHO FCTC, *List of Participants*, WHO Doc A/FCTC/INB6/DIV/2/Rev.2 (26 February 2003) 1–31.

60. Clive Bates, 'Developing Countries Take the Lead on WHO Convention' (2001) 10 *Tobacco Control* 204, 204; Jeff Collin, 'Tobacco Politics' (2004) 47(2) *Development* 91.

61. Jeff Collin and Kelley Lee, 'Globalisation and the Politics of Health Governance: The Framework Convention on Tobacco Control' in Andrew Fenton Cooper and John J Kirton (eds), *Innovation in Global Health Governance: Critical Cases* (Ashgate, 2009) 219, 224.

62. Gregory Jacob, 'Without Reservation' (2004) 5 *Chicago Journal of International Law* 287, 297.

63. Hadii Mamudu and Stanton Glantz, 'Civil Society and the Negotiation of the Framework Convention on Tobacco Control' (2004) 4(2) *Global Public Health* 150, 154.

64. Anna White, 'Controlling Big Tobacco: The Winning Campaign for a Global Tobacco Control Treaty' (2004) 25(1/2) *Multinational Monitor* 13, 14.

65. Brian Simpson, 'Smoke Out!' (2003) Spring *The Magazine of the Johns Hopkins School of Public Health* 26, 34.

66. Ibid 34.

67. Intergovernmental Negotiating Body on the WHO FCTC, *Summary Records*, WHO Doc A/FCTC/INB6/SR 6th sess, 4th plen mtg (1 March 2003) 35.

68. World Health Assembly, *WHO Framework Convention on Tobacco Control*, WHA Res 56.1, 56th sess, 4th plen mtg, WHO Doc A56/VR/4 (21 May 2003).

69. World Health Organization, *History*, above n 35, 26.

70. Ibid.

71. Ibid.

72. Ibid 27.

73. WHO FCTC article 13.

74. WHO FCTC articles 9, 10.

75. WHO FCTC article 11.

76. Ibid.

77. WHO FCTC article 8.

78. WHO FCTC article 6.

79. WHO FCTC article 15.

80. WHO FCTC article 16.

81. WHO FCTC article 17.

82. WHO FCTC article 19.

83. WHO FCTC articles 20–22.

84. WHO FCTC article 4(7).

85. WHO FCTC preamble [18].

86. Hadii Mamudu, Ross Hammond and Stanton Glantz, 'International Trade versus Public Health during the FCTC Negotiations, 1999–2003' (2011) 20(1) *Tobacco Control* e3 <http://www.ncbi.nlm.nih.gov/pmc/articles/PMC3089441/>.

87. Ibid.

88. WHO FCTC preamble [21].

89. Opened for signature 23 May 1969, 1155 UNTS 331 (entered into force 27 January 1980) article 31(1).

90. See, eg, Part II of this volume; Tania Voon, 'Flexibilities in WTO Law to Support Tobacco Control Regulation' (2013) 39 *American Journal of Law & Medicine* 199; Tania Voon and Andrew Mitchell, 'Implications of WTO Law for Plain Packaging of Tobacco Products' in Tania Voon et al (eds), *Public Health and Plain Packaging of Cigarettes: Legal Issues* (Edward Elgar, 2012) 109.

91. *Sessions of the Conference of the Parties to the WHO FCTC*, WHO FCTC <http://www.who.int/fctc/cop/sessions/en/>.

92. Mamudu and Glantz, above n 63, 158.

93. WHO FCTC, *Sessions of the Conference of the Parties*, above n 91.

94. Ibid.

95. Ibid; World Health Organization, 'Rules of Procedure of the Conference of the Parties to the WHO FCTC' r 4.1 *Sessions* (2005) 2.

96. *Guidelines for Implementation of the WHO Framework Convention on Tobacco Control*, WHO FCTC <http://www.who.int/fctc/guidelines/en/>.

97. *Intersessional Groups Established by the Conference of the Parties*, WHO FCTC <http://www.who.int/fctc/guidelines/groups/en/>.

98. *Philip Morris Norway AS v Ministry of Health and Care Services*, Oslo District Court, 14 September 2012 [Tobacco Control Laws trans (2013) <http://www.tobaccocontrollaws.org/litigation/decisions/no-20120914-philip-morris-norway-v.-health>] 16, 19, 26, 28, 29, 50, 60.

99. WHO FCTC Conference of the Parties, *Elaboration of a Protocol on Illicit Trade in Tobacco Products*, FCTC COP Res 2(12), 2nd sess, 4th plen mtg, WHO Doc FCTC/COP2(12) (6 July 2007).

100. WHO FCTC Conference of the Parties, *Elaboration of Protocols (Decision FCTC/COP1(16)): Elaboration of a Template for a Protocol on Illicit Trade in Tobacco Products*, Agenda Item 5.4.1, WHO Doc A/FCTC/COP/2/9 (19 April 2007); WHO FCTC Conference of the Parties, *Elaboration of Protocols (Decision FCTC/COP1(16)): Elaboration of a Template for a Protocol on Cross-border Tobacco Advertising, Promotion and Sponsorship*, Agenda Item 5.4.2, WHO Doc A/FCTC/COP/2/10 (19 April 2007).

101. WHO FCTC Conference of the Parties, *Elaboration of a Protocol on Illicit Trade in Tobacco Products*, COP Dec FCTC/COP2(12), 2nd sess, 4th plen mtg, WHO Doc A/FCTC/COP/2/DIV/9 (6 July 2007), 29–31.

102. *Negotiations of the Protocol to Eliminate Illicit Trade in Tobacco Products*, WHO FCTC <http://www.who.int/fctc/protocol/about/inb/en/index.html>.

103. Opened for signature 10 January 2013, 52 ILM 365 (not yet in force).

104. WHO FCTC Conference of the Parties, *Protocol to Eliminate Illicit Trade in Tobacco Products*, COP Decision FCTC/COP5(1), 5th sess, WHO Doc FCTC/COP/5/DIV/5 (12 November 2012) 3–37.

105. Protocol article 3.

106. See also Chapter 5 of this volume.

107. World Health Organization, 'Report on the Global Tobacco Epidemic, 2013: Enforcing Bans on Tobacco Advertising, Promotion and Sponsorship' (World Health Organization, 2013) 42.

108. Ibid 43.

109. David Levy et al, 'Smoking-related Deaths Averted Due to Three Years of Policy Progress' (2013) 91 *Bulletin of the World Health Organization* 509, 512–15.

110. World Health Organization, 'Banning Tobacco Advertising, Promotion and Sponsorship: What You Need to Know' (World Health Organization, 2013) 12.

3. Guidelines and protocols under the framework convention

Chang-fa Lo

I INTRODUCTION

The *WHO Framework Convention on Tobacco Control* (WHO FCTC)[1] is the first international health treaty concluded under the auspices of the World Health Organization (WHO). It is designed to control, reduce and, hopefully, eliminate the production, transportation, sale and consumption of tobacco products.

The WHO FCTC embodies a 'framework convention' approach. Although there are some substantive rights and obligations included in the convention itself,[2] for many aspects of tobacco control, the treaty identifies only general principles, which are not specific enough to require parties to adopt particular measures or policies.[3] Thus the main contents of the WHO FCTC are to be supplemented by additional legal instruments. Parties have to adopt additional legal instruments under the WHO FCTC so as to implement the principles set forth in the convention.

The parties have adopted a protocol and various sets of guidelines implementing aspects of the WHO FCTC. For some subject matters, parties decided to adopt guidelines to implement the WHO FCTC. For others, they concluded a protocol. It is important to clarify the difference between guidelines and protocols under the WHO FCTC and the policy choice for having some matters dealt with by guidelines and others subject to a protocol. It is also important to note that there are policy and legal implications arising from the use of guidelines or protocols for the effective control of tobacco use and for the interpretation of other international agreements that affect the operation of the WHO FCTC. As will be argued in this chapter, a dual use of guidelines and protocols is preferable for the purpose of effective implementation of the WHO FCTC.

II THE 'FRAMEWORK CONVENTION' APPROACH AND THE USE OF GUIDELINES AND PROTOCOLS

A The Adoption of the 'Framework Convention' Approach and the WHO FCTC as a Living Treaty

The WHO has legislative authority under articles 19 and 21 of the *Constitution of the World Health Organization (WHO Constitution)*[4] to adopt conventions or agreements with respect to any matter within its competence and to adopt regulations concerning sanitary and quarantine requirements and other procedures designed to prevent the international spread of disease. The WHO FCTC was the first treaty negotiated under the auspices of the WHO based on article 19 of the *WHO Constitution*.

As already noted and as evident from the treaty's title, the WHO FCTC adopted a 'framework convention' approach.[5] In the past, this approach was used mainly in the field of international environment law.[6] A framework convention incorporates more general terms and principles, with further development of more specific protocols regarding the steps and measures to be taken left for future stages. The *United Nations Framework Convention on Climate Change*[7] is an example of using a framework treaty as a basis for further supplementation and implementation in later stages. That treaty was later supplemented by the Kyoto Protocol to the *United Nations Framework Convention on Climate Change*[8] to establish obligations for developed countries to reduce their greenhouse gas emissions. Similarly, the WHO FCTC proclaims basic policy objectives and creates governing institutions to make decisions and develop further rules to supplement the convention.[9]

Commentators had certain doubts about the use of a framework convention approach because of concerns that it might not 'increase the effectiveness of domestic laws in the developed world and will not effectively aid the developing world'.[10] Although it might be too early to predict whether such an approach will ultimately become a hurdle to the effective control of tobacco use, it is apparent that countries have been quite active in negotiating and adopting new guidelines and a protocol to implement the WHO FCTC. It is also apparent that the framework convention approach has been quite useful in allowing the WHO FCTC to grow continuously, enriching its content.

From the perspective of the WHO FCTC being continuously supplemented by guidelines and a protocol, it can be considered a living treaty. The WHO FCTC could be one of the fastest growing treaties in practice.

B   The Adoption of Protocols

Many provisions in the WHO FCTC instruct parties to enact or to consider enacting protocols or guidelines to implement its terms. These provisions certainly encourage parties to work towards developing useful protocols and guidelines for the purpose of enhancing the control of tobacco use.

The general provision for the adoption of protocols is in WHO FCTC article 33 (entitled 'Protocols'), which provides:

1. Any Party may propose protocols. Such proposals will be considered by the Conference of the Parties.
2. The Conference of the Parties may adopt protocols to this Convention. In adopting these protocols every effort shall be made to reach consensus. If all efforts at consensus have been exhausted, and no agreement reached, the protocol shall as a last resort be adopted by a three-quarters majority vote of the Parties present and voting at the session. For the purposes of this Article, Parties present and voting means Parties present and casting an affirmative or negative vote.
3. The text of any proposed protocol shall be communicated to the Parties by the Secretariat at least six months before the session at which it is proposed for adoption.
4. Only Parties to the Convention may be parties to a protocol.
5. Any protocol to the Convention shall be binding only on the Parties to the protocol in question. Only Parties to a protocol may take decisions on matters exclusively relating to the protocol in question.
6. The requirements for entry into force of any protocol shall be established by that instrument.

In addition to the general provisions about adopting protocols in article 33, article 23.5 serves as a general basis for the parties to adopt protocols to implement the WHO FCTC. It provides in part:

> The Conference of the Parties shall keep under regular review the implementation of the Convention and take the decisions necessary to promote its effective implementation and may adopt protocols, annexes and amendments to the Convention, in accordance with Articles 28, 29 and 33.

A number of aspects of articles 33 and 23.5 deserve elaboration. First, the subject matters that could be dealt with by a protocol are unrestricted. As long as a party proposes a protocol, the Conference of the Parties will consider its adoption. In other words, those matters currently subject to guidelines can also be subject to a protocol. Second, parties can decide whether to opt in to a protocol. The WHO FCTC does not require its parties to also become parties to a protocol. However, non-parties to the treaty are not allowed to participate in a protocol under the WHO FCTC. Hence, the number of parties to a protocol can be fewer than those of the WHO FCTC. Third, a protocol is binding, but only those parties that have ratified it are bound by it. Parties are not bound by a protocol to which they are not parties.

In addition to the general provisions in the WHO FCTC governing the adoption of a protocol, another provision provides for the use of a protocol to address specific issues. WHO FCTC article 13.8 provides:

> Parties shall consider the elaboration of a protocol setting out appropriate measures that require international collaboration for a comprehensive ban on cross-border advertising, promotion and sponsorship.

However, only the guidelines for implementation of article 13 of the WHO FCTC[11] have been adopted for such purpose. To date, no protocol setting out measures to require international collaboration for a comprehensive ban on cross-border advertising, promotion and sponsorship has been considered and negotiated by the parties.

Although there is no restriction on the scope of subject matters that are suitable for protocols to govern, the practice has been that protocols are not commonly used by the WHO FCTC parties to implement the convention. To date, only the *Protocol to Eliminate Illicit Trade in Tobacco Products* has been adopted (at the fifth Conference of the Parties on 12 November 2012), which is open for signature by the WHO FCTC parties at the time of writing.[12] According to its preamble, this protocol 'builds upon and complements Article 15 of the WHO FCTC, which addresses means of countering illicit trade in tobacco products'.

C   The Adoption of Guidelines

A number of provisions in the WHO FCTC specifically mention the use and the adoption of guidelines. The general rule for adopting guidelines is provided in article 5.4, which states: 'The Parties shall cooperate in the formulation of proposed measures, procedures and guidelines for the implementation of the Convention and the protocols to which they are Parties'. Hence, guidelines are adopted for the purpose of implementing the WHO FCTC.

Some treaty provisions specifically require the adoption of guidelines to address specific tobacco control issues. For example, WHO FCTC article 7 (entitled 'Non-price measures to reduce the demand for tobacco') creates an expectation that parties will adopt guidelines to implement non-price measures for tobacco control. It states:

The Parties recognize that comprehensive non-price measures are an effective and important means of reducing tobacco consumption. Each Party shall adopt and implement effective legislative, executive, administrative or other measures necessary to implement its obligations pursuant to Articles 8 to 13 and shall cooperate, as appropriate, with each other directly or through competent international bodies with a view to their implementation. The Conference of the Parties shall propose appropriate guidelines for the implementation of the provisions of these Articles.

Article 9 (entitled 'Regulation of the contents of tobacco products') provides for parties to adopt guidelines to provide guidance for testing, measuring, and controlling tobacco contents and emissions:

The Conference of the Parties, in consultation with competent international bodies, shall propose guidelines for testing and measuring the contents and emissions of tobacco products, and for the regulation of these contents and emissions. Each Party shall, where approved by competent national authorities, adopt and implement effective legislative, executive and administrative or other measures for such testing and measuring, and for such regulation.

Article 20 (entitled 'Research, surveillance and exchange of information') contemplates parties adopting guidelines for the collection and use of tobacco-related surveillance data:

Parties recognize the importance of financial and technical assistance from international and regional intergovernmental organizations and other bodies. Each Party shall endeavour to: ...

(c) cooperate with the World Health Organization in the development of general guidelines or procedures for defining the collection, analysis and dissemination of tobacco-related surveillance data.

Article 14 (entitled 'Demand reduction measures concerning tobacco dependence and cessation') is rather unique. From the text, it is apparent that each party is expected to adopt guidelines for cessation of tobacco use at the national level. But this provision does not preclude parties from jointly adopting guidelines for the same purpose. As set out below, a set of WHO FCTC guidelines addressing demand reduction issues has already been agreed. Under the guidelines, parties are also expected to develop and disseminate comprehensive tobacco dependence treatment guidelines based on the best available scientific evidence and best practices, taking into account national circumstances and priorities.[13] WHO FCTC article 14.1 states:

Each Party shall develop and disseminate appropriate, comprehensive and integrated guidelines based on scientific evidence and best practices, taking into account national circumstances and priorities, and shall take effective measures to promote cessation of tobacco use and adequate treatment for tobacco dependence.

The Conference of the Parties has adopted seven sets of implementing guidelines, namely guidelines concerning:

- the protection of public health policies with respect to tobacco control from commercial and other vested interests of the tobacco industry;[14]
- protection from exposure to tobacco smoke;[15]
- regulation of the contents of tobacco products and of tobacco product disclosures;[16]
- packaging and labelling of tobacco products;[17]
- education, communication, training and public awareness;[18]
- tobacco advertising, promotion and sponsorship;[19] and
- demand reduction measures concerning tobacco dependence and cessation.[20]

Although guidelines are non-binding, they assist parties to meet their WHO FCTC obligations by urging and recommending the adoption of appropriate implementation measures by individual parties at the national level. Hence guidelines are considered 'a valuable tool in the implementation' of the WHO FCTC.[21]

D When to Use Protocols and Guidelines

Protocols and guidelines are tools for WHO FCTC parties to use for the purpose of achieving the goals of the WHO FCTC. The WHO FCTC does not specify when protocols should be used instead of guidelines or vice versa. For some matters, it might not be appropriate to impose binding obligations on the parties. For instance, it might not be suitable to impose strict and detailed obligations on parties concerning their national cessation strategies and programmes, due to the differences between parties in their levels of tobacco use, their resources, and their legal and institutional structures. In such circumstances, a set of guidelines for parties to consider may be appropriate. Other matters can be dealt with by imposing binding obligations on the parties through a protocol. For instance, WHO FCTC article 5.3 says:

> In setting and implementing their public health policies with respect to tobacco control, Parties shall act to protect these policies from commercial and other vested interests of the tobacco industry in accordance with national law.

This provision does not indicate whether to adopt a protocol or a set of guidelines so as to ensure that parties will act to protect public health policies from the interests of the tobacco industry. Parties have adopted guidelines for implementation of article 5.3 of the WHO FCTC.[22] However, most of the measures recommended in that instrument could also be drafted in a mandatory manner. For instance, principle 2 in the guidelines reads: 'Parties, when dealing with the tobacco industry or those working to further its interests, should be accountable and transparent'. This provision could be drafted so as to *require* parties to be accountable and transparent when dealing with the tobacco industry. Principle 3 in the guidelines reads: 'Parties should require the tobacco industry and those working to further its interests to operate and act in a manner that is accountable and transparent'. This provision could also be drafted to impose *obligations* on parties to require the tobacco industry to operate and act in an accountable and transparent manner. Similarly, principle 4 in the guidelines reads: 'Because their products are lethal, the tobacco industry should not be granted incentives to establish or run their businesses'. This provision could be drafted to prohibit parties from granting incentives to establish or run tobacco businesses.

In short, it is not because of the requirements of the WHO FCTC or because of the nature of the matters to be dealt with that parties decided to adopt guidelines to implement the WHO FCTC instead of adopting protocols for the same purpose. The different degrees of difficulty for concluding a protocol and adopting a set of guidelines affect the selection among these instruments.

III DIFFERENCES BETWEEN AND REASONS FOR USING GUIDELINES AND PROTOCOLS

A The Functions of Guidelines and Protocols for Implementing the WHO FCTC

The function of guidelines is the implementation of the WHO FCTC and its protocols. As mentioned above, WHO FCTC article 5.4 requires parties to cooperate 'in the formulation of proposed measures, procedures

and guidelines for the implementation of the Convention and the protocols to which they are Parties'. Guidelines are commonly adopted to
carry out the objectives specified in the WHO FCTC.

The usual way of implementing an international treaty is to fulfil the
obligations under the treaty. Thus, normally, the implementing rules are
also mandatory. However, the WHO FCTC is different in that it creates a
wide range of expectations but does not make the parties legally
obligated to fulfil them in certain specified manners. Thus, it is up to the
parties to decide whether to conclude a protocol so as to create additional
treaty obligations or to adopt non-binding rules so as to encourage parties
to adopt measures to achieve the goals of the treaty. Both the guidelines
and the protocols have the function of implementing WHO FCTC
parties' obligations under the convention.

B   The Binding or Non-binding Nature of Protocols and Guidelines

Guidelines are essentially non-binding. The commonly used terms in the
guidelines to describe the rules are: 'Parties should', 'Parties should
consider', and 'are recommended'.

For instance, paragraph 17 of the guidelines for implementation of
article 5.3 reads: 'The following important activities *are recommended*
for addressing tobacco industry interference in public health policies'.[23]
The guidelines for implementation of article 11 state in paragraph 9:

> *Parties should consider* requiring, in addition to the health warnings and
> messages referred to in paragraph 8, further health warnings and messages on
> all sides of a package, as well as on package inserts and onserts.[24]

There is no legally binding obligation imposed on the parties under these
provisions. Countries are only expected, urged, or recommended to adopt
certain measures or policies for the purpose of enhancing the achievement of the WHO FCTC.

On the other hand, a protocol establishes legally binding obligations in
addition to the obligations created by the WHO FCTC itself. For
instance, concerning the supply chain control to prevent illicit trade,
article 6 of the *Protocol to Eliminate Illicit Trade in Tobacco Products*
requires parties to prohibit certain manufacturing and trade activities
without a licence. Article 7 of the protocol provides that each party shall
require that all persons engaged in the supply chain of tobacco products
conduct due diligence before commencing such a business relationship.
These are new obligations going beyond the provisions of the WHO
FCTC itself.

However, a protocol may also contain non-binding obligations. For instance, article 17 (entitled 'Seizure payments') of the protocol provides:

> *Parties should*, in accordance with their domestic law, consider adopting such legislative and other measures as may be necessary to authorize competent authorities to levy an amount proportionate to lost taxes and duties from the producer, manufacturer, distributor, importer or exporter of seized tobacco, tobacco products and/or manufacturing equipment.[25]

Under this provision, parties are expected, but not legally required, to adopt some kind of 'penalising' measure so as to collect from illicit traders an amount proportionate to lost taxes.

C   Reasons for Relying on Protocols or Guidelines

As already stated, no strict rule under the WHO FCTC governs the selection of a protocol or a set of guidelines. Generally, it is up to the parties to decide whether to adopt a binding protocol or a non-binding set of guidelines. The selection of a protocol or a set of guidelines depends on the parties' strategic, political and practical judgements.

From a practical and strategic perspective, it appears easier for participating states to agree on non-binding rules. Parties may be more cautious or hesitant in entering into binding obligations and would have to conduct extensive assessment about the possible domestic and international consequences of the new obligations. Such consequences could be legal, political or economic. Parties would also have to persuade stakeholders about assuming additional international legal obligations. The domestic decision-making process could be far longer and more complicated, and consensus could be far more difficult to reach in this context. Parties might therefore decline to participate in negotiating or signing the protocol.

The negotiation process for a protocol may also be longer and more difficult than for a set of guidelines because the parties would have to be more careful about the exact terms used and conditions included.

Parties may have a more efficient decision-making process in negotiating guidelines because they are not assuming international legal obligations and they might not be required to go through a comprehensive domestic consultation and assessment process.

Thus, if creating binding obligations on participating states is critical to successfully implement the WHO FCTC, concluding a protocol is unavoidable. However, if there is no such critical situation requiring the adoption of a protocol, guidelines may be a practical option for the purpose of quickly establishing certain benchmarks and guidance for countries to consider.

IV POLICY IMPLICATIONS FOR TOBACCO CONTROL OF USING GUIDELINES OR PROTOCOLS

A Positive Policy Implications Arising from the Reliance on Guidelines

Due to the difference in the legal consequences of a protocol and guidelines and the consequence that guidelines are easier to negotiate and adopt, there have been far more guidelines completed under the WHO FCTC. The large number of guidelines successfully negotiated and completed is a positive sign indicating the convention's success in bringing the importance of tobacco control to the attention of the general public and policymakers in WHO FCTC parties.

Guidelines are the result of discussions by experts and negotiators about appropriate and effective approaches to tobacco control. Although they are not necessarily legally binding, they still have a high degree of practical authoritative status and are still useful. They serve as benchmarks for the parties to enhance their control of tobacco use. They also serve as valuable guidance for parties, and even for non-parties, when formulating their tobacco control policies.

B Negative Policy Implications Arising from the Reliance on Guidelines

Because guidelines are typically non-binding, many important policy recommendations indicated in the guidelines are not adopted and implemented at the domestic level. For instance, the guidelines for implementation of article 11[26] clearly state that plain packaging:

> may increase the noticeability and effectiveness of health warnings and messages, prevent the package from detracting attention from them, and address industry package design techniques that may suggest that some products are less harmful than others.

These guidelines further recommend that parties consider adopting plain packaging requirements to eliminate the effects of advertising or promotion on packaging. The guidelines for implementation of article 13[27] also suggest that the effect of advertising or promotion on packaging can be eliminated by requiring plain packaging. However, since parties are only recommended to consider adopting plain packaging requirements, this useful policy measure is rarely adopted by the parties. Australia is the only country to have adopted the plain package recommendation to date. However, a limited number of members of the World Trade Organization (WTO), and a tobacco company under a bilateral investment treaty (BIT), have challenged that measure.[28]

V IMPLICATIONS FOR TREATY INTERPRETATION UNDER OTHER TREATY SYSTEMS AND POSSIBLE DUAL USE OF GUIDELINES AND PROTOCOLS

A Implications for Treaty Interpretation by Protocols and Guidelines

Some other treaty systems may affect the operation of the WHO FCTC. The most obvious ones are the WTO's *General Agreement on Tariffs and Trade 1994* (GATT),[29] the *Agreement on Technical Barriers to Trade* (TBT Agreement),[30] and the *Agreement on Trade-Related Aspects of Intellectual Property Rights* (TRIPS Agreement),[31] as well as BITs.

Tobacco control measures could affect international trade in a number of ways. For instance, regulation of the promotion and advertisement of tobacco products could be considered internal rules affecting domestic sales and thus be subject to the national treatment requirement under GATT article III:4. Tax and other price measures for tobacco control are also subject to the national treatment requirement in article III:2. Tracking and tracing mechanisms could affect the importation and exportation of tobacco products and thus be subject to the prohibition on quantitative restrictions under GATT article XI:1. Packaging and labelling requirements may be technical barriers to trade under the TBT Agreement or provisions regarding the protection of trademarks under the TRIPS Agreement. Tobacco control measures may also affect international investment. For instance, Australian plain packaging requirements have been challenged by a tobacco company on the basis that the restrictions constitute indirect expropriation. Because states are often WTO members, WHO FCTC parties, and parties to various BITs, they would have to follow each set of obligations. And because trade and investment rules are binding on such WHO FCTC parties, tobacco control measures are also subject to the scrutiny of the WTO or the BITs. In other words, the operation of the WHO FCTC is practically affected by the WTO and BITs.

In order to reduce the potential conflict between the WHO FCTC and the WTO or BITs, it may be necessary to interpret WTO and BIT terms to take into account the WHO FCTC rules. As explained below, a protocol is preferable to guidelines in helping integrate the WHO FCTC and the WTO or BITs. Tracking and tracing systems will be used as an example to explain the point.

Tracking and tracing mechanisms on tobacco products are required by the *Protocol to Eliminate Illicit Trade in Tobacco Products*. Such mechanisms might be considered import or export restrictions because tobacco products not meeting the tracking and tracing requirements will not be exported or imported. Quantitative import and export restrictions are subject to GATT article XI:1, which provides:

> No prohibitions or restrictions other than duties, taxes or other charges, whether made effective through quotas, import or export licences or other measures, shall be instituted or maintained by any Member on the importation of any product of the territory of any other Member or on the exportation or sale for export of any product destined for the territory of any other Member.

WTO members adopting such mechanisms would have to justify the measure under the GATT. GATT article XX(b) permits measures that are 'necessary to protect human, animal or plant life or health', provided that they are 'not applied in a manner which would constitute a means of arbitrary or unjustifiable discrimination between countries where the same conditions prevail, or a disguised restriction on international trade'.

In deciding whether a measure is necessary for the purpose of GATT article XX(b), a dispute settlement panel of the WTO would employ 'a process of weighing and balancing a series of factors',[32] which usually includes the assessment of: (1) the relative importance of the interests or values furthered by the challenged measure; (2) the contribution of the measure to the realisation of the ends it pursues; and (3) the restrictive impact of the measure on international commerce. Once all those factors have been analysed, a comparison would be undertaken between the challenged measure and reasonably available alternatives that would have an equal contribution to the objective of the measure, in the light of the importance of that objective.[33]

The *Protocol to Eliminate Illicit Trade in Tobacco Products* could affect the application of the 'necessity requirement' under article XX(b) to a tracking and tracing mechanism for tobacco products in three ways. Since tracking and tracing systems are provided for in the protocol, participating states are required to adopt and implement the system to ensure effective control of tobacco use to protect human health and life.

This requirement reflects the consensus on the importance of such mechanisms to protect human health and life. The mandatory nature of these requirements under the protocol also confirm the contribution of tracking and tracing measures to the realisation of the purpose of effective tobacco control (and corresponding health objectives). The mandatory adoption of tracking and tracing mechanisms also shows that other possible alternatives with less trade-restrictive effects are not practically available.

Guidelines might have a similar but possibly lesser effect in applying the necessity requirements under GATT article XX(b) to a tobacco control measure. Let us use the plain packaging requirements as an example. A country requires domestically produced and imported tobacco products to comply with the plain packaging requirements. Tobacco products not meeting the plain packaging requirements are not allowed to be imported (different from the Australian case, in which non-compliant imports are allowed but must then be repackaged before sale). Such requirements are not only in the nature of a technical barrier to trade and a restriction on the use of a trademark, but are also potentially an import restriction subject to GATT article XI:1, mentioned above. From the GATT perspective, the importing country would have to justify its measure under GATT article XX(b). A treaty interpreter would have to decide whether such measures are necessary for the protection of human life or health. Although the ultimate goal of tobacco control is to protect human life or health, the 'contribution of the measure to the realization of the ends pursued by it'[34] might not be absolute and it might not be as easy to argue that there is no possible alternative. That is because of the non-binding nature of the relevant guidelines, which only recommend that parties 'consider' adopting plain packaging requirements, as noted above. In short, treaty interpreters might not be able to infer from the guidelines alone that the adoption of plain packaging requirements is strictly necessary and that there is no appropriate alternative for countries to consider.

B   Possible Dual Use of Guidelines and Protocols

Guidelines are useful in quickly providing guidance to assist parties to discharge their obligations under the WHO FCTC and to build a comprehensive multilateral tobacco control system. They also assist the rapid growth of the multilateral regulatory system. But parties do not always have clear obligations under guidelines. The non-binding nature of guidelines might not be very helpful for parties seeking to persuade domestic legislatures to adopt legislation implementing the guidelines.

Further, other international treaty systems may not take into account non-binding rules. On the other hand, although a protocol may require parties to adopt domestic legislation and may be better recognised by other treaty systems, the process of concluding a protocol is longer and more difficult.

From the WHO FCTC perspective, a given subject matter may be subject to both a protocol and a set of guidelines. In fact, most subject matters are suitable subjects of both types of instrument. For instance, the plain packaging requirements currently referred to in guidelines could also be provided in a protocol. If the plain packaging requirements were provided in a protocol, the parties to the protocol might be able to rely on mandatory provisions therein to persuade domestic legislatures to pass legislation to fulfil their obligations. It would also be more persuasive for such countries to argue that, having acceded to such a protocol, it is 'necessary' for them to implement such requirements, in connection with GATT article XX(b).

If such dual use of a protocol and guidelines was pursued, parties could decide whether to join the protocol group so as to enhance their tobacco control policy and to support their measures under different treaty systems.

VI CONCLUDING REMARKS

This chapter discusses the respective usefulness of protocols and guidelines under the WHO FCTC and their associated difficulties. Guidelines are important for the rapid growth of the WHO FCTC and are useful to guide the parties. Protocols may be more useful in helping obtain domestic legislation and in affecting the consideration of obligations under other treaty systems.

Since the WHO FCTC does not set forth a strict distinction between the use of protocols and guidelines, it is possible for most subject matters to be dealt with either by a protocol or a set of guidelines, or indeed both.

Due to their respective advantages, it is desirable to still rely on guidelines to enhance the rapid growth of the WHO FCTC system and, in addition to that, to incrementally have certain subject matters already covered by guidelines become subject to a protocol. Although fewer parties may sign up to the protocols and although the progress of negotiating a protocol may be slower, it is still desirable to have more protocols negotiated and concluded for the purpose of strengthening the control of tobacco use.

NOTES

1. Opened for signature 16 June 2003, 2302 UNTS 166 (entered into force 27 February 2005).
2. For instance, article 6.3 requires parties to provide rates of taxation for tobacco products and trends in tobacco consumption in their periodic reports.
3. For instance, article 8.2 requires parties to adopt and implement effective measures providing for protection from exposure to tobacco smoke in indoor workplaces and other public places, but the types of measure to be adopted are not prescribed. Article 9 requires parties to adopt and implement effective measures for testing and measuring the contents and emissions of tobacco products, but the scope and standards of testing and measuring are not prescribed. Article 10 requires parties to adopt measures requiring manufacturers and importers of tobacco products to disclose to governmental authorities information about the contents and emissions of tobacco products, but again, the types of measures to be adopted are not prescribed.
4. Adopted 22 July 1946, 14 UNTS 185 (entered into force 7 April 1948).
5. Chang-fa Lo, 'Establishing Global Governance in the Implementation of FCTC: Some Reflections on the Current Two-Pillar and One-Roof Framework' (2006) 1 *Asian Journal of WTO & International Health Law and Policy* 569, from 569.
6. Nele Matz-Lück, 'Framework Conventions as Regulatory Tools' (2009) 1 *Goettingen Journal of International Law* 439, 448.
7. Adopted 29 May 1992, 1771 UNTS 107 (entered into force 21 March 1994).
8. Adopted 10 December 1997, 37 ILM 22 (entered into force 16 February 2005).
9. James Hodge and Gabriel Eber, 'Tobacco Control Legislation: Tools for Public Health Improvement' (2004) 32 *Journal of Law, Medicine & Ethics* 516, 516.
10. Christine Bump, 'Close but no Cigar: the WHO Framework Convention on Tobacco Control's Futile Ban on Tobacco Advertising' (2003) 17 *Emory International Law Review* 1251, 1266–7.
11. WHO FCTC Conference of the Parties, *Guidelines for Implementation of Article 13 of the WHO Framework Convention on Tobacco Control*, WHO Doc FCTC/COP3(12) (November 2008).
12. See <http://www.who.int/fctc/protocol/en/>.
13. WHO FCTC Conference of the Parties, *Guidelines for Implementation of Article 14 of the WHO Framework Convention on Tobacco Control*, WHO Doc FCTC/COP4(8) (November 2010) [23].
14. WHO FCTC Conference of the Parties, *Guidelines for Implementation of Article 5.3 of the WHO Framework Convention on Tobacco Control*, WHO Doc FCTC/COP3(7) (November 2008).
15. WHO FCTC Conference of the Parties, *Guidelines for Implementation of Article 8 of the WHO Framework Convention on Tobacco Control*, WHO Doc FCTC/COP2(7) (July 2007).
16. WHO FCTC Conference of the Parties, *Partial Guidelines for Implementation of Articles 9 and 10 of the WHO Framework Convention on Tobacco Control*, WHO Doc FCTC/COP4(1) (November 2010, amended 2012).
17. WHO FCTC Conference of the Parties, *Guidelines for Implementation of Article 11 of the WHO Framework Convention on Tobacco Control*, WHO Doc FCTC/COP3(1) (November 2008).
18. WHO FCTC Conference of the Parties, *Guidelines for Implementation of Article 12 of the WHO Framework Convention on Tobacco Control*, WHO Doc FCTC/COP4(7) (November 2010).
19. See above n 12.
20. See above n 15.

21. WHO FCTC, *Guidelines for Implementation of the WHO Framework Convention on Tobacco Control* (2013) <http://www.who.int/fctc/guidelines/en/>.
22. See above n 16.
23. Emphasis added.
24. See above n 19 (emphasis added).
25. Emphasis added.
26. See above n 19.
27. See above n 12.
28. See Chang-fa Lo, 'Plain Packaging and Indirect Expropriation of Trademark Rights under BITs' (2012) 32 *Medicine and Law Journal* 521, 521; Chang-fa Lo, 'External Regime Coherence: WTO/BIT and Public Health Tension as an Illustration' (2012) *Asian Journal of WTO and International Health Law and Policy* 263, 275. See also Chapter 14 of this volume.
29. *Marrakesh Agreement Establishing the World Trade Organization*, opened for signature 15 April 1994, 1867 UNTS 3 (entered into force 1 January 1995), annex 1A.
30. Ibid.
31. Ibid annex 1C.
32. Appellate Body Report, *China – Publications and Audiovisual Products*, WTO Doc WT/DS363/AB/R (adopted 19 January 2010) [242], [251] (referring to the necessity analysis in previous disputes).
33. Ibid [242].
34. Ibid [240].

4. The power of the WHO FCTC: understanding its legal status and weight

Jonathan Liberman[*]

I BACKGROUND – LOOKING TOWARDS THE WHO FCTC TEN-YEAR ANNIVERSARY

On 27 February 2015, the *WHO Framework Convention on Tobacco Control* (WHO FCTC)[1] will mark ten years since its entry into force. By that time, it will have at least 177 parties – the number of parties as at the date of writing this chapter.[2] The governing body of the WHO FCTC, the Conference of the Parties (COP), will have met six times, its sixth session scheduled to be held in Moscow, Russian Federation in October 2014, following sessions in Geneva, Switzerland (2006), Bangkok, Thailand (2007), Durban, South Africa (2008), Punta del Este, Uruguay (2010), and Seoul, South Korea (2012).

As well as being times of celebration, major anniversaries can be occasions for reflection, the learning of lessons, and of recommitment, with the integration of lessons learned into future plans and activities. The COP recognised this at its fifth session, noting the upcoming ten-year anniversary, and acknowledging the need 'to examine the impact of the Convention as a tool in promoting public health in general and tobacco prevention in particular' and 'to conduct ... an overall assessment and analysis of the long-term trends in prevalence of tobacco use, as well as implementation levels of comprehensive tobacco control legislation, policies and programmes'.[3] It requested the Convention Secretariat to prepare a report outlining options for conducting an impact assessment of the treaty after ten years of operation. That report will be discussed at the upcoming COP session in Moscow.

In an article published in 2011, after the COP's fourth session, I suggested that the WHO FCTC had:[4]

- raised the global profile of tobacco control;
- strengthened governments in their fight against the tobacco industry, politically and legally;
- reinforced the view that tobacco products are not normal consumer products, contributing to the ongoing de-normalisation of the tobacco industry;
- catalysed the formation and deepening of transnational civil society coalitions;
- facilitated the sharing of experiences, expertise and capacity among and between governments and non-governmental organisations; and
- brought new resources – political, financial and human – into the field.

Two years and one COP on, I think all of this remains true.

Since then, the WHO FCTC has also taken its rightful place on the burgeoning global non-communicable diseases (NCDs) agenda. In the Political Declaration adopted at the landmark September 2011 United Nations (UN) General Assembly High-Level Meeting on the Prevention and Control of NCDs, the 193 UN member states committed to '[a]ccelerate implementation' of the WHO FCTC, recognising that 'substantially reducing tobacco consumption is an important contribution to reducing non-communicable diseases'.[5] They encouraged countries that had not yet done so to consider acceding to the treaty.[6] A new UN Interagency Task Force on the Prevention and Control of NCDs has been established,[7] by way of expanding the mandate of the UN Ad Hoc Interagency Task Force on Tobacco Control, with the World Health Assembly (WHA) recognising the need to 'ensur[e] that tobacco control continues to be duly addressed and prioritised in the new task force mandate'.[8]

In addition, the importance of the WHO FCTC in the defence of tobacco control measures against litigation – both domestic and international – has been further underlined.[9] The treaty is continuing to aid in the interpretation of domestic law and in supporting the constitutionality of tobacco control measures.[10] A World Trade Organization (WTO) panel has referred to the WHO FCTC and its guidelines, notably in a dispute between Indonesia and the United States, neither of which is a party to the treaty.[11] Uruguay[12] and Australia[13] are invoking the WHO FCTC in their defences against lawsuits brought against their tobacco packaging laws by the multinational tobacco company, Philip Morris, under bilateral investment treaties between Uruguay and Switzerland,[14] and Australia and Hong Kong,[15] respectively.

When the impact of the WHO FCTC is considered, such forms of legal significance should be recognised as among the most important indicators. The last few years have seen the tobacco industry expanding its use of lawsuits and legal threats to delay or prevent effective WHO FCTC implementation. The Director-General of the WHO, Dr Margaret Chan, has highlighted the tobacco industry's strategy of pursuing costly, drawn-out litigation and threats of billion-dollar settlements aimed at breaking countries' resolve, and 'instil[ling] fear in countries wishing to introduce similarly tough tobacco control measures'.[16]

Dr Chan noted the difficulty of bearing the financial burden of such litigation, especially for small countries such as Uruguay. In the Seoul Declaration adopted at the COP's fifth session, parties to the WHO FCTC 'not[ed] with concern that the most frequently reported barrier to effective implementation of the WHO FCTC is interference by the tobacco industry'.[17] They declared '[t]heir determination not to allow tobacco industry interference to slow or prevent the development and implementation of tobacco control measures in the interests of public health and in accordance with the Convention and consistent with its guidelines'.[18]

In a legal (and political) sense, the WHO FCTC is the international community's most powerful tool to combat tobacco and the tobacco industry. Yet, as we head towards the treaty's ten-year anniversary, its legal status, weight and utility often appear to be inadequately understood. If this remains the case, its power will never be fully harnessed.

This chapter aims to contribute to that harnessing by addressing some common misapprehensions, focusing on three key points. First, it argues that the WHO FCTC, though originally conceived as a 'framework convention' – which would establish a general governance framework, with detailed content and obligations to be elaborated through protocols – became something quite different through the course of its negotiation. While the treaty will always be evolving, it is not waiting for something further to bring it into full being. Second, it offers a guide to the proper interpretation of the WHO FCTC, in which the individual provisions of the treaty are read in the context of the treaty as a whole, and taking into account its implementation guidelines and other relevant decisions of the COP. Third, it observes that the WHO FCTC's implementation guidelines are often erroneously viewed against a simple dichotomy of 'binding' or 'non-binding', whereas in fact the correct question is how they bear on interpretation of the treaty. The chapter then applies this analysis, and guide to interpretation, to the example of large graphic health warnings, arguing that it is incorrect to claim that WHO FCTC parties implementing large graphic health warnings are acting beyond what is required by the treaty. The chapter concludes by noting that the WHO FCTC, approaching ten years of age, remains young in the broader context of global health governance, and that global health practitioners and researchers are still coming to understand it.

II A FEW KEY POINTS ABOUT THE WHO FCTC AND ITS INTERPRETATION

If the WHO FCTC is to live up to its full, powerful potential as an enabler, supporter, and defender of tobacco control measures, its legal weight and utility need to be better understood than they have been thus far. This entails three major recognitions.

A Not 'Just a Framework Convention' Waiting to Become Complete

In her 1996 article proposing an international legal instrument for tobacco, Allyn Taylor recommended that the WHO initiate negotiations for a tobacco control treaty using the 'framework convention/protocol' approach, which had been used in a range of other areas of international concern.[19] Under this approach, states would first adopt a framework convention calling for international cooperation in realising broadly stated goals, and then parties to the convention 'would conclude separate protocols containing specific measures designed to implement these goals'.[20] Taylor saw a framework convention as 'more likely to secure political consensus and significant action on tobacco control than any other form of binding instrument'.[21]

From its conception, the proposed treaty was viewed as a 'framework convention'. The 1996 WHA resolution (titled 'International Framework Convention for Tobacco Control') that paved the path to a treaty requested the WHO Director-General to 'initiate the development of a framework convention'.[22] Similarly, the formal treaty negotiations were initiated by a resolution titled 'Towards a WHO Framework Convention on Tobacco Control', in which the WHA decided to establish an intergovernmental negotiating body (INB) to draft and negotiate 'the proposed WHO framework convention on tobacco control and possible related protocols'.[23] The resolution referred in a number of places to '*the* WHO framework convention on tobacco control'.

In a briefing document prepared for the early stages of the treaty negotiations, Daniel Bodansky explained that the term 'framework convention' is generally 'used to describe a variety of international agreements whose principal function is to establish a general system of governance for an issue area, and not detailed obligations'.[24] Protocols – separate legally binding agreements made to supplement the framework agreement – may be adopted either concurrently with the framework convention or subsequently, and may be either mandatory or optional for parties to the convention.[25]

Yet what emerged from the hard-fought negotiations conducted through two working group meetings and six sessions of the INB[26] was much more than 'a general system of governance', onto which detailed content would later be added. Even a cursory glance at, for example, articles 8 (protection from exposure to tobacco smoke), 11 (packaging and labelling of tobacco products), 12 (education, communication, training and public awareness), 13 (tobacco advertising, promotion and sponsorship), 14 (demand reduction measures concerning tobacco dependence and cessation) and 16 (sales to and by minors) reveals a number of detailed provisions and strong obligations.

This outcome may have been difficult to foresee when the process towards the treaty was initiated and, indeed, the process may never have commenced had some WHO member states known how it would culminate. But once negotiations commence, they can often generate a momentum that leads to unanticipated results.

In my view, more than 11 years since its entry into force, and nearly 12 years since its adoption by the WHA in May 2003,[27] the treaty suffers from being viewed by some as 'just' a framework convention. The title, associated framing, and perhaps the historical overhang of the framework convention–protocol conception, seem still to convey to some a sense that something more is needed to make it a 'real' treaty. This could be observed in one of the recommendations adopted at the 14th World Conference on Tobacco or Health held in Mumbai in 2009: 'By 2012, the FCTC Protocol on illicit trade in tobacco products will have been adopted, ratified and entered into force and at least one other protocol in negotiation'.[28] A protocol on illicit trade was adopted by the COP at its fifth session,[29] although it has not yet entered into force.[30] But the reference in the Mumbai Declaration to 'at least one other protocol in negotiation', with no mention of what it would relate to, or why it would be needed, suggests an unexamined assumption that further protocols are necessary to 'complete' the treaty.

Today, there is no serious proposal to negotiate another protocol or protocols to the treaty, and the COP is attending to the business of implementation: the ongoing development of normative instruments, the mobilisation of resources,[31] the facilitation of international cooperation,[32] and the strengthening of relationships with key organisations.[33] The treaty is not waiting for further protocols to make it real. It is already a powerful, legally binding instrument of international law.

B The Individual Provisions of the Treaty Must be Read in the Context of the Treaty as a Whole, and Taking its Implementation Guidelines and Other Relevant Decisions of the COP into Account

The rules of treaty interpretation require that each of the WHO FCTC's individual provisions be read within the larger whole of which they form part. The obligations of the WHO FCTC cannot be understood by reading its individual provisions in isolation.

The rules of treaty interpretation under customary international law are generally accepted as being largely codified in the *Vienna Convention on the Law of Treaties* (VCLT).[34] As article 31(1) of the VCLT states: 'A treaty shall be interpreted in good faith in accordance with the ordinary meaning to be given to the terms of the treaty in their context and in the light of its object and purpose'. That 'context', according to article 31(2), includes its preamble. Article 31(3) states that 'together with the context', 'any subsequent agreement between the parties regarding the interpretation of the treaty or the application of its provisions' 'shall be taken into account'.[35]

This means that the accepted rules of treaty interpretation require the interpretation of the WHO FCTC as follows.

The individual provisions of the WHO FCTC should be interpreted in the light of its 'object and purpose',[36] as clearly set out in the treaty's objective:

> The objective of this Convention and its protocols is to protect present and future generations from the devastating health, social, environmental and economic consequences of tobacco consumption and exposure to tobacco smoke by providing a framework for tobacco control measures to be implemented by the Parties at the national, regional and international levels in order to reduce continually and substantially the prevalence of tobacco use and exposure to tobacco smoke.[37]

The WHO FCTC provisions should be interpreted in their 'context',[38] which includes other substantive obligations, such as:

> Each Party shall develop, implement, periodically update and review comprehensive multisectoral national tobacco control strategies, plans and programmes in accordance with this Convention and the protocols to which it is a Party.[39]

> Towards this end, each Party shall, in accordance with its capabilities ...
> adopt and implement *effective* legislative, executive, administrative and/or
> other measures and cooperate, as appropriate, with other Parties in developing
> appropriate policies for preventing and reducing tobacco consumption, nico-
> tine addiction and exposure to tobacco smoke.[40]

> Each Party shall adopt and implement *effective* legislative, executive, admin-
> istrative or other measures necessary to implement its obligations pursuant to
> Articles 8 to 13.[41]

The word 'effective' is highlighted in the above provisions to underline that
parties are legally obliged to adopt and implement 'effective' measures.

The 'context'[42] for interpreting the provisions of the WHO FCTC
includes the treaty's guiding principles, including:

- that '[e]very person should be informed of the health consequences,
  addictive nature and mortal threat posed by tobacco consumption
  and exposure to tobacco smoke';[43]
- the necessity of strong political commitment, taking into account
  'the need' to take measures to: protect all persons from exposure to
  tobacco smoke; to prevent initiation, to promote and support
  cessation, and to decrease consumption; to promote the participation of indigenous individuals and communities; and to address
  gender-specific risks;[44] and
- the importance of international cooperation, particularly transfer of
  technology, knowledge and financial assistance and provision of
  related expertise.[45]

The 'context'[46] for interpreting the WHO FCTC also includes the treaty's
preamble. There is no substitute for reading the preamble in full, but
particularly noteworthy elements include:

- determination 'to give priority to [parties'] right to protect public
  health';
- recognition that 'the spread of the tobacco epidemic is a global
  problem with serious consequences for public health';
- the 'concern of the international community about the devastating
  worldwide health, social, economic and environmental consequences of tobacco consumption and exposure to tobacco smoke';
- serious concern 'about the increase in the worldwide consumption
  and production of cigarettes and other tobacco products, particularly in developing countries, as well as about the burden this
  places on families, on the poor, and on national health systems';

- recognition that 'cigarettes and some other products containing tobacco are highly engineered so as to create and maintain dependence, and that many of the compounds they contain and the smoke they produce are pharmacologically active, toxic, mutagenic and carcinogenic';
- deep concern 'about the escalation in smoking and other forms of tobacco consumption by children and adolescents worldwide, particularly smoking at increasingly early ages';
- alarm at the 'increase in smoking and other forms of tobacco consumption by women and young girls worldwide';
- serious concern about the impact of all forms of advertising, promotion and sponsorship aimed at encouraging the use of tobacco products;
- recall of the *International Covenant on Economic, Social and Cultural Rights* (ICESCR),[47] the Constitution of the WHO,[48] the *Convention on the Elimination of All Forms of Discrimination against Women*,[49] and the *Convention on the Rights of the Child*,[50] and, in particular, article 12 of the ICESCR, which states that 'it is the right of everyone to the enjoyment of the highest attainable standard of physical and mental health', and the preamble to the WHO Constitution, which states that enjoyment of the highest attainable standard of health is one of the fundamental rights of every human being without distinction of race, religion, political belief, economic or social condition; and
- the determination of WHO FCTC parties to promote measures of tobacco control 'based on current and relevant scientific, technical and economic considerations'.

Finally, to the extent that the implementation guidelines and other decisions of the COP constitute 'subsequent agreement(s) between the parties regarding the interpretation of the treaty or the application of its provisions', they '*shall*' be taken into account' in its interpretation.[51]

C It is Wrong to View the WHO FCTC Implementation Guidelines Against a Simple Dichotomy of 'Binding' or 'Non-binding': the Correct Question is How They Bear on Interpretation of the Treaty

The WHO FCTC implementation guidelines are often described (and disparaged or dismissed) as 'non-legally binding'. This description often reflects a misunderstanding of their status, and of their relationship to the treaty.

The WHO FCTC guidelines are adopted by the COP, after considering draft guidelines developed inter-sessionally by working groups of parties established by the COP, and open to all parties. So far, the COP has adopted – by consensus – implementation guidelines on articles 5.3 (protection of public health policies with respect to tobacco control from commercial and other vested interests of the tobacco industry),[52] 8 (protection from exposure to tobacco smoke),[53] 11 (packaging and labelling of tobacco products),[54] 12 (education, communication, training and public awareness),[55] 13 (tobacco advertising, promotion and sponsorship),[56] and 14 (demand reduction measures concerning tobacco dependence and cessation).[57] It has adopted partial implementation guidelines on articles 9 and 10 (regulation of the contents of tobacco products and regulation of tobacco product disclosures)[58] and a set of guiding principles and recommendations for implementation of article 6 (price and tax measures to reduce the demand for tobacco).[59] These are all capable of constituting 'subsequent agreement[s] between the parties regarding the interpretation of the treaty or the application of its provisions'.[60] To the extent that they are subsequent agreements, the rules of treaty interpretation *require* that they be taken into account in the interpretation of the WHO FCTC.

The correct legal question – how the guidelines bear on interpretation of the treaty – cannot be answered at the level of the guidelines generally, or even each set of guidelines individually. Rather, there are differences both between sets of guidelines and between elements of each set of guidelines, according to the precise language used in the guidelines and their relationships to the terms of the treaty itself.[61]

III THE ADOPTION AND IMPLEMENTATION OF LARGE, GRAPHIC HEALTH WARNINGS: AN EXAMPLE OF GOOD FAITH TREATY IMPLEMENTATION

The approach to interpretation described above can be illustrated through the example of large, graphic health warnings. This example is selected here because the tobacco industry routinely claims that, in implementing large, graphic health warnings, parties are acting beyond the requirements of the treaty. In the domestic context, this claim is deployed to characterise proposed measures that are justified in part in terms of implementation of treaty obligations as less important or legitimate, and to diminish the legal significance of the WHO FCTC where the tobacco industry is claiming that large graphic health warnings breach some aspect of domestic law. At the international level, it is argued by the tobacco industry to be significant in the relationship between tobacco control measures and WTO obligations, again in an attempt to diminish the importance of the treaty. The tobacco industry routinely argues, for example, that large graphic health warnings breach WTO obligations, particularly under the *Agreement on Technical Barriers to Trade* (TBT Agreement)[62] and the *Agreement on Trade-Related Aspects of Intellectual Property Rights* (TRIPS Agreement).[63]

In my view, the claim that large graphic health warnings breach WTO obligations is unsound, both because it relies on an erroneous understanding of the way in which the TRIPS Agreement protects trade marks, and because the WTO agreements contain ample flexibilities to allow the implementation of measures designed to protect health, including tobacco control measures. These matters have been extensively canvassed elsewhere[64] and will not be further addressed here. My concern here is with whether large graphic health warnings – such as Thailand's regulations requiring such warnings on 85 per cent of both the front and back of tobacco packaging, presently under legal challenge in Thailand's domestic courts[65] – can fairly be said to be measures beyond the requirements of the FCTC.

The basis for this contention is generally that under article 11.1(b) of the WHO FCTC, warnings and messages 'should be 50% or more of the principal display areas but shall be no less than 30% of the principal display areas' and 'may be in the form of or include pictures or pictograms'. So, the argument goes, pictorial warnings, and warnings larger than 30 per cent of the principal display areas, go beyond what is 'required by' the treaty.

This argument may appear to be superficially sound, but, on closer analysis, it is based on an unjustifiably narrow reading of the treaty's text – on the fallacy of reading individual provisions divorced from the whole of which they form part. When the entirety of article 11.1(b) is read, it can be seen that its essential obligation is that:

> 1. Each Party shall, within a period of three years after entry into force of this Convention for that Party, adopt and implement, in accordance with its national law, *effective* measures to ensure that:
>
> ...
>
> b) each unit packet and package of tobacco products and any outside packaging and labelling of such products also *carry health warnings describing the harmful effects of tobacco use*, and may include other appropriate messages.[66]

This means that the essential article 11.1(b) obligation is to adopt and implement health warnings that 'effectively' 'describ[e] the harmful effects of tobacco use'. Clearly, understandings of effectiveness evolve over time, as evidence develops, and as new practices are adopted and evaluated. The content of the concept of 'effectiveness' is not fixed in time. It was not fixed in May 2003, when the WHO FCTC was adopted by the WHA.[67] Read correctly, the 'should be 50% or more ... but shall be no less than 30%' text, agreed in May 2003, should not diminish the meaning, and evolution over time, of the essential obligation to adopt and implement health warnings that 'effectively' 'describ[e] the harmful effects of tobacco use'.

As noted above, interpretation of the WHO FCTC provisions must take place in their context, which includes other substantive obligations – such as articles 5.2(b) and 7 referred to above – as well as the treaty's objective, guiding principles, and preamble.

Particularly relevant provisions include the guiding principle that '[e]very person should be informed of the health consequences, addictive nature and mortal threat posed by tobacco consumption and exposure to tobacco smoke' and the preambular paragraph recording parties' determination 'to promote measures of tobacco control based on current and relevant scientific, technical and economic considerations'. The latter paragraph underlines the importance and value of scientific evidence – which, by its nature, is constantly evolving – to the way in which measures are adopted and implemented.

Further, to the extent that the article 11 implementation guidelines are 'regarding the interpretation of the treaty or the application of its provisions', they 'shall be taken into account' in its interpretation.[68] The purpose of these guidelines is 'to assist Parties in meeting their obligations under Article 11 of the Convention, and to propose measures that Parties can use to increase the effectiveness of their packaging and labelling measures'.[69] Particularly relevant elements of the guidelines include:

> Well-designed health warnings and messages are part of a range of effective measures to communicate health risks and to reduce tobacco use. Evidence demonstrates that the effectiveness of health warnings and messages increases with their prominence. In comparison with small, text-only health warnings, larger warnings with pictures are more likely to be noticed, better communicate health risks, provoke a greater emotional response and increase the motivation of tobacco users to quit and to decrease their tobacco consumption. Larger picture warnings are also more likely to retain their effectiveness over time and are particularly effective in communicating health effects to low-literacy populations, children and young people. Other elements that

enhance effectiveness include locating health warnings and messages on principal display areas, and at the top of these principal display areas; the use of colour rather than just black and white; requiring that multiple health warnings and messages appear concurrently; and periodic revision of health warnings and messages.[70]

Given the evidence that the effectiveness of health warnings and messages increases with their size, Parties should consider using health warnings and messages that cover more than 50% of the principal display areas and aim to cover as much of the principal display areas as possible.[71]

Evidence shows that health warnings and messages that contain both pictures and text are far more effective than those that are text-only. They also have the added benefit of potentially reaching people with low levels of literacy and those who cannot read the language(s) in which the text of the health warning or message is written. Parties should mandate culturally appropriate pictures or pictograms, in full colour, in their packaging and labelling requirements. Parties should consider the use of pictorial health warnings on both principal display areas (or on all main faces if there are more than two) of the tobacco products packaging.[72]

Evidence shows that, when compared with text-only health warnings and messages, those with pictures:

- are more likely to be noticed;
- are rated more effective by tobacco users;
- are more likely to remain salient over time;
- better communicate the health risks of tobacco use;
- provoke more thought about the health risks of tobacco use and about cessation;
- increase motivation and intention to quit; and
- are associated with more attempts to quit.[73]

Reading the article 11 guidelines as part of the interpretation of article 11 is perfectly consistent with the wording of the COP decision that adopted the article 11 implementation guidelines: 'Emphasizing that the aim of these guidelines is to assist Parties to meet their obligations under Article 11 of the Convention and that they are not intended to increase Parties' obligations under this Article'.[74] The approach outlined here does not 'increase Parties' obligations'. Rather, it assists in clarifying how parties' adoption and implementation of large, graphic health warnings should be understood.

Thus, when article 11.1(b) is read correctly, it is untenable to claim that a party that adopts and implements large graphic health warnings, in good faith, believing, on the basis of sound evidence, that they are likely to effectively describe the harmful effects of tobacco use, is acting beyond the requirements of the treaty. Rather, it is performing its obligations in good faith.

IV CONCLUSION

It is often remarked that the WHO FCTC is the first treaty negotiated under the auspices of the WHO. The WHO was established in 1948.[75] It had been in existence for 55 years by the time the WHO FCTC was adopted, and it will be about to turn 67 when the WHO FCTC reaches its ten-year anniversary. In that broader context, the WHO FCTC remains young, and it is still coming to be understood.

The upcoming ten-year anniversary of the WHO FCTC offers an invaluable opportunity to reflect on what this treaty is and what it can and should be. An important part of this will be developing a fuller understanding of its legal status and weight. Such an understanding will allow the harnessing of the true potential of the WHO FCTC to 'protect present and future generations from the devastating health, social, environmental and economic consequences of tobacco consumption and exposure to tobacco smoke'.[76]

NOTES

*   The author wishes to thank Gian Luca Burci, Alexandra Jones, Benn McGrady and Allyn Taylor for very helpful comments and suggestions on an earlier draft. All views expressed in the chapter are of course those of the author.
1. *WHO Framework Convention on Tobacco Control*, opened for signature 21 May 2003, 2302 UNTS 166 (entered into force 27 February 2005) (WHO FCTC).
2. *Parties to the WHO Framework Convention on Tobacco Control* (27 November 2013) WHO Framework Convention on Tobacco Control <http://www.who.int/fctc/signatories_parties/en/>.
3. WHO FCTC Conference of the Parties, *Impact Assessment of the WHO FCTC*, 4th plen mtg, WHO Doc FCTC/COP5(12) (17 November 2012).
4. Jonathan Liberman, 'Four COPs and Counting: Achievements, Underachievements and Looming Challenges in the Early Life of the WHO FCTC Conference of the Parties' (2012) 21 *Tobacco Control* 215.
5. *Political Declaration of the High-level Meeting of the General Assembly on the Prevention and Control of Non-communicable Diseases*, GA Res 66/2, 66th sess, 3rd plen mtg, Agenda Item 117, UN Doc A/RES/66/2 (24 January 2012, adopted 19 September 2011) annex [43(c)].
6. Ibid.
7. World Health Organization, *UN Interagency Task Force on the Prevention and Control of NCDs* <http://www.who.int/nmh/events/ncd_task_force>.
8. World Health Organization, *Follow-up to the Political Declaration of the High-Level Meeting of the General Assembly on the Prevention and Control of Non-communicable Diseases*, WHO Res WHA66.10, 66th WHA, 9th plen mtg, Agenda Items 13.1 and 13.2, WHO Doc A66/VR/9 (27 May 2013) [2.8].
9. Monique Muggli et al, 'Tracking the Relevance of the WHO Framework Convention on Tobacco Control in Legislation and Litigation through the Online Resource,

Tobacco Control Laws' (4 May 2013) *Tobacco Control* (online first) doi:10.1136/
tobaccocontrol-2012-050854.
10. Ibid 1–2.
11. Panel Report, *United States – Measures Affecting the Production and Sale of Clove
Cigarettes*, WTO Doc WT/DS406/R (circulated 2 September 2011, adopted 24 April
2012).
12. *Philip Morris Brand Sàrl (Switzerland) v Uruguay (Jurisdiction)* (ICSID Arbitral
Tribunal, Case No ARB/10/7, 2 July 2013).
13. *Philip Morris Asia Ltd v Australia (Procedural Order)* (Permanent Court of Arbitration, Case No 2012-12, 31 December 2012).
14. *Agreement between the Swiss Confederation and the Oriental Republic of Uruguay
on the Reciprocal Promotion and Protection of Investments*, signed 7 October 1988,
1976 UNTS 389 (entered into force 22 April 1991).
15. *Agreement between the Government of Hong Kong and the Government of Australia
for the Promotion and Protection of Investments*, signed 15 September 1993, 1770
UNTS 385 (entered into force 15 October 1993).
16. Margaret Chan, 'The Changed Face of the Tobacco Industry' (Speech delivered at the
15th World Conference on Tobacco or Health, Singapore, 20 March 2012) <http://
www.who.int/dg/speeches/2012/tobacco_20120320/en/>.
17. WHO FCTC Conference of the Parties, *Seoul Declaration*, 4th plen mtg, WHO Doc
FCTC/COP5(5) (17 November 2012) preamble.
18. Ibid [5].
19. Allyn Taylor, 'An International Regulatory Strategy for Global Tobacco Control'
(1996) 21 *Yale Journal of International Law* 257.
20. Ibid 294.
21. Ibid.
22. World Health Organization, *International Framework Convention for Tobacco Control*, Resolution WHA49.17, 49th WHA, 6th plen mtg (25 May 1996) [3.1].
23. World Health Organization, *Towards a WHO Framework Convention on Tobacco
Control*, WHO Res WHA52.18, 52nd WHA, 9th plen mtg, WHO Doc A52/7 (24
May 1999) [1.1].
24. Daniel Bodansky, 'The Framework Convention/Protocol Approach', *WHO FCTC
Technical Briefing Series* (1999) WHO Doc WHO/NCD/TFI/99.1, 15.
25. Ibid 33.
26. Documentation of the COP, including the INB, the Working Group, and the
Open-ended Intergovernmental Working Group, is available at WHO Framework
Convention on Tobacco Control, *Documentation in all Official Languages of the
Conference of the Parties* <http://apps.who.int/gb/fctc/E/E_process.html>.
27. World Health Organization, *WHO Framework Convention on Tobacco Control*, WHO
Res WHA56.1, 56th WHA, Agenda Item 13, WHO Doc A66/VR/9 (21 May 2003).
28. 14th World Conference on Tobacco or Health, *Mumbai Declaration* (8–12 March
2009) recommendation 3 <http://www.treatobacco.net/en/uploads/documents/Other%
20Documents/Declarations%2014%20World%20Conference%20Mumbai%202009.
pdf>.
29. WHO FCTC Conference of the Parties, *Protocol to Eliminate Illicit Trade in Tobacco
Products*, WHO Doc FCTC/COP5(1) (12 November 2012).
30. WHO Framework Convention on Tobacco Control, *Signature and Ratification*
<http://www.who.int/fctc/protocol/ratification/en/>.
31. See, eg, WHO FCTC Conference of the Parties, *Financial Resources, Mechanisms of
Assistance and International Cooperation for Strengthening Sustainable Implementation of the WHO FCTC*, WHO Doc FCTC/COP5(14) (17 November 2012); WHO
FCTC Conference of the Parties, *Financial Resources, Mechanisms of Assistance and
International Cooperation*, WHO Doc FCTC/COP4(17) (20 November 2010).

32. See, eg, WHO FCTC Conference of the Parties, *Financial Resources, Mechanisms of Assistance and International Cooperation for Strengthening Sustainable Implementation of the WHO FCTC*, WHO Doc FCTC/COP5(14) (17 November 2012); WHO FCTC Conference of the Parties, *Promoting South–South Cooperation for Implementation of the WHO FCTC*, FCTC/COP5(13) (17 November 2012); WHO FCTC Conference of the Parties, *Promoting South–South Cooperation for Implementation of the WHO Framework Convention on Tobacco Control*, WHO Doc FCTC/COP4(19) (20 November 2010); WHO FCTC Conference of the Parties, *Financial Resources, Mechanisms of Assistance and International Cooperation*, WHO Doc FCTC/COP4(17) (20 November 2010).

33. See, eg, WHO FCTC Conference of the Parties, *Cooperation between the Convention Secretariat, the World Health Organization, the World Trade Organization and the United Nations Conference on Trade and Development*, WHO Doc FCTC/COP5(15) (17 November 2012); WHO FCTC Conference of the Parties, *Cooperation between the Convention Secretariat and the World Trade Organization*, WHO Doc FCTC/COP4(18) (20 November 2010).

34. Opened for signature 23 May 1969, 1155 UNTS 331 (entered into force 27 January 1980) (VCLT).

35. VCLT article 31(3)(a).

36. VCLT article 31(1).

37. WHO FCTC article 3.

38. VCLT articles 31(1), 31(2).

39. WHO FCTC article 5(1). This is one of the treaty's general obligations.

40. WHO FCTC article 5(2)(b) (emphasis added).

41. WHO FCTC article 7 (emphasis added).

42. VCLT articles 31(1), 31(2).

43. WHO FCTC article 4.1.

44. WHO FCTC article 4.2.

45. WHO FCTC article 4.3.

46. VCLT articles 31(1), 31(2).

47. *International Covenant on Economic, Social and Cultural Rights*, opened for signature 19 December 1966, 993 UNTS 3 (entered into force 3 January 1976).

48. 'Constitution of the World Health Organization', *Basic Documents* (45th ed, Supplement, October 2006).

49. *Convention on the Elimination of All Forms of Discrimination against Women*, opened for signature 18 December 1979, 1249 UNTS 13 (entered into force 3 September 1981).

50. *Convention on the Rights of the Child*, opened for signature 20 November 1989, 1577 UNTS 3, 1588 UNTS 530 (entered into force 2 September 1990).

51. VCLT article 31(3)(a).

52. WHO FCTC Conference of the Parties, *Guidelines for Implementation of Article 5.3 of the WHO Framework Convention on Tobacco Control*, WHO Doc FCTC/COP3(7) (22 November 2008).

53. WHO FCTC Conference of the Parties, *Guidelines for Implementation of Article 8 of the WHO Framework Convention on Tobacco Control*, WHO Doc FCTC/COP2(7) (6 July 2007).

54. WHO FCTC Conference of the Parties, *Guidelines for Implementation of Article 11 of the WHO Framework Convention on Tobacco Control*, WHO Doc FCTC/COP3(10) (22 November 2008).

55. WHO FCTC Conference of the Parties, *Guidelines for Implementation of Article 12 of the WHO Framework Convention on Tobacco Control*, WHO Doc FCTC/COP4(7) (20 November 2010).

56. WHO FCTC Conference of the Parties, *Guidelines for Implementation of Article 13 of the WHO Framework Convention on Tobacco Control*, WHO Doc FCTC/COP3(12) (22 November 2008).

57. WHO FCTC Conference of the Parties, *Guidelines for Implementation of Article 14 of the WHO Framework Convention on Tobacco Control*, WHO Doc FCTC/COP4(8) (20 November 2010).

58. WHO FCTC Conference of the Parties, *Partial Guidelines for Implementation of Articles 9 and 10 of the WHO Framework Convention on Tobacco Control*, WHO Doc FCTC/COP4(10) (20 November 2010).

59. WHO FCTC Conference of the Parties, *Set of Guiding Principles and Recommendations for Implementation of Article 6 of the WHO Framework Convention on Tobacco Control (Price and Tax Measures to Reduce the Demand for Tobacco)*, WHO Doc FCTC/COP5(7) (17 November 2012).

60. VCLT article 31(3)(a).

61. Liberman, above n 4, 216.

62. *Marrakesh Agreement Establishing the World Trade Organization*, opened for signature 15 April 1994, 1867 UNTS 3 (entered into force 1 January 1995) annex 1A.

63. *Marrakesh Agreement Establishing the World Trade Organization*, opened for signature 15 April 1994, 1867 UNTS 3 (entered into force 1 January 1995) annex 1C.

64. See, eg, Mark Davison, 'The Legitimacy of Plain Packaging under International Intellectual Property Law: Why There is no Right to Use a Trademark under either the Paris Convention or the TRIPS Agreement' in Tania Voon et al (eds), *Public Health and Plain Packaging of Cigarettes: Legal Issues* (Edward Elgar, 2012) 81; Tania Voon and Andrew Mitchell, 'Implications of WTO Law for Plain Packaging of Tobacco Products' in Tania Voon et al (eds), *Public Health and Plain Packaging of Cigarettes: Legal Issues* (Edward Elgar, 2012) 109; Mark Davison and Patrick Emerton, 'Rights, Privileges, Legitimate Interests, and Justifiability: Article 20 of TRIPS and Plain Packaging of Tobacco' (Monash University Faculty of Law Legal Studies Research Paper No 2013/24, 6 September 2013) <http://papers.ssrn.com/sol3/papers.cfm?abstract_id=2322043>; Tania Voon, 'Flexibilities in WTO Law to Support Tobacco Control Regulation' (2013) 39 *American Journal of Law and Medicine* 199.

65. Ron Corben, 'Thailand's Health Ministry Battles Big Tobacco over Graphic Health Warnings' (8 October 2013) *Voice of America* (online) <http://www.voanews.com/content/thailands-health-ministry-battles-big-tobacco-over-graphic-health-warnings/1765216.html>.

66. WHO FCTC article 11.1(b) (emphasis added).

67. See above n 27 and corresponding text.

68. VCLT article 31(3)(a).

69. WHO FCTC Conference of the Parties, *Guidelines for Implementation of Article 11*, above n 54, annex [1].

70. Ibid annex [7].

71. Ibid annex [12].

72. Ibid annex [14].

73. Ibid annex [15].

74. Ibid preamble.

75. World Health Organization, *History of WHO* (2013) <http://www.who.int/about/history/en/>.

76. WHO FCTC article 3.

5. The European Anti-Fraud Office and the Protocol to Eliminate Illicit Trade in Tobacco Products

Neil Boister[*]

I INTRODUCTION

Over the last ten years the European Anti-Fraud Office (OLAF) has become a significant actor in the global suppression of tobacco smuggling. Its activities reached fruition with the adoption in November 2012, by the fifth Conference of the Parties (COP) to the *WHO Framework Convention on Tobacco Control* (WHO FCTC),[1] of a *Protocol to Eliminate Illicit Trade in Tobacco Products* (*Illicit Trade Protocol* or *Protocol*).[2] The *Illicit Trade Protocol* supplements and fleshes out the general obligations to reduce the illicit trade in tobacco products contained in article 15 of the WHO FCTC. This chapter explores the role that OLAF has played in the development of the *Illicit Trade Protocol*. It examines OLAF's mandate and how OLAF became involved in the negotiation of the *Illicit Trade Protocol*. It analyses the extent to which OLAF used the European Commission's (Commission) agreements with major tobacco manufacturing companies as a model for the substance of the *Protocol*. Finally, the chapter examines whether OLAF has achieved its goals in the negotiation of the *Protocol*, and draws some conclusions about OLAF's role as a norm entrepreneur and about the risks inherent in setting up a system that establishes the tobacco manufacturing industry's role as a regulatory partner.

II OLAF'S MANDATE

OLAF's work against tobacco smuggling arises out of its mandate to protect the financial interests of the European Union (EU). OLAF is an organisational unit of the Commission – a general directorate – but enjoys functional investigative independence.[3] It is authorised to engage in investigations within EU bodies and member states, as well as in third countries,[4] in order to combat 'fraud, corruption and any other illegal activity adversely affecting the EU's financial interests'.[5]

Customs and excise fraud against the EU falls within OLAF's jurisdiction. Tobacco smuggling into the EU avoids customs duty on imports into the EU, the illicit production of tobacco within the EU avoids excise duty imposed on EU goods, and the sale of the tobacco avoids value added tax.[6]

Although established to deal with fraud within the EU, OLAF has become increasingly concerned with fraud emanating from outside the EU.[7] However, in investigations in third countries, OLAF does not have the extensive investigative powers that it enjoys within the EU[8] and must rely on EU agreements on mutual administrative assistance in customs matters with third-party states.

OLAF has played a dominant role in the negotiation of the *Illicit Trade Protocol*. The legal basis of this role is complex. In terms of article 1(2) of *Regulation (EC) No 1073/1999 of the European Parliament and of the Council of 25 May 1999 Concerning Investigations Conducted by the European Anti-Fraud Office (OLAF)* (*OLAF Regulation*),[9] OLAF provides 'member states with assistance from the commission in organising close and regular cooperation between their competent authorities in order to coordinate their activities for the purpose of protecting the European Community's financial interests against fraud'.[10] As noted above, OLAF is formally part of the Commission[11] and thus exercises the Commission's coordinating responsibility in the protection of the EU's financial interests under article 325(3) of the *Treaty on the Functioning of the European Union* (TFEU).[12] OLAF also has the responsibility of developing the Commission's strategy against fraud.[13] Stefanou et al note that 'OLAF represents the Commission in all forums related to its field of competence'.[14]

At the Intergovernmental Negotiating Body (INB) meetings that negotiated the *Illicit Trade Protocol*, OLAF usually spoke on behalf of the Commission. It is difficult for those unfamiliar with the arcane rules of how the EU operates as an international negotiating party to understand why this occurred. The basic principle is that the EU may act under international law only where member states have conferred powers on it to do so. In areas where it has competence, the EU, represented by the Commission, sets the position for all member states.[15] But in areas of shared competence, such as the suppression of fraud, where both the EU and member state interests are involved, the EU, represented by the Commission, and the member states, represented by the Council Presidency, share responsibility. The EU relies on the Commission[16] to shape and present formal EU positions on matters relating to fraud against the EU through the smuggling of tobacco products. On the other hand, provisions for international cooperation in criminal matters are usually entrusted to the European Council Presidency,[17] and member states are required to uphold common positions taken in international forums.[18] In plenary negotiating sessions the minister of the state holding the presidency usually speaks, while in the technical committees a representative from the Commission takes over.[19]

However, although the *Illicit Trade Protocol* involved matters of shared responsibility, OLAF coordinated the European position at the negotiations.[20] OLAF has a 'hybrid' and 'ambiguous status';[21] it is part of the Commission yet enjoys a measure of investigative and budgetary autonomy. This investigative independence does not, however, formally apply when it is acting on behalf of the Commission in the development of anti-fraud strategy.[22] When OLAF is investigating tobacco smuggling cases it is independent of the Commission, but when it is developing strategy against the illicit tobacco trade it *is* the Commission. It has been pointed out that because it was founded as an independent investigative body, there is little power for effective supervision of OLAF within the Commission, through the European Parliament or Council, or through its supervisory committee.[23] It is difficult to know to what extent this limited control of its investigative activities carries through to its role in the negotiation of the *Illicit Trade Protocol*, particularly in regard to technical matters, where it has a monopoly on expertise in comparison with other members of the Commission who may be in attendance.

III OLAF TAKES UP THE STRUGGLE AGAINST TOBACCO SMUGGLING

Tobacco smuggling and the smuggling of counterfeit cigarettes into the EU were identified as priority issues for OLAF in its first report, and it has been actively engaged in investigations into these activities from its formation in 1999, when it established a cigarette smuggling working group.[24] While OLAF enjoyed success against smugglers within EU member states, it took until 2009 for it to obtain a conviction in a foreign state of someone engaged in smuggling cigarettes into the EU.[25] An opportunity to increase its enforcement powers was created when the Commission commenced litigation against major tobacco manufacturers for their supply of the illicit trade,[26] litigation in which the Commission acted in its own right as well as for member states,[27] and to which OLAF 'contributed fully'.[28] In its 1999 report, OLAF noted the inadequacy of mutual assistance agreements with non-member states when it came to assistance in regard to smuggled cigarettes,[29] and later reports prioritised improving cooperation with key countries.[30] In 2002, OLAF stated:

> As OLAF's cooperation with certain third countries increases, the fraudsters move their operations. They select other countries with which the Commission does not presently have cooperation agreements, and/or which have no real interest in helping OLAF to pursue its investigations, or with which effective cooperation is very difficult to establish. ...

> OLAF has coordinated a civil action lodged in New York by the European Community and ten Member States against the American cigarette manufacturers Philip Morris and RJ Reynolds. ... The beneficial effects of the civil action have already been demonstrated by the vastly lower level of smuggling of American cigarettes into the EU in recent years.[31]

The anti-contraband and anti-counterfeit agreement concluded on 9 July 2004 between Philip Morris International (PMI)[32] (PMI Agreement) and the then European Community (EC) (as represented by the Commission) and ten member states settled this litigation. The director of OLAF was designated representative of the EC in the operation of the agreement. The agreement, which runs for 12 years, has three main features: the requirement to make seizure payments; protocols providing for detailed tracking and tracing provisions to determine the point at which diversion of the particular company's products to smugglers occurs; and compliance protocols that provide for strict 'know your customer rules', record-keeping rules, and other due diligence measures. A further agreement settling legal action was signed in 2007 with Japan Tobacco International.[33] Three years later British American Tobacco (BAT) and Imperial Tobacco (ITL) voluntarily signed agreements with OLAF.[34] In OLAF's own words, in 2004 PMI, OLAF and acceding member states entered 'a unique partnership between law enforcement and industry'.[35] One immediate benefit was funding. The Commission notes:

> All 27 Member States have signed the PMI and JTI Agreements, 26 Member States have signed the Agreements with BAT and ITL.[36] ... The four tobacco manufacturers will pay a collective total of $2.15 billion over 20 years, of which 10% is paid to the Commission and the rest is paid to Member States.[37]

After the signing of the PMI Agreement, the then director of OLAF, Franz Bruner, speculated that the money paid by PMI to the EU could cover the costs of running OLAF for years to come.[38] By the end of 2006, PMI had already paid around $425 million, 9.7 per cent of which was paid to the Commission.[39] When in 2005 OLAF established a working group on counterfeiting, technical expertise was also provided by PMI.[40] The Commission is also actively pursuing further agreements.[41]

IV   GLOBALISING THE EU–TOBACCO MANUFACTURER AGREEMENTS

In 2004, OLAF asserted that the PMI Agreement was consistent with the anti-smuggling provisions in the WHO FCTC.[42] OLAF is a law enforcement agency whose strategic goals are heavily influenced by its operational orientation, hence its preoccupation with globalising the tracking and tracing regime pioneered in the PMI Agreement through the *Illicit Trade Protocol*. OLAF views tobacco smuggling as a global phenomenon that can only be suppressed through international cooperation.[43] If enforcement in some states is inadequate, uneven regulation will result in displacement of the problem. The Commission's 'Action Plan to Fight against the Smuggling of Cigarettes and Alcohol Along the EU Eastern Border' highlights the *Illicit Trade Protocol* as an expected part of the measures to fight smuggling.[44]

Tobacco manufacturers party to agreements with the EU also have reason to support an *Illicit Trade Protocol* with a tracking and tracing regime. They are at a commercial disadvantage if some manufacturers go unregulated. The *Illicit Trade Protocol* provides a potential vehicle for moving beyond regulation of a small section of the tobacco industry in a small number of states towards a uniform system of regulation at a global level. Unsurprisingly, the EU has financially supported the *Protocol*'s development process. It committed heavily through the Hercule II programme to the financing of the crucial working group held between INB III and IV, where most of the actual negotiating was done.[45] But the EU was also very sensitive to the necessity of ensuring general financial support for the *Protocol*. One of the issues that came up at INB V was how the *Illicit Trade Protocol* (and in particular the global focal point for the tracking and tracing regime) is to be financed. The EU proposed that the COP pay. Other delegations insisted that the Meeting of the Parties (MOP) to the *Illicit Trade Protocol* pay. The latter delegations' preference is reflected in the wording of article 33(7) of the *Protocol* as adopted.

All this is not to suggest that the EU is alone in its concerns about tobacco diversion to the illicit market. The summary records of the first negotiating session of the INB that settled the WHO FCTC reveal an almost universal concern with the problem.[46] What the diplomatic record reveals, however, is that the EU shaped the content of the *Illicit Trade Protocol* to suit its priorities.

The World Health Organization (WHO) expert group that introduced the idea of an *Illicit Trade Protocol* during the negotiation of the WHO FCTC drew heavily on EU experience.[47] By the fifth session of the INB held in 2002, an OLAF delegate and investigator, Austin Rowan, was attending the INB, and what became draft article 15 of the WHO FCTC already contained basic versions of provisions of the EU's agreements with manufacturers, such as adequate marking of tobacco products to enable tracing.[48] The records of the sixth session of the United Nations (UN) Ad Hoc Interagency Task Force on Tobacco Control took note of statements of the OLAF delegate, Ian Walton-George:[49]

> The participant spoke of the Anti-Contraband and Anti-Counterfeit Agreement between the European Community, certain Member States and Philip Morris International ... However, it is not enough to have an agreement with only one manufacturer. A more global solution is needed, at European or world level. The WHO's FCTC is a vehicle for progress in this regard. A Protocol on Tracking and Tracing, *based on provisions of the Agreement with PMI*, would be a major positive step.[50]

Together with Rowan, Walton-George's head of investigations, he attended the first COP held in 2006, where the decision was taken to elaborate a template for an *Illicit Trade Protocol*.[51] Rowan was then chosen to chair the expert group that drew up the template,[52] where he presented a paper entitled 'Establishing an International Tracking and Tracing Regime for Cigarettes'.[53] At the second COP, the EU delegation pushed for a decision to be made to develop an *Illicit Trade Protocol* on the basis of the template drawn up by the expert group,[54] and on 6 July 2007 the decision was taken to proceed with the negotiation of the *Illicit Trade Protocol*.[55] On 19 September 2007, the European Parliament strongly supported the Commission's 'activities to anchor the Phillip Morris Agreement' in the *Illicit Trade Protocol*.[56] The template, the content of which drew heavily on the EU–tobacco manufacturer agreements, was used as the basis for negotiations in early 2008.[57] It focused on tracking and tracing as the key measure in paragraphs 13–20, as well as licensing in paragraphs 6–10, record-keeping in paragraphs 21–4, and with reference to various due diligence provisions scattered through the document.

At the first INB for the elaboration of the *Illicit Trade Protocol*, Walton-George was elected chairman on the proposal of the WHO's European region on the basis that he was 'a European Community expert ... in combating cigarette smuggling and counterfeiting'.[58] At the end of

INB I he submitted his personal views of the negotiations in a paper emphasising the need for strong supply chain control provisions.[59] During the course of the rest of the negotiations he submitted a number of chairman's texts, which formed the basis for the negotiations; all placed supply chain control, and in particular tracking and tracing, at the centre of the negotiations.[60] Rowan became the voice of the Commission at the negotiations. By INB IV, nine OLAF delegates were attending the negotiations.[61] The draft protocol submitted to the fifth COP in November 2012 included many of the elements for which they consistently advocated.[62] The negotiating history of these elements reveals where OLAF put in its strongest efforts to shape the *Illicit Trade Protocol*.

V LICENSING

Not everything in the *Illicit Trade Protocol* reflects OLAF's preferences. There was, for example, no strong EU support for licensing of participation in the tobacco trade and of tobacco product manufacturing equipment. The EU–tobacco manufacturer agreements did not contain a licensing regime. At INB I, OLAF's Rowan stated that 'licensing was only one of the elements that could be used in the overall control of tobacco products' and emphasised the need for the Protocol to respect the 'diverse licensing systems in the various parties'.[63] At INB II, the EU suggested that the draft licensing provision include the words 'or any control system which guarantees equivalent results'.[64] However, by the end of the process, the EU had given ground and agreed to article 6(1), which provides for an obligation to license manufacturing, importing and exporting of tobacco products and tobacco product manufacturing equipment. Under article 6(2), parties only endeavour to license retailing, commercial growing, transporting, and wholesaling, brokering, warehousing or distribution.

VI DUE DILIGENCE

In the EU–tobacco manufacturer agreements, the manufacturers undertake to know their customers by doing due diligence on all 'contractors' – first purchasers, warehousers, shippers and freight forwarders – that they use to store or ship their products.[65] If the manufacturer is not satisfied that a 'contractor' is able or committed to the smuggling control objectives of the agreement, it undertakes not to do business with them. The manufacturers also undertake to keep searchable databases of first purchasers with information on the first purchaser's name and order number, shipment date, destination of shipment, point of departure from the factory or warehouse, the consignee to whom the product is shipped and the intended market or retail sale.[66] In terms of the agreement, the Commission and relevant EU states' authorities have 'automated query only' access to this database.[67]

The sinews of this detailed scheme were reflected in the due diligence provisions in the template, and were fleshed out in the various revisions of the chair's text. They imposed a due diligence burden on all natural and legal persons who engaged in manufacture, sale, storage, shipment, distribution, import, export of tobacco products and tobacco manufacturing equipment. Due diligence had to be done in respect of first purchasers, who in turn would have been obliged to do due diligence on persons to whom they sold. The informal working group that met between INB IV and INB V settled the provisions on due diligence except in one regard.[68] At INB V, the wording in draft article 6(1) that required each party to ensure the carrying out of due diligence 'in accordance with its national law or legally binding and enforceable agreements' came under scrutiny. India questioned what was meant by implementation of the obligation through 'legally binding and enforceable agreements'.[69] The EU was seeking to preserve its agreements with the tobacco companies as the basis for implementation of the due diligence obligation. OLAF's Rowan rationalised that these agreements imposed obligations in the same way as national law.[70] But the wording implied that the substantive content of the treaty obligation of some of the parties to the *Protocol* would be determined to some extent by the contents of agreements between the party to the treaty and a private 'legal' person (which in terms of that agreement not only bears obligations but also has rights). African states were concerned about the risk of interference by the tobacco industry in the administration of the proposal, and eventually the EU abandoned this wording for an ambiguous formulation that still permits it to implement the *Protocol*'s due diligence provisions through its agreements with manufacturers. In terms of article 7(1) of the *Illicit Trade Protocol*, each party promises to require that all persons engaged in the supply chain: engage in due diligence before the commencement of and during business relationships; monitor sales to ensure they are commensurate with demand in the particular market for which they are intended; and report suspicions.

VII TRACKING AND TRACING

The focus of negotiations during the INB meetings was the provisions enabling the tracking and tracing of tobacco products to identify the point of diversion into the illicit trade. Under the EU–tobacco manufacturer agreements, manufacturers are obliged to mark packs, cartons and master cases to allow OLAF to track and trace their products.[71] At the negotiations of the *Illicit Trade Protocol*, differences emerged as to what form the global tracking and tracing system should take. At INB II, OLAF's Rowan emphasised the need for adoption of an 'international system' of tracking and tracing and explained that the Commission did not want to impose its system based on the EU–tobacco manufacturer agreements on the world and was instead pursuing a system that worked for all, especially developing states.[72] Nevertheless, OLAF did not consider a tax stamp system (such as that used by Brazil) to be an effective international solution.[73] OLAF preferred manufacturer-affixed commercial bar codes. A specific issue that arose was whether tobacco manufacturers should be obliged to provide data on their supply chains to central authorities – data that would be open to interrogation on request by foreign law enforcement authorities. At INB I, Brazil cautioned that 'implementation of a tracking and tracing system should be carried out by the government of the party concerned, without any interference from the tobacco industry'.[74] In Brazil, the government installs and maintains the tax stamp system in factories, and the industry pays for it, while in Canada the distribution of stamps with covert and overt identifiers is also government controlled.[75] OLAF preferred its system, where the information about the supply chain is held by the tobacco manufacturers, and this information is open to interrogation by law enforcement through a computer interface. At INB II, the Brazilian delegate bluntly called 'for a clear decision on whether the international tracking and tracing system would be controlled solely by the parties or in cooperation with the tobacco industry'.[76] At INB III, Walton-George intervened as chair:

> The proposal that I have made in the text is that these data, which are collected by the manufacturers and the importers, are sent to a central point in each party, they are gathered in a database in each of your countries, and they are gathered on a regular basis. ... I have suggested that the second stage is that the data in the national central point should then be passed to an international clearing house that would establish its own database and I have proposed that that database should be run here in Geneva by the Convention Secretariat.[77]

The Commission delegate supported this approach:

The CHAIRPERSON:

The other issue then is the options we have for the tracking and tracing system: whether we start shifting large amounts of data around or whether we try to set up a system that has electronic interfaces with the databases that already exist. ...

Mr ROWAN (European Community):

Yes. We were particularly impressed with the second aspect of your proposal because the problem is that, although the illicit trade in cigarettes represents a very small percentage of the global market, we would be recording vast amounts of information on a daily basis, that would be terrifying for administrations. On the other hand, we must have access to the information which relates to seizures. Hence the idea of it rushing off to go through a central base, perhaps with the Convention Secretariat, and rushing off to the manufacturers so that we can quickly identify where the goods have been diverted and so on, would be very, very important, rather than capturing vast amounts of information that are not really relevant. I am not even sure if the manufacturers would accept it. They might even take legal action against us because if we are capturing all that information, there is a serious risk of leaking business secrets and so on. Whereas all we really want is the information that relates to the illicit trade.[78]

Other delegations remained sceptical about relying on information gathered and stored by tobacco manufacturers. Drafting Group 1, which met in the inter-sessional period between INB III and INB IV, eventually came to a consensus built around autonomous national regimes accessible to each other through an international focal point.[79] At each INB, OLAF fought strenuously to ensure that this package was not changed into something requiring greater government intervention. At INB IV, OLAF's Rowan warned:

three sensitive issues must be addressed in relation to the global interface, namely business secrecy, the need to prevent data mining and other unauthorized access to databases, and data protection.[80]

The EU reassured Brazil that information would not be accessible to tobacco manufacturers,[81] but Brazil questioned whether the tobacco industry could be a competent authority or the EU itself should have access to the information sharing point as it was not a state. The EU responded that it represented its member states[82] and expressed displeasure at Brazil's insinuation that it supported the tobacco industry.[83]

The package was largely unchanged in what became article 8 of the *Illicit Trade Protocol* agreed at INB V. In terms of article 8(1), the global 'tracking and tracing regime' comprising either national or regional systems and a global information-sharing focal point must be established within five years of the entry into force of the *Protocol* and be accessible to all parties, allowing them to make enquiries. In terms of article 8(3), the regime is to be based on the obligation to affix unique, secure and non-removable identification markings which shall indicate *inter alia* the date and place of manufacture, the manufacturing facility, product description, and where applicable the intended market, all in aid of identifying the point of diversion. Article 8(9) governs the making of requests for information, requiring that the response be timely, that requests be made only when the information is necessary for an investigation into illicit trade, and that information not be withheld unreasonably. Answers have to be in accordance with national law, and information must be kept confidential where agreed. Articles 8(10) and 8(11) provide for development of the system and expansion of the scope of enquiries. There are limited safeguards against industry interference. In terms of article 8(12), obligations undertaken by a party shall not be transferred or delegated to the tobacco industry. In terms of article 8(13), each party shall ensure that 'its competent authorities, in participating in the tracking and tracing regime, interact with the tobacco industry and those representing the interests of the tobacco industry only to the extent strictly necessary in the implementation of this Article'. In addition, article 4(2) obliges parties to ensure maximum possible transparency in 'interactions' with the tobacco industry.

The EU proved to be an inflexible negotiator in the WHO FCTC, partly because of the difficult path to a settled EU position, which requires heavy internal negotiation.[84] This unwieldiness also partly explains EU reluctance to change its goals in the negotiation of the *Illicit Trade Protocol*. But it was also restricted by its agreements with tobacco companies. It wanted to lead the world to a position that made for an international extension of these arrangements; it did not want to have to change them because it could not do so unilaterally. The system adopted in the *Illicit Trade Protocol* is a compromise. It does not globalise the European system *in toto*, but it does acknowledge that the industry has a role in suppression of illicit trade. Where they exist, the *Illicit Trade Protocol* leaves national and regional tracking and tracing systems intact, including those used in Europe. It is difficult to know to what extent the EU system will be used as a precedent in the development of tracking and tracing systems in states where such systems do not yet exist, but the implementation of these broadly worded provisions will provide an opportunity for an enhanced role for the tobacco industry in global law enforcement.

VIII OLAF: TRANSNATIONAL ADMINISTRATIVE NORM ENTREPRENEUR

The *Illicit Trade Protocol* sets up a system of mutual administrative assistance, comprising primarily customs cooperation between fiscal investigative authorities. Legalisation projects of this kind always involve the articulation of legal and normative goals; their success depends upon a combination of power, interest and normative vision. The development of the *Illicit Trade Protocol* has adhered fairly closely to the four stages articulated by Koh.[85] At the first stage, a subject-specific interaction based primarily on the model of the Commission's agreement with PMI occurred in a law-declaring forum, the INB. In the second stage, this interaction prompted the interpretation and enunciation of a new global norm, the *Illicit Trade Protocol*, but in particular the international tracking and tracing regime, a process which culminated at COP V when the *Protocol* was adopted. The third stage involves pressure on other parties to internalise the new global norm. This already occurred in negotiations and will continue through assistance in implementation both by OLAF and potentially by tobacco manufacturers. The goal in the fourth stage will be to bind parties to the new norm and thus establish an effective global tracking and tracing and due diligence regime.

In Koh's model, individuals and NGOs operate as transnational normative entrepreneurs, while governmental norm sponsors use their official status to promote these norms. Transnational normative networks composed of both officials and non-officials evolve to promote these norms across borders and resolve problems as they arise. These networks may also serve as interpretative communities to elaborate the meaning and content of these norms and to set standards against which performance may be measured.[86] In the development of the *Illicit Trade Protocol*, OLAF has operated as both norm entrepreneur and governmental norm sponsor. OLAF has also created the possibility for non-officials from the tobacco industry to shape the norm indirectly through input into the model for the norm – the EU–tobacco manufacturer agreements – and now the industry is being established to participate in the interpretative community to elaborate the norm.

IX THE ILLICIT TRADE PROTOCOL, OLAF AND THE DEADLY EMBRACE OF THE TOBACCO INDUSTRY?

Article 5(3) of the WHO FCTC, cited in the preamble to the *Illicit Trade Protocol*, provides that parties shall protect their public health policies 'from commercial and other vested interests of the tobacco industry'. The guidelines that flesh out this article speak of the 'irreconcilable conflict between the tobacco industry's interests and public health interests'.[87] This raises questions about the degree of permissible industry involvement in the suppression of illicit trade. Customs authorities such as OLAF are conflicted, in that they have to facilitate trade in tobacco while policing non-taxed trade. OLAF's relationships with the major tobacco companies have created an epistemic community that has developed specialist knowledge around the tracking and tracing of tobacco products and a mandate to engage with law enforcement personnel. Arguably, the tobacco companies themselves are now transnational administrative norm entrepreneurs in the suppression of illicit tobacco products. Through the *Illicit Trade Protocol*, OLAF has introduced the tobacco industry as a partner in law enforcement activity to the rest of the world. The *Protocol* does not demand that parties embrace the industry, but it does give 'international' sanction to government officials if they decide to establish relationships with these private companies.

Let us return to the agreements themselves to illustrate this point. Recital 1 of the BAT–European Commission agreement states that 'the production of counterfeits and the smuggling of cigarettes into and within the EU causes economic loss to both parties'.[88] Recital 5 recognises that 'the fight against the illicit trade in Cigarettes calls for binding co-operation between the tobacco industry, the Member States and the EU'. Recital 6 acknowledges that 'the Parties' joint intention is to establish ongoing means of cooperation through the mechanics of this Agreement to combat the production of Counterfeits and the smuggling of Cigarettes'. Perhaps most telling is Recital 7, which acknowledges 'that it is the Parties' intention to improve awareness of, and continue to provide training on, measures designed to prevent the illicit trade in Cigarettes among relevant BAT Company employees and appropriate EU and Participating Member States' personnel'. In terms of these agreements, the specific tobacco manufacturer becomes a 'Cooperating Company'.[89] The individual officials within OLAF, and the cigarette manufacturers with whom they have to work under the agreements, have formed partnerships, the main target of which is illicit tobacco trade. The goal of this partnership is not the suppression of the use of tobacco but combating the loss of revenue to the EU from smuggling and the loss of revenue to manufacturers through proliferation of counterfeit products. Moreover, the major tobacco manufacturers now appear to be becoming key financial supporters of transnational law enforcement. In November 2012, INTERPOL announced that it was undertaking a global project against the 'trafficking of illicit goods including tobacco products' that would work with partners including OLAF to 'collect intelligence, develop strategic analytical reports, engage in capacity building and launch joint interdiction operations to target organized crime groups that smuggle illicit and counterfeit products'.[90] PMI pledged €15 million to support the project,[91] a pledge that PMI trumpeted, looking forward to cooperation with INTERPOL.[92] INTERPOL applied to be an official observer for the first time at COP V of the WHO FCTC when the *Illicit Trade Protocol* was adopted, but its application was deferred out of concern about its acceptance of the PMI donation.[93]

Advocates of engagement with the industry in law enforcement may point to increased effectiveness in law enforcement, the commercial advantages of an even global playing field to the tobacco industry,[94] and the retention by government agencies of most if not all of the power in the partnership. Sollier and Mangion, General Counsel and Legal Officer respectively for INTERPOL, sum up the positives of cooperation with the tobacco industry:

> Any success against the ITTP requires that law enforcement and national authorities work together with the legitimate tobacco industry for a number of reasons. Tobacco companies are able to assist in different aspects, including providing resources to enhance capacity, providing technical assistance such as schemes to distinguish genuine tobacco products from counterfeit products and training customs officials in relation to contraband products. Moreover, commitments made in the agreements with the EU provide for technologically enhanced tracking and tracing systems, namely marking, seizure and the recording of information. Tobacco companies also collect a considerable amount of information and intelligence about criminals who target the industry. This has the potential to inform and focus law enforcement efforts to combat the problem worldwide.[95]

While they concede that in relation to the other tobacco control measures in the WHO FCTC the industry has a clear conflict of interest, and counsel caution, these authors rather tentatively argue that alliance with industry 'would perhaps see furtherance of the attempts at curbing the illicit trade of tobacco products, given the resources tobacco companies have at their disposal, and "insider" knowledge and technical expertise on the matter'.[96] It is submitted that the stronger of these two grounds for suggesting that tobacco companies might make a positive contribution to the effort to curb the illicit trade, a ground made even stronger in the age of austerity, arises from access to the tobacco industry's money.

Critics of engagement with the industry in suppressing illicit trade validly point to the long struggle of health authorities with the tobacco industry and the fact that the industry will retain control of information and systems in some key regions, and potentially develop that control in others. For one thing, the technology for marking tobacco products and recording information will be almost entirely within the control of the industry.[97] It will always be in a position at a functional level to push more expensive and sophisticated control systems on individual states parties – systems that law enforcement officers will be able to access but unable to control in terms of the input and output of data. Liberman et al doubt the bona fides of the industry's actions in this regard, noting:

> [T]he tobacco industry is attempting to increase the attention being given to illicit trade and convince policy makers that implementation of tobacco control measures including tax increases, retail display bans and plain packaging will increase illicit trade. The industry's strategy is twofold: dissuade governments from implementing effective tobacco control measures and position itself as a 'legitimate' and 'responsible' partner, ready, willing and able to support and work with governments.[98]

An immediate danger is the diversion of resources within the framework of the WHO FCTC from anti-tobacco industry efforts to the suppression of illicit trade, which serves the industry's purposes.[99] A particular problem that was the subject of heated negotiation was the inclusion of counterfeit cigarettes and tobacco products within the scope of the *Protocol*.[100] This inclusion made sense to OLAF, as it is mandated to suppress the flow of counterfeits into the EU, but action against counterfeits would also have served to make the *Protocol* an instrument for the protection of tobacco manufacturers' intellectual property. Brazil in particular was adamantly opposed to the *Protocol* becoming a vehicle for the extension of international obligations in regard to intellectual property.[101] After negotiation, all references to 'counterfeit' have been expunged from the *Illicit Trade Protocol*, and its preamble notes that 'it does not seek to address issues concerning intellectual property rights'. Nevertheless, the introduction of the industry as a partner is likely to lead to anti-counterfeit measures that will help to give the impression that tobacco products of cooperating manufacturers are somehow less harmful than counterfeit products.

X CONCLUSION

Two questions need to be answered. First, what is the optimal level of industry involvement in the suppression of illicit trade in tobacco? The tobacco industry's interests in maximising profits, antipathy to taxation, linking of taxation to the rise in illicit trade, and overplaying of the importance of the illicit trade[102] suggest great caution is needed in involving the industry. This chapter has shown, however, that the basic premise of law enforcement's acceptance of the involvement of industry appears to have evolved from the position that industry represents a necessary evil to a characterisation of the industry as a positive contributor in the suppression of illicit trade. The *Illicit Trade Protocol* provides an opportunity for the tobacco industry to transform itself from an object of regulation into a subject in the regulatory system. This transformation goes too far in the cause of suppressing illicit trade. Given the nature of its product, the tobacco industry should never be constructed as a partner, but rather only as a source of information that governments have a legitimate right to acquire because of the harm that that information may prevent.

The second question is what is the optimal level of supervision of this relationship? As noted above, the *Illicit Trade Protocol* gives some rough direction here. One might ask, nonetheless, how any party to the *Protocol* can ensure that an enforcement organisation interacts with the tobacco industry only to the extent strictly necessary to implement the tracking and tracing system, as required by article 8(12)? Tobacco manufacturers work to foster relations with government; there is evidence of tobacco manufacturers influencing Commission officials in the past.[103]

At present these questions have been left to states parties. One may only hope that an adequate solution to both questions can be provided prior to the development of guidelines by the MOP to the *Illicit Trade Protocol* demarcating what is legitimate and what is illegitimate intercourse with the industry in the law enforcement relationship, and providing for some mechanism of supervision of that relationship by the MOP itself through specific mandatory reporting duties and assessment processes. A more cautious approach in the development of the *Protocol* itself would have been preferable. Extensive preparatory work was necessary to ensure the development of a firewall between industry involvement in the suppression of illicit trade and the other regulatory functions of the WHO FCTC; no such work was done.

NOTES

* The author attended the negotiating rounds of the *Illicit Trade Protocol* as a consultant for the Framework Convention Alliance on Tobacco Control; the opinions expressed here are, however, his own. Research for this chapter was carried out during a research fellowship at the European University Institute in September 2012. The author wishes to thank the EUI President Professor Marise Cremona in this regard, and Jonathan Liberman and Richard Burchill for their comments.

1. *WHO Framework Convention on Tobacco Control*, opened for signature 16 June 2003, 2302 UNTS 166 (entered into force 27 February 2005) (WHO FCTC).

2. See WHO FCTC Conference of the Parties, *Draft Protocol to Eliminate Trade in Tobacco Products*, 5th sess, WHO Doc FCTC COP/5/6 (11 May 2012); *Protocol to Eliminate Trade in Tobacco Products*, opened for signature 10 January 2013 (not yet in force) (*Illicit Trade Protocol*).

3. *Commission Decision of 28 April 1999 Establishing the European Anti-Fraud Office (OLAF)* [1999] OJ L 136/20, article 7 (*OLAF Decision*); *Regulation (EC) No 1073/1999 of the European Parliament and of the Council of 25 May 1999 Concerning Investigations Conducted by the European Anti-Fraud Office (OLAF)* [1999] OJ L 136/1, article 16 (*OLAF Regulation*).

4. *OLAF Decision* [1999] OJ L 136/20, article 1(1).

5. Ibid.

6. Constantin Stefanou, Simone White and Helen Xanthaki, *OLAF at the Crossroads: Action against EU Fraud* (Hart Publishing, 2011) 129.

7. Ibid xiv.

8. *OLAF Regulation* [1999] OJ L 136/1 articles 5, 7.

9. [1999] OJ L 136/1.

10. See also *OLAF Decision* [1999] OJ L 136/20, article 22; see Simone White, 'EU Anti-Fraud: Strategy and Legislation in a Period of Consolidation' in Celina Nowak (ed), *Fight against EU Fraud: Administrative and Criminal Law Issues* (LEX, 2011) 15, 36.

11. *OLAF Decision* [1999] OJ L 136/20, article 2; see generally Frank Hoffmeister, 'The Contribution of EU Practice to International Law' in Marise Cremona (ed), *Developments in EU External Relations Law* (Oxford University Press, 2008) 37.

12. Jan Inghelram, *Legal and Institutional Aspects of the European Anti-Fraud Office (OLAF): An Analysis with a Look Forward to a European Public Prosecutor's office* (Europa, 2011) 116.

13. *OLAF Decision* [1999] OJ L 136/20, articles 2(3)–(5).

14. Stefanou, White and Xanthaki, above n 6, 27.

15. TEU article 218.

16. Ibid article 17(1).

17. Ibid article 18.

18. Ibid article 34.

19. Hoffmeister, above n 11, 52–3.

20. European Anti-Fraud Office, *The OLAF Report 2011: Twelfth Report of the European Anti-Fraud Office, 1 January to 31 December 2011* (Luxembourg: Publications Office of the European Union, 2012) 30 <http://ec.europa.eu/anti_fraud/documents/reports-olaf/2011/olaf_report_2011_en.pdf>.

21. House of Lords European Union Committee (UK), *Strengthening OLAF, the European Anti-Fraud Office* (House of Lords, Session 2003–04, 139) HL Paper 139 (The Stationery Office, 2004) [29] <http://www.publications.parliament.uk/pa/ld200304/ldselect/ldeucom/139/139.pdf>.

22. Inghelram, above n 12, 117.

23. Ibid 192, 195. See also Stefanou, White and Xanthaki, above n 6, 70.
24. European Anti-Fraud Office, *First Report on Operational Activities 1 June 1999 – 31 May 2000* (23 May 2000) 14 <http://ec.europa.eu/anti_fraud/documents/reports-olaf/rep_olaf_2000_en.pdf>.
25. European Anti-Fraud Office, *Annual Report 2010: European Anti-Fraud Office Summary* (July 2010) 46 <http://ec.europa.eu/anti_fraud/documents/reports-olaf/rep_olaf_2009_en.pdf>.
26. See, in particular, Simone White, 'Operational Effectiveness: Expanding the Civil Route' in Constantin Stefanou, Simone White and Helen Xanthaki (eds), *OLAF at the Crossroads: Action against EU Fraud* (Hart Publishing, 2011) 121.
27. See *Philip Morris International Inc v Commission of the European Communities* (T-377/00, T-379/00, T-380/00, T-260/01, T-272/01) [2003] ECR II-00001, [1].
28. See European Anti-Fraud Office, *Report of the European Anti-Fraud Office (OLAF): Activity Report for the 1 June 2000 to 31 May 2001* (2001) 22 <http://ec.europa.eu/anti_fraud/documents/reports-olaf/rep_olaf_2001_en.pdf>.
29. European Anti-Fraud Office, *First Report on Operational Activities*, above n 24, 35.
30. European Anti-Fraud Office, *Report of the European Anti-Fraud Office (OLAF)*, above n 28, 23.
31. European Anti-Fraud Office, *Report of the European Anti-Fraud Office (OLAF): Third Activity Report for the Year Ending 2002* (2002) 19 <http://ec.europa.eu/anti_fraud/documents/reports-olaf/rep_olaf_2002_en.pdf>.
32. *Anti-Contraband and Anti-Counterfeit Agreement and General Release* (9 July 2004) European Commission <http://ec.europa.eu/anti_fraud/documents/cigarette-smugg-2004/agreement_2004.pdf> (PMI Agreement).
33. European Anti-Fraud Office, *Report of the European Anti-Fraud Office (OLAF): Eighth Activity Report for the Period 1 January – 31 December 2007* (Office for Official Publications of the European Communities, 2008) 5 <http://ec.europa.eu/anti_fraud/documents/reports-olaf/rep_olaf_2007_en.pdf>.
34. The agreements are available at European Anti-Fraud Office, *Cigarette Smuggling* (9 July 2013) European Commission <http://ec.europa.eu/anti_fraud/investigations/eu-revenue/cigarette_smuggling_en.htm>.
35. European Anti-Fraud Office, *Report of the European Anti-Fraud Office (OLAF): Sixth Activity Report for the Period 1 June 2004 to 31 December 2005* (July 2006) 47 <http://ec.europa.eu/anti_fraud/documents/reports-olaf/rep_olaf_2005_en.pdf>.
36. Sweden has not signed the agreements with BAT and ITL.
37. European Commission, 'Impact Assessment Accompanying Document to the Proposal for a Regulation of the European Parliament and the European Council on the Hercule III Programme to Promote Activities in the Field of the Protection of the European Union's Financial Interest' (Commission Staff Working Paper No SEC(2011) 1611 final, 19 December 2011) 6 <http://eur-lex.europa.eu/LexUriServ/LexUriServ.do?uri=SEC:2011:1610:FIN:EN:PDF>.
38. Ibid 3.
39. European Anti-Fraud Office, *Report of the European Anti-Fraud Office (OLAF): Seventh Activity Report for the Period 1 January 2006 to 31 December 2006*, 52 <http://ec.europa.eu/anti_fraud/documents/reports-olaf/rep_olaf_206_en.pdf>.
40. Ibid.
41. European Commission, 'Action Plan to Fight against Smuggling of Cigarettes and Alcohol along the EU Eastern Border' (Commission Staff Working Paper No SEC(2011) 791 final, 24 June 2011) 16 <http://ec.europa.eu/anti_fraud/documents/preventing-fraud-documents/eastern_border_action_plan_en.pdf>.
42. European Anti-Fraud Office, *Report of the European Anti-Fraud Office (OLAF): Fifth Activity Report for the Year Ending June 2004*, 48 <http://ec.europa.eu/anti_fraud/documents/reports-olaf/rep_olaf_2003_2004_en.pdf>.

43. European Anti-Fraud Office, *Eleventh Operational Report of the European Anti-Fraud Office (OLAF): 1 January to 31 December 2010* (2011) 27 <http://ec.europa.eu/anti_fraud/documents/reports-olaf/rep_olaf_2010_en.pdf>.
44. European Commission, above n 41, 6.
45. Ibid 18.
46. See generally Intergovernmental Negotiating Body on the Framework Convention on Tobacco Control, *Summary Records*, 1st sess, WHO Doc A/FCTC/INB1/SR (16–21 October 2000), the European Commission delegate was the first to propose a concrete obligation to combat smuggling (86). The first mention of a possible mechanism to trace the origins of illicit tobacco was made by Canada (88).
47. Working Group on the WHO Framework Convention on Tobacco Control, *Subjects of Possible Protocols and Their Relation to the Framework Convention on Tobacco Control*, WHO Doc A/FCTC/WG1/3 (3 September 1999) 7–11.
48. Intergovernmental Negotiating Body on the WHO Framework Convention on Tobacco Control, *New Chair's Text of a Framework Convention on Tobacco Control*, 5th sess, WHO Doc A/FCTC/INB5/2 (25 June 2002).
49. Then Head of Directorate B, Investigations and Operations II, which included Unit B3, Customs II, dealing with tobacco smuggling. OLAF's internal structure has subsequently been reorganised.
50. United Nations Ad Hoc Interagency Task Force on Tobacco Control, *Report of the Sixth Session* (30 November to 1 December 2005) World Health Organization, 14–15 <http://www.who.int/tobacco/global_interaction/un_taskforce/UNTaskForce_6thSession.pdf> (emphasis added).
51. WHO FCTC Conference of the Parties, *Decisions and Ancillary Documents*, 1st sess, WHO Doc COP/1/2006/CD (17 February 2006) 57.
52. WHO FCTC Conference of the Parties, *Elaboration of Protocols*, 2nd sess, WHO Doc A/FCTC/COP/2/9 (19 April 2007) 2 [5] (*Elaboration of Protocols*).
53. Ibid 2 n 3.
54. WHO FCTC Conference of the Parties, *Verbatim Records of Plenary Meetings*, 2nd sess, WHO Doc A/FCTC/COP2/2007/CD (30 June to 6 July 2007) 28.
55. See WHO FCTC Conference of the Parties, *Decisions*, 2nd sess, WHO Doc A/FCTC/COP/2/DIV/9 (20 December 2009) 29.
56. *European Parliament Resolution of 11 October 2007 on the Implications of the Agreement between the Community, Member States and Philip Morris on Intensifying the Fight against Fraud and Cigarette Smuggling and Progress Made in Implementing the Recommendations of Parliament's Committee of Inquiry into the Community Transit System (2005/2145(INI))* [2008] OJ C 227E/147 A6-0337/2007, [42].
57. *Elaboration of Protocols Elaboration of a Template for a Protocol on Illicit Trade in Tobacco Products*, WHO Doc A/FCTC/COP2/9.
58. WHO FCTC Conference of the Parties, *Report of the Intergovernmental Negotiating Body to the Third Session of the Conference of the Parties on the Progress of its Work*, 3rd sess, WHO Doc FCTC/COP/3/4 (14 November 2008) 2 [7].
59. WHO FCTC Conference of the Parties Intergovernmental Negotiating Body on a Protocol on Illicit Trade in Tobacco Products, *Drafting and Negotiation of a Protocol on Illicit Trade in Tobacco Products*, 1st sess, WHO Doc FCTC/COP/INB-IT/1/7 (15 February 2008).
60. See for example, WHO FCTC Conference of the Parties Intergovernmental Negotiating Body on a Protocol on Illicit Trade in Tobacco Products, *Chairperson's Text for a Protocol on Illicit Trade in Tobacco Products*, 2nd sess, WHO Doc FCTC/COP/INB-IT/2/3 (18 August 2008).

61. WHO FCTC Conference of the Parties Intergovernmental Negotiating Body on a Protocol on Illicit Trade in Tobacco Products, *Summary Records and Decisions*, 4th sess Geneva, WHO Doc FCTC/COP/INB-IT/4/REC1 (14–21 March 2010) 264.

62. WHO FCTC Conference of the Parties, *Draft Protocol on Illicit Trade in Tobacco*, 5th WHO Doc FCTC/COP/5/6 (11 May 2012).

63. WHO FCTC Conference of the Parties Intergovernmental Negotiating Body on a Protocol on Illicit Trade in Tobacco Products, *Summary Records*, 1st sess, WHO Doc FCTC/INB-IT/1/REC/1 (11–16 February 2008) 17.

64. See WHO FCTC Conference of the Parties Intergovernmental Negotiating Body on a Protocol on Illicit Trade in Tobacco Products, *Summary Records*, 2nd sess, FCTC/COP/INB-IT/1/3 (12 December 2007) 19.

65. PMI Agreement, above n 32, article 1 (definition of 'Contractor'), app B protocol 2, entitled 'Know Your Customer', in particular, s 2.03.

66. Ibid app B protocol 3 s 3.03.

67. Ibid.

68. WHO FCTC Conference of the Parties Intergovernmental Negotiating Body on a Protocol on Illicit Trade in Tobacco Products, *Report of the Informal Working Group on the Draft Protocol to Eliminate Illicit Trade in Tobacco Products*, 2nd mtg, WHO Doc FCTC/COP/IWG/2/7 (22 September 2011).

69. WHO FCTC Conference of the Parties Intergovernmental Negotiating Body on a Protocol on Illicit Trade in Tobacco Products, *Summary Records*, 5th sess, WHO Doc FCTC/COP/INB-IT/5/REC/1 (29 March to 4 April 2012) 13ff.

70. Ibid 14.

71. See the PMI Agreement, above n 32, article 5, app D, app D protocol 5 s 5.01, app D protocols 2 (Pack and Carton Marking and Coding), 3 (Master Case Labelling and Scanning).

72. WHO FCTC Conference of the Parties Intergovernmental Negotiating Body on a Protocol on Illicit Trade in Tobacco Products, *Verbatim Records of Plenary Meetings*, 2nd sess, WHO Doc FCTC/COP/INB-IT/2/VR/5 (20–25 October 2008).

73. *Summary Records*, WHO Doc FCTC/INB-IT/1/REC/1, 20.

74. Ibid 19.

75. See ibid, statements of Brazil and Canada.

76. See *Summary Records*, 2nd sess, FCTC/COP/INB-IT/1/3, 7.

77. WHO FCTC Conference of the Parties Intergovernmental Negotiating Body on a Protocol on Illicit Trade in Tobacco Products, *Verbatim Records of Plenary Meetings*, 3rd sess, WHO Doc FCTC/COP/INB-IT/3/REC/2 (28 June to 5 July 2009) 12.

78. Ibid 184–5.

79. See WHO FCTC Conference of the Parties Intergovernmental Negotiating Body on a Protocol on Illicit Trade in Tobacco Products, *Proposals of Drafting Group 1 to the Fourth Session of the Intergovernmental Negotiating Body on Articles 5, 6, 7, 10 and 11 of the Negotiating Text for a Protocol to Eliminate Illicit Trade in Tobacco Products*, WHO Doc FCTC/COP/INB-IT/4/3, draft article 7(1) (13 January 2010).

80. WHO FCTC Conference of the Parties Intergovernmental Negotiating Body on a Protocol on Illicit Trade in Tobacco Products, *Summary Records Decisions*, 4th sess, WHO Doc FCTC/COP/INB-IT/4/REC/1 (14–21 March 2010) 19.

81. Ibid 27.

82. Ibid 46.

83. Ibid 60.

84. See Miriam Faid and David Gleicher, *Dancing the Tango: The Experience and Role of the European Union in Relation to the Framework Convention on Tobacco* (2010) European Commission 14 <http://ec.europa.eu/health/tobacco/docs/tobacco_tango_en.pdf>.

85. Harold Hongu Koh, 'The 1998 Frankel Lecture: Bringing International Law Home' (1998) 35 *Houston Law Review* 623, 644–50.

86. Ibid 647, 648–9.

87. WHO FCTC Conference of the Parties, *Guidelines for Implementation* (2013) 5 <http://www.who.int/fctc/guidelines/adopted/guidel_2011/en/>.

88. *Cooperation Agreement* (15 July 2010) European Commission <http://ec.europa.eu/commission_2010-2014/semeta/headlines/news/2010/07/bat_main_agreement_final.pdf>.

89. Ibid 2.

90. INTERPOL, 'INTERPOL Targets Organised Crime with Global Initiative against Trafficking in Illicit Goods' (Media Release, 22 June 2012) <http://www.interpol.int/News-and-media/News-media-releases/2012/PR050>.

91. Ibid.

92. Philip Morris, 'Philip Morris International Provides 15 Million Euro Contribution to INTERPOL to Fight Trafficking in Illicit Goods' (News Release, 21 June 2012) <http://www.pmi.com/eng/media_center/press_releases/pages/201206210200.aspx>. For greater detail on the project see Joël Sollier and Rosella Mangion, 'INTERPOL – A Partner in Curbing the Illicit Tobacco Trade' (2012) 9(5) *Transnational Dispute Management* 1, 12–14 <http://www.transnational-dispute-management.com/article.asp?key=1876>.

93. See Corporate Accountability International, 'Parties Prevail in Adopting Landmark Illicit Trade Protocol Despite Industry Interference – WHO: Big Tobacco Single Greatest Threat to Tobacco Treaty' (Press Release, 12 November 2012) <http://www.stopcorporateabuse.org/press-release/parties-prevail-adopting-landmark-illicit-trade-protocol-despite-industry-interference>.

94. *Co-operation Agreement* (27 September 2010) European Commission, s 13.13 <http://ec.europa.eu/anti_fraud/documents/cigarette_smug/2010_i/agreement_sept_2010.pdf>.

95. Sollier and Mangion, above n 92, 8.

96. Ibid.

97. See PMI's development of new 'state of the art monitoring systems' for their supply chains, ibid 11.

98. See Jonathan Liberman et al, 'Opportunities and Risks of the Proposed FCTC Protocol on Illicit Trade' (2011) 20 *Tobacco Control* 436, 436.

99. Ibid 437.

100. See Jonathan Liberman, 'Combating Counterfeit Medicines and Illicit Trade in Tobacco Products: Minefields in Global Health Governance' (2012) *Journal of Law, Medicine and Ethics* 326, 339ff.

101. *Summary Records*, 5th sess, WHO Doc FCTC/COP/INB-IT/5/REC/1, 32.

102. Ibid 340.

103. See Asaf Bitton, Mark David Neuman and Stanton A Glantz, *Tobacco Industry Attempts to Subvert European Union's Tobacco Advertising Legislation* (1 April 2002) Centre for Tobacco Research and Education, University of California, 18 <http://www.escholarship.org/uc/item/3r1334mz>, which shows how the Commission's Directorates-General III's head, Martin Bangemann, was courted.

PART II

Tobacco control in the context of international trade and investment

6. The WTO ruling on the United States' flavoured cigarettes ban

Todd Tucker

I INTRODUCTION AND THEORETICAL OVERVIEW

The 'legalisation' of international affairs has attracted significant scholarly attention over the last several decades. According to this research, international regimes are more 'legalised' when states delegate to third parties the ability to determine compliance.[1] By this dimension, the World Trade Organization's (WTO) Dispute Settlement Body (DSB) – where states whose measures are challenged cannot veto the outcome of third-party adjudication – represents 'legalisation' par excellence.[2]

Regimes are also more 'legalised' when more binding and more precise.[3] Here, the status of the WTO is more uncertain. On the one hand, WTO rulings – with the threat of commercial sanctions for non-compliance – are reasonably binding by the lax standards of international legal regimes.[4] On the other hand, powerful nations have flouted rulings for years, apparently assured of their ability to weather the diplomatic and commercial storms.[5] And many key WTO obligations are imprecise and appear to regularly confound respondent governments.[6]

Indeed, subsequent scholarship has questioned the coherence of the 'legalisation' concept,[7] noting that high imprecision and high delegation appear to go together.[8] Moreover, in the absence of a supranational entity with a monopoly of legitimate force, some scholars have suggested that regimes that regularly rule against the preferences of powerful governments will not be able to elicit compliance.[9]

I call this the 'counter-legalisation' problem: delegated authority plus textual imprecision empowers international regimes to fill in textual gaps in ways that states did not intend and do not control. Over time, these regimes increasingly refer to their own case law and logic,[10] but as a consequence may create resistance to compliance. But this does not make 'legalised' entities irrelevant. Their formal determinations continue to exist, serving as a justificatory resource for domestic groups interested in aligning local policy with global determinations. The result is a potential 'legalisation pendulum'. Put differently, state behaviour in response to international legal decisions may be determined by political and structural factors exogenous to the law, but international rulings provide discursive resources that can be used to influence subsequent interactions with states.[11]

It seems that public interest advocacy (such as efforts to regulate tobacco) is particularly susceptible to being curtailed by these pendulum effects. Unlike industry, it does not control jobs or campaign donations that put clear 'costs' and 'benefits' in the minds of policymakers that might justify deviance from international law norms.[12] It is also not the province of the military, where states appear particularly willing to go against international legal determinations.[13] Instead, public interest law may have two strengths: its reliance on empirical evidence and the domestic legitimacy that comes from weighing and balancing different interests. International adjudicatory regimes – which often have their own approach to evidence and balancing – seem well positioned to mimic the strengths of public interest law.

This chapter explores a case study of a potential 'legalisation pendulum' problem. In 2011 and 2012, a WTO Panel and the Appellate Body (AB) ruled against aspects of the United States (US) Family Smoking Prevention and Tobacco Control Act (FSPTCA).[14] Indonesia successfully argued before the WTO[15] that the US policy of banning clove (mostly imported from Indonesia) as a characterising cigarette flavour – while allowing (mostly US-produced) menthol flavourings – constituted discrimination under article 2.1 of the WTO's *Agreement on Technical Barriers to Trade* (TBT Agreement).[16] Commentators have noted that two compliance options would be either to weaken the FSPTCA by allowing cloves or to eliminate differential treatment by banning menthols. Many observers and US policymakers – who appeared to engage in a prolonged balancing act of competing interests to pass and implement the legislation – have responded by criticising the WTO decisions for being out of step with health and regulatory prerogatives.[17] As a consequence, the prospect for near-term US compliance to Indonesia's satisfaction appears to be remote.[18]

I argue that these outcomes should not be surprising. The lack of strong principal-agent controls by states on WTO adjudicators leads to overreaching decisions. As a result, powerful states are unlikely to comply when they lose to weaker states and do not wish to change challenged policies. However, tobacco regulations – public interest regulations with a weak and dispersed base of domestic support – are the type of policy that we might expect to be vulnerable to legalised regimes such as the WTO over the longer term.

II INCREMENTALISM VERSUS LIKENESS

On 22 June 2009, President Obama signed the FSPTCA, which has been called 'the most significant change in federal public health policy in at least a generation'.[19] The bill's purpose section described its objectives as ensuring that the US Food and Drug Administration (FDA) had the authority to address youth tobacco use, while continuing 'to permit the sale of tobacco products to adults'.[20] This approach was tailored to minimise the countervailing impacts of an outright prohibition – a prime concern of the FDA and the United States Supreme Court.[21] The legislation made multiple regulatory distinctions among tobacco products. First, regular tobacco was subject to a host of specific regulatory measures, some of which (such as so-called plain packaging) US federal courts are slapping down.[22] Second, 13 characterising flavours – including strawberry, grape, orange, clove, cinnamon, pineapple, vanilla, coconut, liquorice, cocoa, chocolate, cherry, and coffee – were banned from cigarettes under s 907(a)(1)(A). This provision was developed in 2004 after various US companies had begun marketing candy-flavoured cigarettes aimed at youth.[23] Finally, s 907(e) instructed the newly established Tobacco Products Scientific Advisory Committee (TPSAC) to make a recommendation concerning whether the FDA should ban menthol. One of America's leading anti-tobacco activists described this provision as one that 'gives FDA authority to regulate menthol but to do it in a way based on sound science as opposed to making a political decision without knowing what the impact would be automatically today of eliminating it'.[24] The vast majority of comments (from law enforcement and industry officials) received by the TPSAC advised against a menthol ban out of concern for the potential countervailing effects.[25] Nonetheless, the TPSAC ended up urging a menthol ban,[26] without an independent investigation of such effects.[27] Subsequently, US tobacco companies have challenged the TPSAC recommendation in federal courts.[28]

The distinction between cloves and menthol is the feature of the FSPTCA that created trade problems for the US. Under TBT article 2.1, WTO 'Members shall ensure that in respect of technical regulations, products imported from the territory of any Member shall be accorded treatment no less favourable [TNLF] than that accorded to *like products of national origin* and to like products originating in any other country'.[29]

Despite the fact that the FSPTCA made three major product distinctions for a total of 15 flavour profiles (regular, menthol and the 13 candy flavours), and that any of these flavours can be and have been both domestically produced and imported, the Panel chose to compare only imported *clove* cigarettes with domestic *menthol* cigarettes. Had the United States' treatment of (say) cola cigarettes been compared with that of cloves, there would have been no less favourable treatment: both were banned. It was only through the application of a selective likeness test that a differential (let alone discriminatory) impact could be established.[30]

The likeness test illustrated a major difference between trade law and domestic incrementalist policy. The trade law approach to likeness was driven by a comparison of four dimensions drawn from jurisprudence under the WTO's *General Agreement on Tariffs and Trade 1994* (GATT 1994):[31] (a) the properties, nature and quality of the products; (b) the end-uses of the products; (c) consumers' tastes and habits; and (d) the tariff classification of the products.[32] These factors were then used to determine whether the two products competed with one another and were therefore 'like'. On the question of product characteristics, the Panel saw menthol and clove as each reducing the harshness of tobacco.[33] The Panel determined that both clove and menthol have the end use of being smoked,[34] and that they have similar tariff classifications.[35] The AB did not differ from the Panel significantly on these points. (I will have more to say about the unusual analysis of consumer preference and competition below.)

In contrast, domestic policy is driven by the art of the possible. Regulatory changes affecting small numbers of people are often more politically feasible than those affecting large numbers. Policymakers with significant information gaps and competing demands on their time often avoid regulatory changes with unknown adverse consequences.[36] Where there are known adverse consequences – as with the prohibition of addictive products – policymakers are likely to be even more circumspect. Economists have written that prohibition tends to increase violence, property crime and cartelisation, whilst decreasing the relative quality of drug ingredients.[37] Some organisations have also warned of the negative impact on race relations from paternalistically banning products disproportionately used by African American people.[38] The relative leniency of powder cocaine penalisation compared with freebase cocaine (ie 'crack') penalisation (the latter disproportionately affecting African Americans) remains one of the most contentious criminal and racial justice issues in the country.[39] US law enforcement officials struggle to enforce freebase cocaine prohibition, and there are only 600 000 users of that drug.[40]

Accordingly, the FSPTCA attempted to address a targeted problem among youth that did not affect adults in large numbers. Table 6.1 shows the basic statistics for menthol versus clove smokers. As can be seen, menthol smokers account for nearly a third of all smokers (more than 13 million people), while clove smokers represent a tiny fraction of all smokers. These figures indicate social problems of greatly differing magnitudes. The total population of clove smokers is – at the outer bound[41] – 5 per cent that of menthol smokers, and about 1 per cent that of all smokers. A given youth smoker, however, is 450 per cent more likely to smoke cloves than is a given adult smoker. In contrast, a given youth smoker is only 14 per cent more likely to smoke menthols compared with a given adult smoker. (Insufficient data is available for the 12 other cigarette flavours banned by the FSPTCA, which were targeted on precautionary grounds.)

Table 6.1   US smoking distribution

	Total smokers	of which menthol, %	of which clove, %	Total menthol smokers	Total clove smokers
Youth (12–25)	3 500 000	31.0	5.5	1 085 000	192 500
Adult (over 25)	46 000 000	27.0	1.0	12 420 000	460 000
Total	49 500 000			13 505 000	652 500

Source: Compiled from Appellant submission of the United States, *United States – Measures Affecting the Production and Sale of Clove Cigarettes* (5 January 2012) <http://www.ustr.gov/webfm_send/3225> [32]-[33].

Moreover, over 82 per cent of African American adult smokers smoke menthols, compared with only 23 per cent of white adult smokers. This means that a given African American smoker is more than 3.5 times as likely as a white counterpart to smoke menthols.[42]

There are still other unique attributes of menthol smoking. Recent research into the attitudes of menthol smokers suggests that their demand is relatively price inelastic, meaning that when prices rise they are less likely to reduce consumption or substitute for conventional cigarettes.[43] Indeed, 25 per cent of menthol smokers have stated an intention to simply circumvent any menthol ban.[44] If such survey statistics prove reliable, nearly 3 million people would enter the underground market under a menthol ban. In this context, the WTO ruling may imply compliance options that would be exponentially more difficult to enact than the United States' chosen policy.

III COALITIONS AND WEIGHTS

In its discussion of whether the FSPTCA treated imports less favourably (in light of the United States' concern for countervailing impacts), the Panel made the provocative remark that the bill's effect is 'to impose costs on producers in other Members, notably in Indonesia, while at the same time imposing no costs on any US entity'.[45] This statement seems at odds with evidence that US tobacco companies also owned clove brands,[46] and could potentially market other flavoured brands. These foreclosed opportunities represent real costs. WTO panels are familiar with concepts such as lost expected profits, which undeniably constitute a cost that the domestic companies incurred just as much as foreign producers.[47]

The Panel's commentary did bring to mind, however, a way that WTO panels could help build better policy through forcing countries (through adverse rulings) to internalise uncompensated costs that regulations may impose outside their borders. We know that the process of domestic policymaking involves weighing and balancing distinct interests and risk factors, and ranking the preferences of distinct interests.[48] While the Panel came close to 'speaking the language' of domestic public interest law, it reached a different conclusion by assigning a weight to Indonesia's interests, but not to any others.

Let us contrast and compare these different public interest techniques, and how international regimes might have supplemented in a useful way the domestic process.

First, in light of the Democratic majoritarian politics of the 111th Congress, I would suggest that Republicans carried little weight (even though large numbers of the pre-Tea Party era Republican Party did vote for the bill – a phenomenon that would not hold in today's anti-regulation Congress). Moreover, North Carolina-based tobacco companies were not supportive of reform, but lacked a sufficient political base to get their preferred substitute legislation through.[49]

Instead, the challenge was to hold together the Democratic base. In the brief two-year period (2009–10) when Democrats controlled all three political branches of government (White House, Senate and House of Representatives), policy entrepreneurs paid careful attention to avoiding policy vetoes by factions within the Democratic Party, and deemed some neutralisation of the opposition of affected business interests to be politically necessary.[50] Accordingly, there were essentially three factions: (i) pro-business Democrats, who were responsive to Philip Morris's interests (as the major Virginia-based company not opposing reform);[51] (ii) interventionist public health Democrats responsive to the anti-tobacco groups, whose revealed preference is for any reform;[52] and (iii) the Congressional Black Caucus (CBC), which was influenced by a progressive desire to 'do something', but without singling out African American adults in an overly paternalistic initiative (such as banning menthol), and without overly angering its funders in the tobacco industry.[53] Add to this a fourth group, which is essentially the preference of the policy entrepreneurs such as Representative Henry Waxman (Democrat of California), the powerful chair of the House Energy and Commerce Committee – as committed to tobacco control as he is to getting whatever deal is achievable. Table 6.2 shows these preferences, where each of these four groups can assign five alternative policies (from a total ban to no ban) a rank of 0 (dislike), 1 (modestly like or dislike), or 2 (strongly like).

Table 6.2   Constituencies' rankings under policy alternatives

Constituency	Ban everything	Ban menthols + FSPTCA	FSPTCA	FSPTCA minus cloves	Do nothing
a) Tobacco Dems	0	0	1	1	2
b) Anti-Tobacco Dems	2	2	2	2	0
c) CBC	1	0	1	1	0
d) Waxman	0	0	2	1	0
e) Indonesia	0	0	0	1	1
Balance 1: Domestic (a–d)	3	2	6	5	2
Balance 2: Foreign and Domestic (a–e)	3	2	6	6	3
Balance 3: Producer interest discounted (b–d, with a and e discounted)	3	2	5.5	5	1.5
Balance 4: WTO (only e)	0	0	0	1	1

As this exercise reveals, the FSPTCA was the optimal policy from the domestic bargaining process (ie Balance 1), preferred to a clove exemption and preferred greatly to a menthol ban. It is only when Indonesia's preferences are given equal weight with domestic preferences (ie Balance 2) that the FSPTCA becomes weakly preferred to a clove exemption. However, when both domestic and foreign cigarette producer interests are discounted (ie Balance 3), the FSPTCA again becomes the preferred outcome. In other words, an international deliberative body giving preference to public health outcomes would have produced the same policy outcome as the domestic US process. Even if producer interests were equally weighted with public health interests, an international body would not have been able to state whether the FSPTCA or a clove exemption would be preferred, and some other criterion for decision-making would have had to be adopted. Finally, it is only under the WTO's apparent balancing process (ie Balance 4, where only Indonesia's interests are taken into account) that a clove exemption is strongly preferred to the FSPTCA. However, even 'no regulation' is weakly preferred to an FSPTCA with a clove exemption in this scenario, suggesting that the WTO is unable to provide the US with a clear way forward for its domestic health policy.

IV QUESTIONABLE APPROACH TO EMPIRICAL EVIDENCE

The Panel took an idiosyncratic approach to examining substitutability between cloves and menthols. Economic studies often utilise survey data to examine consumers' willingness to substitute one product for another given different price and availability parameters. Indonesia and the US provided such studies, but the Panel simply stated that the difference in parameters of the studies made it impossible to compare them.[54] Instead, the Panel noted inconclusive remarks from the World Health Organization (WHO), the American Lung Association, TPSAC and other sources about the tobacco industry's rationale for including menthol and other flavours in cigarettes (to mask tobacco, appeal to youth, etc).[55] It used these remarks to conclude that, in 'the mind of youth', cloves and menthol are similar.[56]

This is a substantial logical jump. Industry motivation for marketing flavoured cigarettes in general is very different from establishing the willingness of teens (specific individuals or in general) to substitute one type of flavoured cigarette for another.

In considering the Panel's approach to this question, the AB explicitly noted that the number of users of menthols was not a relevant factor in the likeness/substitutability analysis.[57] Unlike the Panel (which considered only youth smokers), the AB chose to include adult smokers as well (on the basis of their large numbers),[58] but found that the age distribution of the flavoured cigarette smokers did not affect the 'degree of substitutability between clove and menthol'.[59] While asserting that competition and markets are paramount in the likeness analysis,[60] the AB nonetheless found that complainants need not establish actual competition or readily apparent markets.[61] The AB's theory seems to be that if a product *can be* substituted, the products are like. All the more confusing, then, is the repeated references to 'degrees' of substitutability. If one degree is enough, it is unclear why the AB needs a conceptual apparatus allowing for multiple degrees.

While critiquing the Panel's failure to engage extensively with the survey studies, the AB deemed this failure non-determinative, since the Panel had allegedly already established facts showing a sufficiently high degree of substitution and competition.[62] The AB, however, did not mention what these factual findings were, much less demonstrate that they were sufficient. As noted above, the only 'facts' found by the Panel were the conjectures on industry motivation for marketing cigarettes made by the WHO and other sources.

The questionable treatment of empirical evidence was only compounded as the decisions turned towards the TNLF plank of article 2.1. Whereas the likeness test did not turn on empirics, the TNLF test apparently did. The Panel noted that article 2.1 requires TNLF for 'products imported from the territory of *any* Member'.[63] Since, as an empirical matter, Indonesia is the source of most cloves, and most cloves come from Indonesia, the TBT Agreement (under the Panel's interpretation) obliges the US to ensure that 'any' and every WTO member gets TNLF from each domestic regulation.[64] If true, this would require legislators to conduct an exercise – nearly impossible from an incrementalist perspective – of calculating the impact of regulation not just on trade generally, but on the export profiles of each WTO member specifically. If any one member concentrates its exports in a given product, this could be the basis for a WTO claim. The AB essentially upheld this approach, but added the twist that the 12 candy flavours could be included in the article 2.1 analysis. Due to the fact, however, that there were relatively few sold at the time the bill was passed, the competing domestic flavoured cigarettes would still be overwhelmingly menthols. Therefore, the group of Indonesian products would be treated less favourably than the group of US products.[65]

This selective approach to empirical evidence is tilted in a pro-complainant direction. A consistent use of empirical evidence would have shown that menthol and clove are 'unlike' (because of the differing magnitudes and patterns of consumer use and willingness to substitute), even if Indonesian cloves get less favourable treatment than the bulk of domestic flavoured cigarettes. A consistent use of a non-empirical approach would have found candy, cloves and menthol 'like' (because consumer use patterns would not be relevant to theoretical substitutability), but would have found that – because any country *could* produce clove – it is not determinative of a TNLF analysis that Indonesia happens to be the country that *does* produce it. Moreover, the empirical fact of the low market share of the 12 candy flavours would not have been sufficient to discount them in the likeness and TNLF analysis.[66] Either a consistent empirical or non-empirical approach would have found the FSPTCA blameless.[67]

V NON-TEXTUAL ANALYSIS

The WTO's foregoing errors of omission (odd likeness comparisons and poor balancing and empirical techniques) might have been excused on the basis of a relentless commitment to the text of the TBT Agreement. After all, if countries signed up for a TBT Agreement that allowed or even required counterintuitive competitiveness comparisons, should not treaty interpreters respect members' consent?

Loyalty to text did not carry the day. The AB unilaterally modified the underlying article 2.1 obligation, by creating an *ex nihilo* concept: 'detrimental impacts on competitive opportunities stemming exclusively from legitimate regulatory distinctions' (DIOCOSEFLRD) will be considered allowable deviations from TBT obligations.[68] The apparent basis for this conclusion was that not all distinctions can be forbidden (since all technical standards involve distinctions and the TBT Agreement does not forbid all of them); not all trade restrictions can be disallowed (since TBT article 2.2 says that these are acceptable in certain circumstances); and finally, the preamble to the TBT Agreement says that:

> no country should be prevented from taking measures necessary to ensure the quality of its exports, or for the protection of human, animal or plant life or health, of the environment, or for the prevention of deceptive practices, at the levels it considers appropriate, subject to the requirement that they are not applied in a manner which would constitute a means of arbitrary or unjustifiable discrimination between countries where the same conditions prevail or

a disguised restriction on international trade, and are otherwise in accordance with the provisions of this Agreement.

The DIOCOSEFLRD concept is unlikely to satisfy any stakeholder. Respondents will be disappointed because it will be difficult if not impossible to prove in practice that all effects on competition derive *exclusively* from any one thing, let alone a legitimate regulatory distinction. Indeed, the US was unable to use this new exception-like concept in any of its recent battery of TBT cases.[69] On the other side, this interpretative activism goes against the effectiveness principle. The lack of a GATT article XX-style exception in the TBT Agreement (where broad categories of measures are excused from compliance) must be given interpretive weight, but the AB refused. Indeed, despite consulting the preamble to elaborate the DIOCOSEFLRD concept, the AB also failed to give weight to the ending clause of the above-cited sixth recital: 'otherwise in accordance with the provisions of this Agreement'. This provision should be read as a floor requiring the TBT consistency of regulations. The AB's approach introduces significant uncertainty into the scope of members' TBT commitments.

VI PARTING THOUGHTS

The forward trajectory of US tobacco control efforts remains uncertain. Extending a ban to menthol seems unlikely. Tobacco companies have sued to block the FDA from even considering the TPSAC's recommendation to ban menthol,[70] and Waxman and prominent anti-tobacco advocates have urged no weakening of the ban to exempt cloves.[71] Given that other core aspects of the FSPTCA are being whittled away by federal courts (and the Tea Party-era Republican majority is generally anti-regulation), the bill's advocates are perhaps especially likely to defend the incremental gains the FSPTCA gave them in the area of flavoured cigarettes.

In light of this, some scholars have urged the US to simply better justify the regulatory distinction between menthols and cloves in any WTO compliance hearing.[72] While this would do nothing to resolve Indonesia's economic grievances, it is a calculated gamble that by doing nothing but proving more, the WTO can be convinced to backtrack. This alternative has no precedent in the compliance case history.[73] Moreover, both the Panel and the AB gave little to no weight to the United States' underlying regulatory distinctions. Given the overall allergy to evidence, it is unclear on what basis the US would be able to pass the DIOCOSE-FLRD test in subsequent compliance proceedings.

The *Clove Cigarettes* decision has boxed the US into a corner. As it will be politically impossible to ban menthols, the only outcome for genuine compliance will be to weaken the public health policy by exempting additional products (which a Republican Congress might embrace). 'Compliance lite' (further study only) will not resolve Indonesia's grievances.

As of the compliance deadline of 24 July 2013, the US seems poised for the latter course. It has unveiled a new public education campaign warning of the negative impacts of menthol smoking, and a report reviewing the scientific literature on menthol smoking.[74] Moreover, it has requested comments from the public about what future potential menthol regulations should be put in place,[75] without committing to any particular course. Legal experts doubt that these efforts, which stop short of allowing cloves or prohibiting menthols, will convince a compliance panel.[76]

From an international regime perspective, these outcomes illustrate the 'counter-legalisation' problem. First, the lower panel and AB privileged Indonesian over US interests. In so doing, it produced a ruling that the US will almost certainly not comply with to Indonesia's satisfaction. This dynamic echoes the *US – Gambling* and the two other recent TBT cases, where the US 'compliance' response to AB rulings on sensitive anti-gambling, dolphin-safe tuna and country-of-origin labels appears so far to involve primarily more information-gathering, little policy change, and no real improvement in the complainants' export prospects.[77]

Why did the AB and the US behave as they did? One theory suggests that international adjudicatory bodies only rule against states when they can be reasonably assured of compliance, and that states only fail to comply when the benefits of doing so outweigh the costs.[78] While this may partially explain the US motivation, it seems weaker when explaining the AB's motivations. The AB appears to be making a point about the need to make TBT disciplines more useful for developing country exporters.[79] Indeed, influential developing country members including Brazil,[80] Mexico[81] and Turkey[82] (along with Norway[83]) sided with Indonesia in their third-party comments. (Only the European Union sided clearly with the US.[84]) But why would the WTO stretch empirical evidence and textual interpretation to the breaking point, if the only result would be a US shrugging-off of the rulings?

For the US, the division among WTO members in the *Clove Cigarettes* ruling – coupled with the weaker retaliatory punch of some of the affected countries – may lower the costs of non-compliance. This may explain the US response to Indonesia, but it is less able to explain similar non-compliance in the other TBT cases involving major trading partners such as Canada and Mexico. Indeed, the Obama administration appears to be making its own point, despite the retaliation and reputation costs involved in doing so: the WTO should tread lightly on complex administrative and public interest laws that involve delicate weighing and balancing of competing domestic interests and empirical evidence.

For the moment, the AB and US seem content to use these public interest cases to make systemic points about the trade regime's obligations to its members. It is difficult to know whether this is because the costs of doing so are low, or the subject matter is relatively novel in WTO law. The danger to the US regulations is that WTO procedures are structured such that – in the absence of US compliance – the matter will be perpetually on the DSB's agenda.[85] This creates 'legalised' justifications to weaken regulations for future US administrations less committed (for non-international law reasons) to public interest goals.

NOTES

1. Kenneth Abbott et al, 'The Concept of Legalization' (2000) 54 *International Organization* 401, 402.
2. Laurence Helfer and Anne-Marie Slaughter, 'Why States Create International Tribunals: A Response to Professors Posner and Yoo' (2005) 93 *California Law Review* 899, 917.
3. Abbott et al, above n 1.
4. Judith Goldstein and Lisa Martin, 'Legalization, Trade Liberalization, and Domestic Politics: A Cautionary Note' (2000) 54 *International Organization* 603, 623; Krzysztof Pelc and Johannes Urpelainen, 'Buying Out of Violation: When Do International Economic Agreements Allow Countries to Breach-and-Pay?' (Working paper, 3 July 2011) 30.
5. Maria Agius, 'Strategies and Success in Litigation and Negotiation in the WTO' (2012) 17 *International Negotiation* 139, 151.
6. See discussion of US position on article XVI of the *General Agreement on Trade in Services* in the appellant submission of the United States, *United States – Measures Affecting the Cross-Border Supply of Gambling and Betting Services* (14 January 2005) 51 <http://www.ustr.gov/webfm_send/772>.
7. Louis Bélanger and Kim Fontaine-Skronski, '"Legalization" in International Relations: A Conceptual Analysis' (2012) 51 *Social Science Information* 238, 247.
8. Daniel Blake, *Thinking Ahead: Time Horizons and the Legalization of International Investment Agreements* (unpublished thesis, Ohio State University, 2010) 166. This insight was noted by the original 'legalisation' authors, but not thoroughly explored: see Abbott, above n 1, 415.
9. Eric Posner and John Yoo, 'Judicial Independence in International Tribunals' (2005) *California Law Review* 1, 25.
10. For this point with respect to investment law, see Anthea Roberts, 'Power and Persuasion in Investment Treaty Interpretation: The Dual Role of States' (2010) 104

American Journal of International Law 179, 190. For similar points on the role of 'precedent' within WTO law, see Krzysztof Pelc, 'Shaping Precedent in International Trade Law: A Social Network Application' (Paper presented at the *Judicial Institutions: Courts in Domestic and International Affairs* workshop, Princeton, 2012) 6.

11. This corresponds to the *productive* dimension of power, which focuses on discourse, or the social processes that shape how meaning and identities are produced and changed. By defining what counts as 'legal', for instance, powerful actors can shape what courses of actions are taken by states that identify as 'law-abiding'. See Michael Barnett and Raymond Duvall (eds), *Power in Global Governance* (Cambridge University Press, 2005) 12–22.

12. See Pelc and Urpelainen, above n 4.

13. Jack Goldsmith and Eric Posner, *The Limits of International Law* (Oxford University Press, 2005) 73.

14. Panel Report, *United States – Measures Affecting the Production and Sale of Clove Cigarettes*, WTO Doc WT/DS406/R (adopted 24 April 2012) (Panel Report, *US – Clove Cigarettes*); Appellate Body Report, *United States – Measures Affecting the Production and Sale of Clove Cigarettes*, WTO Doc WT/DS406/AB/R (adopted 24 April 2012) (Appellate Body Report, *US – Clove Cigarettes*).

15. For ease of reference, I will call the Panel and AB 'the WTO' when referring to them jointly.

16. *Marrakesh Agreement Establishing the World Trade Organization*, opened for signature 15 April 1994, 1867 UNTS 3 (entered into force 1 January 1995), annex 1A (*Agreement on Technical Barriers to Trade*).

17. See below n 71.

18. Linda Yulisman, 'RI Seeks Damages in Dispute with US', *Jakarta Post* (online), 26 July 2013 <http://www.thejakartapost.com/news/2013/07/26/ri-seeks-damages-dispute-with-us.html>.

19. The bill was passed before the Affordable Care Act, which set a new bar for policy ambition but which represented a similar model of coalition-building, involving at least some industry support: *Patient Protection and Affordable Care Act*, 42 USC 18001 (2010).

20. See *Family Smoking Prevention and Tobacco Control Act,* 21 USC 301 §387 (2009).

21. As the conservative majority on the US Supreme Court noted in the 2000 landmark case striking down an earlier attempt to grant FDA jurisdiction over tobacco, the FDA found that, because of the high level of addiction among tobacco users, a ban would likely be 'dangerous'. In particular, current tobacco users could suffer from extreme withdrawal, the health care system and available pharmaceuticals might not be able to meet the treatment demands of those suffering from withdrawal, and a black market offering cigarettes even more dangerous than those currently sold legally would likely develop. The FDA therefore concluded that, 'while taking cigarettes and smokeless tobacco off the market could prevent some people from becoming addicted and reduce death and disease for others, the record does not establish that such a ban is the appropriate public health response under the act'. See *Food and Drug Administration v Brown & Williamson Tobacco Corp*, 529 US 120, 139 (2000).

22. *RJ Reynolds Tobacco Co v Food and Drug Administration*, F 3d, Nos 11–5332, 12–5063, 2012 WL 3632003 (2012).

23. American Lung Association, *From Joe Camel to Kaui Kolada: The Emergence of Candy-Flavored Cigarettes* (2006) <http://www.lungusa2.org/slati/reports/Candy FlavoredUpdatedAlert.pdf>.

24. Campaign for Tobacco Free Kids, Testimony at Hearing of Committee on Health, Education, Labor, and Pensions, United States Senate, *The Need for FDA Regulation*

of Tobacco, 27 February 2007, 72–3. <http://www.gpo.gov/fdsys/pkg/CHRG-110shrg33769/pdf/CHRG-110shrg33769.pdf>.

25. Seven out of eight of the comments received by TPSAC cautioned against a ban because of the countervailing effects. See US Food and Drug Administration, *Public Submissions for the September 27, 2010 Menthol Report Subcommittee of TPSAC Meeting* (2010) <http://www.fda.gov/AdvisoryCommittees/CommitteesMeeting Materials/TobaccoProductsScientificAdvisoryCommittee/ucm232795.htm>. See also *Letter from Fraternal Order of Police to Federal Drug Administration* (21 September 2011) <http://www.fop.net/publications/archives/letters/2011_0921.pdf>.

26. See Tobacco Products Scientific Advisory Committee, *Menthol Cigarettes and Public Health: Review of the Scientific Evidence and Recommendations* (2011) 225 <http://www.fda.gov/downloads/AdvisoryCommittees/CommitteesMeetingMaterials/Tobacco ProductsScientificAdvisoryCommittee/UCM269697.pdf>.

27. Unfortunately, little independent cost–benefit analysis is on the record, since a thoroughgoing cost–benefit analysis was not required for the Office of Information and Regulatory Affairs. Personal communication between author and an FDA tobacco specialist, 11 September 2012.

28. *Lorillard, Inc v US Food and Drug Administration* 2012 WL 3542228 (DC Cir, 2012).

29. Emphasis added.

30. It is notable that the Panel decided this issue despite the contrary recommendations of the parties, neither of which objected to the Panel broadening the likeness analysis to include other types of cigarette. Nonetheless, the Panel argued that it would be a violation of the due process rights of the parties and of third parties to expand their terms of reference to include additional products. See Panel Report, *US – Clove Cigarettes*, [7.132]–[7.133], [7.144]–[7.147].

31. *Marrakesh Agreement Establishing the World Trade Organization*, opened for signature 15 April 1994, 1867 UNTS 3 (entered into force 1 January 1995), annex 1A (*General Agreement on Tariffs and Trade 1994*).

32. Panel Report, *US – Clove Cigarettes*, [7.121].

33. Ibid [7.182].

34. Ibid [7.198].

35. Ibid [7.239].

36. Andrew Weiss and Edward Woodhouse, 'Reframing Incrementalism: A Constructive Response to the Critics' (1992) 25 *Policy Sciences* 255, 259; David Prindle, 'Importing Concepts from Biology into Political Science: The Case of Punctuated Equilibrium' (2012) 40 *Policy Studies Journal* 21, 33.

37. Jeffrey Miron, 'A Critique of Estimates of the Economic Costs of Drug Abuse' (Report to the Drug Policy Alliance, 2003) 7; Jeffrey Miron and Jeffrey Zwiebel, 'The Economic Case against Drug Prohibition' (1995) 9 *Journal of Economic Perspectives* 175, 190; Gary Becker, Kevin Murphy and Michael Grossman, 'The Economic Theory of Illegal Goods: The Case of Drugs' (National Bureau of Economic Research, 2004) 2.

38. *Letter from National Black Chamber of Commerce to TPSAC*, 15 September 2010 <http://www.fda.gov/downloads/AdvisoryCommittees/CommitteesMeetingMaterials/ TobaccoProductsScientificAdvisoryCommittee/UCM232842.pdf>.

39. See, eg, *Kimbrough v United States*, 552 US 85 (2007).

40. Substance Abuse and Mental Health Services Administration, Office of Applied Studies, *Results from the 2007 National Survey on Drug Use and Health: National Findings* (NSDUH Series H-34, DHHS Publication No SMA 08-4343, 2008) <http://www.oas.samhsa.gov/nsduh/2k7nsduh/2k7Results.cfm#TOC>.

41. Indonesia, in an attempt to downplay the amount of clove smokers for the TBT article 2.2 analysis, argued that the gap between these numbers is even greater –

further emphasising that these are social problems of wildly different magnitudes. See Panel Report, *US – Clove Cigarettes*, [7.390].

42. Ralph Caraballo, 'Menthol and Demographics' (Presentation delivered at the FDA Tobacco Products Scientific Advisory Committee meeting, 30 March 2010) <http://www.fda.gov/downloads/AdvisoryCommittees/CommitteesMeetingMaterials/Tobacco ProductsScientificAdvisoryCommittee/UCM207153.pdf>.

43. John Tauras et al, 'Menthol and Non-menthol Smoking: The Impact of Prices and Smoke-free Air Laws' (2010) 105 *Addiction* 115, 121.

44. Richard O'Connor et al, 'What Would Menthol Smokers Do if Menthol in Cigarettes were Banned? Behavioral Intentions and Simulated Demand' (2012) 107 *Addiction* 1330, 1337.

45. Panel Report, *US – Clove Cigarettes*, [7.289].

46. Indeed, Senator Ted Kennedy (Democrat of Massachusetts) took heat in the press when he exempted cloves during a 2007 mark-up of the FSPTCA. Pundits accused him of caving to Philip Morris, whose parent company had recently invested in a clove brand. See Gardiner Harris, 'Tobacco Bill Includes Compromise and Criticism', *The New York Times* (New York), 17 July 2007.

47. WTO panels would not be able to make an award on such a basis, but could consider such concepts in their debate about whether the costs of regulation are being disproportionately burdensome to certain interests.

48. L Robin Keller, Jay Simon and Yitong Wang (eds), 'Multiple Objective Decision Analysis Involving Multiple Stakeholders' (2009) *Tutorials in Operations Research* 139, 149; Cass Sunstein, *Worst-Case Scenarios* (Harvard University Press, 2009) 8.

49. Interestingly, this alternative legislation exempted both clove and menthol from regulation (see Senate Amendment 1246 s 110(a)(1), which created a prohibition on use of candy terms on packaging, but excluded clove and menthol), but was voted down on 9 June 2009. Barbara Barrett, *Burr Bucks Efforts for FDA Regulation of Tobacco Industry* (3 June 2009) McClatchy <http://www.mcclatchydc.com/2009/06/03/69362/burr-bucks-efforts-for-fda-regulation.html#.UaNG3-lYsop>; Mark Binker, 'Burr, Hagan Continue Tobacco Fight against Odds' (9 June 2009) *News & Record* <http://www.cigarettesflavours.com/smoking-prevention/hagan-battle-against-odds-for-tobacco/>.

50. Jacob Hacker, 'The Road to Somewhere: Why Health Reform Happened' (2010) 8 *Perspectives on Politics* 861, 869; Craig Volden and Alan Wiseman, 'Breaking Gridlock: The Determinants of Health Policy Change in Congress' (2011) 36 *Journal of Health Politics, Policy and Law* 227, 257.

51. Contrary to the views of some commentators, the menthol exclusion was not an instance of straightforward legislative capture. A case study of the FSPTCA process shows that the FDA, liberals in Congress and anti-tobacco groups had amplified political clout following a decade of awful publicity for the tobacco industry. In this context, Philip Morris was not driving the regulatory process, but attempting to react to and anticipate it. Indeed, the fact that Philip Morris was blamed alternately for the 2009 clove inclusion and the 2007 clove exemption shows the weakness of a crude capture model. See Harris, above n 46; Kevin Gauntt Barker, 'Thank You for Regulating: Why Philip Morris's Embrace of FDA Regulation Helps the Company but Harms the Agency' (2009) 61 *Administrative Law Review* 197, 200. But see Mariano-Florentino Cuéllar, 'Coalitions, Autonomy, and Regulatory Bargains in Public Health Law' in Daniel Carpenter and David Moss (eds), *Preventing Capture: Special Interest Influence in Regulation and How to Limit It* (Tobin Project, 2013).

52. Their true preference ranking more closely resembles a strongly monotonic set, where 'much reform' is preferred to 'some reform' to 'little reform', but it is assumed that progressive groups lack sufficient bargaining power to affect policy at such a

detailed level. Rather, progressive groups can typically only tip the scales when the policy process is already moving in pro-reform directions for exogenous reasons.

53. VB Yerger and RE Malone, 'African American Leadership Groups: Smoking with the Enemy' (2002) 11 *Tobacco Control* 336, 337.
54. Panel Report, *US – Clove Cigarettes*, [7.210].
55. Ibid [7.218]–[7.231].
56. Ibid [7.232].
57. Appellate Body Report, *US – Clove Cigarettes*, [131].
58. Ibid [137].
59. Ibid [144].
60. Ibid [137].
61. Ibid [142].
62. Ibid [145], [154].
63. Panel Report, *US – Clove Cigarettes*, [7.275] (emphasis added).
64. Ibid.
65. Appellate Body Report, *US – Clove Cigarettes*, [194]–[200].
66. The inconsistent approach towards empiricism manifested itself later in the AB's decision as well. In its section evaluating whether the US passed the 'detrimental impacts on competitive opportunities stemming exclusively from legitimate regulatory distinctions' test, the AB questioned why the US would not simply ban menthol in addition to cloves, and suggested that the countervailing impacts would not be significant, since menthol smokers could simply substitute regular cigarettes [225]. This significant statement is made without any reference to studies showing demand elasticity of menthol smokers, or reference to the actual magnitudes of smokers in one versus another category.
67. Such disregard for quantitative research appears to be fairly widespread in AB decisions, prompting one scholar to write: 'more prominently requiring and basing its findings on quantitative studies would enhance predictability and base "competitive relation" determinations – competitiveness in the marketplace after all being the criterion selected by the AB itself – on more objective, empirically established facts of competition rather than the intuition and deductive logic of judges comparing two products in the isolation of a WTO meeting room': Joost Pauwelyn, 'The Use, Nonuse and Abuse of Economics in WTO and Investor-State Dispute Settlement' in Jorge Huerta Goldman, Antoine Romanetti and Franz Stirnimann Fuentes (eds), *WTO Litigation, Investment and Commercial Arbitration: Cross-fertilization and Reciprocal Opportunities* (Kluwer, 2013).
68. Appellate Body Report, *US – Clove Cigarettes*, [182].
69. These were Appellate Body Report, *US – Clove Cigarettes*; Appellate Body Report, *United States – Measures Concerning the Importation, Marketing and Distribution of Tuna and Tuna Products*, WTO Doc WT/DS381/AB/R, (16 May 2012); Appellate Body Report, *United States – Certain Country of Origin Labelling (COOL) Requirements*, WTO Docs WT/DS384/AB/R and WT/DS386/AB/R (29 June 2012).
70. *Lorillard, Inc v US Food and Drug Administration,* WL 3542228 (2012) slip op, 3.
71. *Letter from Robert R Block et al to Ron Kirk, United States Trade Representative*, 23 April 2012 <http://www.cpath.org/sitebuildercontent/sitebuilderfiles/support_final_us_position_4-24-12.pdf>; Harry A Waxman, *Rep. Waxman Statement on the WTO Ruling on Clove Cigarettes*, 4 April 2012, Democrats Committee on Energy and Commerce <http://democrats.energycommerce.house.gov/index.php?q=news/rep-waxman-statement-on-the-wto-ruling-on-clove-cigarettes>.
72. Robert Howse, comment on Simon Lester, *Implementing the Clove Cigarettes Ruling* (17 April 2012), International Economic Law and Policy Blog <http://worldtradelaw.typepad.com/ielpblog/2012/04/implementing-clove-cigarettes.html>.

73. Todd Tucker, *Memo: Summarizing WTO Appellate Body Decision on US Flavored Tobacco Ban* (27 April 2012) Public Citizen 17–19 <http://www.citizen.org/documents/memo-appellate-body-clove-ruling-04-12.pdf>.
74. US Food and Drug Administration, 'Preliminary Scientific Evaluation of the Possible Public Health Effects of Menthol Versus Nonmenthol Cigarettes' (24 July 2013) <http://www.fda.gov/downloads/ScienceResearch/SpecialTopics/PeerReviewof ScientificInformationandAssessments/UCM361598.pdf>.
75. *Menthol in Cigarettes, Tobacco Products*, 78 Fed Reg 44,484 (24 July 2013).
76. 'US Claims Compliance in Clove Cigarettes Case, Some Experts Skeptical' (26 July 2013) *Inside US Trade* (online).
77. On the gambling case, see Agius, above n 5. On the other TBT cases, see 'New US Draft Tuna Labeling Rule May not Satisfy Mexico in WTO Case' (11 April 2013) *Inside US Trade* (online); 'Mexico Will Pursue Compliance Talks in Tuna Case, Gears up to Retaliate' (18 July 2013) *Inside US Trade* (online); 'Canada Preparing to Request Compliance Panel in US COOL Dispute' (27 June 2013) *Inside US Trade* (online). While violations of national treatment do not necessarily require a remedy of more market access, clearly most complainants have the latter in mind.
78. Clifford Carrubba and Matthew Gabel, 'Courts, Compliance, and the Quest for Legitimacy in International Law' (2013) 14 *Theoretical Inquiries in Law* 505, 526–8.
79. This has been a longstanding concern in the research on development. See OECD, 'Analysis of Non-Tariff Barriers of Concern to Developing Countries' (2005) 16 *OECD Trade Policy Papers* [22] <http://dx.doi.org/10.1787/223281783722>.
80. Appellate Body Report, *US – Clove Cigarettes*, [63].
81. Ibid [70].
82. Ibid [75].
83. Ibid [73].
84. Ibid [67]. Colombia and Guatemala had offered more muted support at the lower panel level.
85. Obligation to pay rather than perform could be an important safety valve for the WTO. However, because the WTO formally requires performance, the matter will not go away. See Joost Pauwelyn, 'How Strongly Should We Protect and Enforce International Law' (Paper presented at the University of Chicago Law School Workshop, March 2006) 43–57. See also Pelc and Urpelainen, above n 4.

7. The WHO FCTC as an international standard under the WTO Agreement on Technical Barriers to Trade

Lukasz Gruszczynski[*]

I INTRODUCTION

The legality of national tobacco control measures is increasingly being tested in different international forums. A subsidiary of Phillip Morris recently initiated an arbitration proceeding under a bilateral investment treaty (BIT) against Australia, seeking compensation for unlawful expropriation resulting from the introduction of a new law on plain packaging. A similar complaint was lodged against Uruguay under the Swiss-Uruguay BIT concerning the size and content of mandatory pictorial warnings on tobacco product packages. The World Trade Organization (WTO) has also become an important arena wherein international tobacco companies indirectly challenge various municipal health measures.[1] At the beginning of 2012, as discussed in Chapter 6 of this volume, the WTO adjudicating bodies were required to decide a dispute relating to the United States' (US) ban on the production, sale and importation of flavoured cigarettes (including clove cigarettes). More recently, a number of WTO members initiated a formal dispute settlement proceeding against Australia in response to its plain packaging law. Other disputes, relating to the contents of cigarettes and other tobacco-related regulatory measures, lie ahead.

The *Agreement on Technical Barriers to Trade* (TBT Agreement)[2] is probably the most important piece of WTO law when it comes to assessing national tobacco control measures.[3] Although it acknowledges WTO members' broad regulatory discretion, it also establishes certain parameters for national technical regulations, having regard to their effect on international trade. As part of this overall framework, the TBT Agreement encourages international harmonisation by offering certain legal advantages to those technical measures which comply with international standards. Insofar as concerns tobacco control measures, the major potential source of such standards is the *WHO Framework Convention on Tobacco Control* (WHO FCTC, or Convention)[4] and its guidelines, as elaborated in Chapter 2 of this volume. This is also the main focus of this chapter, which is aimed at enquiring into whether the WHO FCTC and its guidelines can be in fact regarded as relevant international standards under the TBT Agreement.

This chapter proceeds as follows: Part II gives a short overview of relevant provisions of the TBT Agreement. Part III moves on to the WHO FCTC and explains its basic disciplines. Part IV connects both instruments by examining the WHO FCTC and its guidelines in the light of the criteria proposed by the Appellate Body in one of its recent reports. The aim of this part is to determine whether the WHO FCTC and/or accompanying guidelines could qualify as relevant international standards under the TBT Agreement. The final part of the chapter briefly outlines the practical consequences of qualifying the WHO FCTC and its guidelines as international standards for current and future WTO disputes.

II　THE TBT AGREEMENT

The TBT Agreement is a part of WTO law that aims at disciplining national technical standards. This broad category encompasses technical regulations, standards and conformity assessments, but excludes sanitary and phytosanitary measures (article 1.5), which are regulated by the *Agreement on the Application of Sanitary and Phytosanitary Measures* (SPS Agreement).[5] In practice, the majority of national tobacco control measures qualify as technical regulations. A 'technical regulation' is defined by the TBT Agreement as a 'document which lays down product characteristics or their related processes and production methods, including the applicable administrative provisions, with which compliance is mandatory'. It may include such aspects as terminology, symbols, packaging, marking or labelling requirements as they apply to a product, process or production method (annex 1.1).[6]

The TBT Agreement includes its own variations of basic principles of international trade law, such as most favoured nation and national treatment principles (article 2.1)[7] and the necessity requirement (article 2.2), which precludes measures being more trade-restrictive than necessary to achieve a legitimate objective. The list of such objectives is open-ended and includes the prevention of deceptive practices, protection of human health or safety and animal or plant life or health, as well as environmental protection. The above requirements are supplemented with an elaborate set of procedural rules intended to increase the transparency of national regulatory processes (article 2.9). Consequently, WTO members are expected to publish a notice of a proposed technical regulation, notify other members about a draft, and allow a reasonable time for other members to make comments and discuss them. Comments as well as the outcomes of the discussion need to be taken into account (but not necessarily reflected) when adopting a final measure.

As already mentioned, the TBT Agreement promotes standardisation in the field of technical regulations by requiring WTO members to use international standards as a basis for their measures. This obligation arises whenever relevant international standards exist or their completion is imminent. The obligation is not absolute, however, and a WTO member may deviate from international standards if 'such international standards or relevant parts would be an ineffective or inappropriate means for the fulfilment of the legitimate objectives pursued' (article 2.4). On the other hand, a member that conforms to international standards obtains the benefit of a rebuttable presumption that the measure is in conformity with article 2.2.[8] In addition, according to article 2.9, such a measure is relieved from the procedural obligations discussed above.

Unfortunately, the TBT Agreement is rather opaque with respect to the issue of what should be considered an international standard. In contrast to the SPS Agreement, it does not enumerate any specific organisations whose standards are relevant within its context. Instead it includes two separate definitions of an 'international body or system' and a 'standard'. The first is understood as a body or system whose membership is open to the relevant bodies of at least all WTO members (thus the list of relevant international standard-setting bodies is open-ended). A standard, on the other hand, is described as a:

> document approved by a recognized body that provides, for common and repeated use, rules, guidelines or characteristics for products or related processes and production methods, with which compliance is not mandatory. It may also include or deal exclusively with terminology, symbols, packaging, marking or labelling requirements as they apply to a product, process or production method.[9]

This definition is supplemented by the explanatory note, which provides, *inter alia,* that '[f]or the purpose of this Agreement[,] standards are defined as voluntary ... Standards prepared by the international standardization community are based on consensus. This Agreement covers also documents that are not based on consensus'.

Moreover, an introductory note to annex 1 stipulates that its terms, unless defined otherwise in the TBT Agreement, shall have the same meaning as those included in the 1991 sixth edition of the *ISO/IEC Guide 2 (General Terms and Their Definitions Concerning Standardization and Related Activities)*. The latter includes a definition of an 'international standard' and characterises it as a 'standard that is adopted by an international standardizing/standards organization and made available to the public'.[10] In addition, the Committee on Technical Barriers to Trade (TBT Committee), an entity created as a platform for WTO members for consultations on any matters relating to the operation of the TBT Agreement and the furtherance of its objectives, adopted the *Decision on Principles for the Development of International Standards* (Decision on International Standards, or Decision),[11] which elaborates on some of the above requirements. In particular, the Decision enumerates certain principles and procedures that should characterise the work of an international standard-setting body.

This complex and multi-layered structure is not easily translatable into one operational definition. To some extent this was accomplished by the Appellate Body in its *US – Tuna II (Mexico)* report,[12] where a number of criteria for qualifying a specific rule as an international standard were identified. These requirements will be examined in more detail in Part IV below. For the moment it is sufficient to note that the Appellate Body identified the Decision as a 'subsequent agreement between the parties regarding the interpretation of the treaty or the application of its provisions' as provided for in article 31.3(a) of the *Vienna Convention on the Law of Treaties* (VCLT).[13] Consequently, WTO adjudicating bodies are obliged under article 3.2 of the *Understanding on Rules and Procedures Governing the Settlement of Disputes* to take this Decision into account when interpreting specific provisions of the TBT Agreement (that is, definitions of an 'international body' and 'standard').[14]

III THE FRAMEWORK CONVENTION ON TOBACCO CONTROL

The WHO FCTC is a legally binding international treaty adopted in 2003 under the auspices of the World Health Organization (WHO). In particular, the organisation relied, for the first time in its history, on article 19 of the WHO Constitution,[15] which gives the authority to the World Health Assembly (WHA) to adopt conventions with respect to any matter falling within the competence of the WHO, subject to a two-thirds majority vote. The Convention eventually entered into force on 27 February 2005 after the necessary number of ratifications (40 countries) was reached. It is a framework agreement, meaning that it establishes only general rules, which require further elaboration in subsequent instruments such as protocols[16] or guidelines. The WHO FCTC currently has 177 parties and is one of the most widely accepted UN treaties.[17] It should be noted, however, that neither the US nor Switzerland has ratified the Convention.

The aim of the WHO FCTC is to contribute to the protection of human health from the consequences of smoking and exposure to tobacco smoke. This is accomplished through the establishment of a set of framework rules to be implemented by the state parties. The Convention includes provisions aimed at reducing both the demand for, and supply of, tobacco products. The first group, aimed at reducing demand, encompasses price and tax measures (article 6), regulations protecting against exposure to tobacco smoke (article 8), measures on the contents of tobacco products (article 9) and their disclosure (article 10) and packaging and labelling requirements (article 11), as well as rules on tobacco advertising, promotion, and sponsorship (article 13). The supply-related provisions concern illicit trade in tobacco products (article 15), sales to minors (article 16), and the provision of support for economically viable alternative activities for tobacco workers and growers (article 17).

The WHO FCTC also establishes two bodies: a permanent Convention Secretariat and a Conference of the Parties to the WHO FCTC (COP). The Secretariat takes care of the daily management of the Convention. The COP, composed of all parties to the Convention, is responsible for supervising the implementation of the Convention. It may also adopt additional protocols to the Convention (article 33), which regulate specific aspects of tobacco control policies, and develop guidelines for the implementation of different provisions of the WHO FCTC (article 7). Until now, the COP has adopted seven guidelines. In the context of this chapter, of particular importance are the partial guidelines for implementation of articles 9 and 10 (on the contents of tobacco products and tobacco product disclosures),[18] guidelines for implementation of article 11 (on the packaging and labelling of tobacco products),[19] and guidelines for implementation of article 13 (on tobacco advertising, promotion and sponsorship).[20] Contrary to the Convention itself, however, the guidelines are non-binding and are aimed at assisting the parties in meeting their obligations under the WHO FCTC.

IV   THE WHO FCTC AS AN INTERNATIONAL STANDARD UNDER THE TBT AGREEMENT

The WTO adjudicating bodies have not yet analysed whether the WHO FCTC could be considered a 'relevant international standard' within the framework of the TBT Agreement. The only case that touched upon the relevance of the WHO FCTC rules under the TBT Agreement was *US – Clove Cigarettes*.[21] The panel, however, did not discuss these guidelines in the context of article 2.4, but rather used them as evidence of international consensus on specific aspects of tobacco control policies and the existence of underlying concerns (for example, risks connected with the use of flavoured cigarettes). This was not a legal omission on the part of the panel inasmuch as none of the parties maintained that there were relevant international standards applicable to the measure at hand. However, while there is no case law which has determined whether the WHO FCTC (and its guidelines) are relevant international standards, the recent report of the Appellate Body in *US – Tuna II (Mexico)* may be helpful in this regard. One of the issues that was extensively discussed by the Appellate Body was whether two resolutions[22] adopted within the framework of the 1999 *Agreement on the International Dolphin Conservation Program*[23] could qualify as an international standard. In this context, the Appellate Body set out some general criteria that need to be met in order to consider a particular rule as an international standard for the purpose of the TBT Agreement:

- a rule is adopted by a body that has recognised activities in standardisation (although those activities could be its secondary function);[24]
- a 'body' is understood as 'a legal or administrative entity that has specific tasks and composition'. While it does not need to be an international organisation,[25] it needs to be of an international character;[26]
- 'standardization activity' means an activity of establishing provisions for common and repeated use. Such provisions can take the form of rules, guidelines or characteristics for products, or related process and production methods (including packaging, marking and labelling requirements);[27] and
- membership in such a body is open to the relevant bodies of at least all WTO members.[28] As explained by the Appellate Body, in order to consider such a body 'open', it must be open at every stage of the development of standards on a non-discriminatory basis (for

example, provisions for accession cannot disadvantage the bodies of some WTO members as compared with other members).[29]

A high level of participation of WTO members in a particular body may suggest that its activities in standardisation are recognised.[30] Moreover, when determining whether a body is open to the relevant bodies of WTO members and whether it has 'recognized activities', one should also consider the extent to which such a body follows the principles and procedures established by the TBT Committee in its Decision on International Standards. In particular:

- a standardising body needs to be open to WTO members (as explained above);[31]
- a standard-setting process has to be transparent (that is, providing essential information to members at all stages, offering the possibility of making comments, publication of a standard upon its adoption), impartial (with respect to access to participation in working groups, submission of comments on drafts, revision of standards) and based on consensus (but only in the sense that the views of all parties are taken into account and conflicting arguments are reconciled);
- standards must be effective and relevant, meaning that they need to respond to the regulatory and market needs of WTO members; this also requires that they be up to date (that is, corresponding with scientific and technological developments) and capable of review if necessary, and that an international standardising body has procedures in place aimed at improving its communication with the WTO;
- the standardising process must be coherent and consistent with the work of other standardising bodies;
- a standardising body must undertake efforts to ensure the effective participation of developing countries in the development of standards.[32]

The Appellate Body did not address in its report two questions that may also be relevant when determining what should be regarded as an international standard under the TBT Agreement: (i) whether an international standard must be based on consensus; and (ii) whether it has to be made available to the public.[33] This was done by the panel in the same case which concluded, with reference to the explanatory note, that consensus was not an element of an international standard.[34] This conclusion is also supported by the Decision of the TBT Committee, which, as explained above, only requires taking into account all views and reconciling conflicting arguments.[35] With regard to the availability of a standard to the public, the panel stated rather generally that this requires the dissemination of information on adopted standards to market operators and other interested entities.[36]

The question thus arises: to what extent do the WHO FCTC and its guidelines meet the above criteria? There seem to be good grounds for arguing that both instruments can be regarded as international standards for the purpose of the TBT Agreement. The WHO FCTC was adopted by the WHO (through its WHA) – an international organisation (that is, a legal body) with a specific composition (almost all states) and specific tasks in the area of international health. This is also true for the guidelines. As explained above, they are adopted by the COP – an entity that has specific tasks (for example, to adopt protocols and guidelines necessary for the implementation of the Convention) and composition (that is, all parties to the Convention). The latter also indicates that the COP is of an international character (that is, it solely consists of countries with the exception of the European Union). Moreover, the Appellate Body has already identified a similar type of entity (that is, a meeting of the parties to the *Agreement on International Dolphin Conservation Program*) as a 'body'.

The development of guidelines by the COP can be regarded as a form of standardising activity. The activities of the COP consist of establishing common provisions (that is, by all state parties) for repeated (permanent) use, and take the form of guidelines for products (for example, cigarettes). Various guidelines relate to both the characteristics for products and packaging, and marking and labelling requirements as they apply to the products. The first group includes those provisions that require the parties to prohibit or restrict ingredients that may be used to increase the palatability of tobacco products and those with colouring properties or that create the impression that tobacco products have some health benefits. The second group encompasses those provisions that require the disclosure of various properties of tobacco products and specific packaging and labelling of tobacco products: that is, size of health warnings; use of pictures and pictograms on tobacco products packaging; content and language of warning messages; information on constituents and emissions of tobacco products; prevention of packaging and labelling that is misleading or deceptive (for example, low tar or ultra light); and plain packaging. At the same time, however, it seems that some of the guidelines will not pass this requirement. For example, the guidelines for implementation of article 5.3 are concerned with the protection of public health policies with respect to tobacco control from commercial and other vested interests of the tobacco industry.[37] As a consequence, they do not deal with characteristics for products, or packaging, marking and labelling requirements. The same is true for the guidelines for implementation of article 12, which regulate issues such as education, communication, training, and public awareness.[38]

The same conclusion can be reached with respect to the WHO as such. One of the main functions of the organisation is adoption of 'standards with respect to the safety, purity and potency of biological, pharmaceutical and similar products moving in international commerce', and 'advertising and labelling of biological, pharmaceutical and similar products moving in international commerce'.[39] Indeed, the organisation has been quite active in this field.[40] Although the WHO FCTC as a convention was based on a different legal basis (that is, article 19 rather than 31), there is nothing in the Appellate Body report that would prevent considering its adoption as a part of standardising activities performed by the WHO (irrespective of whether such activities are channelled through article 19 or 31). Consequently, one may conclude that the activities of the WHO consist of establishing common provisions (that is, by all WHO members) for repeated use, and take the form of standards or binding norms for various products. As far as the WHO FCTC is concerned, similarly to the guidelines, a number of its provisions relate to products and packaging characteristics, as well as marking and labelling requirements as they apply to the products (for example, articles 9, 10 and 11).

In this context, one may also ask whether the legal status of the WHO FCTC guidelines is relevant when it comes to their assessment under the TBT Agreement. As mentioned above, the guidelines, unlike the Convention, are of a non-binding nature – they are issued in order to assist the state parties in the implementation of the specific provisions of the Convention. From the perspective of general international law, they can be regarded at best as a form of soft law and do not impose any legally binding obligations on the parties. This, however, is irrelevant under the TBT Agreement. In fact, standards are specifically defined as non-binding documents ('with which compliance is not mandatory'), and only the TBT Agreement confers on them a quasi-normative authority by recognising them as a reference point for national regulatory measures.[41]

As clarified by the Appellate Body, standardisation activities need to be recognised by WTO members. One of the factors that may suggest such recognition is a high level of participation of WTO members in a particular body. This is the case for both the WHO and the COP. The former has 194 member states, which includes almost all WTO members,[42] while 177 states are parties to the Convention (and as a consequence members of the COP), with the vast majority of them also being

WTO members.[43] These levels of participation strongly suggest that both the WHO's and the COP's activities are widely recognised.

More problematic is the question of 'openness'. On the one hand, the WHO is an open international organisation. As a general rule, all member states of the United Nations can become WHO member states simply by signing or otherwise accepting the WHO Constitution.[44] The same is true for the Convention. According to its article 35, the WHO FCTC is open for accession from the day after the date on which the Convention is closed for signature. There is no precondition for accession, nor any need to obtain prior consent from the COP (an element that was fatal in the *US – Tuna II (Mexico)* dispute, where a formal invitation was required). In the context of the WHO FCTC, the whole process is automatic, and participation in the Convention is wholly dependent on the decision of an acceding state. Having said this, it must be conceded that not every WTO member can become a WHO member state or a state party to the Convention, as both structures are in principle limited to states, while WTO membership is also available to non-sovereign entities such as separate customs territories. In this regard, article 3 of the WHO Constitution clearly provides that the organisation is open to states only.[45] Although regional integration organisations can participate in the WHO FCTC (the European Union is in fact one of the parties), special administrative regions (for example, Hong Kong) or non-state territorial entities (for example, Taiwan), which are separate custom territories, are excluded (as in the case of the WHO). To some extent, the inability of Hong Kong to be a party to the Convention was remedied by the notification of China that was deposited on 11 October 2005 with the Secretary-General of the United Nations (the depository of the Convention), extending the application of the WHO FCTC (and corresponding guidelines) to the Hong Kong and Macao Special Administrative Regions.[46]

Taiwan unsuccessfully applied for WHO membership twice, in 2007 and 2008. In 2009 it was eventually invited, as Chinese Taipei, to participate in the meetings of the WHA as an observer (without voting rights). Since then this status was renewed for each subsequent year, but no progress has yet been made with respect to its WHO membership.[47] As far as the WHO FCTC is concerned, the ratification process at the domestic level was completed as early as March 2005. However, the instrument of accession that was sent to the Secretary-General was left without any further consideration, due to the general opposition from the Chinese Government.[48] As a consequence, Taiwan is currently not a party to the Convention. An attempt to grant it observer status at the meetings of the COP failed.[49] At the same time, Taiwan has adopted some of the most stringent regulations in the world in order to comply with the provisions of the WHO FCTC.

Thus, although from a formal point of view neither the WHO nor the WHO FCTC is open to all WTO members, a certain degree of flexibility and pragmatism is required here. A literal interpretation of the openness requirement would remove the majority (if not all) international standard-ising bodies from the scope of the TBT Agreement. Usually, inter-governmental organisations and standardising bodies are not open to non-state actors, while the WTO is one of the rare organisations that accepts separate customs territories as members. Therefore, narrow reading will clearly go against the spirit of the agreement, which is the promotion of international harmonisation in the technical regulations in trade field. Moreover, the practice of WTO members in the TBT Committee (for example, when it comes to notifications of technical regulations that deviate from ISO/Codex standards) seems to indicate that the open membership requirement is not absolute. The International Organization for Standardization and the Codex Alimentarius Commis-sion (Codex Commission) are generally regarded by WTO members as relevant standard-setting bodies, and yet Taiwan is not a member of either of them. In addition, a parallel treaty – the SPS Agreement – explicitly recognizes certain entities, including the Codex Commission, as relevant international standard-setting bodies.[50] None of them is open for Taiwan. It would be odd to consider Codex Commission standards as relevant under one WTO agreement and to refuse such recognition under the other.

The above conclusions as to the recognised character of standard-isation activities and the openness of both the WHO and the COP find additional support if one tests their operations against the various principles and procedures contained in the Decision on International Standards. The whole process of WHO FCTC adoption was fully transparent and open at each stage. The special working group respons-ible for preparing draft elements of the Convention, as well as the intergovernmental negotiating body (together with its own internal work-ing groups), were open to all WHO member states.[51] Indeed, they attracted a high number of state participants.[52] It is also worth adding that all documents relevant for the discussions (for example, experts' papers, official statements by WHO member states, materials of the Secretariat) were distributed before meetings and countries could comment on all proposed solutions. In addition to that, the WHO organised intersessional consultations for its member states in regions and sub-regions, giving them an additional opportunity to express their opinions.[53] Although it would be sufficient for the adoption of the Convention to secure a two-thirds vote of the WHA, in reality the whole process was highly consensual, and the WHO FCTC was eventually adopted unanimously.[54]

Transparency and openness are probably even more notable when it comes to guidelines. Technical drafting is done within special working groups that are established by the COP, and each state party may join a particular group on an equal basis. The outcome of their work is reported to the COP, where additional discussion takes place. The COP can make any and all necessary suggestions, ask for amendments, and limit or extend the mandate of a particular working group. The COP formally adopts guidelines, so, in this sense, it has the final word. All adopted guidelines are subsequently published in hard copy and on the WHO FCTC webpage, which also suggests that the WHO FCTC complies with the requirement of making standards available to the public. The decision-making process in working groups is informal and based on consensus. Although a decision of the COP can be taken by a three-fourths majority vote of the parties present and voting, the consensual nature of its decision-making process is highlighted in the *Rules of Procedure of the COP*.[55] In particular, rule 50.2 provides that 'the Conference of the Parties shall make every effort to reach agreement by consensus' while rule 50.3 envisages majority voting only if all efforts to reach consensus have been exhausted and no agreement has been reached.[56] This clearly meets the requirement of the Decision of the TBT Committee, which only calls for taking into account the views of all parties and reconciling conflicting arguments. In any case, to date all guidelines have been adopted by consensus.

The WHO FCTC and guidelines are effective and respond to the regulatory and market needs of WTO members. This is evidenced by the high level of participation of countries in the activities of specific working groups (for example, 56 countries take part in the working group on article 6)[57] and in the Convention as such. Neither the WHO FCTC nor the guidelines would appear to 'distort the global market, have adverse effects on fair competition, or stifle innovation and technological development'.[58] To the contrary – when one considers that WTO members would introduce diverse tobacco control measures independently of the Convention (and its guidelines), their adoption can be seen as a factor that contributes to the restoration of the global market (that is, by creating a common set of rules for all countries). Since regulatory measures proposed by the WHO FCTC (and guidelines) apply to all tobacco products, irrespective of their origin, they do not seem to affect competition. Although some requirements may stifle innovation (for example, by prohibiting development of new tobacco products), they also force technological improvements necessary for adjustment of products

to changing regulatory frameworks (for example, introducing new production methods for blended cigarettes to avoid using additives). Both the
WHO FCTC and the guidelines are also based on solid scientific
evidence and can be reviewed if the Parties consider that they are
obsolete, inappropriate or ineffective.[59] For example, the preamble to the
partial guidelines for implementation of articles 9 and 10 stress 'the
provisional nature of the guidelines and the need for periodic reassess-
ment in light of the scientific evidence and country experience'.[60]

Both the WHO and the Convention Secretariat maintain a number of
communication channels with the WTO. Although no formal agreement
has been signed between these two organisations, the WHO enjoys
observer status in various WTO committees and councils (for example,
the TBT Committee and TRIPS Council). The WTO Secretariat holds the
same status in various bodies operating within the institutional framework of the WHO (for example, the Intergovernmental Working Group
on Public Health, Innovation and Intellectual Property). The WTO is also
involved as a member in the Inter-Agency Task Force on Tobacco
Control, an entity that was established by the United Nations Economic
and Social Council under WHO leadership to ensure coordination
between different international organisations in the field of tobacco
control, and particularly in the context of adoption of the WHO FCTC.[61]
This cooperation is also visible at the level of the Convention. A
representative of the WTO Secretariat is always present at the meetings
of the COP, while a representative of the WHO, as mentioned above,
attends the meetings of the TBT Committee (representing the Convention
Secretariat). In addition, the COP, during its fourth session, adopted a
special decision on the cooperation between the WHO FCTC and the
WTO.[62] This decision, among other things, calls for the Convention
Secretariat to prepare a report on the possible modes of cooperation with
the WTO on trade-related tobacco control issues, cooperate with the
WTO Secretariat, and monitor disputes regarding trade-related issues of
relevance to the implementation of the WHO FCTC.

The standardising process run by the WHO and the COP does not
seem to be incompatible with the work of other standardising bodies.
There is neither duplication nor overlap with the work of other international standardising bodies. To this end, article 24.3(e) of the WHO
FCTC specifically obliges the Convention Secretariat to ensure that the
necessary coordination between relevant international and regional intergovernmental organisations and other bodies takes place.

The WHO took various steps to facilitate the participation of the least
developed countries at the different stages of development of the Convention. To this end, it provided financial support for representatives from

such countries participating in the meetings of the WHO FCTC working group[63] and the intergovernmental negotiating body.[64] A special trust fund was also created to enable other developing countries to take part in meetings.[65] The WHO FCTC as such also undertakes efforts to ensure the effective participation of developing countries in the development of guidelines. The operation of the Convention is financed through voluntary payments by the state parties, with the developed countries responsible for a majority of contributions. Participation in the COP's meetings of delegates from low- and lower-middle-income countries is financed from the WHO FCTC budget.[66] If one looks at the composition of specific working groups elaborating draft guidelines, the developing countries constitute a majority of their members.

V   CONSEQUENCES FOR CURRENT AND FUTURE DISPUTES

The above analysis shows that there are good grounds for regarding the WHO FCTC and its guidelines as 'relevant international standards' for the purpose of the TBT Agreement. Accordingly, it is worthwhile to look at the practical consequences of such recognition for both ongoing and potential future WTO disputes. This issue can be particularly relevant in the context of the Canadian and Brazilian measures regulating the content of cigarettes and the Australian law on plain packaging. All those measures, except for the Canadian one,[67] have been notified as required by the TBT Agreement. Although this suggests that members do not yet recognise the existence of relevant international standards, it cannot be decisive in deciding whether the WHO FCTC and its guidelines should be qualified as such. The notification undertaken can be viewed as a prudential response to the fact that no formal recognition (for example, from the WTO adjudicating bodies) of international standards in the field has yet taken place.

The Canadian *Cracking Down on Tobacco Marketing Aimed at Youth Act*,[68] which was introduced in 2009, prohibits the use of certain additives in tobacco products (for example, colouring agents, sweeteners, and certain flavouring substances, but not menthol). The goal of the regulation is to reduce the attractiveness of tobacco products for young and first-time consumers.[69] The Brazilian measure is even more stringent as it establishes a complete ban on the use of almost all types of additives, including flavouring agents and menthol, in tobacco products.[70] The rationale is the same as in the case of the Canadian law,[71] but the list of prohibited additives is more comprehensive (in principle, the only permitted ingredients are tobacco itself, water and sugar). Both regulations have been heavily criticised by other WTO members at the meetings of the TBT Committee. In particular, it is argued that the measures could violate articles 2.1 and 2.2 of the TBT Agreement.[72]

The third measure that would likely be affected by recognition of the WHO FCTC and its guidelines as relevant international standards is the plain packaging law[73] that has recently been passed by Australia and was fully implemented on 1 December 2012. The law requires all tobacco products to be marketed in standardised packs and prohibits the use of any trademarks or other marks on the retail packaging of tobacco products except for 'the brand, business or company name for the tobacco products, and any variant name for the tobacco products' provided in a form prescribed by the law.[74] According to Australia, the plain packaging requirement will diminish the attractiveness of cigarettes, particularly to young people, and make the health warnings more visible, thus increasing their deterrence effect. Although the main concerns with respect to the plain packaging regulation arise out of the *Agreement on Trade-Related Aspects of Intellectual Property Rights*,[75] the TBT Agreement is also relevant. In particular, five WTO members (Ukraine, Honduras, the Dominican Republic, Cuba and Indonesia) have initiated formal dispute settlement proceedings, claiming that the measure violates articles 2.1 and 2.2 of the TBT Agreement.[76]

On their face, all the above-cited measures seem to be based on the WHO FCTC and its guidelines. For example, WHO FCTC article 9 and the relevant guidelines recognise that 'from the perspective of public health, there is no justification for permitting the use of ingredients, such as flavouring agents, which help make tobacco products attractive'[77] and that '[p]arties should regulate, by prohibiting or restricting, ingredients that may be used to increase palatability in tobacco products'.[78] The same is true for ingredients that have colouring properties or are used to create the impression that products have health benefits (for example, vitamins).[79] As far as the Australian plain packaging law is concerned, the guidelines for implementation of article 13 are particularly relevant. They provide that '[p]arties should consider adopting plain packaging requirements to eliminate the effects of advertising or promotion on packaging'.[80] In a similar vein, the guidelines for implementation of article 11 stipulate that '[p]arties should consider adopting measures to restrict or prohibit the use of logos, colours, brand images or promotional information on packaging, other than brand names and product names, played in a standard colour and font style'.[81]

As explained above, if the WHO FCTC guidelines are qualified as international standards, measures that are based on them will benefit from the presumption of consistency with article 2.2 of the TBT Agreement and will be excused from the transparency obligations provided in article 2.9. Since all the above-cited measures (except for Canadian one) have been properly notified, the most important consequence in the context of the above trade disputes is activation of the presumption of consistency with the necessity requirement.

Before speculating whether this will work out in practice, however, one needs to await a decision of the Appellate Body on the status of the WHO FCTC (and its guidelines) under the TBT Agreement (which may happen already in the *Australia – Tobacco Plain Packaging* dispute). From a national point of view, such recognition would be more than welcome. The possibility of relying on guidelines will guarantee necessary regulatory space for WTO members when it comes to tobacco control measures, ensuring at the same time a high level of health protection. Allowing the WHO FCTC and its guidelines to qualify as international standards is also beneficial for systemic reasons, as it will improve the predictability of the system created by the TBT Agreement and the consistency between different legal regimes (that is, the WTO and the WHO FCTC).[82] At the same time, if the presumption of article 2.5 does not apply here, the situation is not fatal for a defending WTO member. First, the WHO FCTC provisions could be regarded as relevant rules of international law applicable in the relations between the parties in the sense of article 31.3(c) of the VCLT (assuming that 'parties' are understood by WTO adjudicating bodies as parties to the dispute, and not all the parties to agreements).[83] Second, both the WHO FCTC and the guidelines may be used as a 'fact' that will help to confirm existence of certain risks to health, and the importance and legitimacy of national measures as well as their necessity and proportionality.[84] As mentioned above, this approach was actually taken by the panel in the *US – Clove Cigarettes* dispute. In other words, if national measures do not benefit from the presumption, the WHO FCTC and its guidelines can remain an important element in the demonstration of certain factual assertions (and as a consequence influence subsequent legal determinations).

NOTES

* An earlier version of this chapter appeared in the special issue, 'Legal Issues in Tobacco Control' (2012) 5 *Transnational Dispute Management*, online. The research was financed by the Polish National Science Center pursuant to grant number 2012/07/B/HS5/03767: *Tobacco Control Measures in International Law: Finding a Balance between Competing Interests.*

1. Note that only WTO members themselves can initiate a formal dispute settlement proceeding. In reality, however, some complaints are indirectly initiated and subsequently supported by private operators affected by the contested measures. For instance, a complaint by Antigua and Barbuda against the US ban on Internet gambling was backed up by the gaming industry, for details see Jane Kelsey, *Serving Whose Interests? The Political Economy of Trade in Services Agreements* (Routledge, 2008) 174–80.

2. *Marrakesh Agreement Establishing the World Trade Organization*, opened for signature 15 April 1994, 1867 UNTS 3 (entered into force 1 January 1995), annex 1A (*Agreement on Technical Barriers to Trade*).

3. Other relevant WTO agreements include: *General Agreement on Tariffs and Trade*, LT/UR/A-1A/1/GATT/2 (signed 30 October 1947), as incorporated in *Marrakesh Agreement Establishing the World Trade Organization*, opened for signature 15 April 1994, 1867 UNTS 3 (entered into force 1 January 1995) annex 1A (*General Agreement on Tariffs and Trade 1994*); *Marrakesh Agreement Establishing the World Trade Organization*, opened for signature 15 April 1994, 1867 UNTS 3 (entered into force 1 January 1995), annex 1B (*General Agreement on Trade in Services*); *Marrakesh Agreement Establishing the World Trade Organization*, opened for signature 15 April 1994, 1867 UNTS 3 (entered into force 1 January 1995), annex 1C (*Agreement on Trade-Related Aspects of Intellectual Property Rights*).

4. *World Health Organization Framework Convention on Tobacco Control*, opened for signature 16 June 2003, 2302 UNTS 166 (entered into force 27 February 2005).

5. *Marrakesh Agreement Establishing the World Trade Organization*, opened for signature 15 April 1994, 1867 UNTS 493 (entered into force 1 January 1995), annex 1A (*Agreement on the Application of Sanitary and Phytosanitary Measures*). For an extensive discussion on the applicability of the SPS and TBT Agreements, see Lukasz Gruszczynski, *Regulating Health and Environmental Risks under WTO Law. A Critical Analysis of the SPS Agreement* (Oxford University Press, 2010) 63–8.

6. Cf Appellate Body Report, *European Communities – Measures Affecting Asbestos and Asbestos-Containing Products*, WTO Doc WT/DS135/AB/R (adopted 5 April 2001) [67]–[69] (defining technical regulations).

7. Article 2.1 provides that 'Members shall ensure that in respect of technical regulations, products imported from the territory of any Member shall be accorded treatment no less favourable than that accorded to like products of national origin and to like products originating in any other country'.

8. Article 2.5 specifically provides that such a measure 'shall be rebuttably presumed not to create an unnecessary obstacle to international trade'. In order to benefit from the presumption, such a measure also needs to be prepared, adopted or applied for one of the legitimate objectives explicitly elaborated in article 2.2.

9. TBT Agreement annexes 1.4 and 1.2 respectively.

10. International Organization for Standardization, *ISO/IEC Guide 2: 1991 – General Terms and Their Definitions Concerning Standardization and Related Activities* (6th ed, 1991) [3.2.1] (*ISO/IEC Guide 2*).

11. *Decisions and Recommendations Adopted by the WTO Committee on Technical Barriers to Trade Since 1 January 1995*, WTO Doc G/TBT/1/Rev.10 (9 June 2011) 46.

12. Appellate Body Report, *United States – Measures Concerning the Importation, Marketing and Sale of Tuna and Tuna Products*, WTO Doc WT/DS381/AB/R (adopted 13 June 2012) (*US – Tuna II (Mexico)*).

13. Ibid [372]. Article 31.3(a) of the VCLT provides: 'There shall be taken into account [when interpreting a treaty], together with the context: (a) any subsequent agreement between the parties regarding the interpretation of the treaty or the application of its

provisions' *Vienna Convention on the Law of Treaties*, opened for signature 23 May 1969, 1155 UNTS 331 (entered into force 27 January 1980).

14. *Marrakesh Agreement Establishing the World Trade Organization*, opened for signature 15 April 1994, 1867 UNTS 3 (entered into force 1 January 1995), annex 2 *(Understanding on Rules and Procedures Governing the Settlement of Disputes)*.

15. *Constitution of the World Health Organization*, signed on 22 July 1946, 14 UNTS 185 (entered into force 7 April 1948).

16. Only one protocol has been adopted to date: the *Protocol to Eliminate Illicit Trade in Tobacco Products*. The protocol was open for signature by the parties to the WHO FCTC for the period of one year, starting from 10 January 2013, and will enter into force 90 days following the date of deposit of the 40th instrument of its ratification (article 43 of the Protocol): see WHO FCTC Conference of the Parties, *Decision: Protocol to Eliminate Illicit Trade in Tobacco Products*, 5th sess, WHO Doc FCTC/COP5(1) (12 November 2012).

17. The list of the countries that are parties to the Convention is available on the WHO FCTC webpage: see World Health Organization, *Parties to the WHO Framework Convention on Tobacco Control* (25 March 2014) <http://www.who.int/fctc/signatories_parties>.

18. WHO FCTC Conference of the Parties, *Partial Guidelines for Implementation of Articles 9 and 10 of the WHO Framework Convention on Tobacco Control*, WHO Doc FCTC/COP4(10) (20 November 2010) *(Partial Guidelines for Implementation of Articles 9 and 10)*.

19. WHO FCTC Conference of the Parties, *Guidelines for Implementation of Article 11 of the WHO Framework Convention on Tobacco Control*, WHO Doc FCTC/COP3(10) (22 November 2008) *(Guidelines for Implementation of Article 11)*.

20. WHO FCTC Conference of the Parties, *Guidelines for Implementation of Article 13 of the WHO Framework Convention on Tobacco Control (Tobacco Advertising, Promotion and Sponsorship)*, WHO Doc FCTC/COP3(12) (22 November 2008) *(Guidelines for Implementation of Article 13)*.

21. Panel Report, *United States – Measures Affecting the Productions and Sale of Clove Cigarettes*, WTO Doc WT/DS406/R (adopted 24 April 2012).

22. See Parties to the Agreement on the International Dolphin Conservation Program, *Resolution to Adopt the Modified System for Tracking and Verification of Tuna*, 5th mtg, AIDP Doc A-01-01 (20 June 2001); Parties to the Agreement on the International Dolphin Conservation Program, *Resolution To Establish Procedures For AIDCP Dolphin Safe Tuna Certification*, 5th mtg, AIDP Doc A-01-02 (20 June 2001).

23. Opened for signature 15 May 1998, (1998) 37 ILM 1246 (entered into force 15 February 1999).

24. Appellate Body Report, *US – Tuna II (Mexico)*, [362].

25. The term 'body' was defined by the Appellate Body with reference to the *ISO/IEC Guide 2*, see ibid [355]–[356].

26. Ibid [359].

27. Ibid [360].

28. Ibid [364].

29. Ibid [374].

30. Ibid [363].

31. Ibid [374].

32. Decision on International Standards, WTO Doc G/TBT/1/Rev.10, [3]–[13].

33. Appellate Body Report, *US – Tuna II (Mexico)*, [353].

34. Panel Report, *United States – Measures Concerning the Importation, Marketing and Sale of Tuna and Tuna Products*, WTO Doc WT/DS381/R (adopted 24 April 2012) [7.676] *(US – Tuna II (Mexico))*.

35. Decision on International Standards, WTO Doc G/TBT/1/Rev.10, [8]. A similar approach was adopted under the SPS Agreement, cf Panel Report, *EC Measures Concerning Meat and Meat Products (Hormones), Complaint by the United States*, WTO Doc WT/DS26/R (adopted 13 February 1998) [8.69].

36. Panel Report, *US – Tuna II (Mexico)*, [7.694]–[7.695].

37. WHO FCTC Conference of the Parties, *Guidelines for Implementation of Article 5.3 of the WHO Framework Convention on Tobacco Control*, WHO Doc FCTC/COP3(7) (22 November 2008).

38. WHO FCTC Conference of the Parties, *Guidelines for Implementation of Article 12 of the WHO Framework Convention on Tobacco Control*, WHO Doc FCTC/COP4(7) (20 November 2010).

39. WHO Constitution article 31.

40. See, eg, 'Guidelines for Assuring the Quality of Pharmaceutical and Biological Products Prepared by Recombinant DNA Technology' (Technical Report Series No 814, annex 3, World Health Organization, 1991).

41. Note, however, that the WTO case law suggests that the legal nature of an international standard (whether it is binding or non-binding) is of secondary importance. In *US – Tuna II (Mexico)*, the binding character of the two resolutions did not prevent the panel from analysing whether they could have been qualified as international standards: see Panel Report, *US – Tuna II (Mexico)*, [7.666]–[7.740].

42. Information available on the official WHO webpage, see World Health Organization, *Countries* <http://www.who.int/countries>.

43. Note that only 12 of the 155 WTO members are not parties to the WHO FCTC.

44. *WHO Constitution* article 4. There is also a separate procedure for non-UN member states (cf *WHO Constitution* article 6 and ch XIV), but since almost all countries are UN member states this remains a rather theoretical option.

45. Note, however, that the WHA, in its resolution initiating the process of WHO FCTC adoption, explicitly permitted regional economic integration organisations to participate in the drafting and negotiating process: see World Health Organization, *Towards a WHO Framework Convention on Tobacco Control*, WHO Res WHA52.18, 52nd WHA, 9th plen mtg, WHO Doc A52/7 (24 May 1999) [1.3].

46. Information available in the United Nations Treaty Collection database, see United Nations Treaty Collection, *WHO Framework Convention on Tobacco Control* (14 May 2013) <http://treaties.un.org/Pages/ViewDetails.aspx?src=TREATY&mtdsg_no=IX-4&chapter=9&lang=en>.

47. Sigrid Winkler, 'Taiwan's UN Dilemma: To Be or Not to Be' (2012) 9 *Taiwan-U.S. Quarterly Analysis* <http://www.brookings.edu/research/opinions/2012/06/20-taiwan-un-winkler>.

48. See generally Michael Sheng-ti Gau, 'The Legal Controversies between China and Taiwan in the WHO from the Perspectives of an International Law Scholar in Taiwan' (2008) 1 *Journal of East Asia & International Law* 159.

49. Ibid 160.

50. The relevant international standard-setting bodies under the SPS Agreement are: the Codex Commission, the World Organization for Animal Health and the *International Plant Protection Convention*, opened for signature 17 November 1997, 2367 UNTS 223 (entered into force 2 October 2005).

51. World Health Organization, *Towards a WHO Framework Convention on Tobacco Control*, WHO Res WHA52.18, 52nd WHA, 9th plen mtg, WHO Doc A52/7 (24 May 1999) [1.1]–[1.2].

52. Cf, eg, Intergovernmental Negotiating Body on the WHO Framework Convention on Tobacco Control, *List of Participants*, WHO Doc A/FCTC/INB1/DIV/2 Rev.1 (18 October 2000).

53. Cf World Health Organization, *Intersessional Consultations* <http://www.who.int/tobacco/fctc/consultations/en/print.html>. In addition, the WHO organised public hearings on issues related to the proposed Convention, in which 160 different organisations participated.

54. World Health Assembly, *WHO Framework Convention on Tobacco Control*, WHA Res WHA56.1, 5th plen mtg, WHO Doc A56/8 (21 May 2003).

55. World Health Organization, *WHO Framework Convention on Tobacco Control: Rules of Procedure of the Conference of the Parties* (World Health Organization, 2006).

56. Ibid.

57. This high level of participation reflects the real interest of countries in the development of WHO FCTC tobacco control standards.

58. Decision on International Standards, WTO Doc G/TBT/1/Rev.10, [10].

59. The WHO FCTC envisages a special procedure for amending its provisions (cf WHO FCTC article 28).

60. *Partial Guidelines for Implementation of Articles 9 and 10*, above n 18, 1.

61. United Nations Economic and Social Council, *Ad Hoc Inter-Agency Task Force on Tobacco Control, Report of the Secretary-General*, UN Doc E/2000/21 (1 May 2000) 4.

62. WHO FCTC Conference of the Parties, *Cooperation between the Convention Secretariat and the World Trade Organization*, 4th sess, 10th plen mtg, WHO Doc FCTC/COP4(18) (20 November 2010).

63. Working Group on the WHO Framework Convention on Tobacco Control, *Report of the First Meeting of the Working Group*, 1st mtg, WHO Doc A/FCTC/WG1/7 (28 October 1999) [89]–[90] (*Report of the First Meeting of the Working Group*).

64. Intergovernmental Negotiating Body on the WHO Framework Convention on Tobacco Control, *Summary of Records of Plenary Meetings*, 1st sess, WHO Doc A/FCTC/INB1/SR 16 (16–21 October 2000).

65. *Report of the First Meeting of the Working Group*, WHO Doc A/FCTC/WG1/7, [89].

66. Cf WHO FCTC Conference of the Parties, *Harmonization of Travel Support Available to Parties to the WHO Framework Convention on Tobacco Control in Line with Current World Health Organization Administrative Policies for Travel Support*, 4th sess, WHO Doc FCTC/COP4(21) (15–20 November 2010).

67. See, eg, Committee on Technical Barriers to Trade, *Minutes of the Meeting of 5–6 November 2009*, WTO Doc G/TBT/M/49 (22 December 2009) [8]–[18] (*TBT Minutes of Meeting November 2009*).

68. SC 2009 c 27.

69. Committee on Technical Barriers to Trade, *Minutes of the Meeting 24–25 March 2011*, WTO Doc G/TBT/M/53 (26 May 2011) [226].

70. Committee on Technical Barriers to Trade, *Minutes of the Meeting of 20–21 March 2012*, WTO Doc G/TBT/M/56 (16 May 2012) [114]. The final version of the act was published on 16 March 2012 as Resolution RDC 14/2012 of the Brazilian National Agency for Sanitary Surveillance.

71. It seems that the Brazilian Government is also concerned with the health effects of additives, as they can make cigarettes more addictive or risky. This would indicate that there was a second objective, apart from the reduction in attractiveness, consisting in elimination of those additives which are harmful themselves (cf *TBT Minutes of Meeting November 2009*, WTO Doc G/TBT/M/49 [59]).

72. See, eg, ibid [12]–[13].

73. *Tobacco Plain Packaging Act 2011* (Cth).

74. Ibid s 20.

75. See above n 3.

76. See, eg, Request for the Establishment of a Panel by Ukraine, *Australia – Certain Measures Concerning Trademarks and Other Plain Packaging Requirements Applicable to Tobacco Products and Packaging*, WTO Doc WT/DS434/11 (17 August 2012).
77. *Partial Guidelines for Implementation of Articles 9 and 10*, above n 18, [1.2.1.1].
78. Ibid [3.1.2.2]. However, it may be disputed whether the Canadian measure is based on WHO FCTC standards inasmuch as it excludes menthol from the scope of its prohibition.
79. Ibid [3.1.2.2(ii)]–[3.1.2.2(iii)].
80. *Guidelines for Implementation of Article 13*, above n 20, [17].
81. *Guidelines for Implementation of Article 11*, above n 19, [46].
82. One should, however, acknowledge that there could be some negative systemic implications resulting from recognising the WHO FCTC guidelines as relevant international standards. Many WTO members may become wary about participating in any similar future activities or become persistent objectors.
83. For the discussion on this issue see Lukasz Gruszczynski, 'Customary Rules of Interpretation in the Practice of WTO Dispute Settlement Bodies' in Ole Kristian Fauchald and André Nollkaemper (eds), *The Practice of International and National Courts and the (De-)Fragmentation of International Law* (Hart Publishing, 2012) 46–52.
84. Cf World Health Organization, *Confronting the Tobacco Epidemic in a New Era of Trade and Investment Liberalization* (World Health Organization, 2012) 73.

8. Disputes regarding tobacco control measures under investor-state arbitration

Tsai-yu Lin

I INTRODUCTION

That tobacco consumption and exposure to tobacco smoke cause death, disease and disability is well established by scientific evidence. The global tobacco epidemic has become a pressing public health issue.[1] Over the years, various tobacco control measures have been put in place around the world. This can be attributed to the adoption of the *WHO Framework Convention on Tobacco Control* (WHO FCTC),[2] the most important public health treaty on tobacco. Disputes between tobacco companies and countries implementing active tobacco control measures have increased with the implementation of such measures.[3] Recently, tobacco company Philip Morris initiated investor-state arbitration under bilateral investment treaties (BIT) challenging Uruguay and Australia's tobacco packaging laws.[4] This action has created concerns regarding potential conflicts between the WHO FCTC and BITs. In 2010, Philip Morris filed claims against Uruguay at the International Centre for Settlement of Investment Disputes (ICSID) under the BIT between Switzerland and Uruguay.[5] In 2011, another Philip Morris entity filed a claim against Australia under a BIT between Hong Kong and Australia[6] and invoked the United Nations Commission on International Trade Law Arbitration Rules (UNCITRAL Arbitration Rules)[7] to govern the arbitration proceedings. In the view of Philip Morris, the tobacco packaging measures at issue unlawfully interfere with its use of trademarks and intellectual property – the central investments protected by the BITs – and therefore constitute a violation of several obligations under the BITs.[8] Philip Morris seeks relief in the form of substantial financial compensation as well as the suspension of the challenged regulations.

Controlling the packaging and labelling of tobacco products constitutes an integral part of the tobacco control measures under the WHO FCTC related to the reduction of the demand for tobacco.[9] The ongoing investment disputes between Philip Morris and Uruguay and Australia have for the first time brought tobacco control measures modelled on the WHO FCTC under scrutiny in treaty-based investment arbitrations. Treaty-based investor-state investment arbitration is a prominent element of modern BITs. Its uniqueness lies in the involvement of the host state and the associated public interest implications. Despite the involvement of states, the *ICSID Rules of Procedure for Arbitration Proceedings* (ICSID Arbitration Rules)[10] and *UNCITRAL Arbitration Rules* – the two most popular arbitral rules applied to investment disputes – are originally modelled on or designed for the resolution of international commercial disputes between private parties. As a result, whether investor-state arbitral proceedings can sufficiently take account of public interest concerns is of great concern to the public health community. In addition to controversial substantive issues that have arisen,[11] the process of the arbitral proceedings and the possible awards that may be made in relation to tobacco control will have significant implications for the host state's right to regulate tobacco products, the WHO FCTC's future development, and global public health.

Against this background, and by looking at some procedural arrangements in terms of the ICSID Arbitration Rules and the UNCITRAL Arbitration Rules, this chapter argues that as a dispute settlement mechanism, investor-state arbitrations might not provide a suitable forum in which to resolve investment disputes involving tobacco control measures. In promoting the protection of public health and the settlement of relevant disputes, BIT parties, including the investor's home state, might play some useful roles in the course of investor-state arbitration.

II ARBITRATING INVESTMENT DISPUTES REGARDING TOBACCO CONTROL UNDER INVESTOR-STATE ARBITRATION: AN INAPPROPRIATE FORUM?

After making a brief comparison between the ICSID and UNCITRAL Arbitration Rules, this section examines issues regarding non-disputing parties' access to arbitration proceedings, the lack of appellate review of awards, and the potential for resistance from host states in relation to compliance with the tobacco control aspects of the award.

A   Non-disputing Parties' Access to Arbitration Proceedings

The international arbitration community generally accepts the increasing importance of transparency in treaty-based investment arbitration because of its public dimension.[12] Public participation in arbitral proceedings, as one element of transparency,[13] can contribute to establishing a more credible system of arbitration and a higher quality of arbitral awards. The ICSID and UNCITRAL Arbitration Rules have different rules regarding public participation.

The ICSID Arbitration Rules, as amended in 2006, provide for two specific instances of non-disputing party participation. The first allows a non-disputing party to file a written submission with the tribunal as amicus curiae. In accordance with r 37(2), after consulting both parties, the tribunal may allow a non-disputing party to file a written submission in respect of a matter within the scope of the dispute. In determining whether an amicus curiae submission should be accepted, the tribunal is instructed to consider the extent to which:

(a)   the non-disputing party submission would assist the Tribunal in the determination of a factual or legal issue related to the proceeding by bringing a perspective, particular knowledge or insight that is different from that of the disputing parties;

(b)   the non-disputing party submission would address a matter within the scope of the dispute; [and]

(c)   the non-disputing party has a significant interest in the proceeding.[14]

In addition, the tribunal is required to ensure that the amicus curiae submission 'does not disrupt the proceeding or unduly burden or unfairly prejudice either party, and that both parties are given an opportunity to present their observations on the non-disputing party submission'.[15] Given this, the ICSID tribunal is empowered to accept or consider amicus curiae submissions without having to obtain the prior approval of one or both of the disputing parties. Such submissions may provide more useful information to the tribunal beyond the disputing parties' submissions.

The second instance of non-disputing party participation relates to hearings. Rule 32(2) provides:

Unless either party objects, the Tribunal, after consultation with the Secretary-General, may allow other persons, besides the parties, their agents, counsel and advocates, witnesses and experts during their testimony, and officers of the Tribunal, to attend or observe all or part of the hearings, subject to appropriate logistical arrangements. ...

The openness of a hearing is therefore subject to the agreement of the disputing parties. Tribunals are not entitled to open hearings over the objection of a disputing party.

In contrast, the current UNCITRAL Arbitration Rules contain more limited provisions on transparency.[16] There is no explicit provision giving a non-disputing party the right to make an amicus curiae submission. However, the tribunal has an implied procedural power to accept amicus curiae briefs on a case-by-case basis.[17] In this regard, article 17(1) provides:

> the arbitral tribunal may conduct the arbitration in such manner as it considers appropriate, provided that the parties are treated with equality and that at an appropriate stage of the proceedings each party is given a reasonable opportunity of presenting its case. The arbitral tribunal, in exercising its discretion, shall conduct the proceedings so as to avoid unnecessary delay and expense and to provide a fair and efficient process for resolving the parties' dispute.

As to rules on hearings, article 28(3) provides that hearings are to be held 'in camera' unless the parties agree otherwise. Either disputing party can therefore block public access to the hearings.[18]

In light of the above discussion, under the ICSID system, non-disputing parties might be afforded with more opportunity to participate in investment arbitration. On the part of the tribunals, the observations in amicus briefs from non-governmental organisations or civil society could be useful because they may present perspectives and expertise independent of those provided by the parties. By allowing the relevant legal issues or claims to be examined in a broader context, the wider public interest is more likely to be taken into account by tribunals.[19] This point is of particular importance to disputes that contain significant public interest ramifications. As the Philip Morris cases have shown, investment disputes over tobacco control measures may concern the legality of tobacco packing regulations, a host state's right to regulate tobacco products, and broader questions of public health. The subject matter of the disputes goes beyond a mere investment issue, and the decision of the tribunal may affect other countries that have adopted or are contemplating similar tobacco control measures as envisioned by the WHO FCTC. Viewed in this light, if the investment tribunal hearing a tobacco control claim can accept or consider amicus curiae briefs and the information and arguments contained in the submissions, it might lead to greater acceptance of arbitral awards by the public.[20] In this regard, whether the World Health Organization (WHO) itself can qualify as an amicus curiae[21] to attend an arbitration seems unclear. Also, whether other parties to the

WHO FCTC could be given amicus status or some procedural privilege as a non-disputing state party may also need some clarification.[22]

Nevertheless, the availability of amicus curiae briefs alone could not necessarily increase or ensure the legitimacy of an award.[23] Whether and to what extent the amicus brief influences the arbitral decision would be left to the discretion of the tribunal in a given case. Importantly, as shown in ICSID practices, tribunals have been quite conservative regarding the participation of non-disputing parties at oral hearings and their access to documents such as pleadings or witness statements.[24] In such circumstances, it is questionable whether the amicus could appropriately address the substantive issues in dispute and assist the tribunal in reaching its decision.

B   The Lack of Appellate Review of Awards

The finality of an award rendered by a tribunal lies at the centre of investment arbitration. Article 53(1) of the *Convention on the Settlement of Investment Disputes Between States and Nationals of Other States* (ICSID Convention)[25] explicitly establishes the final and binding nature of ICSID awards. The awards rendered are therefore in principle not subject to any appeal or other remedy 'except those provided for in the Convention'. Therefore it is possible to seek certain limited review of awards made under ICSID.[26] For instance, according to article 52(1) of the ICSID Convention, either party can request the ad hoc committees to annul awards based on the grounds that the tribunal was not properly constituted; the tribunal manifestly exceeded its powers; there was corruption on the part of a member of the tribunal; there has been a serious departure from a fundamental rule of procedure; or the award has failed to state the reasons on which it is based. An ICSID award therefore could be annulled on the basis of procedural deficiencies.[27] ICSID annulment proceedings differ from judicial appeals.[28] For instance, a successful challenge will result in the award being annulled, but the award cannot be modified. An ad hoc committee is not empowered to review the merits of the original award, regardless of whether there is error of fact or law in the award.[29]

Article 32 of the UNCITRAL Arbitration Rules provides that all awards shall be final and binding on the parties and that the parties shall carry out all awards without delay. Generally, arbitral proceedings conducted in accordance with the UNCITRAL Arbitration Rules apply the law of the seat of arbitration.[30] Therefore, the review of UNCITRAL awards will be left to national courts at the seat of arbitration in accordance with the applicable national laws. In some cases, the applicable laws are based on the UNCITRAL Model Law on International Commercial Arbitration (UNCITRAL Model Law).[31] According to article 34 of the UNCITRAL Model Law, the courts will undertake only limited review on grounds such as invalidity of the arbitration agreement; lack of notice to a party or other inability to present the case; non-arbitrability of the subject matter; and violation of domestic public policy. There is no *de novo* review of either the facts or the law as determined by the tribunal.

Accordingly, neither ICSID nor UNCITRAL awards are subject to real appellate review. The arbitral tribunal is the only authority to decide the merits of a dispute. As a result, matters involving a vital public interest might be subject to incorrect or defective arbitrations without the opportunity of a second opinion concerning the factual and substantive aspects of the award. The risks arising from inaccurate or inconsistent awards in connection with tobacco control might be greater than in other investment disputes. For example, Philip Morris has alleged that Uruguayan and Australian tobacco labelling/packaging laws significantly impair its use of trademarks and amount to indirect expropriation of its property rights, entitling it to damages. To determine this claim, the respective tribunals might need to consider how to draw the dividing line between legitimate regulatory measures and compensable indirect expropriation – a difficult question in investment arbitrations. Tribunals have taken different approaches to determining whether a measure constitutes indirect expropriation, such as examining the effect of a regulatory measure on investment (the 'sole effects doctrine') or engaging in proportionality analysis, and generally they have excused bona fide measures from classification as indirect expropriation.[32] In addition, the role of the WHO FCTC and its related legal instruments (such as guidelines or declarations) in interpretation of BIT provisions could also pose an unprecedented challenge to the arbitration tribunal. The challenged (and WHO FCTC-modelled) tobacco control measures therefore face some legal uncertainty.

C   Possible Resistance to Compliance with the Awards

The ICSID system contains effective compliance and enforcement mechanisms. In the event of non-compliance by a host state with an adverse ICSID award, the award creditor has multiple avenues to enforce the award. The award creditor may seek recognition and enforcement in the courts of all contracting states to the ICSID Convention. As set out in article 54 of the ICSID Convention, contracting states are obliged to recognise the finality of an ICSID award and enforce the monetary obligations imposed in the award as if it were a final judgment of the state's own courts. Accordingly, the award creditor can identify contracting states where the losing state has attachable assets and request that the contracting state's courts recognise and enforce the award.[33] Alternatively, the award creditor may resort to its home state for diplomatic protection under article 27[34] or may bring an international claim against the offending state before the International Court of Justice (ICJ) under article 64.[35] Given these mechanisms, ICSID contracting parties have generally voluntarily complied with adverse awards.[36] Judicial enforcement proceedings have taken place on only a few occasions.[37]

An UNCITRAL award is binding in that the parties are required to honour its terms. The UNCITRAL Arbitration Rules themselves do not contain mechanisms to enforce an award. However, in most cases, where a host state refuses to comply with an award made under the UNCITRAL Arbitration Rules, the award creditor may seek to enforce the award in the national courts of the state party to the *Convention on the Recognition and Enforcement of Foreign Arbitral Awards* (New York Convention)[38] if the losing state is also a party to that convention. The New York Convention generally applies to arbitral awards made in a state other than the state where recognition and enforcement are sought.[39] The enforcing courts must enforce an UNCITRAL award in accordance with basic requirements set out in the New York Convention. The successful creditor can enforce awards across multiple jurisdictions. However, article V of the New York Convention enumerates certain grounds under which enforcement of the award may be declined. In particular, article V(2)(b) provides that a national enforcing court can refuse enforcement if it finds that 'the enforcement of the award would be contrary to the public policy of that country'. Therefore, UNCITRAL awards are subject to policy review by the courts of the country in which enforcement is sought.

Upon receiving an adverse award made in either ICSID or UNCITRAL proceedings, the host state is obliged to honour the award and pay the award creditor. In the case of tobacco control, that might result in the host state having to pay compensation to a tobacco company for tobacco control measures. It is possible that the host state might find itself confronted by community opposition to using public funds to pay compensation for the state's enforcement of tobacco control measures enacted in line with the WHO FCTC.

In the face of a host state's refusal to comply with an ICSID award, a tobacco company, acting as an award creditor, is entitled to invoke the enforcement mechanisms provided under the ICSID system. This may create some practical problems. For instance, the tobacco company might find it difficult to overcome a claim by the host state that the assets sought to be attached are immune from execution. If the tobacco company seeks recognition and enforcement of the ICSID award in the territory of the offending state, the court might deny that request if the state has refused to pay based on consideration of its tobacco control policy. Additionally, it might be unclear whether the tobacco company's home state will be willing to initiate diplomatic measures or ICJ lawsuits against the non-complying state for the purpose of enforcing the award. This might particularly be the case where the investor's home state is also a party to the WHO FCTC.

The tobacco company might also face practical challenges if it seeks to enforce an UNCITRAL award under the New York Convention. If the enforcement would deviate from the public policy of the state, the court could refuse to enforce the award. In this regard, whether WHO FCTC-modelled tobacco control policy could constitute 'transnational public policy'[40] capable of empowering the court to decline to enforce an award might merit consideration.[41] The WHO FCTC has broad world-wide acceptance, with 177 parties. This fact demonstrates that the control of tobacco for health reasons is an internationally recognised pre-eminent value. Therefore, the enforcement of an UNCITRAL award against a WHO FCTC-modelled tobacco control measure might be considered a violation of transnational public policy, justifying the court's refusal to enforce the award under the New York Convention. If the court's state is also a party to the WHO FCTC, there might be stronger grounds for such a refusal.

Accordingly, if a host state fails to comply with an adverse investment award related to tobacco control on grounds of public policy, the tobacco company claimants may find pursuant to both the ICSID Arbitration Rules and the UNCITRAL Arbitration Rules that enforcement of the award is impossible or impracticable. As a result, investor-state arbitrations might not effectively settle investment disputes involving tobacco control.

III   A SUGGESTION REGARDING THE INVOLVEMENT OF BIT CONTRACTING PARTIES IN INVESTMENT DISPUTES REGARDING TOBACCO CONTROL

Investment disputes concerning tobacco control concern regulatory barriers to tobacco-related activities created by a host state's tobacco control policy as opposed to the regulatory measures targeting specific investments or investors. Tobacco control measures are frequently implemented to comply with the host country's commitments under the WHO FCTC. In contrast, the tobacco company, acting as an investor, can assert rights directly and independently against a host state when it believes that a violation of the BIT has taken place, regardless of the attitude of its home country.[42] From the perspective of the resolution of the dispute, as noted above, investor-state arbitrations might prove ineffective. For the purpose of protecting public health and settling the dispute, the contracting party to the BIT might consider assuming a role in the investor-state arbitration.

A   Investor's Home State Involvement in the Course of the Investor-State Arbitration

If the tobacco investor's home country shared the international view as to the importance of tobacco control and opposed the investor's position in the dispute (and particularly if it is a party to the WHO FCTC), it might consider intervening in the investor-state arbitration proceedings between the tobacco company and the host state. Parties to the WHO FCTC have a legal obligation to perform their treaty obligations in good faith, in accordance with article 26 of the *Vienna Convention on the Law of Treaties* (VCLT).[43] The good faith requirement requires the parties to act in a manner that is objectively compatible with the meaning, object and purpose of the treaty.[44] The investor's home state, at a minimum, might assume a duty to respect the conduct of its fellow WHO FCTC party (the host country) to further its commitment to implementing effective tobacco control programmes under the WHO FCTC. In this respect, article 4.3 of the WHO FCTC states:

> international cooperation, particularly transfer of technology, knowledge and financial assistance and provision of related expertise, to establish and implement effective tobacco control programmes, taking into consideration local culture, as well as social, economic, political and legal factors, is an important part of the Convention.

There are therefore justifiable grounds for the investor's home state to intervene in the investor-state proceedings. Practically, for instance, it might consider submitting an amicus curiae brief as a non-disputing party in the interests of global public health. Further, in the case of a failure of a host state to comply with the ICSID award, the investor's home state might not give diplomatic support to the tobacco company's claims for monetary compensation and might maintain its cooperative relationship with the host state in relation to tobacco control. The home state might opt not to recognise and enforce an UNCITRAL award on the grounds of transnational public policy in respect of tobacco control.

B Issues of Interpretative Clarification by BIT Contracting Parties to Guide the Conduct of the Arbitral Tribunal

Recourse to state-state dispute settlement, a separate mechanism contained in most BITs, might help mitigate the tension arising from investor-state disputes involving tobacco control. State-state dispute settlement usually applies to disputes between contracting parties concerning the interpretation or application of the BIT. Before resorting to formal arbitration proceedings, contracting parties are typically required to attempt to settle the dispute by consultation, negotiation or diplomatic means.[45] Therefore, contracting parties (the host state and the investor's home state) may engage in discussions or negotiations to establish a common understanding regarding the interpretation or application of the BIT with respect to the contested measure. By virtue of this, contracting parties can not only preserve their overall relationship, but can also seek and ascertain their true real intention as to how specific BIT provisions should be applied or interpreted. For instance, in the case that both BIT contracting parties are also WHO FCTC parties, such a consultation process could be used to clarify whether WHO FCTC-modelled tobacco control measures should be considered legitimate measures falling within a state's right to regulate rather than amount to compensable indirect expropriation. In this regard, it should be noted that the *Declaration on the Implementation of the WHO Framework Convention on Tobacco Control*[46] made under the WHO FCTC states that 'measures to protect public health, including measures implementing the WHO FCTC and its guidelines fall within the power of sovereign States to regulate in the public interest, which includes public health'. Given that declaration, BIT parties have justifiable grounds for reaching such agreements on the interpretation of BITs.

Legally, a common understanding or subsequent interpretation regarding specific provisions established by BIT contracting parties through consultation or negotiation may enjoy the status of a subsequent agreement between the parties under VCLT article 31(3)(a).[47] Such subsequent agreements might be used as an interpretative clarification to guide the overall application of the BIT and to help the tribunals handling investor-state disputes to appropriately interpret relevant provisions.[48] Such agreements might move disputes toward 'healthier' outcomes.

BIT contracting parties might also include provisions in BITs requiring the exclusive use of state-state dispute settlement to deal with investment disputes involving tobacco control. That is, investor-state arbitration could not be used for investment disputes with respect to tobacco control. Tobacco companies would be precluded from directly challenging the WHO FCTC-modelled tobacco control measures under the BIT. In such a case, it is the home country of an investor, not the investor, who would evaluate the possible conflicts regarding the interpretation or application of the BITs and the application of tobacco control measures. In this way, investor-state arbitration would no longer be used as a potent strategic tool by tobacco companies to disrupt the host state and other WHO FCTC parties in the implementation of tobacco control policy.

IV CONCLUDING REMARKS

The Philip Morris challenges against Uruguay and Australia mark one of the first attempts by tobacco companies to use investor-state arbitration provided for in a BIT as a tool to seek substantial monetary compensation and the suspension of tobacco control measures. As shown in this chapter, investor-state arbitration by its procedural design might not result in a credible award in terms of tobacco control concerns, which might intensify concerns over the loss of the sovereign power of host states to regulate public health.[49] Given the urgent tobacco problem prevalent worldwide, and the importance of tobacco control for public health, BIT contracting parties need to reconsider the relationship between foreign investment, investor-state dispute settlement and the WHO FCTC.

NOTES

1. According to the World Health Organization (WHO), tobacco use causes nearly 6 million deaths annually through heart disease, cancer, respiratory diseases, childhood diseases and others. By the year 2030, the annual death toll could increase to more than 8 million worldwide. WHO, *Tobacco Industry Interference: A Global Brief* (WHO/NMH/TFI/12.1, 2012) 5.
2. Opened for signature 16 June 2003, 2302 UNTS 166 (entered into force 27 February 2005).
3. For instance, in the context of the World Trade Organization, some countries, which are also WHO FCTC contracting parties, initiated dispute settlement cases with Australia concerning its plain packaging requirements in 2012. See WTO disputes WT/DS434 (complaint by Ukraine), WT/DS435 (complaint by Honduras), WT/DS441 (complaint by the Dominican Republic) and WT/DS458 (complaint by Cuba). It has been argued that Australia's obligations under the *Agreement on Trade-Related Aspects of Intellectual Property Rights, the Agreement on Technical Barriers to Trade and the General Agreement on Tariffs and Trade 1994* would be of

relevance. In this regard, Philip Morris is reportedly providing legal advice and funding to the Ukraine and Honduras governments: see Melissa Sweet, *A Wrap of Reaction to the High Court Decision on Plain Packaging* (16 August 2012) Crikey <http://blogs.crikey.com.au/croakey/2012/08/15/a-wrap-of-reaction-to-the-high-court-decision-on-plain-packaging/>.

4. See *Tobacco Plain Packaging Act 2011* (Cth). Under Australian law, tobacco products must be sold in drab packages with graphic images of tobacco-related diseases and without logos. In addition to Australia, countries such as the United Kingdom, New Zealand, Canada, Belgium, France, and the European Union have been considering adopting similar plain packaging requirements. See Quit Victoria, Cancer Council Victoria, *Plain Packaging of Tobacco Products: A Review of the Evidence* (May 2011), 4–5, 16, 23.

5. *Agreement between the Swiss Confederation and the Oriental Republic of Uruguay on the Reciprocal Promotion and Protection of Investments*, dated 7 October 1988, 1976 UNTS 389 (entered into force 22 April 1991).

6. *Agreement between the Government of Hong Kong and the Government of Australia for the Promotion and Protection of Investments*, signed 15 September 1993, 1748 UNTS 385 (entered into force 15 October 1993).

7. UNCITRAL, *UNCITRAL Arbitration Rules (As Revised in 2010)* (April 2011); *UNCITRAL Arbitration Rules As Revised in 2010*, GA Res 65/22, UN GAOR, 65th sess, 57th plen mtg, UN Doc A/RES/65/22 (6 December 2010).

8. For instance, Uruguay requires that 80 per cent of the surface of cigarette packs sold in Uruguay be devoted to pictures and warnings about the dangers of smoking. Philip Morris alleged that the restriction will severely limit the space on packages available for branding and prevent it from making effective use of its trademarks. Phillip Morris also contended that Uruguay's regulation prohibiting it from marketing more than one type of cigarette per brand (eg Marlboro, Marlboro Lights, and Marlboro Extra Lights) breaches its trademarks, resulting in a loss of market share. Philip Morris argued that Uruguay had breached its obligations under the Switzerland–Uruguay BIT not to hinder the management, use, enjoyment, growth or sale of investments through unreasonable or discriminatory measures (article 3(1)); to refrain from acts of illegitimate expropriation (article 5(1)); and to provide fair and equitable treatment to the investments (article 3(2)).

9. Article 11 of the WHO FCTC covers three main areas: (1) government-mandated health warnings; (2) labelling of tobacco constituents and emissions; and (3) the removal of misleading information from the package. More specifically, the WHO FCTC provides that health warnings on cigarette packages should cover 50 per cent or more of package surface and that product labelling should not directly or indirectly leave the false impression that 'light' or 'extra light' cigarettes are less harmful. With respect to plain packaging, the guidelines for implementation of article 13 of the WHO FCTC recommend that parties consider adopting plain packaging requirements to eliminate the effects of advertising or promotion on packaging. Also, the guidelines for implementation of article 11 of the WHO FCTC encourage the use of plain packaging requirements.

10. See ICSID, *ICSID Convention, Regulations and Rules* (ICSID/15, April 2006) 99 <https://icsid.worldbank.org/ICSID/StaticFiles/basicdoc/CRR_English-final.pdf>.

11. See generally Andrew Mitchell and Sebastian Wurzberger, 'Boxed in? Australia's Plain Tobacco Packaging Initiative and International Investment Law' (2011) 27(4) *Arbitration International* 623; Tania Voon and Andrew Mitchell, 'Time to Quit? Assessing International Investment Claims Against Plain Tobacco Packaging In Australia (2011) 14(3) *Journal of International Economic Law* 515.

12. Whether private commercial arbitration is also in need of transparency remains an open question, given that privacy and confidentiality are perceived as important features of commercial arbitration proceedings.
13. On transparency, ICSID Administrative and Financial Regulations, reg 22 requires ICSID to disclose the existence of disputes. In practice, the registration of a request for arbitration is listed on the ICSID website. As the case progresses, certain updated information is made publicly available, indicating the procedural stage, the subject matter, and the appointment of the arbitrators. With regard to the publication of the award, r 48(4) of the ICSID Arbitration Rules prohibits ICSID from publishing the final award without the consent of both parties, but ICSID shall 'promptly' include in its publications excerpts of the legal reasoning of the tribunal.
14. ICSID Arbitration Rules r 37(2).
15. Ibid.
16. For instance, UNCITRAL Arbitration Rules r 34(5) states that 'an award may be made public with the consent of all parties or where and to the extent disclosure is required of a party by legal duty, to protect or pursue a legal right or in relation to legal proceedings before a court or other competent authority'. The UNCITRAL Working Group II (Arbitration and Conciliation) has been working for two years to improve rules on transparency. At the 58th session of February 2013, it published the final draft text of rules on transparency in treaty-based investment arbitration: UNCITRAL Working Group II, *Report of Working Group II (Arbitration and Conciliation) on the Work of its Fifty-eighth Session,* UN Doc A/CN.9/765 (13 February 2013).
17. For instance, one tribunal ruled, on the basis of article 15(1) of the UNCITRAL Arbitration Rules (1967), that it had the power to accept written amicus curiae submissions from each of the petitioners: *Methanex Corporation v United States, Decision on Amici Curiae* (Ad Hoc Arbitral Tribunal, UNCITRAL Rules, 15 January 2001) [47]. A similar position was adopted in *United Parcel Service of America Inc v Government of Canada (Award on the Merits)* (2007) 46 ILM 922.
18. The finalised draft on rules on transparency presented by UNCITRAL Working Group II will provide for open oral hearings as well as the publication of key documents, including notices of arbitration, pleadings, transcripts, and all decisions and awards issued by the tribunal: Luke Eric Peterson, 'UN Working Group Finalizes UNCITRAL Transparency Rules, but They Won't Apply Automatically to Stockpiles of Existing Investment Treaties' (14 February 2013) *Investment Arbitration Reporter* (online) <http://www.iareporter.com/articles/20130215_4>.
19. As at 2010, non-disputing parties had made submissions in five ICSID cases. For instance, in *Biwater Gauff Ltd v Tanzania (Award)* (ICSID Arbitral Tribunal, Case No ARB/05/22, 24 July 2008) [361], the tribunal authorised five non-governmental organisations, including those with expertise in environmental, human rights, and sustainable development issues, to file a joint written submission based on r 37(2) of the ICSID Arbitration Rules. See Lucy Reed, Jan Paulsson and Nigel Blackaby, *Guide to ICSID Arbitration* (Kluwer Law International, 2011) 141.
20. The WHO FCTC formally recognises the importance of civil society in article 4.7, which states 'the participation of civil society is essential in achieving the objective of the Convention and its protocols'. Additionally, in *United States – Measures Affecting the Production and Sale of Clove Cigarettes (US – Clove Cigarettes)*, the US prohibition on the production or sale of cigarettes containing certain additives, including clove, but permitting the production and sale of other cigarettes, including cigarettes containing menthol, was found to violate certain WTO rules (see Chapter 6 of this volume). In that case, two amicus curiae briefs were received by the appellate body: one from the Campaign for Tobacco-Free Kids, the American Academy of Pediatrics, the American Cancer Society, the American Cancer Society Cancer Action

Network, the American Lung Association, the American Medical Association, and the American Public Health Association; and the other from the O'Neill Institute for National and Global Health Law at the Georgetown University Law Center: Appellate Body Report, *US – Clove Cigarettes*, WTO Doc WT/DS406/AB/R (adopted 24 April 2012) [10].

21. The European Commission was granted permission to intervene as amicus curiae in *AES Summit Generation Limited v The Republic of Hungary* (ICSID Case No ARB/07/22, 23 September 2010). See Christina Knahr, 'The New Rules on Participation of Non-Disputing Parties in ICSID Arbitration: Blessing or Curse?' in Chester Brown and Kate Miles (eds), *Evolution in Investment Treaty Law and Arbitration* (Cambridge University Press, 2011) 319, 330–33.

22. Under WTO dispute settlement rules, WTO members other than disputants are given some procedural rights to attend the proceedings as third parties. See *Understanding on Rules and Procedures Governing the Settlement of Disputes* article 10.

23. Nigel Blackaby and Caroline Richard, 'Amicus curiae: A Panacea for Legitimacy in Investment Arbitration?' in Michael Waibel et al (eds), *The Backlash against Investment Arbitration: Perceptions and Reality* (Kluwer Law International, 2010) 253, 254.

24. The tribunal is concerned with the tension between increasing transparency and maintaining the procedural integrity and efficiency of the hearing. See *Biwater Gauff*, above n 19.

25. 575 UNTS 159 (concluded 18 March 1965, entered into force 14 October 1966).

26. See article 50(1) of the ICSID Convention regarding the interpretation of the award and article 51(1) regarding the revision of an award.

27. A number of ICSID awards have been subjected to annulment proceedings. These proceedings might be strategically used as a delaying method by the non-complying state. See generally Tsai-yu Lin, 'Systemic Reflections on Argentina's Non-Compliance with ICSID Arbitral Awards: A New Role of the Annulment Committee at Enforcement?' (2012) 5 *Contemporary Asia Arbitration Journal* 1.

28. During the ICSID amendment process, some contracting states called for the establishment of an ICSID appellate mechanism similar to the WTO Appellate Body, but did not gain sufficient support. The main concerns about such a mechanism related to prolonging and undermining the efficiency of the arbitration process. But see Tsai-yu Lin, 'Compulsory License for Access to Medicines, Expropriation and Investor-State Arbitration under Bilateral Investment Agreements: Are There Issues Beyond the TRIPS Agreement?' (2009) 40 *IIC-International Review of Intellectual Property and Competition Law* 167.

29. Reed, Paulsson and Blackaby, above n 19, 162–3.

30. Stephen Jagusch and Jeffrey Sullivan, 'A Comparison of ICSID and UNCITRAL Arbitration: Areas of Divergence and Concern' in Waibel et al, above n 23, 90.

31. See GA Res 40/72, UN GAOR, 40th sess, 112th plen mtg (11 December 1985); GA Res 61/33, UN GAOR, 61st sess, 64th plen mtg, Agenda Item 77, UN Doc A/RES/61/33 (4 December 2006).

32. See generally Santiago Montt, *State Liability in Investment Treaty Arbitration: Global Constitutional and Administrative Law in the BIT Generation* (Hart, 2009) ch 5.

33. Loukas Mistelis (ed), *Concise International Arbitration* (Kluwer Law International, 2010) 144.

34. Article 27(1) of the ICSID Convention reads: 'No Contracting State shall give diplomatic protection, or bring an international claim, in respect of a dispute which one of its nationals and another Contracting State shall have consented to submit or

shall have submitted to arbitration under this Convention, unless such other Contracting State shall have failed to abide by and comply with the award rendered in such dispute'.

35. Article 64 of the ICSID Convention reads: 'Any dispute arising between Contracting States concerning the interpretation or application of this Convention which is not settled by negotiations shall be referred to the International Court of Justice by the application of any party to such dispute, unless the States concerned agree to another method of settlement'. As at September 2010, no ICSID contracting state had exercised their rights under article 64: Reed, Paulsson and Blackaby, above n 19, 190.

36. It is generally believed that the high cost of non-compliance by the state, in terms of losing its reputation as an investment-friendly environment in the international business community, and the possible negative impact on its access to World Bank funding or credit, contributes to this practice: Lin, above n 28, 2.

37. Mistelis, above n 33, 145.

38. 330 UNTS 3 (opened for signature 10 June 1958, entered into force 7 June 1959).

39. New York Convention, article 1.

40. The term 'international public policy' refers to a country's domestic public policy applied in an international context: Mark Buchanan, 'Public Policy and International Commercial Arbitration' (1998) 26 *American Business Law Journal* 514.

41. Professor Chang-fa Lo suggests that there must be some criteria developed to decide the scope of transnational public policy. In this respect, public policy concerning human rights protection, public policy concerning any other international treaty that outlaws certain behaviour and urges countries to cooperate with one another, and public policy concerning international ethical rules should constitute the contents of transnational public policy: Chang-fa Lo, 'Principles and Criteria for International and Transnational Public Policies in Commercial Arbitration' (2008) 1 *Contemporary Asia Arbitration Journal* 82.

42. The investor's home state may be unable to control the investor's claims because the investor has been conferred substantive rights by the BIT. See *Corn Products International, Inc. v The United Mexican States* (ICSID Case No ARB(AF)/04/01, 15 January 2008), [169].

43. 1155 UNTS 331 (adopted 22 May 1969).

44. Malgosia Fitzmaurice and Dan Sarooshi, *Issues of State Responsibility before International Judicial Institutions* (Hart, 2004) 92. In addition, the WHO FCTC in its opening language mentions that 'Member States that have signed the Convention indicate that they will strive in good faith to ratify, accept, or approve it, and show political commitment not to undermine the objectives set out in it'.

45. For instance, article 37 of the US-Uruguay BIT (entitled 'State-State Dispute Settlement') provides in para 1 that: 'Subject to paragraph 5, any dispute between the Parties concerning the interpretation or application of this Treaty that is not resolved through consultations or other diplomatic channels shall be submitted on the request of either Party to arbitration for a binding decision or award by a tribunal in accordance with applicable rules of international law. In the absence of an agreement by the Parties to the contrary, the UNCITRAL Arbitration Rules shall govern, except as modified by the Parties or this Treaty'.

46. World Health Organization, 'Declaration on the implementation of the WHO Framework Convention on Tobacco Control' (No FCTC/COP/4/DIV/6, 6 December 2010).

47. Article 31(3) of the VCLT provides: 'There shall be taken into account, together with the context: (*a*) any subsequent agreement between the parties regarding the interpretation of the treaty or the application of its provisions'.

48. The Free Trade Commission of the *North American Free Trade Agreement* (opened for signature 17 December 1992, 32 ILM 289, 605 (entered into force 1 January 1994) is authorised to oversee the implementation of provisions and resolve disputes regarding the interpretation or application of the treaty. According to article 1132(2) of the NAFTA, the Commission can issue 'interpretation' of relevant provisions that binds arbitral tribunals dealing with investor-state disputes.

49. The legitimacy of investor-state arbitration has been subject to significant criticism. See generally Waibel et al, above n 23. In January 2012, following Bolivia and Ecuador, the Bolivarian Republic of Venezuela denounced the ICSID Convention. Argentina has also announced plans to withdraw. The Australian Government has recently adopted a policy against the use of investor-state arbitration in trade agreements and BITs, including the Trans-Pacific Partnership negotiations.

9.   Tobacco control in ASEAN

Locknie Hsu

I INTRODUCTION

Almost 30 per cent of the adult population of the Association of Southeast Asian Nations (ASEAN) smokes. All but one of the ASEAN members are currently parties to the *WHO Framework Convention on Tobacco Control* (WHO FCTC).[1] The outlier is Indonesia, the most populous of the ten ASEAN countries. Multilaterally, all ten ASEAN members are World Trade Organization (WTO) members and subject to its trade rules. Regionally, ASEAN is in the process of accelerated economic integration, with the aim of establishing the ASEAN Economic Community (AEC) in 2015.[2] A Common Effective Preferential Tariff (CEPT) system, set up under the ASEAN Free Trade Area (AFTA) arrangement, has existed since 1992,[3] propelling members towards trade liberalisation and elimination of tariffs. At the same time, ASEAN has been negotiating trade and investment treaties with external partners, which have separate liberalisation targets and implications. In tandem, the overarching ASEAN Strategic Framework on Health and Development (2010–15)[4] was established under the ASEAN Socio-Cultural Community (ASCC) Blueprint,[5] to introduce and implement health-related initiatives in ASEAN. One area of focus of this framework is healthy lifestyles.[6] In 2010, under these auspices, ASEAN health ministers committed to addressing tobacco control as a priority to promote healthy living. As a result, legislative and non-legislative initiatives have been introduced. In July 2012, ASEAN health ministers announced that tobacco would not be included in tariff liberalisation of the AFTA.

ASEAN's mosaic of tobacco control laws and regulations is therefore a work in progress, as the region continues to step up economic integration and liberalisation aggressively while managing important health issues such as those relating to tobacco control. This chapter examines the tobacco-related laws and policies of this dynamic and diverse region, including both tariff and non-tariff means of control.

II ASEAN AS AN ECONOMIC COMMUNITY

ASEAN is a vast economic market. Realisation of the economic potential and attraction of this market led leaders to begin a process of economic integration in the early 1990s, with the first significant, legally binding step in this direction being the establishment of the AFTA in 1992.[7] This established, among other arrangements, the CEPT system of tariffs within ASEAN to promote a freer flow of goods in the region.

The agreements establishing the AFTA provided for gradual integration among its members. The six founding members of ASEAN – Brunei Darussalam, Indonesia, Malaysia, Philippines, Singapore and Thailand – committed to speedier dismantling of trade barriers than the four members who joined ASEAN later – Cambodia, Lao PDR, Myanmar and Vietnam. Members were permitted to provide for a number of exclusions and limitations, depending on their areas of economic sensitivity. At various stages over the years, timelines for tariff reductions or elimin-ations and other forms of liberalisation have been provided to move the integration process forward.[8]

In 2003, in Bali, ASEAN leaders signed the *Declaration of ASEAN Concord II* treaty (the *Bali Concord*) to establish an 'ASEAN Community … comprising three pillars, namely political and security cooperation, economic cooperation, and socio-cultural cooperation'.[9] In 2007, the ASEAN Economic Blueprint was published to further flesh out the roadmap for implementation of the *Bali Concord* objectives.[10] Of the three pillars, the economic pillar is most pertinent for present purposes, as it deals with economic barriers and initiatives that have a bearing on tobacco control within ASEAN. However, as health-related issues fall under the socio-cultural pillar, some decisions thereunder are pertinent to tobacco control as well.

To implement the AEC, members entered into the *ASEAN Trade in Goods Agreement* (ATIGA)[11] to accelerate integration in trade in goods.

A Tobacco Trade and ASEAN

ASEAN members have maintained import and other barriers to tobacco products, as have many other countries. At the time of establishment of the AFTA and, later, the ATIGA, there was no specific discussion of economic integration and its relationship with tobacco control.[12] With the tobacco control issue increasingly moving to the forefront globally (partly due to implementation obligations of countries under the WHO FCTC and partly due to the prominent legal challenges brought against certain states for their tobacco control laws), it became a formal topic of discussion and for action for ASEAN health ministers in 2012. In July 2012, the health ministers announced that members would withdraw tobacco products from the tariff liberalisation plan under the AFTA.[13]

This would be significant for two reasons: it would represent a departure from the liberalisation exercise of the AFTA, and it would expressly recognise tobacco control as a legitimate health measure at an ASEAN-wide level. It would also have a significant impact on certain ASEAN members (such as Indonesia) where there are both domestic and foreign-owned tobacco product companies, which currently enjoy the zero or low tariffs on such products in the region due to the CEPT scheme.[14] However, there appear to have been no further public statements on the implementation of this 2012 announcement so far. The ATIGA therefore continues to include tariff commitments on tobacco products, as can be seen from the ASEAN members' ATIGA Tariff Schedules of 2009.[15]

It should be noted that article 19.2(h) (read with article 22.2) of the ATIGA expressly allows a member state to exclude products placed in Schedule H from tariff commitments for reasons provided under article 8 (a general exceptions provision). Article 8(b), in particular, is an exception resembling article XX of the *General Agreement on Tariffs and Trade 1994* (GATT 1994),[16] in that it covers measures necessary for the protection of human health. Hence, article 19 clearly provides ASEAN members with the means to exclude from tariff concessions products that affect human health.

Below is a summary of the ASEAN members' ATIGA commitments on tariffs for tobacco products, based on their published schedules:

1. Brunei Darussalam has committed to reduce all tobacco tariffs to zero as of 2010.
2. Cambodia has committed to reduce all tobacco tariffs to 0–5 per cent by 2015.
3. Indonesia has committed to reduce all tobacco tariffs to zero as of 2012.
4. Lao People's Democratic Republic has committed to reduce all tobacco tariffs to 5 per cent by 2015.
5. Malaysia has committed to reduce all tobacco tariffs to 5 per cent as of 2010.
6. Myanmar has committed to eliminate tariffs completely on several tobacco products as of 2013. For the remaining products, the commitment is to reduce tariffs (depending on the product line) to between 0 and 5 per cent by 2015.

7. The Philippines has committed to reduce all tobacco tariffs to zero as of 2010.
8. Singapore has committed to apply zero tariffs to tobacco products from the date of entry into force of the ATIGA, ie May 2010.
9. Thailand has committed to reduce all tobacco tariffs to zero as of 2012.
10. Vietnam has scheduled all tobacco products under 'category H', identified in article 19(2)(h) of the ATIGA as goods not subject to import duties reduction or elimination, by virtue of reasons under article 8 (the general exceptions provision). It is the only ASEAN member to have scheduled all its tobacco products under 'category H' to date.

Should the health ministers' announcement of July 2012 become a reality, one might expect to see a change to the schedules of the nine members which have so far not scheduled tobacco products as category 'H' exclusions.

Apart from intra-ASEAN obligations under the ATIGA, ASEAN member states have trade liberalisation obligations to non-ASEAN trade partners in separate free trade agreements (FTA).[17] These contain separate liberalisation commitments that may include tobacco-related products, services and investments.

ASEAN is presently negotiating *a Regional Comprehensive Economic Partnership* (RCEP) agreement.[18] ASEAN states are also pursuing FTA negotiations as individual states, while a small number of others (Brunei Darussalam, Malaysia, Singapore and Vietnam) are participating in negotiations for a Trans-Pacific Partnership Agreement (TPP), which includes the United States, a tobacco-exporting country.

B   WTO Obligations and ASEAN

All ASEAN members are members of the WTO and subject to obligations under its multilateral agreements. These include the GATT 1994, the *General Agreement on Trade in Services* (GATS),[19] the *Agreement on Sanitary and Phytosanitary Measures* (SPS Agreement)[20] and the *Agreement on Technical Barriers to Trade* (TBT Agreement).[21] Some disputes relating to ASEAN members with regard to tobacco control measures have arisen, both under the original GATT 1947[22] system and under the WTO system. Under the GATT 1947 system, the US complained about Thailand's fiscal measures before a panel in *Thailand – Cigarettes*.[23] As a result of this action, Thailand had to amend its measures to ensure that they were non-discriminatory. More recently, under the WTO system, the

Philippines successfully challenged Thailand's measures affecting imported cigarettes in *Thailand – Customs and Fiscal Measures on Cigarettes from the Philippines*.[24] The TBT Agreement was used in a tobacco-related challenge in the WTO brought by Indonesia against the United States. In *US – Clove Cigarettes*,[25] Indonesia challenged US regulations affecting the import of Indonesian clove cigarettes. This culminated in a decision by the Appellate Body requiring the US to bring its measures into conformity with the TBT Agreement.[26]

SPS Agreement and TBT Agreement-type commitments that may have a bearing on tobacco control measures also exist in certain ASEAN FTAs. An example is the *ASEAN–Australia–New Zealand Free Trade Area*, in which ASEAN members and their trade partners, Australia and New Zealand, reaffirm the SPS Agreement and TBT Agreement rights and obligations, making such rights and obligations applicable under the FTA.[27]

III   ASEAN-WIDE TOBACCO CONTROL INITIATIVES

The ASCC has produced a number of tobacco control initiatives. For example, the *2009 ASEAN Strategic Framework on Health and Development (2010–2015)* included the promotion of healthy lifestyles within ASEAN for implementation under the ASCC Blueprint, with tobacco control as one of six focus areas mentioned.[28] In March 2012, a specific initiative was announced at the World Conference on Tobacco or Health held in Singapore, namely, the ASEAN Focal Points on Tobacco Control,[29] to help implement the ASCC and to promote a smoke-free ASEAN. Pursuant to that initiative, a group has met annually since 2010 to discuss health cooperation initiatives.[30] An ASEAN Bi-Annual Work Plan on Tobacco Control was also launched at the conference.[31]

Separately, a non-governmental alliance known as the Southeast Asia Tobacco Control Alliance (SEATCA) has been working across different sectors to promote and accelerate tobacco control within the ASEAN region. SEATCA has been highly active with various initiatives, including the ASEAN Focal Points on Tobacco Control, which aim to help member states implement the WHO FCTC recommendations and tobacco control 'best practices'.

The ASEAN Community has evolved in such a way that public health issues – such as tobacco control – fall within a separate pillar from the AEC, and are part of the ASCC, under the control of the ASEAN health ministers. In 2002, the Regional Action Plan on Healthy ASEAN Lifestyles was announced, in which tobacco control was expressly identified as a 'priority area'.[32] The 'Programme of Work' in the plan stated the following broad target:

> Tobacco control – to develop and implement national action consistent with the Framework Convention on Tobacco Control, as appropriate, for example, on smuggling, taxation, product advertising, distribution, sale, and agricultural production ...

At the same time, ASEAN's participation in the WTO and in multiple FTAs necessarily complicates the introduction of trade and investment-related measures affecting tobacco products and related services. Assessing the legality of a contemplated measure is a multi-factorial exercise requiring consideration of all relevant provisions and any applicable exceptions or carve-outs.

There is a need therefore to ensure coherence between the work of economic officials and health officials, at both regional and multilateral levels. Within ASEAN, officials implementing the AEC and ASCC need to work collaboratively in dealing with tobacco control measures under the economic and socio-cultural 'pillars'. In trans-regional negotiations such as those regarding the TPP, as well as in multilateral discussions in the WTO and WHO, ASEAN needs to develop a coherent and united stand with regard to the place of tobacco control and the WHO FCTC within trade negotiations.

IV AN OVERVIEW OF NATIONAL TOBACCO CONTROL METHODS IN ASEAN MEMBERS

ASEAN members employ a number of national measures in tobacco control. These include border measures such as tariffs, as well as internal measures such as taxes and sale, packaging and use restrictions.

A Tax Measures

ASEAN countries utilise a variety of fiscal tools for tobacco control. These include excise taxes, value-added or goods and services taxes, and others.[33] Except in Brunei Darussalam and Singapore, import tariffs are also imposed on top of these taxes. These measures can significantly affect the affordability of cigarettes and related products.[34]

However, establishment of the AFTA and its CEPT tariff scheme (and more recently, the ATIGA) have, as mentioned, created pressure and commitments on ASEAN members to reduce or eliminate their import tariffs on tobacco products, allowing for more affordable imports to enter their borders.[35]

B   Non-Tax Measures

While the import of cigarettes and other common tobacco products is permitted in ASEAN, some tobacco products are specifically prohibited. In Singapore, for example, the import and sale of chewing tobacco is prohibited.[36]

Like other countries, authorities have to deal not only with more familiar tobacco products but also emerging products with health risks associated with the use of tobacco or nicotine in them. One such example is the relatively new product 'electronic cigarettes' (or 'e-cigarettes'). The treatment of such products within ASEAN is not presently uniform.

In Singapore, for example, the importation of 'imitation tobacco products' is prohibited.[37] Section 16(1) of the *Tobacco (Control of Advertisements and Sale) Act* defines such products as follows:

> any confectionery or other food product or any toy or other article that is designed to resemble a tobacco product or the packaging of which is designed to resemble the packaging commonly associated with tobacco products.[38]

Within this provision, the authorities include items such as e-cigarettes, which mimic many features of conventional cigarettes but do not contain all the chemical substances in them.[39]

In contrast, e-cigarettes are permitted (and increasingly popular) in the Philippines, although the authorities are becoming more concerned about their use.[40]

Other non-tax means of control reflect various aspects of the WHO FCTC such as the use and expansion of smoke-free zones within each country; prohibiting advertisements; prohibiting misleading information on packaging, promotional and sponsorship activities; strict packaging requirements; ingredient controls; point-of-sale controls; age controls.[41] Within some of these measures, some difficult issues arise due to modern technology and communication tools, such as the possibility and ease of cross-border advertising through the Internet and the availability of such advertisement on common devices such as personal computers and mobile telephones. Such matters are discussed later in relation to challenges for ASEAN states.

Within ASEAN, packaging requirements are well established, though with differing levels of stringency.

Table 9.1   Overview of ASEAN pictorial warning measures

ASEAN member	Main tobacco control legislation	Whether pictorial warning mandatory and if so, minimum percentage of packaging front and back
Brunei Darussalam	*Tobacco Order 2005 and Regulations*	Yes, 75% (from September 2012)[1]
Cambodia	*Tobacco Control Act 2010****	Yes, 30%
Indonesia	*Law No 36/2009 on Health**[2]	Yes (40%, with new 2012 Regulations, to take effect from June 2014)[3]
Lao PDR	*Law of Tobacco Control 2009 and Decision on Printing of Health Warnings on Cigarette Packets and Cartons**[4]	No*
Malaysia	*Control of Tobacco Products Regulation 2004*	Yes, top 40% for front and top 60% for back
Myanmar	*Control of Smoking and Consumption of Tobacco Product Law 2006*[5] *(effective 4 May 2007)**	No*
Philippines	*Tobacco Regulation Act 2003**	No*
Singapore	*Tobacco (Control of Advertisements and Sale) Act 2011* and *Tobacco (Control of Advertisements and Sale) (Labelling) Regulations 2012*	Yes, 50%
Thailand	*Tobacco Products Control Act 1992; Non-Smokers' Health Protection Act 1992*[6]	Yes, 85% (2013)[7]
Vietnam	*Tobacco Control Law of 2012,* Decision No 1315/QD-TTg[8]	Yes, from 1 May 2013, 50%[9]

* *Source:*   Author's compilation from Southeast Asia Tobacco Control Alliance, *The ASEAN Tobacco Control Report* (June 2012) 5.

Notes:
1   *Tobacco (Labelling) (Amendment) Regulations 2012* (Brunei Darussalam).
2   See Arientha Primanitha, 'Tobacco Bill Requires Graphic Warnings to be Displayed on Cigarette Packaging in Indonesia', *Jakarta Globe* (online), 9 January 2013; Tommy Dharmawan, 'A New Breakthrough on Tobacco Control', *Jakarta Post* (online), 26 January 2013; Sara Schonhardt, 'Is Indonesia, One of Big Tobacco's Last Frontiers, Closing?', *The Christian Science Monitor* (online), 4 March 2013.

3   *Tobacco Regulation Peraturan Pemerintah/PP No 109 of 2012, Protection of Materials Containing Form of Addictive Substances Tobacco Products for Health*, effective 24 December 2012, <http://www.depkes.go.id/downloads/InfoTerkini_PP109_2012_Tentang_Tembakau.pdf>.

4   Lao People's Democratic Republic, Ministry of Health, *Decision on Printing Health Warnings on Cigarette Packets and Cartons* (23 May 2006) <http://seatca.org/dmdocuments/Laos%20-%20Decision%20on%20Health%20Warnings.pdf>.

5   Southeast Asia Tobacco Control Alliance, *The ASEAN Tobacco Control Report 2012* (June 2012) 4 <http://seatca.org/dmdocuments/ASEAN%20Tobacco%20Control%20Report%202012.pdf>.

6   BE 2535 (1992), available at Tobacco Control Laws <http://www.tobaccocontrollaws.org/files/live/Thailand/Thailand%20-%20Non-smokers%20HPA%20.pdf>.

7   Southeast Asia Tobacco Control Alliance, *Regional Alliance Congratulates Thailand's Health Minister on 85% Health Warnings on Cigarette Pack* (11 March 2013) Tobacco Control Resource Center <http://seatca.org/?p=2213>.

8   Southeast Asia Tobacco Control Alliance, *The ASEAN Tobacco Control Report 2012* (June 2012) 4 <http://seatca.org/dmdocuments/ASEAN%20Tobacco%20Control%20Report%202012.pdf>.

9   C Quyen, 'Health Warnings in Pictures to be Printed on Cigarette Packs', *VietnamNet Bridge* (29 January 2013) <http://english.vietnamnet.vn/fms/society/58290/health-warnings-in-pictures-to-be-printed-on-cigarette-packs.html>.

V   CHALLENGES FACING ASEAN: WHO FCTC IMPLEMENTATION AND OTHER ISSUES

A   Diversity within ASEAN

A number of challenges face ASEAN members in implementing WHO FCTC obligations, where they apply. Within the ten ASEAN members, there is a wide diversity in cultures, languages spoken and economic means (and, accordingly, differences in public funding available for tobacco control initiatives). There are also differences in the business interests of member states; some members have tobacco growers and state-run monopoly tobacco bodies, while others do not.[42]

It has also been reported that in Asian countries, including the ASEAN states, 'tobacco has an important cultural role, and in particular among men, the exchange of cigarettes is often used in social interactions'.[43] In addition, children and teenagers may be exposed to tobacco products through easy access at points of sale (especially where there is no minimum age requirement for purchase, such as in Indonesia)[44] and through family members, and thus may be tempted to begin smoking.

These cultural and familial aspects may signal a challenge for which legislation may not be the most effective solution. Instead, 'soft' non-legal approaches to inculcate change may be necessary.[45]

B Levels of Corruption

Another challenging problem within ASEAN states that may affect tobacco control is corruption.[46] According to the Corruption Perceptions Index 2012 published by Transparency International,[47] ASEAN's rankings are as shown in Table 9.2.

Table 9.2 ASEAN corruption perception rankings

Global rank	Country
5	Singapore
46	Brunei Darussalam
54	Malaysia
88	Thailand
105	Philippines
118	Indonesia
123	Vietnam
157	Cambodia
160	Lao PDR
172	Myanmar

With significant corruption perception levels in several ASEAN countries, the possibility of interference with policymaking is real and needs to be tackled effectively.

C Possible Next Steps

Relatively up-to-date report cards dating from 2011–12 provided by all ASEAN members to the WHO (except for Indonesia, which remains outside the WHO FCTC) show that the implementation of tobacco control measures under the WHO FCTC recommendations has been proceeding at non-uniform speed within ASEAN, with Singapore and Thailand being among those leading with more wide-ranging measures than others.[48]

Some have questioned the legal status of the recommendations in the guidelines for implementing the WHO FCTC articles – and hence whether they are binding – because specific steps in the recommendations are being challenged in international arbitrations, as being violations of investment treaty commitments (such as expropriations of intellectual property through plain packaging) or as being unconstitutional.

1   Point-of-sale display prohibitions

A number of countries have taken steps to ban visual displays of such products at their point of sale. These measures have given rise to legal actions. The tobacco industry has sought to challenge such a measure within the European Free Trade Area (EFTA)[49] after Norway, an EFTA member, chose to introduce such a ban.[50] In September 2011, the EFTA Court ruled in favour of a visual display ban in the European Economic Area (EEA) states in *Philip Morris Norway AS v The Norwegian State*, provided certain prerequisites were met.[51]

A number of ASEAN members such as Singapore are now considering prohibiting the display of tobacco products at points of sale.[52] Within ASEAN, Thailand has already introduced such a ban.[53] No doubt the litigation elsewhere will offer ASEAN valuable insight into the types of arguments raised, and the reasoning used by the deciding tribunals.

2   Plain packaging

So far, no ASEAN member has announced that it will introduce plain packaging. No doubt, ASEAN members are keenly observing the disputes being faced by Australia and Uruguay in this regard. Australia's introduction of mandatory plain packaging for cigarettes in 2012 has so far been challenged in three forums: in the Australian national court system, in investment treaty arbitration and, most recently, at the WTO. Except for the national court action, the disputes are ongoing. In the case of the national court challenge, the Australian measures were challenged, unsuccessfully, as being unconstitutional.[54] Australia is also facing investment treaty arbitration brought against it under the Australia–Hong Kong Bilateral Investment Treaty,[55] and trade actions under the WTO brought by the Dominican Republic, Honduras, Ukraine, Cuba and, most recently, Indonesia.[56]

With the numerous bilateral investment treaty and FTA obligations of ASEAN and its component states, these disputes will offer invaluable lessons on the applicability of various provisions and exceptions which may be *in pari materia* with those affecting ASEAN states.

3   Control of advertising and promotion through the Internet, social media, films and educational institutions

(a)   Domestic   By now, most ASEAN states have some form of restrictions over the domestic advertising of tobacco products.[57] This includes

even Indonesia, the only non-WHO FCTC party, which passed a new tobacco control law in January 2013.[58] In Indonesia, however, sponsorship of cultural and sporting events, with blatant accompanying publicity for tobacco brands, remains possible.[59]

(b) Cross-border Article 13 of the WHO FCTC requires a 'comprehensive ban of all tobacco advertising, promotion and sponsorship' where this is constitutionally possible. This includes the prohibition of cross-border advertising, promotion and sponsorship. The guidelines on implementing article 13 state that the ban should include the placing of advertisements 'on the Internet or another cross-border communications technology by any person or entity *within* the territory of a Party'[60] and to 'any person or entity that broadcasts tobacco advertising, promotion and sponsorship that could be received in another State'.[61] The guidelines also elaborate on the requirement to ban cross-border advertising, promotion and sponsorship from *entering* a Party's territory under article 13.7 of the WHO FCTC. Australia, for example, introduced a prohibition on Internet advertising of tobacco products in September 2012. This includes dissemination through the Internet via a computer as well as via a mobile telephone.[62]

While ASEAN members do control 'mainstream' domestic advertising of tobacco products, such as advertisements in print and on radio and television,[63] advertising on the Internet and social media (such as Facebook and Twitter) remains largely unregulated. Such use of the Internet remains available, and promotional clips or scenes on the use of tobacco products are easily viewable.[64]

In Singapore, the *Smoking (Control of Advertisements and Sale of Tobacco) Act* prohibits advertising of tobacco products, and the prohibition turns on what amounts to 'publishing' matters covered by the Act. The Act defines 'publish' as follows:

'publish', with its grammatical variations, in relation to an advertisement, includes issuing, showing, displaying, exhibiting or making known an advertisement in any manner whatsoever.[65]

Relatedly, the Act defines an 'advertisement' as follows:

'advertisement' includes any notice, circular, pamphlet, brochure, programme, price-list, label, wrapper or other document and any announcement, notification or intimation to the public or any section thereof or to any person or persons made –

(a) orally or in writing;

   (b) by means of any poster, placard, notice or other document affixed, posted up or displayed on any wall, billboard or hoarding or on any other object or thing;

   (c) by means of producing or transmitting sound or light and whether for aural or visual reception or both;

   (d) by means of any writing on any vehicle, ashtray, calendar, cigarette-lighter, clock or any other object or thing; or

   (e) in any other manner whatsoever ...[66]

Unlike the Australian provision mentioned earlier, this definition makes no express reference to advertising conveyed via the Internet or mobile telephony. While para (c) could possibly be invoked, and para (e) is literally wide enough to include such advertising, the opening paragraph itself appears to be rather limited, judging from the illustrative words given.[67]

During a recent parliamentary debate, questions on Internet advertising of tobacco products and on-screen smoking received a relatively non-committal answer from the then health minister, which suggests that the existing advertising provisions mentioned above may not cover Internet advertising.[68]

Increasing restrictions on traditional promotion channels will be likely to cause tobacco entities to use social and new media more. A potential challenge is how to pre-empt this before it takes root in currently unregulated media such as Facebook, Twitter, and YouTube videos. This is one issue already foreseen by the New Zealand Government as it considers more tobacco control regulations.[69]

A related issue is online, cross-border sale of tobacco products. As Internet purchasing increases, the variety of goods available and their accessibility across borders will grow. A review of popular Internet purchasing sites revealed that a variety of cigarettes, cigars and related products are available for order online. Article 11 of the *Protocol on Illicit Trade in Tobacco Products* attempts to address such Internet sales and suggests regulatory measures.[70]

(c) Smoking in films and radio and television programmes   There is no evident control over the screening of films or television containing smoking scenes. From Hollywood to Bollywood, heroes and villains are often shown to be smoking on screen. While some calls on film-makers have been made, this is largely unaddressed within ASEAN at the moment.[71] By contrast, it has been reported that China has restricted smoking in films and television programmes.[72]

(d) Sponsorship through 'corporate social responsibility' programmes – tobacco promotion control in leisure activities and in educational institutions   While tobacco-linked sponsorship has been restricted or prohibited in ASEAN, some forms of sponsorship of education programmes can still be observed.[73] For developing countries in ASEAN, educational opportunities are highly prized. The link between tobacco and education is therefore particularly dangerous, given that there could be a strong temptation to promote education through tobacco sponsorship, whether through financial support or scholarships in the name of tobacco entities.

In Singapore, such sponsorship is not permitted. Further, to address the risk of children and youths being exposed to smoking addiction, Singapore law specifically prohibits the use of tobacco products by persons below 18 years of age, as well as the sale or *giving* of tobacco to them.[74] This addresses exposure risks both in and outside of educational institutions.

With the recent introduction of compulsory financial contributions by tobacco entities to national 'tobacco control funds' in ASEAN states (such as those newly established in Lao People's Democratic Republic and Vietnam), if such funds could be used to help support educational institutions, it would alleviate the need for direct sponsorship by tobacco entities. Such funds could also strongly promote aggressive non-smoking initiatives among those most vulnerable or susceptible to adopting the smoking habit in that particular community, such as children and youths.

4   Other specific issues within ASEAN
Apart from the above challenges, there are further challenges which relate to the economic profile or regulator's position in some ASEAN states.

(a) Members that are host to tobacco growers or tobacco businesses   Within ASEAN, Indonesia, Malaysia, the Philippines and Thailand are tobacco growers, apart from being host to tobacco sale and export companies.[75] With the exception of Malaysia, where the grower industry is much less significant in terms of output and employment, such states have an additional, real challenge of ensuring that efforts to comply with the WHO FCTC and its guidelines are not hampered by the interests of tobacco businesses.

(b) State bodies in potential conflict of interest positions   In some ASEAN countries, there are state-related bodies that are involved in the tobacco trade, and conflicts of interest can arise in the state's regulation

of tobacco. In Thailand, with a long history beginning in 1939, the Thailand Tobacco Monopoly (TTM), a state enterprise, operates under the auspices of the Ministry of Finance. Thai law previously granted the TTM a monopoly to produce cigarettes within Thailand, but this changed following pressure from trade partners such as the United States.[76]

D   Health Exceptions: A Regulatory and Negotiating Strategy for FTAs

With tobacco industry entities raising legal challenges frequently against state actions on tobacco control, an important consideration for ASEAN would be whether general exceptions of the kind found in GATT article XX can offer legal protection.

There are major general exceptions relating to public health in ASEAN trade and investment treaties.[77] These include the following:

1.   article 9 of *the Agreement on the Common Effective Preferential Tariff (CEPT) Scheme for the ASEAN Free Trade Area (AFTA)* (CEPT Agreement);[78]
2.   article 12 of *the Framework Agreement on Enhancing ASEAN Economic Cooperation 1992*;[79]
3.   the 1995 Protocol to amend the CEPT Agreement included all manufactured and agricultural goods within the CEPT Scheme (see amended article 3 of the CEPT Agreement);
4.   article 8(b) of ATIGA and Chapter 8 of the SPS Agreement, especially article 81(3); and
5.   article 17 of the ASEAN *Comprehensive Investment Agreement.*

Some ASEAN treaties signed with external partners, such as the *ASEAN–China Comprehensive Investment Agreement*, also contain a general exception provision which protects necessary health measures.[80] It has been rightly pointed out that ASEAN countries should be mindful of the 'necessity' requirement under public health exceptions resembling article XX(b) of the GATT 1994, when formulating or introducing tobacco control measures.[81]

Interestingly, in a side letter relating to the Services Chapter of the *Australia–United States Free Trade Agreement*,[82] the following was expressly noted by the two signatories, with reference to their negotiations on Chapter 10 (Investment) and Chapter 11 (Cross-Border Trade in Services):

During the negotiations, the Parties discussed the objectives behind the regulation of *retail trade services of tobacco products*, alcoholic beverages, and firearms. *Such regulations will typically fall within the exceptions provided under the sub-paragraphs (a), (b) and (c)(iii) of Article XIV of GATS, as incorporated in the Agreement.*[83]

As the above is expressed by the signatories to be an integral part of the FTA, it forms an important express link between each party's regulation of trade services of tobacco products, and *inter alia*, the *health* exception of GATS article XIV(b). By contrast, there is no equivalent statement regarding the general exception in article 22.1 of the FTA, which incorporates article XX of the GATT 1994 and its interpretative notes. Nonetheless, this side letter language forms an interesting basis for other negotiating parties to argue for a parallel, express linkage between regulation of trade of tobacco *products* and an article XX(b) GATT-type provision, as a minimum.

In the ASEAN–Japan FTA,[84] tobacco products have been excluded altogether from the tariff liberalisation commitments of some ASEAN member states.[85]

The negotiating parties to the TPP comprise Australia, Brunei Darussalam, Canada, Chile, Japan, Malaysia, Mexico, New Zealand, Peru, Singapore, Vietnam and the United States, with the most recent additions being Canada, Mexico and Japan. The following points are noteworthy within this group:

1. Only four are ASEAN members – Brunei Darussalam, Malaysia, Singapore and Vietnam (and are therefore subject to ASEAN treaty commitments).
2. Among the ASEAN participants, Brunei Darussalam and Singapore do not apply tobacco import tariffs, but otherwise have strong tobacco control laws.
3. Some participating countries have strong private interests in tobacco production and export, such as the US and Japan.
4. Of the 12 participating countries, only the US, though a signatory, is not a party to the WHO FCTC.[86]

In a press release of May 2012, the United States Trade Representative (USTR) set out a proposal on how the TPP might approach tobacco products.[87] Three salient points from this proposal are mentioned here. First, that tariff phase-outs would be applicable to such products under the TPP. Although subsequent to this proposed position, there have been calls for the TPP to exclude tobacco products from tariff elimination requirements, there has been no change from the initial announcement on this point.[88]

Secondly, it was proposed that the TPP 'would explicitly recognize the unique status of tobacco products from a health and regulatory perspective'. It is not clear what this would entail, although it appears to at least have been intended to pave the way for an express statement separating tobacco products in some way from other products under the TPP.

Thirdly, the following 'safe harbour' was put forward:

> The proposal would include language in the 'general exceptions' chapter that allows health authorities in TPP governments to adopt regulations that impose origin-neutral, science-based restrictions on specific tobacco products/classes in order to safeguard public health. This language will create a safe harbor for FDA tobacco regulation, providing greater certainty that the provisions in the TPP will not be used in a manner that would prevent FDA from taking the sorts of incremental regulatory actions that are necessary to effectively implement the Tobacco Control Act, while retaining important trade disciplines (national treatment, compensation for expropriations, and transparency) on tobacco measures.[89]

Since this proposal, polarised views have emerged, and there appears to have been no official negotiating draft tabled on this as yet. One concern arising from the above proposal by its specific reference to 'health authorities' – as opposed to any government authority – is that non-health authority tobacco control measures, such as tax and intellectual property measures, would be excluded from this 'safe harbor'.[90]

In August 2013, the United States made a new proposal on tobacco for the negotiations, maintaining the market access element. The proposal also envisages a general exception for matters necessary to protect human life or health, and a provision that states that the TPP parties understand that the general exception applies to tobacco health measures. The proposal further provides that prior to challenging a TPP party's tobacco regulatory measure, health authorities of the concerned parties are to meet to discuss the measure.[91] Malaysia has reportedly provided a counter-proposal, which seeks to carve tobacco out from the TPP.[92] The issue of tobacco in the TPP is discussed further in Chapter 10 of this volume.

Finally, in some treaties, indirect expropriation is defined and limited to exclude non-discriminatory regulatory action taken to protect health.[93]

For ASEAN, therefore, it is imperative that a clear negotiating stance on tobacco control measures and any applicable exceptions, whether in the form of a general health exception similar to GATT article XX(b) or a specific exception applicable to tobacco products and their regulation, be developed and implemented.

VI CONCLUSION

Tobacco control in ASEAN has been growing steadily, thanks to national initiatives and to participation in the WHO FCTC and its associated initiatives. The relatively recent focus on tobacco control at the ASEAN health ministers' level and ASEAN-wide actions to regulate tobacco, particularly under the auspices of the ASCC, are important new directions. As the majority of ASEAN members continue to implement the requirements of the WHO FCTC, one can expect more measures to be introduced. Domestically, the majority of ASEAN members will be grappling with further implementation of WHO FCTC obligations in various aspects of tobacco control. An area receiving relatively little attention in ASEAN at the moment but vital in the tobacco control discussion is the use of the Internet, social media and films for cross-border advertising, promotion and sale of tobacco products, especially among younger consumers. The discrepant resources and priorities within ASEAN states create a potential hurdle to a unified approach on this front.

At the same time, forces that may act to promote the sale and use of tobacco products such as trade-liberalising FTAs form part of ASEAN's calculus in tackling tobacco control. Such agreements aim to reduce barriers to movement of goods, services and investments, including those related to tobacco, with the potential result of greater access to such goods by consumers in ASEAN.

Though the ongoing TPP negotiations involve only a small number of ASEAN countries, they are critical because the treatment of tobacco control in a final TPP agreement will have implications for both the tobacco-exporting and tobacco-importing participants, for future acceding parties, as well as for future treaties should the TPP be used as a sort of negotiating 'template'. There is therefore an important and urgent opportunity in these negotiations to fashion provisions that satisfactorily take into account participants' tobacco regulatory expectations (and, indeed, obligations, such as those under the WHO FCTC) and the public health dimension to such a trade treaty. The ongoing bilateral and multilateral tobacco control disputes will offer important legal and policy lessons, and these developments, together with initiatives such as the TPP, are no doubt being keenly watched by ASEAN.

NOTES

1. Opened for signature 16 June 2003, 2302 UNTS 166 (entered into force 27 February 2005) (WHO FCTC).
2. See *Declaration of ASEAN Concord II (Bali Concord)*, signed 7 October 2003, and ASEAN Economic Blueprint, adopted by ASEAN leaders at the 13th ASEAN Summit, 20 November 2007, Singapore.
3. *Agreement on the Common Effective Preferential Tariff (CEPT) Scheme for the ASEAN Free Trade Area*, signed and entered into force 28 January 1992.
4. Endorsed by the 10th ASEAN Health Ministers Meeting, 22 July 2010, Singapore.
5. Endorsed by the 14th ASEAN Summit on 1 March 2009, Thailand.
6. ASEAN, *Operationalisation of ASEAN Strategic Framework on Health Development 2010–2015* <http://www.globinmed.com/index.php?option=com_content&view=article&id=103894:operationalisation-of-asean-strategic-framework-on-health-development-2010-2015&catid=265&Itemid=316>.
7. *Framework Agreement on Enhancing ASEAN Economic Cooperation*, signed 28 January 1992 (entered into force 28 January 1992*); Agreement on the Common Effective Preferential Tariff Scheme for the ASEAN Free Trade Area*, signed 28 January 1992 (entered into force 28 January 1992).
8. See Chia Siow Yue, 'Accelerating ASEAN Trade and Investment and Integration: Progress and Challenges' in Philippe Gugler and Julien Chaisse (eds) *Competitiveness of the ASEAN Countries, Corporate and Regulatory Drivers* (Edward Elgar Publishing, 2010); Hadi Soesastro, 'Implementing the ASEAN Economic Community (AEC) Blueprint' in Hadi Soesastro (ed) *Deepening Economic Integration – The ASEAN Economic Community and Beyond* (Research Project Report 2007-1-2, ERIA, 2008) 47 <http://www.eria.org/publications/research_project_reports/images/pdf/PDF%20No.1-2/No.1-2-part2-3.pdf>. For a discussion of tobacco control efforts in Asia generally, see Judith MacKay, Bungon Rithhiphakdee and K Srinath Reddy, 'Tobacco Control in Asia' (2013) 381(9877) *The Lancet* 1581.
9. *Bali Concord*, above n 2.
10. *Bali Concord*, above n 2.
11. *ASEAN Trade in Goods Agreement (ATIGA)*, signed 26 February 2009, entered into force 17 May 2010.
12. For an overview of the position in ASEAN as at 2002, see William Onzivu, 'The Public Health Implications of the Association of Southeast Asian Nations (ASEAN) Legal Regime on Tobacco Control' (2002) 4(2) *Australian Journal of Asian Law* 160.
13. 'ASEAN Agrees to Withdraw Tobacco from AFTA', *The Star Online*, 9 July 2012 <http://www.thestar.com.my/News/Nation/2012/07/09/Asean-agrees-to-withdraw-tobacco-from-Afta.aspx>.
14. See above n 3.
15. See, eg, *Annex 2: Tariffs under the ASEAN Trade in Goods Agreement (ATIGA) Cambodia* <http://www.asean.org/images/2012/Economic/AFTA/annex/Annex2-Cambodia.pdf>, which shows a commitment to reduce the tariffs to 0–5 per cent by 2015.
16. *General Agreement on Tariffs and Trade*, LT/UR/A-1A/1/GATT/2 (signed 30 October 1947), as incorporated in *Marrakesh Agreement Establishing the World Trade Organization*, opened for signature 15 April 1994, 1867 UNTS 3 (entered into force 1 January 1995) annex 1A (*General Agreement on Tariffs and Trade 1994*).
17. ASEAN has signed FTAs with Australia and New Zealand, China, Korea, Japan and India. The texts of these FTAs are available at: International Enterprise Singapore, *About FTAs* <http://www.fta.gov.sg/sg_fta.asp>.

18. The RCEP negotiating states comprise ASEAN and those trade partners mentioned in n 17; see generally International Enterprise Singapore, *Factsheet: The Regional Comprehensive Economic Partnership (RCEP)* <http://www.fta.gov.sg/press_release%5CFACTSHEET%20ON%20RCEP_final.pdf>.

19. *Marrakesh Agreement Establishing the World Trade Organization*, opened for signature 15 April 1994, 1867 UNTS 3 (entered into force 1 January 1995) annex 1B (*General Agreement on Trade in Services*).

20. *Marrakesh Agreement Establishing the World Trade Organization*, opened for signature 15 April 1994, 1867 UNTS 3 (entered into force 1 January 1995) annex 1A (*Agreement on the Application of Sanitary and Phytosanitary Measures*).

21. *Marrakesh Agreement Establishing the World Trade Organization*, opened for signature 15 April 1994, 1867 UNTS 3 (entered into force 1 January 1995), annex 1A (*Agreement on Technical Barriers to Trade*).

22. *General Agreement on Tariffs and Trade*, opened for signature 30 October 1947, 55 UNTS 187 (entered into force 1 January 1948).

23. Panel Report, *Thailand – Restrictions on Importation of and Internal Taxes on Cigarettes*, WTO Doc DS10/R – 37S/200 (adopted 7 November 1990) (*Thailand – Cigarettes*).

24. Appellate Body Report, *Thailand – Customs and Fiscal Measures on Cigarettes from the Philippines*, WTO Doc WT/DS371/AB/R (adopted 15 July 2011).

25. Appellate Body Report, *United States – Measures Affecting the Production and Sale of Clove Cigarettes*, WTO Doc WT/DS406/AB/R (adopted 24 April 2012).

26. See Chapter 6 of this volume.

27. *Agreement Establishing the ASEAN–Australia–New Zealand Free Trade Area* (AAN-ZFTA), signed 27 February 2009, [2010] ATS 1 (entered into force 1 January 2010) ch 5.

28. See ASEAN, above n 6.

29. See Secretary-General of ASEAN, 'ASEAN Secretary-General towards the Vision of a Smoke-Free ASEAN' (Speech delivered at the 15th World Conference on Tobacco or Health, Singapore, 22 March 2012) <http://www.asean.org/news/asean-secretariat-news/item/asean-secretary-general-towards-the-vision-of-a-smoke-free-asean>.

30. See, eg, 'AFPTC Meets in Cambodia' (31 May 2013) 3 *ASEAN e-Health Bulletin* (online) 2: <http://www.asean.org/images/3rd%20issue%20of%20asean%20e-health%20bulletin%20f.pdf>.

31. 15th *World Conference on Tobacco or Health*, Singapore (20–24 March 2012).

32. ASEAN, *Regional Action Plan on Healthy ASEAN Lifestyles* <http://www.asean.org/communities/asean-socio-cultural-community/item/regional-action-plan-on-healthy-asean-lifestyles>.

33. Raphaella Prugsamatz et al, *ASEAN Tobacco Tax Report Card* (29 February 2012) Southeast Asia Initiative on Tobacco Tax, Table 4 <http://seatca.org/dmdocuments/ASEAN%20tax%20Report%20card%202012.pdf>, which sets out the various component taxes applicable in each ASEAN country.

34. For a study on excise taxes and affordability within certain ASEAN countries, see Sophapan Ratachena and Ulysses Dorotheo, *Affordability of Cigarettes and the Impact of Raising Excise Taxes in Southeast Asia: Cambodia, Indonesia, Lao PDR, the Philippines, Thailand and Vietnam* (January 2012) Southeast Asia Initiative on Tobacco Tax <http://seatca.org/dmdocuments/Affordability-final-11-01-56-web.pdf>.

35. For a discussion on the effect of the AEC, its liberalisation requirements and objectives, and tobacco control, see Sophapan Ratanachena, *The AEC's Impact on Tobacco Tax in ASEAN and its Threat to Public Health* (26 July 2012) ICIRD <http://www.icird.org/2012/files/papers/Sophapan%20Ratanachena2.pdf>.

36. *Tobacco (Control of Advertisements and Sale) Act* (Singapore, ch 309, 2011 rev ed).

37. See ASEAN, *Singapore* <http://www.asean.org/communities/asean-economic-community/item/singapore-3>.
38. *Tobacco (Control of Advertisements and Sale) Act* (Singapore, ch 309, 2011 rev ed).
39. See Health Sciences Authority (Singapore), *Highlights: Prohibition on Certain Products* (8 May 2013) <http://www.hsa.gov.sg/publish/hsaportal/en/health_products_regulation/tobacco/legislation/highlights___prohibition.html>.
40. See Sheila Crisostomo, 'E-cigarettes not Advisable for Smokers – DOH', *Philippine Star* (online) (21 January 2013).
41. See, eg, Health Promotion Board (Singapore), *National Tobacco Control Programme (NTCP)* (12 September 2012) <http://www.hpb.gov.sg/HOPPortal/article?id=428>; Health Promotion Board (Singapore), *Smoking Control Programmes for Adults* (3 April 2013) <http://www.hpb.gov.sg/HOPPortal/programmes-article/2490#4>.
42. See Isra Sarntisart, 'ASEAN Regional Summary Report: AFTA and Tobacco' (Southeast Asia Tobacco Control Alliance, July 2006) <http://www.smoke-free.ca/trade-and-tobacco/Thailand/ASEAN%20Regional%20Summary%20Report_AFTA%20and%20Tobacco.pdf>.
43. Louisa Picco et al, 'Smoking and Nicotine Dependence in Singapore: Findings from a Cross-Sectional Epidemiological Study' (2012) 2012 41 *Annals Academy of Medicine* 325, 330.
44. Kate Hodal, 'Indonesia's Smoking Epidemic – an Old Problem Getting Younger', *The Guardian* (online), 23 March 2012 <http://www.guardian.co.uk/world/2012/mar/22/indonesias-smoking-epidemic>.
45. See, eg, 'Buying "Double Happiness" Reveals China's Tobacco Battle', *Bloomberg Businessweek* (online), 5 February 2013 <http://www.businessweek.com/news/2013-02-05/buying-double-happiness-reveals-china-s-tobacco-battle>.
46. See, eg, Campaign for Tobacco-Free Kids, *Indonesia: Tobacco Control Advocates Expose Corruption after Tobacco Clause Found Missing from the National Health Bill* <http://global.tobaccofreekids.org/en/industry_watch/case_studies/indonesia_tobacco_control_advocates>.
47. Transparency International Sri Lanka, *Sri Lanka Placed 79th in Global Corruption Perception Index* (5 December 2012) Transparency International <http://www.transparency.org/news/pressrelease/20121205_sri_lanka_placed_79th_in_global_corruption_perception_index>.
48. For the reports of the nine ASEAN members who are party to the WHO FCTC, see *Parties' Reports*, WHO Framework Convention on Tobacco Control <http://www.who.int/fctc/reporting/party_reports/en/index.html>.
49. EFTA states comprise Lichtenstein, Iceland, Norway and Switzerland.
50. *Act Relating to the Prevention of the Harmful Effects of Tobacco 1973*, Act No 14 of 9 March 1973, Norway, s 5: < http://www.regjeringen.no/en/dep/hod/Subjects/the-department-of-public-health/norways-national-strategy-for-tobacco-co.html?id=451948>.
51. *Philip Morris Norway AS v Ministry of Health and Care Services* (E-16/10) [2011] EFTA (12 September 2011).
52. In 2013, the Singapore Government gave indications that it was considering the banning of point-of-sale displays (Statement by the Singapore Minister for Health in Parliament, 12 March 2013). For other countries permitting point-of-sale displays such as the Philippines, see 'Advertising at Point-of-Sale Gone Berserk, A Case for Pack Display Ban' (November 2012) 10 *Tobacco Industry Surveillance* (online): <http://www.healthjustice.ph/uploads/F_POS_Handout_Nov2012.pdf>.
53. See Ministry of Public Health, Thailand, *Directive Procedures for Distribution of Tobacco Products* <http://www.tobaccocontrollaws.org/files/live/Thailand/Thailand%

20-%202005%20POS%20Directive.pdf>; *Advertisement, Sale Promotion and Sponsorship ban in Thailand*, WHO Country Office for Thailand <http://www.whothailand.org/en/Section3/Section104_312.htm>.

54. *JT International SA v Commonwealth*; *British American Tobacco Australasia Ltd v Commonwealth* [2012] HCA 43 (5 October 2012).

55. *Agreement between the Government of Hong Kong and the Government of Australia for the Promotion and Protection of Investments*, 1748 UNTS 385 (signed 15 September 1993, entered into force 15 October 1993).

56. See DS434, initiated by Ukraine (http://www.wto.org/english/tratop_e/dispu_e/cases_e/ds434_e.htm); DS435, initiated by Honduras (http://www.wto.org/english/tratop_e/dispu_e/cases_e/ds435_e.htm); DS441, initiated by the Dominican Republic (http://www.wto.org/english/tratop_e/dispu_e/cases_e/ds441_e.htm); and DS458 initiated by Cuba (http://www.wto.org/english/tratop_e/dispu_e/cases_e/ds458_e.htm).

57. For the nine ASEAN states that are party to the WHO FCTC, reports on their regulation over domestic advertising, promotion and sponsorship can be found here: *Reporting on the Implementation of the Convention*, WHO FCTC <http://www.who.int/fctc/reporting/en/>.

58. See *Global Tobacco Control Updates: Tobacco Control Regulation an Important Step Forward for Indonesia* (25 Jan 2013) Campaign for Tobacco-Free Kids <http://global.tobaccofreekids.org/en/global_updates/detail/2013_01_25_indonesia>.

59. See Sarah Schonhardt, 'Is Indonesia, One of Big Tobacco's Last Frontiers, Closing?', *CNBC* (online), 4 March 2013 <http://www.cnbc.com/id/100516212>.

60. WHO, *WHO Framework Convention on Tobacco Control: Guidelines for Implementation* (WHO, 2013) 102–3.

61. Ibid 102.

62. *Tobacco Advertising Prohibition Amendment Act 2012* (Cth) s 15A.

63. See, eg, *Smoking (Control of Advertisements and Sale of Tobacco) (Foreign Newspapers) (Consolidation) Notification 2000* (Singapore).

64. For a discussion of cross-border Internet advertising and promotion of tobacco products, see Andrew T Kenyon and Jonathan Liberman, 'Controlling Cross-Border Tobacco: Advertising, Promotion and Sponsorship – Implementing the FCTC' (Legal Studies Working Paper No 161, Center for Media and Communications Law, University of Melbourne, August 2006) <http://papers.ssrn.com/sol3/papers.cfm?abstract_id=927551>.

65. *Tobacco (Control of Advertisements and Sale) Act* (Singapore, ch 309, 2011 rev ed).

66. Ibid.

67. This is notwithstanding the use of 'includes' in this paragraph, if one were to apply the well-known *ejusdem generis* rule of interpretation.

68. Statement by the then Singapore Minister for Health in Parliament (19 July 2010).

69. For discussions on tobacco control and social media, see *Tobacco Product Marketing on the Internet* (28 November 2011) Campaign for Tobacco-Free Kids <http://www.tobaccofreekids.org/research/factsheets/pdf/0081.pdf>.

70. The protocol was agreed by the Intergovernmental Negotiating Body of the Conference of the Parties of the WHO FCTC in April 2012 and adopted by the Conference of the Parties in November 2012: see *About the Protocol to Eliminate Illicit Trade in Tobacco Products*, WHO FCTC <http://www.who.int/fctc/protocol/about/en/>. The protocol is not yet in force at the time of writing.

71. See, eg, *Malaysian Health Minister Calls for Non-smoking Films* (31 May 2011) ASEAN-China Free Trade Area <http://www.asean-cn.org/Item/2926.aspx>.

72. See Wendy Zeldin, *China: More Control on Smoking on Screen* (23 February 2011) Library of Congress <http://www.loc.gov/lawweb/servlet/lloc_news?disp3_l20540 2534_text>; Agence France-Presse, *China Restricts Smoking in Films, TV* (13

February 2011) xinmsn entertainment <http://entertainment.xin.msn.com/en/celebrity/buzz/hollywood/article.aspx?cp-documentid=4639252>.

73. In Malaysia, for example, the British American Tobacco Institute provides educational scholarships and other charitable causes: see *British American Tobacco Malaysia Foundation* (3 April 2012) British American Tobacco Malaysia <http://www.batmalaysia.com/group/sites/BAT_7RYJ8N.nsf/vwPagesWebLive/DO7SUKR2?opendocument&SKN=1>.

74. *Tobacco (Control of Advertisements and Sale) Act* (Singapore, ch 309, 2011 rev ed) ss 10, 11.

75. For information on Malaysia tobacco growers, see 'Nothing Positive about Tobacco Farming', *The Star Online* (online), 4 September 2012 <http://biz.thestar.com.my/news/story.asp?file=/2012/9/4/business/11962646&sec=business>.

76. The two pieces of legislation passed in Thailand to reform tobacco control in 1992 are the *Tobacco Products Control Act*, BE 2535 and *The Non-Smokers Health Protection Act*, BE 2535. See generally Naowarut Charoenca et al, 'Success Counteracting Tobacco Company Interference in Thailand: An Example of FCTC Implementation for Low- and Middle-income Countries' (2012) 9 *International Journal of Environmental Research and Public Health* 1111.

77. For a summary of the ASEAN health-protection treaty provisions as at 2002, see Onzivu, above n 12, 168–70.

78. See above n 3.

79. See above n 7.

80. *Agreement on Investment of the Framework Agreement on Comprehensive Economic Cooperation between the People's Republic of China and the Association of Southeast Asian Nations*, signed 15 August 2009, entered into force 15 February 2010, article 16.1(b).

81. World Health Organization, *Confronting the Tobacco Epidemic in a New Era of Trade and Investment Liberalization* (2012) 53–4.

82. *Australia–United States Free Trade Agreement* (AUSFTA), signed 18 May 2004, [2005] ATS 1 (entered into force 1 January 2005).

83. *Letter from Robert Zoellick to Mark Vaile* and vice versa, 18 May 2004. Text of letters available at: <http://www.ustr.gov/sites/default/files/uploads/agreements/fta/australia/asset_upload_file537_3899.pdf> (emphasis added).

84. *ASEAN Japan Comprehensive Economic Partnership* (AJCEP), signed 14 April 2008, entered into force 1 December 2008 (except for Indonesia).

85. See for example Malaysia's, Thailand's and Vietnam's Schedules of Commitments and explanatory Headnotes, available at *Overview of ASEAN JAPAN Comprehensive Economic Partnership*, Singapore Government <http://www.fta.gov.sg/fta_ajcep.asp?hl=38>.

86. See *Parties to the WHO Framework Convention on Tobacco Control*, WHO FCTC <http://www.who.int/fctc/signatories_parties/en/>.

87. See below n 89.

88. See, eg, *No Free Trade for Cigarettes* (8 March 2013) *Framework Convention Alliance* <http://fctc.org/index.php?option=com_content&view=article&id=970:no-free-trade-for-cigarettes&catid=229:general-news&Itemid=233>; *Conflict between the TPP and the FCTC*, Southeast Asia Tobacco Control Alliance <http://seatca.org/dmdocuments/TPP%20&%20FCTC_Brief_Final.pdf>.

89. Information of 18 May 2012, originally available at USTR website (no longer available as at September 2013). See, eg, Stanton Glantz, *USTR Abandons Plan to Protect Tobacco Control Measures under Trans-Pacific Partnership Trade Agreement* (16 August 2013) Center for Tobacco Control Research & Education <http://www.tobacco.ucsf.edu/ustr-abandons-plan-protect-tobacco-control-measures-under-trans-pacific-partnership-trade-agreement>.

90. See, eg, *Letter from Ginny Lyons and Kathleen Keenan to Ambassador Ron Kirk* (25 July 2012) <http://ash.org/wp-content/uploads/2012/08/Vermont-Letter.pdf>.

91. See *Fact Sheet: New US Proposal on Tobacco Regulation in the Trans-Pacific Partnership* (21 August 2013) United States Trade Representative <http://www.ustr. gov/about-us/press-office/fact-sheets/2013/august/fact-sheet-tobacco-and-tpp>. See also Thomas Bollyky, *The Tobacco Problem in US Trade* (5 September 2013) Council on Foreign Relations <http://www.cfr.org/trade/tobacco-problem-us-trade/ p31346>.

92. See *TPP Agreement Negotiations and Tobacco* (18 September 2013) O'Neill Institute for National & Global Health Law <http://www.oneillinstituteblog.org/tpp-agreement-negotiations-tobacco/>.

93. The 2012 US Model BIT reflects such an exception: 'Except in rare circumstances, non-discriminatory regulatory actions by a Party that are designed and applied to protect legitimate public welfare objectives, such as public health, safety, and the environment, do not constitute indirect expropriations'; see Office of the Spokesperson, 'United States Concludes Review of Model Bilateral Investment Treaty' (Media Note, 2012/611, 20 April 2012); see also, eg, AANZFTA annex.

10. International trade policy and tobacco products under the Obama administration

Jamie Strawbridge[*]

I INTRODUCTION

Ever since the creation of the World Trade Organization (WTO) in 1995, administrations of the United States (US) – Democratic and Republican alike – have argued that binding WTO rules help to rationalise international commerce while still allowing WTO members sufficient 'policy space' to put in place measures designed to promote public health. Under President Obama, that longstanding assertion was put to an early and rigorous test. Less than a year after Obama signed into law the *Family Smoking Prevention and Tobacco Control Act*[1] (*Tobacco Control Act*) – a landmark achievement for the president that gave the federal government much greater ability to regulate the US tobacco industry – Indonesia launched a legal challenge, alleging that the Act violated WTO rules. That litigation prompted some officials within the administration to begin pushing for additional legal safeguards in order to ensure that tobacco control measures such as the *Tobacco Control Act* do not run into legal difficulties under trade agreements. Specifically, this effort arose in the context of the Trans-Pacific Partnership (TPP) negotiations, the president's signature trade initiative and the economic component of his 'pivot' to Asia.[2] After contentious interagency deliberations, the White House signed off on a draft legal 'safe harbour' proposal for tobacco control regulations in the TPP that was unlike anything the United States had developed before in international trade policy.[3]

The reaction to the proposal from US tobacco companies, business associations and agricultural groups, has been intense. Together, they have launched a concerted campaign to convince the White House to scrap it entirely, arguing that 'special treatment' for tobacco as formulated in the TPP proposal would not only lower the economic ambition of the regional trade agreement, but would undermine the very assumptions upon which the current framework of international trade rules relies by implying that existing safeguards in the WTO or past US bilateral and regional trade accords are insufficient to protect public health measures, including tobacco control measures. Public health advocates, on the other hand, strongly support the draft proposal. While confessing that they are a bit underwhelmed by its narrow scope, they nonetheless recognise the draft proposal as an important first step toward their ultimate goal of 'carving out' tobacco products from trade agreements altogether. As of April 2013, the administration still appeared committed to advancing some version of its 'safe harbour' proposal in the TPP talks, which some business sources say would be unusual in light of the level of opposition that the proposal faces. At the same time, the opposition has had an effect. While the administration was initially going to table the proposal at a formal TPP round in May 2012, the White House appears to have made a last-minute political decision to hold off until the TPP talks are closer to completion, perhaps in order to avoid an unnecessary confrontation with the business community. Although the administration has said it wants to wrap up TPP negotiations in 2013, this appears exceedingly unlikely; in fact, most Washington-based observers believe the talks will likely drag on well into 2014 at least.

II ORIGINS OF THE TPP TOBACCO 'SAFE HARBOUR'

The TPP negotiations were started in the waning days of the George W Bush administration and resumed in earnest under Obama in the fall of 2009. As of May 2013, the effort involved the United States and 11 other countries: Australia, New Zealand, Brunei, Singapore, Chile, Peru, Malaysia, Vietnam, Canada, Mexico, and Japan. The negotiations seek to create a 'regional' agreement among these countries, although the administration says the TPP will be crafted as a 'living' agreement that could eventually expand to encompass an even larger group of countries in the Asia-Pacific region.[4] From the start, the administration has said that the TPP will be a 'twenty-first-century' agreement that improves upon rules contained in past US accords. Unlike other areas, however, the administration has not publicly trumpeted its tobacco 'safe harbour' approach as an important innovation in trade policy. In fact, the proposal had a fairly clandestine origin. Tobacco industry sources say the administration did not consult with them at all when initially crafting it, and that they first heard of it when news leaked out to them through informal channels. By the fall of 2011, the draft proposal was still formally a secret, although many in the business and public health communities knew the administration was considering something aimed specifically at the treatment of tobacco products in the TPP.

There are several reasons why the administration may have decided to consider new language for tobacco products in the TPP negotiations, although perhaps the most important relates to the WTO legal challenge mounted by Indonesia against the *Tobacco Control Act*. Among other things, that 2009 Act banned flavoured cigarettes – including clove cigarettes imported from Indonesia – but exempted all menthol cigarettes from that general ban. In 2012, the Appellate Body determined that clove and menthol cigarettes are 'like' products under article 2.1 of the WTO's *Agreement on Technical Barriers to Trade* (TBT Agreement)[5] and that the US law afforded 'less favorable' treatment to imported clove cigarettes from Indonesia than to menthol cigarettes produced in the United States within the meaning of that provision. The administration condemned the decision, arguing that the findings could limit the ability of governments to regulate in the public interest. 'The result in this dispute should be of grave concern to any Member regulating for the benefit of public health', it warned at a meeting of the WTO's Dispute Settlement Body (DSB) in Geneva in April 2013. The Appellate Body's analysis, the administration maintained, is 'insufficient to allow for the type of legitimate incremental regulation commonly applied to situations such as the one presented here'.[6]

But beyond the pronouncements in Geneva, the outcome of this legal dispute unsettled some administration officials, especially those within the Department of Health and Human Services (HHS). HHS houses the Food and Drug Administration (FDA), which is the division of the US Government directly responsible for regulating the manufacture, distribution and marketing of tobacco products pursuant to the *Tobacco Control Act*.[7] HHS and FDA officials are generally perceived as wary of instances in which international trade obligations could inhibit their ability to regulate as they see fit, and the outcome in the *Clove Cigarettes* case raised this precise issue. Even before the final Appellate Body decision was released, this WTO challenge reinforced the desire of HHS officials to secure unique treatment for tobacco products in the TPP, partly to ensure that the new regional trade agreement could not serve as a future forum for legal challenges against regulations issued pursuant to the 2009 law. Early on in the interagency process, HHS officials were even more ambitious, privately arguing in favour of a complete 'carve out' for tobacco products in the TPP, meaning that these products would not be subject to, or affected by, any provisions under a final TPP agreement, including tariff reductions. Officials from the Office of the United States

Trade Representatives (USTR), on the other hand, strongly resisted this idea and worked to scale it back substantially. After an intensive deliberative process, the White House ultimately endorsed a compromise that falls far short of a full 'carve out' but does endorse the concept that tobacco products pose unique public health risks and that certain tobacco regulations should benefit from unique legal safeguards in a final TPP agreement.

While the *Clove Cigarettes* case appears to be a leading reason why HHS began agitating for 'special' tobacco provisions, it is likely not the only one. As an initial matter, it is important to note that the idea of unique treatment for tobacco products in trade agreements is not new; public health advocates have long urged USTR to adopt this position and, in the specific context of the TPP, the Campaign for Tobacco Free Kids (an advocacy group) called on the administration to exclude tobacco products from the scope of a TPP agreement as far back as January 2010, nearly two years before the *Clove Cigarettes* panel report was released.[8] But opinions vary somewhat on the more crucial question of what other factors led the Obama administration to endorse this position. The director of the HHS Office of Global Health Affairs (a division within HHS that deals specifically with trade-related issues) has argued that, under President Obama, HHS has played a larger role in the formation of trade policy than ever before.[9] According to this logic, the fact that HHS – which, unlike the USTR, is focused specifically on promoting public health – has engaged more in trade policy discussions inevitably altered the nature of trade policies that were approved through the interagency process. Business representatives generally agree that this explanation has some merit, although they add that HHS was, overall, a more powerful division of the Obama administration than USTR during the president's first term, and argue that this helped to tip the balance in HHS's favour. These representatives also believe that the USTR did not push back against the HHS drive to 'single out' tobacco as forcefully as it might have, something they attribute to a lack of leadership at the USTR and a failure to recognise the full implications of special treatment. Public health advocates say that blaming the USTR makes little sense because the USTR clearly worked to scale back the scope of HHS's initial demands. Some advocates also say that the aggressive strategy[10] launched by Philip Morris and some WTO members to challenge tobacco control measures under trade agreements provided additional momentum behind the notion that new 'safeguards' for tobacco measures should be included in the TPP.

III DETAILS OF THE PROPOSAL

The US proposal would include language in a TPP 'general exceptions' section stating that, notwithstanding other provisions in the agreement, health authorities are permitted 'to adopt regulations that impose origin-neutral, science-based restrictions on specific tobacco products/classes in order to safeguard public health', according to a summary of the proposal released by USTR in May 2012.[11] According to the USTR, this will 'create a safe harbor for FDA tobacco regulation, providing greater certainty that the provisions in the TPP will not be used in a manner that would prevent FDA from taking the sorts of incremental regulatory actions that are necessary to effectively implement the Tobacco Control Act'. At the same time, according to the summary, 'important trade disciplines' such as national treatment, compensation for expropriations and transparency would continue to apply to tobacco measures. The proposal would also 'explicitly recognize the unique status of tobacco products from a health and regulatory perspective'. According to stake-holders briefed by USTR officials, the proposal does not explicitly reference the WHO *Framework Convention on Tobacco Control* (WHO FCTC),[12] an international treaty aimed at driving down the use of tobacco products, likely because the United States is not a party to that treaty.[13]

The purpose of the proposal is to provide shelter from legal challenge for tobacco regulations issued by health authorities in general and the FDA in particular.[14] It is meant to ensure that, although Indonesia successfully challenged provisions of the *Tobacco Control Act* under the auspices of the WTO, TPP members would have a tougher time challenging FDA regulations issued pursuant to that Act within the confines of a final TPP agreement.[15] However, the proposal does not go nearly as far as it could have, even setting aside the fact that it does not 'carve out' tobacco products from the TPP. In fact, its scope is limited in three key ways that appear difficult to justify if the underlying purpose of the proposal is to safeguard the ability of TPP governments to impose measures related to tobacco control.

First, the 'safe harbour' would apply to tobacco regulations but does not apply to statutes passed by legislative bodies. This is somewhat curious because much of the ongoing debate regarding the intersection of trade rules and tobacco control measures relates to laws, including the debate surrounding Australia's plain packaging law[16] or even the *Tobacco Control Act* that Indonesia successfully challenged in the *Clove Cigarettes* case. From an intellectual standpoint, it makes little sense to distinguish between laws and regulations, especially as they at times perform similar functions. Through the *Tobacco Control Act*, for instance, the US Congress delegated vast new regulatory powers over tobacco products to the FDA, and the FDA has since developed and issued regulations pursuant to that law. That is one model of how legislation can operate. Other sections of the 2009 law, however, do not delegate broad authority to the FDA, but rather take specific 'regulatory' steps; for instance, the law bans flavoured cigarettes, including clove cigarettes. The effect of the 'safe harbour' TPP proposal, therefore, would be to provide comparatively broader protections to those TPP partners that address tobacco control through regulatory rather than statutory means, even if the end result were the same.

A second limitation of the US proposal is that it would apply only to regulations issued at the national level. That is, the proposal would not cover regulations passed at the sub-central level, which public health advocates say is a noteworthy limitation because sub-central authorities often play a role in tobacco regulation. While certain responsibilities remain firmly under the jurisdiction of the federal government, including regulation over warning labels on cigarette packs, US states have the authority to take other measures to complement those federal actions, such as prohibiting the placement of tobacco products and tobacco product ads near cash registers.[17] These state-level regulations would receive no new protections under the TPP 'safe harbour' proposal.

Third, the proposal only covers regulations issued by national health authorities, but would not have any direct relevance for regulations issued by other divisions of TPP national governments. Again, this offers mixed results for anti-smoking advocates, who point out that consumer protection agencies often have a role in tobacco regulation. Historically, this has also been true in the United States; while the 2009 law consolidated powers to regulate tobacco products under the FDA, other divisions of the US Government have historically played a leading role in tobacco regulation.[18]

In light of these limitations, many in the US public health community privately doubt that the proposal would, in and of itself, do much to help promote tobacco control. After all, they point out, it is narrowly tailored to address a specific situation in the United States (FDA regulations issued pursuant to the *Tobacco Control Act*), would not shield tobacco products from tariff cuts (which advocates say drive up consumption by lowering prices thanks to increased competition in the marketplace), and would still allow for the possibility of legal challenges against many tobacco control measures in TPP countries.

Even for regulations that fall under the scope of the proposal, some supporters say it is not entirely clear how much 'shelter' it would actually provide. For instance, two terms included in the proposal – 'science-based' and 'origin-neutral' – are new terms of art that are not included in either WTO rules or the texts of past US bilateral trade agreements, and so their interpretation is uncertain.

Concerning the 'science-based' standard, article 2 of the WTO's *Agreement on the Application of Sanitary and Phytosanitary Measures* (SPS Agreement)[19] generally requires WTO members to ensure that an SPS measure 'is based on scientific principles and is not maintained without sufficient scientific evidence'. But tobacco regulations would most likely fall under the auspices of the TBT Agreement, where there is no explicit reference to 'science' at all. The apparent reason behind this formulation in the US proposal is to limit the scope of the regulations that it would shield from legal challenge to only those measures with scientific validation, but some believe the proposal would in fact introduce new legal uncertainties if the term 'science-based' ever came before a TPP legal tribunal for interpretation.[20]

Likewise, WTO rules do not contain any disciplines related to measures that are 'origin-neutral' that could serve as a reference point were a legal tribunal to be convened under the TPP. Instead, WTO rules tend to focus on the idea of non-discrimination as formulated in, for instance, article III:4 of the *General Agreement on Tariffs and Trade 1994* (GATT 1994).[21] That article states that imports from other WTO members 'shall be accorded treatment no less favourable than that accorded to like products of national origin in respect of all laws, regulations and requirements affecting their internal sale, offering for sale, purchase, transportation, distribution or use'. Similar language appears in article 2.1 of the TBT Agreement. The US proposal, by contrast, offers something totally new: specific exemptions for regulations that are 'origin-neutral', a distinct term used by the USTR to describe the relevant provision of the 2009 law that was successfully challenged by Indonesia under the auspices of the WTO.[22] It is possible that the introduction of this new term is meant to ensure that the proposal covers regulations that are non-discriminatory on their face even if the effect of those regulations is to harm imports more than domestic products. This would represent a direct response to the *Clove Cigarettes* case: while the *Tobacco Control Act* was non-discriminatory on its face, the WTO Appellate Body still found that it was an example of de facto discrimination and ruled against it. It is possible that an arbitral panel convened under the TPP could conclude that the 'safe harbour' (if included in a final TPP deal) provides additional protections for all regulations that are facially non-discriminatory, even if the effect of those regulations is to harm imports more than domestic products, but that is unclear.[23] If this is the intention of the proposal, public health advocates argue, the administration should alter the proposal and state this explicitly.

IV   REACTIONS TO THE PROPOSAL

Despite these limitations and uncertainties, public health organisations such as the Campaign for Tobacco Free Kids, Action on Smoking and Health and the American Cancer Society – as well as public health leaders in Congress such as Representative Henry Waxman (District of California) – are eager for the Obama administration to table the proposal. Most fundamentally, they praise the administration's embrace of the principle that tobacco products are unique and should be treated differently than other products in the context of trade agreements, and believe that establishing this concept in the TPP would serve as a critical first step toward rethinking the ways in which trade deals and tobacco control measures intersect. They also believe that, if the United States were to formally table the proposal in the negotiations, other TPP members may then be willing to propose amendments that would broaden its scope and make it more meaningful. For these advocates, ensuring that the United States formally tables its proposal is also crucial in light of their failure to convince other TPP members to 'go first' and table their own tobacco control proposals. If the ultimate goal is to 'carve out' tobacco from trade agreements so that tariff reductions do not help to drive up consumption and tobacco companies cannot use these agreements as legal forums to challenge tobacco control measures, these advocates believe that the US proposal in the TPP at least represents a good first step.

US business associations and tobacco companies oppose the proposal for several reasons. Most basically, they argue that going ahead with the proposal amounts to a poor negotiating tactic that could harm US export interests in other sectors. For instance, if the United States demands an exemption from trade rules for tobacco control regulations, other US negotiating partners – including other TPP members – might demand their own special exemptions from trade rules for alcoholic beverages or genetically modified foods, making it harder to use trade agreements to mount legal challenges against market access barriers that crop up in these areas. Worse, some business groups fear that the US proposal could even make it harder for the United States to resist demands for special exemptions from trade disciplines for reasons that have nothing to do with public health and everything to do with protecting sensitive industries from import competition. In this view, a US insistence on an exemption from general TPP rules for tobacco regulations could lead Japan to insist on special treatment for sensitive agricultural products such as rice in the TPP goods market access discussions.

The fundamental objection of the business community, however, is that the TPP proposal represents a shift away from the stringent trade disciplines enshrined in the WTO and a move toward a more precautionary approach under which regulations that might not pass muster in Geneva would nonetheless be protected from legal challenge. Business groups point out that WTO disciplines have helped past administrations enforce free trade around the world. In a February 2013 letter to President Obama, for instance, 31 leading US agricultural groups signalled their fear that the TPP proposal could ultimately make it more difficult for the United States to challenge foreign restrictions on genetically modified foods or the sale of meat from animals treated with artificial growth hormones, both of which are trade barriers that the United States has successfully challenged under the WTO in the past.[24]

Rather than granting countries more leeway under trade rules to take measures in the name of public health, business representatives would prefer to stick with the existing balance enshrined in article XX(b) of the GATT 1994, which allows WTO members to take measures that are 'necessary to protect human, animal or plant life or health', so long as those measures are not 'applied in a manner which would constitute a means of arbitrary or unjustifiable discrimination between countries where the same conditions prevail' and do not amount to a 'disguised restriction on international trade'. For the US business community, the TPP proposal lowers this standard by allowing TPP health authorities to put in place regulations that, rather than being 'necessary' to achieve a public health objective, are merely taken 'in order to safeguard public health'. They say there is no need to alter the existing balance between commercial obligations and public health considerations; moreover, they note that administration officials are unable to explain why the 'necessary' standard in article XX would not cover any regulations that the FDA may develop pursuant to the 2009 *Tobacco Control Act*, or any other legitimate public health measure the United States may want to implement in the future.[25] Even if the scope of the proposal itself is narrow, it represents something much larger: a shift away from the assumption that existing rules are sufficient. In June 2012, four former USTRs raised this very point, noting that they 'consistently took the position that trade and investment agreements entered into by the United

States permit participating governments substantial latitude to adopt sound, science-based regulation in the public interest'. Given that history, they wrote, 'we do not understand why the Administration believes that is no longer the case with respect to tobacco regulation'.[26]

Legal experts tend to side with the business community. In general, they believe that product-specific rules should be avoided in trade agreements whenever possible. Whether legislating at the domestic or international level, they argue, it is best to write the rules of the game as broadly as possible, in part for logistical reasons – after all, it would be impossible to craft specific rules for every possible situation that could arise. This is not to say that international trade agreements have not contained product-specific exceptions in the past – the WTO's *Agreement on Agriculture*,[27] for instance, is little more than an exemption from subsidies' disciplines contained in the WTO's *Agreement on Subsidies and Countervailing Measures*.[28] But these exemptions from general rules are best seen as political necessities, these experts argue: instances where trading partners were simply unable to agree to subject sensitive areas to normal trading rules and were forced to settle on alternative language. These situations inevitably arise, as trade negotiations cannot escape political considerations; however, the goal should always be to avoid product-specific rules whenever possible.

Like business lobbyists, most WTO lawyers also believe that the general exceptions contained in article XX of the GATT 1994 already provide sufficient leeway for governments to put in place statutes and regulations that are designed to promote public health objectives. But even if the United States considered WTO rules to be fundamentally lacking when it comes to protecting the ability of governments to put in place public health measures – and this is not the view of the Obama administration – these lawyers argue that the US proposed approach makes little sense. First, they argue that the proposal is confusing from the point of view of consistency and logic. Speaking hypothetically, they reason that if public health were really at risk due to international trade rules – a view these experts do not espouse – it would make sense for the United States to address the problem across the board, not just with respect to tobacco products. After all, cigarettes are harmful to the consumer, but there are plenty of other products that pose a risk to human health. If existing trade rules really needed to be bolstered – and if the United States wanted to take the first step in that direction in the TPP – it would make sense to ensure that new exemptions and 'safe harbours' apply not only to tobacco but also to all other products that are harmful to human health, they say. Thus, many scholars contend that there is an unsettling inconsistency to the US proposal. Even if one accepts the premise that international trade rules need to be changed to make it easier to defend public health objectives – which WTO lawyers generally do not – the exclusive focus of the United States on tobacco products is confusing and illogical, they say.

Some legal experts also question whether the proposal might inadvertently weaken the ability of TPP governments to put in place public health regulations in other areas that would otherwise withstand scrutiny if challenged under TPP dispute settlement procedures. They say it is possible that the US proposal could act to narrow the scope of any general public health exceptions, along the lines of those contained in article XX of the GATT 1994, that are included in a final TPP deal. After all, if a TPP deal affords special protections for tobacco regulations, a legal tribunal may conclude that other types of public health regulations are not protected to the same degree, even if they fall under the broader article XX-like exemptions – otherwise, the tobacco 'safe harbour' would serve no purpose. While a TPP deal could look to mitigate this effect by stressing that the tobacco-specific provisions are for 'clarification purposes only', the very existence of special rules for tobacco implies that TPP members are not convinced that the general exemptions are sufficient, they say.

On the other hand, these experts say it is unlikely that the US proposal, if included in a final TPP deal, would do anything to affect the outcome of litigation under the WTO between TPP members on tobacco control regulations. While there is no clear guidance from the Appellate Body on this precise issue, most WTO legal experts believe that WTO rules can only be altered through a formal WTO amendment and cannot be changed by subsequent international agreements to which WTO parties agree. Proponents of this view point out that applicable law for WTO panels is already narrowly drawn under article 7 of the Dispute Settlement Understanding (DSU),[29] which tasks WTO panels with examining complaints referred to them 'in the light of the relevant provisions' of the WTO covered agreements cited by the parties to the dispute, not other non-WTO treaties. Article 3 of the DSU further states that the dispute settlement system 'serves to preserve the rights and obligations of Members under the covered agreements', and states explicitly that recommendations and rulings of the Dispute Settlement Body 'cannot add to or diminish the rights and obligations provided in the covered agreements'. Even some experts who believe WTO members can sign subsequent agreements that alter the WTO rights that they apply to one another say the US proposal would likely not have this effect because it is so specifically drawn as an exemption from TPP rules – not WTO rules – and makes no reference to the WTO at all.

Thus, the proposal would not affect WTO litigation (all TPP members are also members of the WTO), and appears to only increase the ability of TPP members to defend tobacco control regulations in the context of a state-to-state legal challenge pursued under the auspices of a final TPP agreement. This is an important point because state-to-state arbitration under US bilateral and regional trade agreements has hardly ever been used, partly due to the fact that the WTO is still seen as the premier venue for settling trade disputes. In essence, then, the proposal relates to a type of legal challenge that hardly ever comes up. On the other hand, business representatives fear that the proposal could also make it harder for companies to challenge tobacco regulations under an investor–state dispute settlement mechanism that will likely be included in a final TPP agreement; after all, they note, it would make little sense to safeguard a measure in the state-to-state context, but then not do the same in the investor–state context. In private briefings, USTR officials have down-played this concern, although legal experts say it is hard to evaluate what effect, if any, the proposal would have on investor–state disputes without seeing the proposal's legal language, which the administration is with-holding.[30]

V TOBACCO AND THE TRANSATLANTIC TRADE AND INVESTMENT PARTNERSHIP

Even as the administration continues to hold off on tabling the proposal in the TPP negotiations, business associations and public health advocates are already considering how inclusion of a 'safe harbour' in the TPP could impact US trade policy generally and the US negotiating position in talks with the European Union specifically. President Obama announced his intention to negotiate a new agreement with Europe in his State of the Union Address in February 2013,[31] and the USTR formally notified Congress of its intention to enter into these negotiations – dubbed the Transatlantic Trade and Investment Partnership (TTIP) negotiations – roughly one month later.[32] The European Commission is hoping to conclude the negotiations by the end of 2014, although that appears to be an ambitious target.[33] Officials on both sides of the Atlantic have stressed that much of the focus of the talks will be on regulatory issues that stifle international commerce, as tariffs in the United States and EU are already generally low.

From a tobacco policy standpoint, both US business representatives and public health advocates see an intimate connection between the TPP and the TTIP negotiations. Even some opponents of the TPP 'safe harbour' proposal recognise that, if the United States insists on its inclusion in the TPP, it will likely become part of the US trade 'template' under the Obama administration, meaning the White House will also seek its inclusion in the TTIP. In this scenario, one business representative explained, the main task of the US business community would be to ensure that the administration does not seek something even more far-reaching than its TPP proposal.

Public health advocates, on the other hand, see the TTIP negotiations as an opportunity to take another 'step forward' on the issue of tobacco control in trade agreements, perhaps even going beyond whatever gains they make in the TPP. They note that the European Commission initiated a process in December 2012 to revamp the existing Tobacco Products Directive (TPD) in Europe, which acts as a framework for member state legislation on tobacco products.[34] The proposed TPD revision – which, according to the Commission, could enter into force from 2015–16[35] – would implement a suite of dramatic reforms that are designed to make smoking less attractive and drive down initiation rates among young people. The proposal is strongly supported by tobacco control advocates, who see this reform effort not only as a positive development in and of itself but also as a hopeful indication that EU negotiators will be sympathetic to their arguments in the TTIP context. On the other hand, some trade experts within the Commission appear wary of the notion of 'singling out' tobacco products for special treatment in trade agreements and would likely oppose this proposal were it to arise in the TTIP talks; thus, it is unclear which position the Commission as a whole would end up taking on the matter.

The TPD revision as proposed by the Commission has several key provisions. Unlike the *Tobacco Control Act*, it would ban all cigarettes with a 'characterizing flavor' without providing any exemption for menthol cigarettes. It would also ban 'slim' cigarettes that have a diameter of less than 7.5 mm. According to the Commission, this ban is necessary because users of slim cigarettes – often young women – believe they are less dangerous and associate the product with femininity or elegance and weight loss; thus, these slim cigarettes are considered misleading. The revision would also require a minimum content of 20 cigarettes in each pack, which is meant to ensure that cheap 'kiddy packs' containing fewer cigarettes are no longer available. The revision would also strengthen labelling requirements for cigarette packs. In particular, it would mandate that a 'combined warning' – meaning a picture showing the hazards of smoking plus text warning against smoking – must cover 75 per cent of the external area of both the front and back surface of the unit packet, with further health warnings covering

50 per cent of the surfaces of the lateral sides.[36] The proposed TPD revision would not require member states to adopt plain packaging laws, although it would explicitly authorise member states to put in place such laws, provided that they did not conflict with the TPD revision itself.[37]

US tobacco companies are not even trying to enlist the support of the Obama administration to protest these proposed changes in Europe; they say the administration is simply not interested in fighting tobacco policies abroad, and cite in particular the fact that business groups were unable to convince the administration to weigh in against Australia's plain packaging legislation.[38] Alongside WTO members such as Malawi and the Dominican Republic, US tobacco companies and business associations are criticising the Commission's proposal directly, alleging that it is not based on sound science, may violate WTO rules, and 'calls into question the capacity to achieve regulatory commitments that are essential to a successful and meaningful US–EU trade agreement'.[39] While business groups have not publicly explained why they believe the proposal may violate WTO rules, tobacco industry representatives privately suggest that the ban on slim cigarettes, for instance, is not backed by sound science and is therefore 'more trade-restrictive than necessary' under article 2.2 of the TBT Agreement. Industry representatives also suggest that the requirement that graphic warning labels cover 75 per cent of the front and back of cigarette packs, while not as onerous as plain packaging, might nonetheless still constitute a violation of WTO rules because it unduly restricts the use of their intellectual property.[40] The Commission dismisses these arguments, saying that the TPD proposal has been carefully analysed and fully complies with WTO rules.

Legal experts examining these claims say it is not clear whether the proposal, as originally unveiled by the Commission, could be successfully challenged under WTO rules. At the very least, they point out that such a legal case would likely be less clear-cut than Indonesia's challenge against the *Tobacco Control Act* because the TPD revision is non-discriminatory on its face; for instance, menthol cigarettes are not exempted from the general ban on flavoured cigarettes. While tobacco companies and some WTO members may allege violations under article 2.2 of the TBT Agreement, these experts also note that the Appellate Body in past cases has appeared hesitant to fault measures under this provision, perhaps because it is somewhat difficult to determine whether a given measure is more trade-restrictive than necessary. But the WTO-consistency of the proposal is difficult to judge, especially because there is still not a definitive ruling in the Australian plain packaging WTO case and because the European Parliament, which is now considering the proposal, could amend the proposed revision that the Commission has put forward. Still, the fact that the proposal is coming under such criticism this early in the process could make some EU officials more interested in the idea of additional legal protections for tobacco control measures in the context of the TTIP.

VI CONCLUSION: THE CHALLENGE FACING THE OBAMA ADMINISTRATION

When it comes to the nexus of international trade obligations and tobacco control efforts, the Obama administration has worked itself into a difficult position. While sympathetic to the idea that tobacco products should receive new, unique protections in the TPP, the administration appears uninterested in taking that position to its logical conclusion and arguing that these new protections are needed because disciplines in past trade deals were insufficient. This hesitancy comes as little surprise; after all, such an admission could spark calls for the renegotiation of past US bilateral and regional trade agreements and raise questions about why new safeguards are necessary for tobacco products, but not for other harmful products. Such an admission could also undermine confidence in WTO rules, something that the administration would likely want to avoid in light of its continued strong support for WTO rules and their enforcement in Geneva. By holding off on its proposal in the TPP negotiations, the administration has bought itself some time, but it will eventually have to start explaining why the proposal is necessary or why it should be abandoned. Either way, its decision on this issue will be important for the future of US international trade policy.

NOTES

* The author's views are his own. Much of the information in this chapter is culled from private conversations, and the author was compelled to use 'background' attributions in several sections of this chapter.
1. *Family Smoking Prevention and Tobacco Control Act*, 21 USC § 301 (2009).
2. See Mark Manyin et al, 'Pivot to the Pacific? The Obama Administration's "Rebalancing" Toward Asia' (Congressional Research Service, 28 March 2012) <http://www.fas.org/sgp/crs/natsec/R42448.pdf>.
3. See Jamie Strawbridge, 'Cigarettes, TPP, and the Wisdom of Product-Specific Rules in Trade Deals' (2012) 9 *Transnational Dispute Management* (online).
4. For more information, see Office of the United States Trade Representative, *Outlines of the Trans-Pacific Partnership Agreement* (November 2011) <http://www.ustr.gov/about-us/press-office/fact-sheets/2011/november/outlines-trans-pacific-partnership-agreement>.

5. *Marrakesh Agreement Establishing the World Trade Organization*, opened for signature 15 April 1994, 1867 UNTS 3 (entered into force 1 January 1995), annex 1A (*Agreement on Technical Barriers to Trade*).

6. Mission of the United States, Geneva, Switzerland, *Statements by the United States at the April 24, 2012 DSB Meeting* (24 April 2012) <http://geneva.usmission.gov/2012/04/25/statements-by-the-united-states-at-the-april-24-2012-dsb-meeting/>.

7. See US Food and Drug Administration, *Overview of the Family Smoking Prevention and Tobacco Control Act: Consumer Fact Sheet* (2013) <http://www.fda.gov/TobaccoProducts/GuidanceComplianceRegulatoryInformation/ucm246129.htm>.

8. *Letter from Campaign for Tobacco-Free Kids to the United States Trade Representative*, 25 January 2010 <http://www.regulations.gov/#!documentDetail;D=USTR-2009-0041-0095>.

9. 'HHS Highlights Role in Formulating Tobacco, IPR Aspects of Trade Policy' (26 April 2013) 31(17) *Inside US Trade* (online).

10. As of May 2013, the Dominican Republic, Cuba, Honduras and Ukraine had all initiated WTO legal proceedings against the Australian law. In addition, Philip Morris Asia has initiated legal proceedings against the legislation under the auspices of a bilateral investment treaty signed between Australia and Hong Kong.

11. Office of the United States Trade Representative, *Fact Sheet: TPP Tobacco Proposal* (May 2012).

12. Opened for signature 16 June 2003, 2302 UNTS 166 (entered into force 27 February 2005).

13. The US Government signed the treaty in 2004, but the US Senate has not ratified it.

14. Washington-based observers say it is not entirely clear to them whether the proposal would also apply to regulations issued by the HHS, rather than the FDA, although this would presumably be the case.

15. While the proposal was drafted to safeguard FDA regulations, the draft language would apply to national health authorities in other TPP countries as well.

16. *Tobacco Plain Packaging Act 2011* (Cth). The Act prohibits the use of logos, brand imagery, and promotional text on tobacco products and packaging, and includes restrictions on colour, size, format and materials of packaging, as well as the appearance of brand and variant names.

17. See Campaign for Tobacco Free Kids, *The Impact of the New FDA Tobacco Law on State Tobacco Control Efforts* (21 June 2010) <http://www.tobaccofreekids.org/research/factsheets/pdf/0360.pdf>.

18. In the case of the United States, the Federal Trade Commission was previously responsible for issuing regulations to implement new tobacco control legislation. For instance, it issued regulations in 1965 stating that all cigarettes and tobacco advertisements had to carry warning labels (*Federal Cigarette Labeling and Advertising Act*, 15 USC §§ 1333, 1334 (1965)). In 1986, it issued regulations governing the format and display of health warnings on smokeless tobacco packages and advertising (*Comprehensive Smokeless Tobacco Health Education Act*, 15 USC §§ 4402, 4406 (1986)).

19. *Marrakesh Agreement Establishing the World Trade Organization*, opened for signature 15 April 1994, 1867 UNTS 3 (entered into force 1 January 1995), annex 1A (*Agreement on the Application of Sanitary and Phytosanitary Measures*).

20. Benn McGrady has argued that most of the SPS Agreement is concerned with 'whether there is scientific evidence of the existence of a risk' as demonstrated through a risk assessment. He believes that the US proposal, by relying on the term 'science-based', may instead suggest that a TPP member 'would have to show scientific evidence of the effectiveness of the measure, or of the contribution it makes to tobacco control'. See Benn McGrady, 'US Proposal on Tobacco in Trans-Pacific Partnership' on *O'Neill Institute Trade, Investment & Health Blog* (18 May 2012)

<http://www.oneillinstitutetradeblog.org/us-proposal-on-tobacco-in-trans-pacific-partnership/>.

21. *General Agreement on Tariffs and Trade*, LT/UR/A-1A/1/GATT/2 (signed 30 October 1947), as incorporated in *Marrakesh Agreement Establishing the World Trade Organization*, opened for signature 15 April 1994, 1867 UNTS 3 (entered into force 1 January 1995) annex 1A (*General Agreement on Tariffs and Trade 1994*).

22. In its legal briefs in the WTO *US – Clove Cigarettes* dispute, the US argued that measures that are 'origin-neutral' and apply equally to domestic and imported products are not necessarily inconsistent with national treatment obligations, so long as there is a legitimate reason why the measure has a more harmful impact on imports than domestically produced products in practice. See First Written Submission of the United States of America, *United States – Measures Affecting the Production and Sale of Clove Cigarettes*, WTO Doc WT/DS406 (16 November 2010) [199]–[201].

23. This precise issue was raised in the *US – Clove Cigarettes* dispute. The Appellate Body interpreted TBT Agreement article 2.1 as prohibiting both de jure and de facto discrimination against imported products, but permitting 'detrimental impact on competitive opportunities for imports that stems exclusively from legitimate regulatory distinctions'. Ultimately, it faulted the US measure in part because it was not persuaded that the decision to ban clove cigarettes but allow menthol cigarettes stemmed from a 'legitimate regulatory distinction': see Appellate Body Report, *United States – Measures Affecting the Production and Sale of Clove Cigarettes*, WTO Doc WT/DS406/AB/R (adopted 24 April 2012).

24. *Letter from the American Beverage Association et al to President Barack Obama*, 1 February 2013 <http://insidetrade.com/iwpfile.html?file=feb2013%2Fwto2013_0584a.pdf>.

25. *Letter from the Emergency Committee for American Trade et al to the United States Trade Representative*, 9 May 2012 <http://insidetrade.com/iwpfile.html?file=jun2012%2Fwto2012_1405e.pdf>.

26. *Letter from Bill Brock et al to the United States Trade Representative*, 22 June 2012 <http://insidetrade.com//index.php?option=com_iwpfile&file=jun2012/wto2012_1383.pdf>.

27. *Marrakesh Agreement Establishing the World Trade Organization*, opened for signature 15 April 1994, 1867 UNTS 3 (entered into force 1 January 1995), annex 1A (*Agreement on Agriculture*).

28. *Marrakesh Agreement Establishing the World Trade Organization*, opened for signature 15 April 1994, 1867 UNTS 3 (entered into force 1 January 1995), annex 1A (*Agreement on Subsidies and Countervailing Measures*).

29. *Marrakesh Agreement Establishing the World Trade Organization*, opened for signature 15 April 1994, 1867 UNTS 3 (entered into force 1 January 1995), annex 2 (*Understanding on Rules and Procedures Governing the Settlement of Disputes*).

30. For a more detailed analysis on the possible relevance of the TPP proposal for investor–state challenges, see Strawbridge, above n 3, 10.

31. See President of the United State of America, 'Remarks by the President in the State of the Union Address' (Speech delivered at the State of the Union Address, Washington DC, 12 February 2013) <http://www.whitehouse.gov/the-press-office/2013/02/12/remarks-president-state-union-address>.

32. *Letter from the United States Trade Representative to John Boehner*, 20 March 2013 <http://www.ustr.gov/sites/default/files/03202013%20TTIP%20Notification%20Letter.PDF>.

33. See 'Dutch Vice Minister Sees Mid-2016 Conclusion for U.S.–EU Trade Deal' (2013) 31(9) *Inside US Trade* (online).

34. See European Commission, *Revision of the Tobacco Products Directive* (2013) <http://ec.europa.eu/health/tobacco/products/revision/>.

35. Ibid.

36. See European Commission, 'Questions and Answers: Towards a New EU Law on Tobacco Products' (Press Release, MEMO/12/1005, 19 December 2012) <http:// europa.eu/rapid/press-release_MEMO-12-1005_en.htm#footnote-2>.

37. In correspondence with the author, a Commission spokesman downplayed this aspect of its revision, saying that it is 'nothing new' because the current directive, which is silent on the issue, would not preclude member states from pursuing 'plain packaging' laws.

38. See 'Business Groups Seek USTR Help in Fighting Australian Cigarette Law' (2011) 29(25) *Inside US Trade* (online).

39. *Letter from Bob Stallman, American Farm Bureau Federation et al to HE João Vale de Almeida, Delegation of the European Union to the United States*, 5 April 2013 <http://insidetrade.com/iwpfile.html?file=apr2013%2Fwto2013_1207a.pdf>.

40. These tobacco representatives say they do not object to provisions in the *Tobacco Control Act* that call for 50 per cent of the front and back of cigarette packs to be taken up by health warnings.

PART III

Tobacco control around the world

11. Tobacco control in Europe: the potential for plain packaging

Peter K Henning and Leonid Shmatenko[*]

I INTRODUCTION

> The caption was done in distinctive cigarette-pack typeface, 'Hysterica Bold', they called it at the office. It said, WARNING: SOME PEOPLE WILL SAY ANYTHING TO SELL CIGARETTES.[1]

Ever since it was scientifically proven that smoking harms your health, legislators around the world have tried to enforce stricter tobacco control policy on the grounds of public health. Tobacco manufacturers, on the contrary, try to undermine this policy. The newest trend in tobacco control policy is the so-called plain packaging, a package with a standardised appearance containing large health warnings. Trademarks, logos, etc, are not allowed. Canada was the first government to try to introduce plain packaging in 1994. The introduction failed due to concerns regarding the trademark rights of the tobacco manufacturers. Concerns regarding violations of obligations under the law of the World Trade Organization (WTO)[2] and the *North American Free Trade Agreement*,[3] in particular, caused the Canadian Government to abandon the plans. A few years later, the United Kingdom wanted to introduce plain packaging. However, almost the same considerations led to the cancellation of these plans. Additionally, the British Government considered that the measures would possibly violate the prohibition on restrictions on free movement of goods within the European Union (EU) pursuant to article 34 of the *Treaty on the Functioning of the European Union* (TFEU).[4] On 28 November 2013, however, the British Department of Health requested an independent review of the current public health evidence on plain packaging. This review shall help the government to reach a renewed decision on plain packaging during 2014.[5]

Finally, Lithuania was the most recent EU member to try to introduce plain packaging, without success in Parliament.[6]

Despite the aforementioned failures, the EU is revising its Tobacco Product Directive[7] to give an opportunity for member states to introduce plain packaging.[8] This revision was supposed to be launched on 22 August 2012 so as to receive the Commission's approval in November 2012, just in time to be included in the European Parliament's (EP) work programme for 2013. However, the directive proposal was finally introduced on 19 December 2012.[9] The next step is the discussion of the proposal in the EP and in the Council of Ministers. It can be expected that the reformed Directive 2001/37/EC will be adopted in 2014 and will come into effect between 2015 and 2016.[10]

The proposal includes new regulations regarding ingredients and emissions, traceability and security features, tobacco for oral use, cross-border distance sales of tobacco products, novel tobacco products, nicotine-containing products and herbal products for smoking, as well as labelling and packaging. Even though it is not as intrusive as the current proposal, the 2001 Tobacco Product Directive has faced legal proceedings.[11] Thus, it might be assumed that the same will happen to the revision.

This chapter will focus on the labelling and packaging options proposed. Being the harshest option in the revised Directive, plain packaging will be examined in relation to compatibility with EU law, with special regard to article 34 TFEU and the *Charter of Fundamental Rights of the European Union* (CFRE).[12] The chapter will also evaluate the decisions of the Court of the European Free Trade Association (EFTA Court) in the context of food product labelling. If plain packaging is consistent with EU law, the consequence *argumentum a fortiori* is that any less severe measure is consistent with EU law as well.

II COMPETENCE OF THE EU TO INTRODUCE PLAIN PACKAGING

Upon being introduced, the first legal obstacle that plain packaging can expect is the threshold question of the competence of the EU Commission and the Parliament.

A Competence of the EU

A possible legal basis for plain packaging is article 114 TFEU or article 168 TFEU. Article 114 TFEU represents the most important article for the introduction of plain packaging as 'it empowers the EU to replace, by qualified majority vote, divergent national legislations with a common rule applicable across the whole territory'.[13] Contrary to the specific and tailored legal bases for fundamental freedoms or for certain political areas, article 114 TFEU must be construed broadly.[14] According to article 114(3) TFEU, the European legislator has special competence in relation to the amendment of existing directives, if for example there is a pre-eminent change in public and political opinion in relation to public health.[15] Even if competence is derived from article 114(3) TFEU, the power to legislate is still derived from article 114(1) TFEU.[16] Hence, when introducing plain packaging, the EU has to follow the prerequisites set forth in article 114 TFEU, that is, to guarantee formal and substantive legality of the proposed regulation.

B Formal Legality

The European Commission has the right to propose measures in regard to law coordination.[17] Whenever the European Commission makes a proposal according to article 114(1) TFEU, the European Parliament has to be heard. Thus, the common legislative procedure according to articles 289(1) and 294 TFEU has to be observed. Furthermore, the 'European Economic and Social Committee' must be consulted. Subsequently, the European Council votes on the regulation. Only if a qualified majority according to article 16(3) of the *Treaty on European Union* (TEU)[18] is reached will the regulation be enacted. There is no doubt that the European Commission will ensure these standards when passing a regulation on plain packaging. Hence, it can be assumed that plain packaging will be formally legal.

C Material Legality

When determining the material legality, an extensive test according to article 114 TFEU has to take place. This test requires: (a) the realisation of the aims set forth in article 26 TFEU, (b) through certain measures, (c) for the harmonisation of the legislation in the member states, (d) to achieve the creation and functioning of the internal market. Article 26(1) TFEU states that '[t]he Union shall adopt measures with the aim of establishing or ensuring the functioning of the internal market, in accordance with the relevant provisions of the Treaties'. Plain packaging ensures the functioning of the internal market, as harmonisation of tobacco regulations does in general. This issue has been subject to previous decisions of the Court of Justice of the European Union (ECJ).[19] According to article 288 TFEU, the EU's competences include regulations, directives, decisions, recommendations and opinions. As plain packaging would be introduced through an amendment of the existing Directive 2001/37/EC, this requirement would also be fulfilled.

Harmonisation means the subject-related approximation of national statutes to a harmonised European law standard. The main aim is the elimination of legal differences and the resulting distortion of competition.[20] It is evident that different EU members, although having adopted Directive 2001/37/EC, have different packaging requirements. For example, Spain has already introduced health warnings including coloured pictures,[21] whereas German regulations only require health warnings.[22] A mandatory common plain packaging layout would harmonise the fragmented national laws, thereby assisting with the functioning of the internal market. The discretion of member states has resulted in fragmentation. Thus, it is preferable that the EU makes plain packaging obligatory.

D   German Peculiarities Concerning the Relationship to EU Law

The ECJ and the *Bundesverfassungsgericht* (German Constitutional Court, or GCC) have diverging opinions on the direct application of EU law and domestic law. Especially in regard to the relationship between German constitutional law and EU law, some peculiarities have to be taken into account. The problem of a conflict of laws, however, arises only in the case of a direct application of EU law. Such cases are particularly EU regulations, which are directly applicable according to article 288(2) TFEU. The case for EU directives is slightly different. According to article 288(3) TFEU, directives must be transferred into domestic law. Subsequently, they form a part of national law and become directly applicable. The cornerstone of the dispute on the conflict of laws results from the lack of a dedicated regulation in the area. Hence, the courts have to decide how to treat such cases.

It is the ECJ's opinion that EU law prevails over national law, whether the national law is simple majority law or constitutional law.[23] In its first decision, the GCC adopted a comparable point of view. It held, however, that only directly applicable EU law prevails over national law. Whenever regulations subject to EU law are in dispute, the GCC does not have the competence to decide upon the matter.[24] In cases where courts are doubtful whether the national law violates EU law, they have the option to initiate proceedings at the ECJ pursuant to article 267 TFEU for a preliminary ruling.

Only three years later, the GCC amended and clarified its view in the so-called '*Solange-I*' (literally: 'as long as') case.[25] It still considered that EU law represented *lex specialis* to national law. However, as long as the

EU law did not guarantee comparable standards of protection of fundamental rights as the German *Grundgesetz* (Constitution), the boundaries of EU law were to be determined by the fundamental rights in the Constitution.[26] This evolution was confirmed in 1986 by the '*Solange-II*' case.[27] Any claims arising out of EU law, thus, should be claimed at the ECJ, as the GCC lacks competence.[28] This precedent has been followed by the GCC in its later cases and has been strengthened further.[29] Holding that EU law still provides the necessary standards of protection of fundamental rights, the GCC dismissed a case relating to Commission Regulation 2257/94/EC ('bendy banana law') in 2000.[30]

In this regard, special attention should be paid to the precedent of the *Treibhaus-Emissionsberechtigungen* of the GCC.[31] In this decision, the GCC ruled that if an EU member state does not have any discretion in regard to the implementation of an EU directive, the national courts should examine whether the EU law is compatible with the CFRE. Where necessary, the national courts should initiate a preliminary ruling according to article 267 TFEU.

With this insight into the rather complicated relationship between the GCC with European fundamental rights standards and its (absolute) aspirations regarding its own competence whenever fundamental rights are violated, the question becomes 'What does this mean for the case of plain packaging in regard to German constitutional law?' Assuming plain packaging is introduced by an amendment of the Directive 2001/37/EC, it will have to be transferred into national law. Thus, when making a claim pursuant to national law, tobacco manufacturers would first have to initiate proceedings at the GCC. The GCC would evaluate whether the national law was consistent with the fundamental rights of the Constitution[32] and the CFRE.[33] However, if the tobacco manufacturers aimed for the nullification of the directive, the GCC would have to initiate a preliminary ruling according to article 267 TFEU or a nullification proceeding according to article 263 TFEU at the ECJ. Here, the ECJ again would have to evaluate whether the directive violates any fundamental rights of the CFRE.

III RESTRICTIONS UNDER PRIMARY EU LAW

When introducing plain packaging, the EU legislator has to bear in mind restrictions of primary EU law. It would have to comply mainly with the CFRE and article 34 TFEU.[34] To date two disputes have reached the ECJ,[35] but neither of them dealt with fundamental rights or European freedoms. Instead, the cases dealt mainly with the competence of the EU to make regulations. Therefore, the next part of this chapter covers issues that any European court would have to consider when deciding on plain packaging.

A   Binding Nature of the Charter of the Fundamental Rights of the European Union and the European Freedoms

By the *Treaty of Lisbon*,[36] the CFRE became primary EU law according to article 6(1) TEU.[37] In its consistent precedent, the ECJ has established that the CFRE forms an integral part of the European Principles of Law. Thus, only measures complying with these rights can be regarded as legal.[38] However, the protection can be guaranteed only if the EU authority is competent and the measure taken by the legislator transnational.[39] Article 51(2) CFRE does 'not establish any new power or task for the Community or the Union, or modify powers and tasks defined by the Treaties'. A binding introduction of plain packaging in the EU member states would affect all tobacco manufacturers in the EU. Further, it would affect not only trade inside a single state, but also trade in the broader EU market. Therefore, the introduction of plain packaging would be a transnational task lying within EU competence.[40] As a result the CFRE would apply.

However, plain packaging may also interfere with the free movement of goods according to article 34 TFEU as part of the European freedoms. These are, like the CFRE, primary EU law, and they aim to protect trading inside the European internal market. The ECJ has repeatedly held that not only European member states but also EU legislators are bound by the European freedoms.[41]

B   Scope of Protection of Fundamental Rights in the CFRE

Any dispute arising from such an EU regulation – be it before a German court or the ECJ – would have to deal with three different fundamental rights: freedom of expression (article 11 CFRE), the right to property (article 17 CFRE), and the right to engage in work (article 15 CFRE). The extent to which these fundamental rights are violated by plain packaging is discussed in the following section.

1   Freedom of expression
According to article 11(1) CFRE, '[e]veryone has the right to freedom of expression', including 'freedom to hold opinions and to receive and impart information and ideas without interference by public authority and regardless of frontiers'. Article 11(1) CFRE closely replicates article 10

of the *European Convention on Human Rights* (ECHR).[42] According to article 52(3) CFRE, these provisions have the same 'meaning and scope'. Consequently, case law and scholarly works on article 10 ECHR can be consulted for the interpretation of article 11 CFRE.[43] Before evaluating the compatibility of plain packaging with the latter, it is important to distinguish between the different measures that would be introduced through plain packaging. In the context of article 11(1) CFRE and article 10 ECHR, the legitimacy of the extended health warnings and the messages associated with the plain packaging are relevant.

In relation to the scope of protection of article 11 CFRE, both the GCC and the ECJ dogmatically distinguish between a personal and an object-ive scope of protection.[44] These scopes determine the general applic-ability of the fundamental right with regard to the person claiming the infringement of the freedom of expression and to the facts of the case. The personal scope protects citizens of the European Union as well as legal entities thereof.[45] In contrast, the objective scope protects the freedom of expression itself. This principle is recognised within the ECHR and can also be transferred to the CFRE.[46] Regarding the objective scope of protection, the ECHR has established that the freedom of expression is guaranteed without making any distinction as to whether the aim of the statement is profit-making or not.[47] Therefore, commercial advertising is said to be included in the scope of application.[48] Thus, the present case of tobacco packaging enjoys the full protection of the freedom of expression.

The prescription of designs for cigarette packages and what may permissibly be written on them restricts tobacco manufacturers' freedom of speech and falls within the scope of application of article 11(1) CFRE.[49] However, whether the provision is violated has to be determined on a case-by-case basis. This involves an investigation into whether the EU legislator violates freedom of speech by prohibiting certain designs and by prescribing the print of health warnings.

2 The right to property

In addition to the enlargement of warning pictures and messages, plain packaging typically prohibits or restricts the use of logos, colours, brand images and brand names.[50] Those are trademarks of the respective tobacco manufacturers and thus their intellectual property. A prohibition to use them is a possible violation of their property rights. According to article 17(1) CFRE, '[e]veryone has the right to own, use, dispose of and bequeath his or her lawfully acquired possessions. No one may be deprived of his or her possessions, except in the public interest ... The use of property may be regulated by law in so far as is necessary for the general interest'. Additionally, article 17(2) CFRE clarifies that '[i]ntellectual property shall be protected'.

The personal scope of application of article 17 CFRE is comparable to that of article 11 CFRE. Article 1(1) of the *Protocol No 1 to ECHR on the Protection of Human Rights and Fundamental Freedoms*[51] provides that '[e]very natural or legal person is entitled to the peaceful enjoyment of his possessions',[52] thus protecting legal entities. Article 17(2) CFRE explicitly includes intellectual property such as patents and trademark rights.[53]

3   Freedom to conduct a business

Further, plain packaging might violate the right of the tobacco producers to freely conduct their business. As stated in article 16 CFRE, '[t]he freedom to conduct a business in accordance with Community law and national laws and practices is recognized'. According to scholars, article 16 CFRE is an autonomous right and *lex specialis* to article 15 CFRE,[54] especially protecting freedom of competition and advertising.[55] To secure effective protection of fundamental rights, freedom of advertising and freedom of expression as stipulated in article 11 CFRE can be applied simultaneously.[56]

Even though the scope of the rights guaranteed by article 16 CFRE has not yet been expressly determined by the ECJ, it can be derived from the relevant case law, which suggests a broad scope of application.[57] Applying this broad understanding, plain packaging falls within the scope of article 16 CFRE.

C   Infringements through Plain Packaging

Following the Guidelines for Implementation (Guidelines) of the WHO *Framework Convention on Tobacco Control* (WHO FCTC),[58] plain packaging should be considered by 'adopting measures to restrict or prohibit the use of logos, colors, brand images or promotional information on packaging other than brand names and product names displayed in a standard color and font style'.[59] Australia followed this guidance faithfully and was promptly sued by *Philip Morris*. Once introduced in the EU, the same could happen to the European Commission.

By dictating that tobacco manufacturers use plain packaging, the legislator prohibits tobacco producers from creating their individual cigarette packages. Indeed, producers are obliged to print health warnings and messages that do not correspond to their views. Additionally, the brand name is presented in a standardised style, and graphic logos are prohibited. Such measures are severe violations of tobacco manufacturers' freedom of expression.[60] As discussed above, both are protected by article 11(1) CFRE.

The most severe violation of the right to property possible according to article 17(1) CFRE is an expropriation, meaning the complete and permanent deprivation of property.[61] Plain packaging, however, only prohibits the use of logos and brand names on cigarette packs. This means that they can still be used by the tobacco manufacturers for any other form of marketing allowed in the relevant jurisdiction, for example posters, postcards, bookmarks, pens, etc, as well as for internal use. As there is no further limitation, plain packaging alone does not constitute a complete and permanent deprivation of trademarks. However, one might argue that such a prohibition of usage amounts to a so-called de facto expropriation.[62] This – in contrast to a formal expropriation – does not require the deprivation of ownership but instead requires that the position of the property owner is reduced to a minimum, such that an exploitation of rights is no longer possible.[63] This requires that a court 'look behind the appearances and investigate the realities of the situation',[64] that is, a case-by-case decision. Tobacco manufacturers are deprived of 'any reasonable method of marketing'[65] with respect to the use of their brand names and logos on cigarette packs. However, there are no other prohibitions interwoven with plain packaging, as brand names and logos can still be used for other marketing purposes.[66] In view of this fact, it seems difficult to find a de facto expropriation through plain packaging, despite contrary arguments by some legal scholars.[67]

Measures having a direct effect on a right holder, for example penalty payments, constitute an infringement of article 16 CFRE[68] if they have 'a sufficiently direct and significant effect on freedom to exercise a trade'.[69]

The ECJ has stated that:

[t]rade mark rights are … an essential element in the system of undistorted competition which the Treaty seeks to establish and maintain. Under such a system, an undertaking must be in a position to keep its customers by virtue of the quality of its products and services, something which is possible only if there are distinctive marks which enable customers to identify those products and services.[70]

Based on this argument, some German and Austrian legal scholars assume that plain packaging would constitute a sufficiently direct and significant effect on freedom to exercise a trade.[71] Further, if trademarks are less significant, this may lead to isolation of national markets. Introduction of tobacco products into new markets would be hindered, as customers may lose the capability to distinguish between different tobacco brands.[72] Indeed, packaging is said to be vital in tobacco marketing,[73] as it is very difficult for smokers to distinguish the brands just by the taste of the cigarette.[74]

However, if the measure affects the right holder only indirectly, or if the effect of the legislative act is collateral, an infringement is not made out,[75] because the measure only affects economic development and not the right holder itself. This is part of the entrepreneurial risk.[76]

Two cases decided by the ECJ concerning wine labelling are noteworthy in this respect. In both cases, the ECJ stated that even minor regulations in regard to labelling amount to interferences with the freedom to conduct a business and thus require justification.[77] The provisions at issue in *SMW Winzersekt v Land Rheinland-Pfalz* laid down general rules for the description of sparkling wines and aerated sparkling wines.[78] The ECJ stated in that regard that:

> provisions affect only the arrangements governing the exercise of that right and do not jeopardize its very existence … It is for that reason necessary to determine whether those provisions pursue objectives of general interest, do not affect the position of producers such as Winzersekt in a disproportionate manner and, consequently, whether the Council exceeded the limits of its discretion in this case.

However, those provisions were considerably less intensive than plain packaging, which requires a certain layout for the whole cigarette package. In consequence, as plain packaging is more intrusive than the regulations discussed in *SMW Winzersekt v Land Rheinland-Pfalz*, it is likely that the ECJ would discern an infringement and require a justification.

D   Justification

Plain packaging constitutes a severe violation of tobacco manufacturers' rights. However, the CFRE allows the justification of such measures according to article 10(2) ECHR, article 17(1) CFRE and article 16 CFRE. In regard to freedom of expression, the relevant justification is stipulated in article 10(2) ECHR, which provides that '[t]he exercise of … freedoms … may be subject to such formalities, conditions, restrictions or penalties as are prescribed by law and are necessary in the interests of … public safety [and] the protection of health or morals'.

In *Vereinigte Familiapress Zeitungsverlags- und vertriebs GmbH v Heinrich Bauer Verlag*,[79] the ECJ held that the justification of article 10(2) ECHR on the grounds of public health also applies to article 11(1)

CFRE. This leads to the conclusion that the violation of freedom of expression according to article 11(1) CFRE is justifiable on the grounds of public health as well.

Further, the requirements of article 52(1) and (2) CFRE have to be read in addition to the justification possibilities, which can be derived from the corresponding articles.[80] However, due to article 52(3) CFRE, these justification requirements do not apply to article 11 CFRE in connection with article 10(2) ECHR.[81]

Article 16 CFRE requires 'accordance with Community law and national laws and practices'. This gives the legislator a wide scope to limit the right to conduct a business.[82]

Additionally, the freedoms contained in article 16 CFRE may be limited subject to the justification requirements contained in article 52(1) and (2) CFRE, which provide:

1. Any limitation on the exercise of the rights and freedoms recognised by this Charter must be provided for by law and respect the essence of those rights and freedoms. Subject to the principle of proportionality, limitations may be made only if they are necessary and genuinely meet objectives of general interest recognised by the Union or the need to protect the rights and freedoms of others.

2. Rights recognised by this Charter for which provision is made in other Parts of the Constitution shall be exercised under the conditions and within the limits defined by these relevant Parts.

Hence, article 52(1) CFRE requires the maintenance of a minimum level of protection; ie a person may not be completely deprived of the relevant right.[83] Thus, per se, a measure is only unjustified if the essence of the freedom or right is undermined. However, it still is unclear what the essence of those rights and freedoms is.[84]

Even though it is likely that there is an infringement of article 16 CFRE, tobacco manufacturers are still able to use the trademark for other purposes.[85] Hence, the infringement is not so severe as to leave an empty shell and deprive the right of its essence.

As discussed above, there is no infringement of article 17(1) CFRE. However, even if one assumes such an infringement, it is justifiable by the exceptions in article 17(1) CFRE and article 1(1) of the Protocol No 1 to ECHR in connection with article 52 CFRE. These provisions declare that the right to property can be restricted in the 'public interest', ie public health, subject to a three-step test requiring the suitability, necessity and proportionality of the relevant measure.[86]

1 Suitability

In introducing new regulations, legislators have a wide discretion in selecting suitable measures.[87] Although tobacco manufacturers still challenge the suitability of plain packaging, this measure clearly affects individuals looking at cigarette packages,[88] thus making it not completely unsuitable to protect public health. Nevertheless, some European scholarly opinions state that plain packaging is not suitable due to the fact that all cigarette packs would have the same appearance, diminishing the deterrent effect.[89] Even in 1995 there were already numerous studies providing evidence that plain packaging is likely to reduce tobacco use.[90] These studies were recently confirmed.[91] Thus, this argument is unconvincing.

2 Necessity

Necessity means that the measure may not go beyond what is necessary to achieve its declared objective, that is, protection of public health.[92] Thus, the crucial question is whether an alternative measure exists that can achieve the same level of protection of public health as plain packaging, while being less intrusive than the latter.[93] Alternative measures include display bans in shops and malls or tobacco tax increases. However, when applying a critical point of view, it is clear that both alternatives would also limit the fundamental rights of tobacco manufacturers.[94]

Further, the business value of any tobacco manufacturer lies in its packaging, making it the most important feature in the marketing process, especially when trying to attract young people. Once opened, packages are often used and then regularly presented in public.[95] Thus packaging is a form of 'mobile advertising of the brand'.[96] This effect cannot be prevented by a display ban or a tax increase. Therefore, there is no other suitable measure.

3 Proportionality

Additionally, plain packaging has to be proportional, which requires weighing the burdens against the objectives that the measure pursues.[97] In the case of plain packaging, the interest of the EU legislator is to protect public health, while the interest of tobacco manufacturers is to increase sales and market share.

According to a decision of the ECJ, 'the protection of public health ... must take precedence over economic considerations'.[98] Therefore, there are high hurdles to overcome for tobacco manufacturers' freedom of expression to prevail over public health.[99] Considering the dangerous nature of tobacco products, extended health warnings are not an unacceptable burden for tobacco manufacturers.[100] An extension of warning measures is more lenient than a complete ban on sales.

With regard to freedom of expression, it is also important for the purpose of marketing and advertising to distinguish between statements and messages of individuals and those expressed by legal entities, which receive lesser protection. As stated by the ECJ, 'particularly in a field as complex and fluctuating as advertising', the review of the measure is 'limited'[101] and the protection of rights can be reduced.[102] Thus, tobacco manufacturers may not rely on the full scope of protection in regard to their advertising activities.

Plain packaging can diminish the effect of tobacco marketing on children and adolescents.[103] Recent studies regarding advertisements demonstrate that children and adolescents are not capable of evaluating advertisements.[104] Previous studies dealing with the advertisement of the Camel brand with Joe Camel showed that children watching the advertisement were more likely to report prior exposure to the Joe Camel cartoon character than children who did not watch the advertisement, and were better able to identify the type of product being advertised and the Camel cigarette brand name than other cigarette brand names.[105] Further, in 1991, children found the Camel cigarette advertisements more appealing than other cigarette advertisements, and the share held by Camel of the illegal children's cigarette market in five regions of the United States increased from 0.5 per cent to 32.8 per cent in three years, representing sales estimated at US$476 million per annum.[106] This shows the significance of advertisements and cigarette packs and their impact upon children and adolescent cigarette consumption. Such an impact has to be prevented, to ensure that the protection of public health prevails over economic considerations. Thus, plain packaging represents a proportional measure to prevent not only adults from smoking, but also children and adolescents.[107]

4 Additional requirements

Additional to the requirements mentioned above, article 17(1) CFRE calls for reasonable compensation in the case of the deprivation of rights (but not other interferences). This payment has to be made in 'good time' and is part of the test of adequacy.[108] It is yet to be determined if the European legislator will offer compensation to tobacco manufacturers, and no political discussion has been initiated on this topic.

E   Free Movement of Goods

Plain packaging, as envisioned by the EU Commission, might also violate the free movement of goods stipulated in article 34 TFEU. According to this provision, '[q]uantitative restrictions on imports and all measures having equivalent effect shall be prohibited between Member States'.

1   Scope of protection of article 34 TFEU

The scope of protection of article 34 TFEU has objective and personal elements. The personal scope of protection, however, is not applicable to plain packaging, because the provision only protects the free movement of goods.[109] The objective scope of protection is defined by the term 'goods' mentioned in article 28(2) TFEU.[110] Goods are 'products which can be valued in money and which are capable, as such, of forming the subject of commercial transactions'.[111] Correspondingly, tobacco products as well as their packs are goods within the meaning of article 34 TFEU and thus fall within the objective scope of protection.

2   Infringement of the free movement of goods

Infringements of article 34 TFEU cover (a) restrictions upon import quantities[112] and (b) 'measures having equivalent effect'.[113] Plain packaging does not quantitatively restrict the importation of cigarettes or cigarette packets.

Thus, the requirements of article 34 TFEU would be fulfilled only if plain packaging is a 'measure having equivalent effect'. As stated by the ECJ, equivalent measures are able to weaken the European trade flow, whether this effect is direct or indirect, actual or potential (*Dassonville*).[114] Plain packaging is aimed at reducing the number of active smokers and thus also tends to reduce trade in cigarettes in general. Therefore, it is able to potentially weaken the European trade flow indirectly and thus represents an equivalent measure.

Since its *Keck* decision, the ECJ additionally distinguishes in this regard between selling arrangements and product-bound measures. As the cigarette pack, however, is so closely related to the actual product, the introduction of plain packaging must be seen as a product-bound measure requiring a justification.[115]

3   Justification

An infringement of article 34 TFEU can be justified on grounds of public health according to article 36 TFEU. However, again, the requirements of the three-step test of adequacy have to be met.[116] Article 36 TFEU sets forth that the measure 'shall not ... constitute a means of arbitrary discrimination or a disguised restriction on trade between Member States'.

(a) Three-step test of adequacy As shown, plain packaging is suitable, necessary and proportional.[117] For article 36 TFEU, however, the protection of human health plays a major role. In the EFTA Court decision *Philip Morris Norway AS v Staten v/Helse- og omsorgsdepartementet* addressing a tobacco display ban, the court stated regarding article 13 of the Agreement on the European Economic Area (EEA),[118] which is similar to article 36 TFEU:

> [a]ccording to settled case-law, the health and life of humans rank foremost among the assets or interests protected by Article 13 EEA ... Legislation which aims at controlling the consumption of tobacco with a view to preventing the harmful effects caused to the health of humans by tobacco products clearly reflects, in the view of the Court, health concerns recognised by Article 13 EEA.[119]

Even though the ECJ is not bound by the decision of the EFTA Court, particularly in regard to the *Philip Morris Norway AS v Staten v/ Helse- og omsorgsdepartementet* case, which addressed display bans of tobacco products, it can be assumed that the European Economic Area (including the European Union) pays special attention to public health concerns. Thus, the judgment of the EFTA Court might nevertheless influence future decisions of the ECJ. It might also be assumed that the ECJ will adopt similar reasoning in assessing the justification for plain packaging.

(b) Disguised restriction and arbitrary discrimination A disguised restriction can only be assumed if the intended purpose of the measure is protectionism.[120] However, this is not the intention of plain packaging. Finally, the standards for arbitrary discrimination are high as it has to be unambiguous.[121] Plain packaging aims for the harmonisation of cigarette packs throughout the EU and it is not to be expected that tobacco manufacturers would face discrimination by competitive distortions. Thus, as the requirements of article 36 TFEU are met, one has to assume that in case of a decision the ECJ will not establish a violation of the free movement of goods.

IV CONCLUSION

As *Dalligate*[122] has passed, the new European Commissioner for Health and Consumer Policy Tonio Borg inherited the invidious task to enforce the WHO FCTC Guidelines into European legislation without becoming a victim of heavy lobbying. Although the current proposal of the reformed Directive 2001/37/EC is much less severe than expected and feared by tobacco manufacturers, it still empowers member states to introduce plain packaging. Even if plain packaging is not introduced, the proposal provides regulations prescribing combined warnings (picture plus text) of 75 per cent displayed on both sides of the packages of tobacco products, presented in rotation. Such a design of tobacco packs may provoke legal proceedings against the European Commission.

Hence, plain packaging is not unproblematic in the EU legal context. It involves an apparent infringement of fundamental rights of the tobacco manufacturers. Thus, its introduction will be a balancing act between regulatory measures and fundamental rights, as trademarks are valuable to their owners. However, public health is also a public good, which may be protected by almost any means, making plain packaging justifiable.

Bearing this in mind, the EU is proceeding with the implementation of the WHO FCTC Guidelines, by reforming Directive 2001/37/EC. The main aim of the EU will be to survive the legal war of the tobacco manufacturers, who will be using all available instruments such as lobbying, investment claims and aggressive advertising campaigns to undermine plain packaging. Once a court decision permitting plain packaging has been made, the way for plain packaging will be definitively cleared.

NOTES

*   This chapter is an extended version of the article: Peter K Henning and Leonid Shmatenko, 'Plain Packaging on its Way to Europe: Competence Issues and Compatibility with European Fundamental Rights' (2012) 9 *Transnational Dispute Management*, <http://www.transnational-dispute-management.com/article.asp?key=1888>. The authors would like to thank Heiko Sauer and Andrew Hammel for their rich feedback on this chapter.

1.   Christopher Buckley, *Thank You for Smoking* (Allison & Busby, 2003) 9.
2.   For the compatibility of plain packaging with WTO law cf Tania Voon and Andrew D Mitchell, 'Implications of WTO Law for Plain Packaging of Tobacco Products' in Tania Voon, Andrew D Mitchell and Jonathan Liberman with Glyn Ayres (eds), *Public Health and Plain Packaging of Cigarettes: Legal Issues* (Edward Elgar, 2012) 109.

3. *North American Free Trade Agreement*, opened for signature 17 December 1992, 32 ILM 289, 605 (1993) (entry into force 1 January 1994); Report of the Standing Committee on Health, *Towards Zero Consumption – Generic Packaging of Tobacco Products* (June 1994); Expert Panel Report Prepared at the Request of Health Canada, *When Packages Can't Speak: Possible Impacts of Plain and Generic Packaging of Tobacco Products* (March 1995) <http://www.legacy.library.ucsf.edu/documentStore/r/c/e/rce50d00/Srce50d00.pdf>; Excerpt of the Statement of the Minister of Health of Canada David Dingwall at the House of Commons of Canada from 6 December 1996 (1996) <http://www.parl.gc.ca/Content/HOC/Archives/Committee/352/sant/evidence/25_96-12-06/sant25_blk-e.html>.

4. Treaty on the Functioning of the European Union, opened for signature 7 February 1992, [2009] OJ C115/199 (entered into force 1 November 1993) (TFEU); HM Government, *A Smokefree Future – A Comprehensive Tobacco Control Strategy for England* (2010) 39 No 3.26 <http://webarchive.nationalarchives.gov.uk/20100509080731/http://dh.gov.uk/prod_consum_dh/groups/dh_digitalassets/@dh/@en/@ps/documents/digitalasset/dh_111789.pdf>.

5. Parliamentary Under Secretary of State, United Kingdom Department of Health, *Written Ministerial Statement: Tobacco Control Update* (28 November 2013) United Kingdom Parliament <http://www.parliament.uk/documents/commons-vote-office/November-2013/28%20November/7-Health-TobaccoControl.pdf>; United Kingdom Department of Health, 'Independent Review of Standardised Packaging for Tobacco' (Press Release, 28 November 2013) <https://www.gov.uk/government/news/independent-review-of-standardised-packaging-for-tobacco>.

6. Kristina Janušauskaitė, 'Litauen – A Proposal to Introduce "Plain Packaging Requirement" in the Law on Tobacco Control Fails in Parliament' (2010) 10 *Gerwerblicher Rechtsschutz und Urheberrecht Internationaler Teil* 908.

7. *Council Directive 2001/37/EC of the European Parliament and of the Council of 5 June 2001 on the Approximation of the Laws, Regulations and Administrative Provisions of the Member States Concerning the Manufacture, Presentation and Sale of Tobacco Products* [2001] OJ L 194/26.

8. *European Commission Proposal for a Directive of the European Parliament and of the Council on the Approximation of the Laws, Regulations and Administrative Provisions of the Member States Concerning the Manufacture, Presentation and Sale of Tobacco and Related Products of 19 December 2012*, COM/2012/0788. See also Reinhard Pauling, 'Nichtraucherschutz in der EU soll verbessert werden' (2010) 2 *Europäische Zeitschrift für Wirtschaftsrecht* 42; 'Europäische Union – Kommission erwägt Einführung genormter Einheitsverpackungen' (2010) 12 *Gewerblicher Rechtsschutz und Urheberrecht Internationaler Teil* 1110; Fabian Ziegenaus, 'No Logo? Pläne der EU-Kommission zu Zigaretten in Einheitsverpackungen auf dem Prüfstand' (2010) 21 *Gewerblicher Rechtsschutz und Urheberrecht. Praxis im Immaterialgüter – und Wettbewerbsrecht* 475; Alberto Alemanno, 'Out of Sight, Out of Mind – Towards a New EU Tobacco Products Directive' (2012) 18 *Columbia Journal of European Law* 197.

9. European Commission, 'Tobacco Products: Towards Bigger Health Warnings and Ban of Strong Flavourings', 19 December 2012, <http://www.europa.eu/rapid/press-release_IP-12-1391_en.htm#PR_metaPressRelease_bottom>.

10. Ibid.

11. *The Queen v Secretary of State for Health, ex parte British American Tobacco (Investments) Ltd and Imperial Tobacco Ltd* (C-491/01) [2002] ECR I-11453.

12. *Charter of Fundamental Rights of the European Union*, opened for signature 7 December 2000, [2000] OJ C 364/01 (entered into force 1 December 2009).

13. Nicolas de Sadeleer, 'Procedures for Derogation from the Principle of Approximation of Laws under Article 95 EC' (2003) 40 *Common Market Law Review* 889; see also Alemanno, above n 8.
14. Christian Tietje in Eberhard Grabitz Meinhard Hilf and Martin Nettesheim (eds), *Das Recht der Europäischen Union* (CH Beck, 46th ed, 2011), commentary on article 114 TFEU, margin no 3.
15. *British American Tobacco* (C-491/01), above n 11, [80].
16. Tietje, above n 14, article 114 TFEU, margin no 113.
17. Wolfgang Kahl in Christian Callies and Matthias Ruffert (eds), *EUV/AEUV: Das Verfassungsrecht der Europäischen Union mit Europäischer Grundrechtecharta – Kommentar* (CH Beck, 4th ed, 2011), commentary on article 115 TFEU, margin no 32.
18. *Consolidated Version of the Treaty on European Union*, opened for signature 7 February 1992, [2012] OJ C326/01 (entered into force 1 November 1993).
19. Cf also Alemanno, above n 8, 4.
20. See also, with further references: Kahl, above n 17, article 115 TFEU, margin no 13.
21. Tobacco Labeling Resource Center, Spain <http://www.tobaccolabels.ca/countries/spain>.
22. Tobacco Labeling Resource Center, Germany <http://www.tobaccolabels.ca/countries/germany>.
23. *Flaminio Costa v ENEL* (C-6/64) [1964] ECR I-1251, 1269, margin no 8 et seq, 12; *Amministrazione delle finanze dello Stato v Simmenthal* (C-106/77) [1978] ECR I-629, 643 et seq.
24. *Milchpulver*, Bundesverfassungsgericht [German Constitutional Court], 2 BvR 255/69, 9 June 1971 reported in (1971) 31 BVerfGE 145, 173 et seq.
25. *Internationale Handelsgesellschaft von Einfuhr- und Vorratsstelle für Getreide und Futtermittel ('Solange-I')*, Bundesverfassungsgericht [German Constitutional Court], BvL 52/71, 29 May 1974 reported in (1974) 37 BVerfGE 271.
26. Ibid 279.
27. *Re Wuensche Handelsgesellschaft ('Solange-II')*, Bundesverfassungsgericht [German Constitutional Court], 2 BvR 197/83, 22 October 1986 reported in (1986) 73 BVerfGE 339.
28. Cf ibid 366 et seq.
29. *Maastricht*, Bundesverfassungsgericht [German Constitutional Court], 2 BvR 2134, 2159/92, 12 October 1993 reported in (1993) 89 BVerfGE 155.
30. Cf *Bananenmarktverordnung*, Bundesverfassungsgericht [German Constitutional Court], 2 BvL 1/97, 7 June 2000 reported in (2000) 102 BVerfGE 147.
31. *Treibhausgas-Emissionsberechtigungen*, Bundesverfassungsgericht [German Constitutional Court], 1 BvF 1/05, 13 March 2007, reported in (2007) 118 BVerfGE 79, 97.
32. On the compatibility of plain packaging with German constitutional law see Leonid Shmatenko, 'Verfassungsmäßigkeit von Einheitsverpackungen (*Plain Packaging*) bei Zigaretten' (2013) 35 *Jura* 74.
33. See above n 31.
34. Hans Jarass, *EU-Grundrechte* (CH Beck, 2005) 27.
35. *Salamander AG, Una Film "City Revue" GmbH, Alma Media Group Advertising SA & Co Partnership, Panel Two and Four Advertising SA, Rythmos Outdoor Advertising SA, Media Center Advertising SA, Zino Davidoff SA and Davidoff & Cie SA v European Parliament and Council of the European Union* (T-172/98 and T-175/98 to 177/98) [2000] ECR II-02487; *Federal Republic of Germany v European Parliament and Council of the European Union* (C-380/03) [2006] ECR I-11573.

36. *Treaty of Lisbon*, opened for signature 17 December 2007, OJ [2007] C 306/01 (entered into force 1 December 2009).
37. Eckhard Pasche and Franziska Roesch 'Europäischer Grundrechtsschutz nach Lissabon – die Rolle der EMRK und der Grundrechtecharta in der EU' (2008) *Europäische Zeitschrift für Wirtschaftsrecht* 519.
38. *J Nold, Kohlen- und Baustoffgroßhandlung v Commission of the European Communities* (C-4/73) [1974] ECR 491, margin no 13.
39. Hans-Werner Rengeling and Peter Szczekalla, *Grundrechte in der Europäischen Union – Charta der Grundrechte und Allgemeine Rechtsgrundsätze* (Carl Heymanns Verlag, 2004) 22.
40. See above section II C.
41. See also, with further references, Michael Schweitzer, Yves Bock and Werner Schroeder, *EG-Binnenmarkt und Gesundheitsschutz – Am Beispiel der neuen Tabakrichtlinie der Europäischen Gemeinschaft* (Verlag Recht und Wirtschaft, 2002) 110.
42. *European Convention on Human Rights*, opened for signature 4 November 1950, European Treaty Series 5 (entered into force 3 September 1953).
43. Dirk Ehlers, 'Allgemeine Lehren der Unionsgrundrechte' in Dirk Ehlers (ed), *Europäische Grundrechte und Grundfreiheiten* (Walter de Gruyter, 3rd ed, 2009) 443, 445.
44. Cf Christian Callies in Callies and Ruffert, above n 17, commentary on article 11 CFRE, from margin no 3 et seq.
45. Dirk Ehlers, *European Fundamental Rights and Freedoms* (Walter de Gruyter, 2007) sec 7, margin no 101.
46. *Vereinigte Familiapress Zeitungsverlags- und vertriebs GmbH v Heinrich Bauer Verlag* (C-368/95) [1997] ECR I-3689; Juergen Kuehling, 'Kommunikationsfreiheit (Meinungsäußerungs- und Informationsfreiheit)' in Sebastian Heselhaus and Carsten Nowak (eds), *Handbuch der Europäischen Grundrechte* (CH Beck, 2006) 664.
47. *Coca v Spain* (1994) 285 Eur Court HR (ser A) margin no 35 et seq.
48. Kuehling, above n 46, 686.
49. Cf Schweitzer, Bock and Schroeder, above n 41, 94 et seq.
50. World Health Organization, *Guidelines for Implementation of the WHO Framework Convention on Tobacco Control* (2013) 59 <http://apps.who.int/iris/bitstream/10665/80510/1/9789241505185_eng.pdf>.
51. *Protocol to the Convention for the Protection of Human Rights and Fundamental Freedoms*, opened for signature 20 March 1952, European Treaty Series 9 (entered into force 18 May 1954).
52. Cf also Jarass, above n 34, article 17 CFRE, margin no 17.
53. Rengeling and Szczekalla, above n 39, 632.
54. See also, with further references: Nowak, above n 46, 664; Jarass, above n 34, article 16 CFRE, margin no 4.
55. Nowak, above n 46, 664.
56. Ruffert, 'Grundrecht der Berufsfreiheit' in Ehlers, above n 43, 581.
57. Ibid 585, with further references to case law.
58. Opened for signature 16 June 2003, 2302 UNTS 166 (entered into force 27 February 2005).
59. *Guidelines for Implementation of the WHO Framework Convention on Tobacco Control*, above n 50, 59.
60. Matthias Horst and Joachim Bergmann, 'Erklärung des Rechtsausschusses des Bundes für Lebensmittelrecht eV (BLL) zu Einheitspackung als Instrument des Vebraucherschutzes' (2012) 4 *Zeitschrift für das gesamte Lebensmittelrecht* 405, 416 et seq.
61. See also, with further references, Jarass, above n 34, article 17 CFRE, margin no 18.

62. Alemanno, above n 8, at 39.
63. *Sporrong and Lönnroth v Sweden* (1982) 52 Eur Ct HR (Ser A), margin no 63; Jarass, above n 34, article 17 CFRE, margin no 18.
64. Jarass, above n 34, margin no 18.
65. *Regione autonoma Friuli-Venezia Giulia and Agenzia regionale per lo sviluppo rurale (ERSA) v Ministero delle Politiche Agricole e Forestali* (C-347/03), [2005] ECR I-3785, margin no 122.
66. Cf Alemanno, above n 8, 39.
67. Horst and Bergmann, above n 60, 390; Schroeder, above n 60, 412 et seq.
68. *Metronome Musik GmbH v Music Point Hokamp GmbH* (C-200/96) [1998] ECR I-1953, margin no 28.
69. *Zeitungsverlag Niederrhein GmbH & Co Essen KG and Axel Springer AG v Hans-Jürgen Weske* (C-435/02 and C-103/03) [2004] ECR I-8663, margin no 49.
70. *SA CNL-SUCAL NV v HAG GF AG* (C-10/89) [1990] ECR I-3711, margin no 13.
71. Horst and Bergmann, above n 60, 391; Schroeder, above n 60, 417.
72. Horst and Bergmann, above n 60, 391; Schroeder, above n 60, 417.
73. Henry Aubin, 'Are "Generic" Packs Cigarettes' Future?', *The Gazette* (Canada), 8 November 1989, Legacy Tobacco Documents Library, <http://legacy.library.ucsf.edu/tid/per26a99>.
74. British American Tobacco, *The Vanishing Media* (1978), Legacy Tobacco Documents Library, <http://www.legacy.library.ucsf.edu/tid/jlf17a99/pdf>.
75. Jarass, above n 34, article 16 CFRE, margin no 13. See also Carsten Nowak, 'Unternehmerische Freiheit und Wettbewerbsfreiheit' in Heselhaus and Nowak, above n 46, 893.
76. Jarass, above n 34, article 16 CFRE, margin no 13.
77. *Staatsanwalt [Public Prosecutor] Freiburg v Franz Keller* (C-234/85), [1986] ECR I-2897, margin no 3; *SMW Winzersekt GmbH v Land Rheinland-Pfalz* (C-306/93), [1994] ECR, I-5555, margin no 24.
78. *Staatsanwalt [Public Prosecutor] Freiburg v Franz Keller* (C-234/85), [1986] ECR I-2897, margin no 3.
79. *Vereinigte Familiapress Zeitungsverlags- und vertriebs GmbH v Heinrich Bauer Verlag* (C-368/95), above n 46, margin no 26; Schweitzer, Bock and Schroeder, above n 41, 94–7.
80. Sebastian Heselhaus, 'Eigentumsgrundrecht', in Heselhaus and Nowak (eds), above n 46, 929.
81. Christian Callies in Christian Callies and Matthias Ruffert (eds), above n 17, commentary on article 11 CFRE, margin no 28 (with further references).
82. Jarass, above n 34, article 16 CFRE, margin no 18.
83. See, eg, *Hubert Wachauf v Federal Republic of Germany, represented by the Bundesamt für Ernährung und Forstwirtschaft (Federal Office for Food and Forestry)* (C-5/88), [1989] ECR, 2633 [17]; *Hermann Schräder HS Kraftfutter GmbH & Co KG, Ochtrup (Federal Republic of Germany) v Hauptzollamt Gronau* (C-265/87), [1989] ECR 2263 [15]; *Federal Republic of Germany v Council of the European Union* (C-280/93), [1994] ECR I-4973 [78].
84. Thorsten Kingreen in Christian Callies and Matthias Ruffert (eds), above n 17, commentary on article 52 CFRE, margin no 64.
85. See above section III A.
86. Rengeling and Szczekalla, above n 39, 247 with further references to case law of the European Court of Human Rights.
87. Schweitzer, Bock and Schroeder, above n 41, 97.
88. Denying the impact of health warnings on customers, see Felix Hardach and Markus Ludwigs, 'Die Novellierung der Warnhinweispflicht für Tabakerzeugnisse

im Lichte der negative Meinungsfreiheit – Eine grundrechtliche Neubewertung' (2007) 7 *Die Öffentliche Verwaltung* 288, 294.

89. Schroeder, above n 60, 414 citing H Sattler, 'Einheitspackungen und Konsumentenverhalten', (Speech delivered at the seminar 'Plain Packaging', Frankfurt am Main, Germany, 28 June 2012, sponsored by British American Tobacco and Philip Morris GmbH).

90. Rob Cunningham and Ken Kyle, 'The Case for Plain Packaging', (1995) 4 *Tobacco Control* 80, 81.

91. Daniella Germain, Melanie Wakefield and Sarah Durkin, 'Adolescents' Perceptions of Cigarette Brand Image: Does Plain Packaging Make a Difference?' (2010) 46 *Journal of Adolescent Health* 385; D Hammond, '"Plain Packaging" Regulations for Tobacco Products: The Impact of Standardizing the Color and Design of Cigarette Packs' (2010) *Salud Pública de México* 52.

92. Rengeling and Szczekalla, above n 39, 247; *Maizena Gesellschaft mbH v Bundesanstalt für landwirtschaftliche Marktordnung (BALM)* (C-137/85), [1987] ECR 4587, margin no 15.

93. Hans Jarass, *New Dimensions of Tobacco Regulation and Fundamental Rights and Freedoms: Basic Questions of Brand Packaging, Product Display and Product Ingredients* (lexxion, 2012) 107.

94. See further Shmatenko, above n 32.

95. Alberto Alemanno and Enrico Bonadio, 'Do You Mind My Smoking? Plain Packaging of Cigarettes under the TRIPS Agreement' (2011) 10(3) *The John Marshall Review of Intellectual Property Law* 451, 455.

96. Ibid 451, 454.

97. Jarass, above n 93, 106.

98. *Affish BV v Rijksdienst voor de Keuring van Vee en Vlees* (C-183/95), [1997] ECR I-4362, margin no 43.

99. Cf also *United Kingdom v Commission of the European Communities* (C-180/96 R), [1996] ECR I-3903, margin no 93; *Warnhinweise für Tabakerzeugnisse*, Bundesverfassungsgericht [German Constitutional Court], 2 BvR 1915/91, 22 January 1997 reported in (1997) 95 BVerfGE 173, 184.

100. Cf Helmut Siekmann 'Verfassungsmäßigkeit eines umfassenden Verbots der Werbung für Tabakprodukte' (2003) 16 *Die Öffentliche Verwaltung* 662.

101. *Herbert Karner Industrie-Auktionen GmbH v Troostwijk GmbH* (C-71/02), [2004] ECR I-3054, margin no 51.

102. Cf Siekmann, above n 100, 662.

103. Ibid.

104. Anne van Aaken, *Begrenzte Rationalität und Paternalismusgefahr: Das Prinzip des schonenden Paternalismus* (Max Planck Society, 2006) 1; Crawford Moodie et al, 'Young People's Perceptions of Cigarette Packaging and Plain Packaging: An Online Survey' (2012) 1 *Nicotine & Tobacco Research* 98; Janne Scheffels and Gunnar Sæbø, 'Perceptions of Plain and Branded Cigarette Packaging Among Norwegian Youth and Adults: A Focus Group Study' (2012) 2 *Nicotine & Tobacco Research* 450.

105. Joseph Di Franza et al, 'RJR Nabisco's Cartoon Camel Promotes Camel Cigarettes to Children' (1991) 22 *The Journal of the American Medical Association* 3149.

106. Ibid.

107. For detail regarding the prevention see Simone Susanne Hilgers, *Plain Packaging, Vereinbarkeit mit deutschen, unionsrechtlichen und völkerrechtlichen Vorgaben* (Dr Kovac, 2013), 53 et seq; for a diverging opinion see Jarass, above n 93, 101 et seq.

108. Rengeling and Szczekalla, above n 39, 641; Alemanno, above n 8, 42.

109. With further references to the current state of discussion: Stefan Leible and Thomas Streinz in Grabitz, Hilf and Nettesheim, above n 14, commentary on article 34 TFEU, margin no 32.
110. Ibid, article 34 TFEU, margin no 28.
111. *Commission of the European Communities v Italian Republic* (C-7/68), [1968] ECR 423, 428.
112. Leible and Streinz, above n 109, article 34 TFEU, margin no 51 et seq.
113. Ibid, margin no 53 et seq.
114. *Procureur du roi (Public Prosecutor) v Benoit and Gustave Dassonville* (C-8/74), [1974] ECR 837, margin no 5; cf also *Eugen Schmidberger, Internationale Transporte und Planzüge v Republik Österreich* (C-112/00), [2003] ECR I-5659, margin no 56.
115. Alemanno, above n 8, 45.
116. Walter Frenz, *Handbuch Europarecht Vol 1 – Europäische Grundfreiheiten* (Springer, 2004), margin no 1051 et seq.
117. Cf above section III A.
118. *Agreement on the European Economic Area*, opened for signature 2 May 1992, [1994] OJ L 1/3 (entered into force 1 May 1995).
119. *Philip Morris Norway AS v The Norwegian State, represented by the Ministry of Health and Care Services* (E-16/10), [2012] OJC C 291/14.
120. See also, with further references, Leible and Streinz, above n 109, article 36 TFEU, margin no 53.
121. Ibid, article 36 TFEU, margin no 52.
122. The resignation of former Health Commissioner John Dalli took place after alleged cash-for-influence from the tobacco industry in 2012. See Marc Hall and Jeremy Fleming, 'Parliament Seeks Secret Dalli File, Mulls Special Inquiry' (11 January 2013)   <http://www.euractiv.com/health/parliament-seeks-secret-dalli-do-news-516971>.

12. Tobacco control in Canada

Rob Cunningham

I INTRODUCTION

Canada has seen tremendous progress in tobacco control. Current smoking (daily or occasional) among Canadians aged 15+ has decreased from 50 per cent in 1965 to 25 per cent in 1999 to 17 per cent in 2011, while daily smoking has decreased from 42 per cent in 1965 to 21 per cent in 1999 and 14 per cent in 2011.[1] Among 15–19-year-olds, current smoking was 46 per cent in 1965 and 51 per cent in 1974, decreasing to 28 per cent in 1999 and to 12 per cent in 2011.[2] In the early 1970s and early 1980s, Canada had the highest per capita cigarette consumption in the world.[3] Since then, tobacco use has decreased considerably, as governments in Canada have sought to implement a comprehensive strategy that includes taxation, legislation and programming. Canada (population 35 million) is a federal country, with ten provinces[4] and three territories.[5] Tobacco control legislation has been enacted at both federal and provincial/territorial levels. In addition, municipalities have adopted bylaws, particularly regarding smoke-free places. Twelve of Canada's provinces/territories are common-law jurisdictions. The thirteenth, predominantly French-speaking Quebec, has a civil code.

The constitutional division of powers between the federal government and the provinces dates from 1867, the year Canada was formed.[6] In 1982, the *Canadian Charter of Rights and Freedoms*[7] became part of the Canadian Constitution, providing a new means for laws to be potentially invalidated as unconstitutional. The Supreme Court of Canada is Canada's highest court.[8] The tobacco industry in Canada has long been dominated by three companies: Imperial Tobacco Canada Ltd (a British American Tobacco subsidiary); Rothmans, Benson & Hedges Inc (a Philip Morris International subsidiary);[9] and JTI-Macdonald Corp (a Japan Tobacco International subsidiary since 1999, previously named RJR-Macdonald when a subsidiary of RJ Reynolds Tobacco Company). As in many countries, the tobacco industry has strongly opposed most types of tobacco control legislation. In Canada, the tobacco industry has also often turned to the courts seeking to invalidate legislation. This chapter will provide an overview of Canada's success with tobacco control legislation, and how this legislation has been achieved despite domestic constitutional challenges, and in some cases despite claims that proposed legislation infringed international trade agreements. Canada's successful experience provides an example for many other countries.

II REGULATORY MEASURES

A General Restrictions on Advertising and Promotion

Canada has extensive restrictions on tobacco advertising and promotion, but not a complete ban. Pursuant to the 1997 federal *Tobacco Act*,[10] tobacco advertising and promotion is banned, except for permitted types, which include:

- advertising in direct mail to an identified adult aged 18+;
- signs in places where persons under 18 are prohibited by law (eg bars);
- price/availability information (eg signs) and displays at retail (although provincial/territorial legislation deals with this);
- placing tobacco brand names/logos on some non-tobacco goods (eg lighters, matches);
- advertising/promotion within the tobacco trade (eg between manu-facturers and retailers);
- incoming cross-border advertising (eg foreign magazines, Internet, broadcasts of sponsored events), but not if the advertising is placed by someone in Canada; and
- packaging.[11]

To be legal, permitted advertising in direct mail and in bars may not be 'lifestyle' advertising, appealing to youth, or misleading; nor may it include a testimonial.[12] There is no federal requirement for permitted advertising to include health warnings. The provisions in the *Tobacco Act*, as amended, include:

- a ban on tobacco advertising for television, radio, publications (including print and Internet), billboards, transit, and other media not explicitly permitted;[13]
- a ban on tobacco sponsorship promotions, whether using a brand name or a corporate name;[14] and

- a ban on free distribution, coupons, rebates, incentive promotions (eg contests, games, gifts, frequent purchaser programmes).[15]

Historically, in 1964, some weak tobacco advertising restrictions were implemented through the industry's voluntary code.[16] In 1972, following voluntary code amendments, cigarette advertising was removed from television and radio, and a weak, small text warning was placed on many remaining tobacco advertisements.[17] The tobacco industry subsequently expanded sponsorship of sports and arts events to avoid the broadcast ban.[18] In 1988, following an intensive lobbying battle, Parliament adopted the *Tobacco Products Control Act*[19] to ban tobacco advertising. Two manufacturers quickly filed a constitutional challenge in the Quebec Superior Court.[20] Ultimately, in 1995, in *RJR-MacDonald*,[21] the Supreme Court of Canada held that the legislation was within federal jurisdiction under the criminal law power.[22] However, the Court, by a 5:4 majority, concluded that a total advertising ban was an unjustified infringement of freedom of expression and struck down the Act's advertising ban.[23] The Court concluded that at the trial (held in 1990–91) the federal government had not brought forward sufficient evidence to justify a total ban.[24]

With the advertising ban invalidated, the tobacco industry resumed direct advertising.[25] In a public relations effort to discourage strong replacement legislation, the industry again introduced a new voluntary code.[26] In 1997, following another intensive lobbying battle, Parliament adopted the *Tobacco Act.* The partial advertising restrictions in the *Tobacco Act* sought to follow the guidance of the Supreme Court of Canada in *RJR-Macdonald* as to measures that would be considered constitutional. Nonetheless, the three major manufacturers each quickly commenced a constitutional challenge to the new legislation.[27] Ultimately, in 2007, a unanimous (9:0) Supreme Court of Canada in *JTI-Macdonald*[28] upheld the *Tobacco Act*'s advertising restrictions and sponsorship ban in their entirety, concluding that the provisions were a reasonable and justifiable limitation on freedom of expression.[29] The judgment's wording was strong, and provided further encouragement to health organisations that a comprehensive tobacco advertising ban would now be constitutionally justifiable in Canada.[30]

At the provincial level, most provinces do not have advertising restrictions outside the retail environment, although some do. In Quebec, brand names/logos on non-tobacco goods are banned, and there are no exceptions allowing direct mail to an identified adult or allowing signs in bars.[31] In 2008, Quebec adopted a regulation requiring a boxed health warning in the top left corner of permitted print advertising,[32] though 2009 federal legislative amendments banned print advertising.[33] In 1971,

British Columbia adopted legislation banning tobacco advertising.[34] The legislation was upheld as being within provincial jurisdiction.[35] Nonetheless, in 1972, the advertising ban was replaced with partial restrictions.[36]

B Restrictions on Retail Displays

All provinces/territories have legislation prohibiting tobacco displays at retail, although legislative wording varies. Most have exemptions of some manner allowing displays in specialty tobacconists. Legislation in four provinces/territories contain exemptions allowing displays in premises where minors are prohibited, though in practice only a very small percentage of tobacco retailers use this exemption. All provinces have significant restrictions on permitted signage at retail.[37] Saskatchewan was the second jurisdiction worldwide to ban tobacco retail displays, from 11 March 2002[38] (after Iceland, from 1 August 2001).[39] Rothmans, Benson & Hedges quickly brought a constitutional challenge arguing that the Saskatchewan display ban was invalid because it went further than federal tobacco legislation.[40] In 2005 the Supreme Court of Canada unanimously (9:0) upheld the Saskatchewan legislation, concluding that the Saskatchewan and federal laws were complementary and not in conflict.[41] In 2013, the Nova Scotia Provincial Court concluded that the provincial display ban was justified as a reasonable limit on freedom of expression.[42] The Alberta Provincial Court reached a similar conclusion in 2012.[43]

C Packaging and Labelling Requirements

Canada has been a world leader when it comes to advances in package health warnings. Canada was the first country to require picture-based health warnings (in 2001),[44] and the first to require sizes of 20 per cent (1989),[45] 35 per cent (1994)[46] and 50 per cent (2001)[47] of the package, front and back. As of June 2012, warnings cover the top 75 per cent of the front and back of cigarette packages.[48] Canada has among the largest cigarette package warnings in the world.[49]

Historically, starting in 1972, a voluntary text warning appeared on a lateral side of cigarette packages.[50] From 1989, mandatory text warnings (four in rotation) covered 20 per cent of the front and back of the package.[51] From 1994, eight rotated black and white text warnings covered about 35 per cent of the front and back of the package at the top.[52] From 2001, 16 rotated warnings with colour pictures covered the top 50 per cent of the package (front and back), alongside 16 rotated interior text messages either on an insert or on the slide of 'slide and shell' packages.[53] The requirements from 2012 include 16 rotated warnings with colour pictures covering the top 75 per cent of the package front and back, with a national toll-free quitline number and a web address included in the exterior warnings, and eight new interior messages with colour pictures.[54]

Warning requirements for tobacco products other than cigarettes and little cigars continue to be covered by earlier regulations. Picture warnings are required for roll-your-own tobacco, tobacco sticks, kreteks, cigars (including little cigars), and pipe tobacco, while text warnings are required for bidis, chewing tobacco and snuff. The minimum warning size for these other tobacco products is generally 50 per cent, although some packages of cigars and pipe tobacco have a smaller mandated size.[55]

As of June 2012, a series of four rotated black on white toxic emission text messages must appear on a lateral side of cigarette packages.[56] Machine yield numbers for tar, nicotine and other substances are no longer required on packages.[57] National regulations adopted in 2011 ban 'light' and 'mild' descriptors for cigarettes, roll-your-own tobacco, and some other tobacco products.[58] These regulations were preceded by settlement agreements in 2006 between the federal Competition Bureau and each of the three major tobacco manufacturers (and later some smaller tobacco manufacturers) to remove 'light' and 'mild' descriptors.[59] The federal Minister of Health had initially proposed a ban on 'light' and 'mild' descriptors in 2001,[60] prompting tobacco industry arguments that this would infringe international trade agreements:[61] specifically the *North American Free Trade Agreement* (NAFTA),[62] the World Trade Organization (WTO) *Agreement on Technical Barriers to Trade* (TBT Agreement),[63] and the WTO *Agreement on Trade-Related Aspects of Intellectual Property Rights* (TRIPS Agreement).[64]

The tobacco industry has brought several legal challenges against Canada's package warnings. In 1995, a 5:4 majority of the Supreme Court of Canada held that requiring health warnings to be unattributed (eg not attributed to 'Health Canada') was an unjustified infringement of freedom of expression.[65] In 2000, in response to the judgment, the next round of requirements gave tobacco manufacturers the option of attributing warnings to 'Health Canada'.[66] In 2007, the Supreme Court of Canada upheld 50 per cent picture warnings, dismissing a claim that such warnings were an unjustified infringement of freedom of expression.[67] In 2011, the tobacco industry opposed the then proposed 75 per cent warning size, claiming that the size constituted an infringement of

NAFTA, the *Paris Convention for the Protection of Intellectual Property*,[68] and the TRIPS Agreement.[69] The federal government adopted the new 75 per cent warning size despite the industry claims.

Canada has not yet required 'plain' or standardised packaging without colours/logos, although regulatory authority to do so exists federally[70] and in several provinces.[71] In 1994, the House of Commons Standing Committee on Health recommended plain packaging.[72] This Committee's recommendation was made despite tobacco industry claims that plain packaging was an unjustified infringement of freedom of expression, and that plain packaging infringed international trade agreements.[73]

D   Requirements for Smoke-Free Spaces

Canada has among the world's strongest smoke-free legislation. Legislation prohibits smoking in all indoor workplaces and public places, although workplaces in private homes are normally exempt (especially if only residents use the workplace), and some provinces allow designated smoking rooms in nursing homes for seniors. Most of the applicable smoke-free legislation is at the provincial/territorial level, but federal legislation[74] applies to the approximately 10 per cent of workplaces that are federally regulated.

Starting in the 1970s and strengthened over time, many municipalities have adopted bylaws, often preceding stronger provincial/territorial action.[75] Nine provinces/territories have prohibited smoking in vehicles with children.[76] Four Canadian provinces/territories have prohibited smoking on patios of restaurants and bars, as have a number of municipalities.[77] Smoking is prohibited not only on the inside of all federal and provincial prisons, but also on all outside prison grounds.[78] A growing number of municipalities are prohibiting smoking in specified outdoor areas, such as parks, playgrounds, sports fields/facilities, beaches, and grounds of municipal buildings.[79] Smoking is banned on elementary and secondary school property in all provinces, either through legislation or administrative policy.[80] A growing number of hospital policies prohibit smoking on hospital property.[81] Some universities and colleges have policies to prohibit smoking on campus,[82] while others limit smoking to designated outdoor areas.[83] Canada was a world leader for smoke-free airlines, prohibiting smoking on domestic airline flights of two hours or less in 1987, on all domestic flights in 1989, and, in a world precedent, on all flights (including international flights) of its domestic airlines in 1994.[84]

Most legal challenges to smoke-free laws have been unsuccessful, although some were threatened or commenced with great fanfare. While legal challenges to municipal authority to adopt smoking bylaws have mainly been dismissed,[85] a few municipal bylaws were invalidated as being unauthorised by the municipality's enabling statute.[86] Such judgments invalidating bylaws (or parts of bylaws) were typically followed by provincial legislative amendments expanding municipal authority to enable adoption of such bylaws. Legal challenges claiming that the federal government did not have administrative authority to ban smoking inside prisons[87] or on outdoor prison grounds[88] have been dismissed. Prison smoking bans have been held to not constitute a breach of life, liberty and security of the person,[89] or cruel and unusual punishment,[90] or discrimination infringing equality rights.[91] Similarly, courts have dismissed claims that smoking bans in restaurants and bars infringed freedom of association[92] or constituted discrimination infringing equality rights.[93]

E   Restrictions on Flavoured Tobacco Products

National legislation prohibits flavouring and other additives in cigarettes, little cigars and blunt wraps, with an exemption for menthol. This legislation was implemented by Bill C-32, in force at retail on 5 July 2010.[94] At the time of its adoption, Bill C-32 was world-precedent-setting, containing the most extensive ban on flavours and additives of any jurisdiction.

The tobacco industry strongly opposed Bill C-32. The industry in part argued that Bill C-32 would ban US-style cigarettes (eg Marlboro), but with legislation in place US-style cigarettes continue to be sold in Canada.

Among tobacco industry arguments was a claim that Bill C-32 infringes the TBT Agreement and NAFTA, with Philip Morris International making such arguments before a Senate Committee.[95] The tobacco industry also raised legal arguments elsewhere.[96] The issue was also raised by various countries at the WTO Committee on Technical Barriers to Trade.[97] However, no legal proceedings have been commenced in Canada or at the WTO.[98]

Little cigars are defined in Bill C-32 as being 1.4 g or less, or as having a cigarette filter.[99] Following implementation of Bill C-32, several companies marketed 'resized' little cigars in many flavours and weighing just over 1.4 g.[100]

Several provinces have regulatory authority (so far unused) to restrict or ban flavoured tobacco products. Ontario has banned flavoured little cigars, with provisions similar to federal legislation.[101]

F   Restrictions on the Number and Type of Retail Locations

All provinces/territories except British Columbia have prohibited tobacco sales in pharmacies and establishments containing a pharmacy (eg some grocery stores).[102] In Ontario, the courts held that such legislation does not infringe freedom of expression.[103] In Quebec in 1998, the Quebec Professions Tribunal ruled that selling tobacco in pharmacies was exercising a business incompatible with the pharmacy profession, even if tobacco was sold separately from the dispensary.[104]

Depending on the province, tobacco sales are prohibited in college and university campuses; restaurants; bars; casinos; athletic or recreational facilities; temporary, outdoor or movable locations; hospitals and other healthcare facilities; residential care facilities; and provincial and municipal government buildings.[105]

Most provinces/territories require tobacco retailers to have a tobacco retail licence.[106] Only two provinces require a licence fee.[107] A number of municipalities, especially in Ontario and Alberta, have tobacco retailer licence requirements, with the highest licence fee being in St Albert, Alberta at $700 per store per year, effective 2013.[108]

G   Restrictions on Youth Access

Since 1994, federal legislation has prohibited tobacco sales to persons under age 18.[109] Seven provinces/territories have their own legislation prohibiting tobacco sales to minors with a minimum age of 19.[110] Four have a minimum age of 18,[111] and two have no such legislation.[112] Retailers are required to comply with both federal and provincial/territorial legislation.

Federal legislation prohibits vending machines except in bars,[113] while six provinces/territories have banned vending machines altogether.[114] Since 1994, federal legislation has also prohibited self-serve displays (eg on a counter-top).[115]

With new and better legislation governing sales to minors introduced in the 1990s, and greater government enforcement action, compliance has improved. National evaluations involving underage youth attempting to purchase cigarettes found that 48 per cent of stores refused to sell to 15–17-year-old test shoppers in 1995, while 84 per cent refused in 2009.[116]

Legislation prohibiting sales to minors has been held to be within both provincial and federal jurisdiction.[117]

The Ontario Court of Appeal has held that using random test shopping, even without a reasonable suspicion that the person monitored is selling tobacco to minors, is a valid enforcement approach that does not constitute entrapment.[118]

H Reporting Requirements

Canada has among the most detailed reporting regulations in the world. The federal *Tobacco Reporting Regulations*,[119] adopted in 2000, require tobacco manufacturers to report to Health Canada information for all tobacco products, including:

- unit sales volumes on a brand-by-brand basis for each province/ territory;
- promotional activities including marketing expenditures;
- additives/ingredients on a brand-by-brand basis;
- manufacturing procedures;
- research;
- product constituents; and
- toxic emission yields in smoke.

A tobacco industry constitutional challenge to the reporting regulations was dismissed.[120] The industry had argued that the reporting requirements constituted an unreasonable search and seizure, constituted an unjustified infringement of freedom of expression, and were within exclusive provincial (and not federal) jurisdiction.[121]

I Other Regulatory Measures

A few other measures are worth noting:

- Five nicotine replacement products (NRT) are sold in Canada following approval by Health Canada (gum, patch, lozenge, inhaler, mouth spray). These products may be advertised and may be widely sold on a non-prescription basis, although in Quebec these products may still be sold only in pharmacies (without a prescription). Marketing restrictions regarding NRT have become more relaxed over time, and indicated uses have become more extensive (eg partial substitution of cigarettes for NRT, instead of only quitting altogether).[122]
- Canada was the first country and second jurisdiction (after New York state) to adopt a cigarette flammability standard to reduce fire risk.[123]
- In 1998, the *Tobacco Fee Act*[124] was adopted in British Columbia to recover from tobacco manufacturers the annual cost of the provincial government's tobacco control strategy. Each company's fee would be based on the strategy's annual cost (eg $20 million) multiplied by the company's market share (eg 60 per cent). This legislation, however,

was never proclaimed into force, and was repealed when a new government took office.[125]

III TOBACCO TAXATION

In Canada, both federal and provincial/territorial governments impose tobacco taxes, and these taxes have been increased for the purpose of reducing tobacco use.[126]

A Contraband, Fines and Unpaid Taxes

In 1994, the federal government and five provinces rolled back tobacco tax rates in response to high contraband levels.[127] At the time, the three major tobacco manufacturers were exporting vast quantities of tobacco products to the US, without taxes, knowing that these products would be smuggled back into Canada.[128] The 1994 reduction in tobacco taxes had a very adverse effect on progress to reduce smoking.[129]

The contraband of the early 1990s prompted significant legal proceedings. In 1998, a US company in the RJR group was convicted in the US of contraband relating to Canada, with a US$15 million penalty.[130] In 1999, the Canadian Government filed a *Racketeer-Influenced and Corrupt Organizations Act* (RICO)[131] civil claim in US federal court against RJ Reynolds, RJR-Macdonald and related companies, but US courts dismissed Canada's claim on jurisdictional grounds.[132] In response, in August 2003, the Canadian Government filed a $1.5 billion civil claim in Ontario Superior Court against RJ Reynolds, RJR-Macdonald and related companies.[133] In February 2003, the Royal Canadian Mounted Police (RCMP) filed criminal prosecutions against JTI-Macdonald, related companies and eight individual executives.[134] On 11 August 2004, Quebec ordered JTI-Macdonald to pay $1.36 billion in unpaid tobacco taxes, penalties and interest, which prompted JTI-Macdonald on 24 August 2004 to seek and obtain bankruptcy protection.[135]

Eventually in 2008–10, each of the three major companies were convicted of contraband on guilty pleas, and also agreed to civil settlements[136] with federal and provincial governments. Total fines were $525 million (the largest in Canadian history), while civil payments were $1.175 billion,[137] with an overall total of $1.7 billion.

The amounts obtained by the Government were significantly less than the government revenue lost due to contraband, the tobacco tax rollback, and interest. The settlements were criticised as being severely inadequate.[138] Indeed, in the JTI-Macdonald bankruptcy protection proceedings, federal and provincial governments gave notice of contraband-related claims against JTI-Macdonald alone of $9.6 billion, not including interest and various other claims.[139]

B Tobacco Taxation and First Nations

In Canada, status natives purchasing tobacco products on First Nation reserves are not required to pay provincial tobacco taxes, federal goods and services tax or equivalent (5 per cent), or provincial sales taxes.[140] This exemption does not apply to off-reserve purchases by status natives[141] nor to on-reserve purchases by non-natives.[142] Federal tobacco taxes do apply to on-reserve purchases by status natives.[143] There are more than 600 First Nations with reserve territories in Canada.[144] The exemption for status natives has encouraged smoking among First Nations, provided an incentive for product diversion and illegal sales, and prompted considerable enforcement activity and related litigation.[145]

C Other Tax Measures

Canada also has several other tobacco taxation measures not commonly found internationally:

- The federal government imposes an export tax to impede the type of contraband that occurred in the early 1990s.[146]
- Shipments of tobacco products to consumers between provinces or by mail are prohibited.[147]
- The federal government imposes a surtax on tobacco manufacturer profits, in addition to regular corporate income tax.[148]
- Federal (but not provincial) tobacco tax is imposed on tobacco products sold in Canadian duty-free stores.[149]
- Each province has its own tobacco tax marking.[150]

IV FURTHER LITIGATION AGAINST TOBACCO CONTROL MEASURES

A Expropriation

There have been several cases claiming that tobacco control legislation constitutes expropriation under domestic Canadian law. Each of these cases has been dismissed, including for legislation: (i) requiring 50 per cent picture warnings on tobacco packages;[151] (ii) prohibiting tobacco advertising, including the use of registered trademarks in advertising;[152] (iii) prohibiting designated smoking rooms, including existing ones;[153] and (iv) prohibiting cigarette packages containing less than 20 cigarettes.[154]

B Injunctions

When legal challenges to legislation have been commenced, sometimes there have also been attempts to suspend (stay) implementation of the legislation until after the legal challenge has been completed. The leading Canadian case on staying legislation is *RJR-Macdonald* (1994),[155] where tobacco companies sought to stay new, larger package warnings. The Supreme Court of Canada dismissed the application.[156]

Since *RJR-Macdonald* (1994), applications to stay tobacco control legislation have consistently been dismissed, including legislation:

- banning tobacco sales in pharmacies (Ontario, 1994);[157]
- restricting tobacco advertising and promotion (national, 1997);[158]
- requiring picture warnings covering 50 per cent of the front and back of tobacco product packages (national, 2000);[159]
- prohibiting tobacco sponsorship of the Montreal Grand Prix Formula One auto race (national, 2003);[160]
- prohibiting smoking at restaurants and bars, including on outdoor patios (city of Kingston, Ontario, 2003);[161] and
- prohibiting smoking in bars (Quebec, 2006).[162]

C Relevance of the WHO Framework Convention on Tobacco Control

Canada played a leadership role prior to and during negotiations for the *WHO Framework Convention on Tobacco Control* (WHO FCTC).[163] Canada ratified the WHO FCTC on 26 November 2004.

Though not legally required, all provinces/territories supported WHO FCTC ratification by the federal government. The Quebec Government went further, adopting a decree declaring that it was bound by the WHO FCTC.[164] Health organisations have issued several 'shadow reports' urging a more robust WHO FCTC implementation in Canada.[165]

The WHO FCTC has been cited with approval in two Canadian constitutional cases. In *JTI-Macdonald* (2007), the Supreme Court of Canada cited the WHO FCTC in upholding federal advertising restrictions and also the 50 per cent package warning size.[166] In 2013, the Nova

Scotia Provincial Court upheld the constitutional validity of the provincial tobacco display ban, citing WHO FCTC article 13 and the guidelines for implementation of that article.[167]

V PRODUCT LIABILITY LITIGATION

Tobacco product liability litigation in Canada is more significant than in any other country apart from the United States. Of prime importance are class actions and government Medicare cost-recovery lawsuits.

A Class Actions in Quebec

In March 2012, the trial began in Quebec Superior Court in two massive broad-based product liability class actions seeking $27 billion from the three major Canadian tobacco manufacturers. These cases were initially filed in 1998, certified to proceed as class actions in 2005,[168] and heard together in a common trial.

One of the class actions is *Conseil québécois sur le tabac et la santé and Jean-Yves Blais v JTI-Macdonald Corp.*[169] As part of the case, $100 000 in compensatory damages and an additional $5000 in punitive damages is sought for each Quebec resident who prior to 20 November 1998 smoked at least 36 500 cigarettes (equal to 20 cigarettes per day for five years) and who prior to 12 March 2012 developed lung cancer, throat cancer or emphysema.[170]

The other class action is *Cécilia Létourneau v JTI-Macdonald Corp.*[171] The claim is brought on behalf of Quebec residents who, as of 30 September 1998, had been smoking for at least four years, were addicted to the nicotine in the cigarettes of the defendant tobacco companies, were daily smokers of these cigarettes, and were still smoking as of 21 February 2005 or until their death if earlier than 21 February 2005. For each of these individuals, $5000 is sought in compensatory damages and an additional $5000 in punitive damages.[172]

In the class actions, the tobacco industry named the federal government as a Defendant in Warranty, arguing that the federal government should reimburse the industry for all or some of the damages that might be awarded. The federal government, however, successfully brought a motion to be removed as Defendant in Warranty.[173]

Materials from the case are being placed on the Internet, including exhibits, transcripts, and preliminary court rulings.[174] Blogs have been providing daily trial reports.[175] The trial is projected to continue into 2014.

B Medicare Cost-recovery Lawsuits

All ten provinces, as well two territories,[176] have adopted legislation[177] to facilitate a Medicare cost-recovery lawsuit against the tobacco industry.[178] Nine provinces have filed lawsuits.[179] The remaining province (Nova Scotia) and Nunavut have announced an intention to file a lawsuit.[180]

Ontario is seeking $50 billion in damages, while Quebec is seeking $60 billion.[181] Not all provincial lawsuits specifically indicate the amount of damages sought.

The US experience is part of the inspiration for provincial governments. In the US, state government health care cost-recovery lawsuits resulted in out-of-court settlements, with US$246 billion payable to state governments over 25 years, more than 40 million pages of internal tobacco company documents being made public, new marketing restrictions, and other measures.[182]

In Canada in 1997, British Columbia was the first province to adopt Medicare cost-recovery legislation,[183] with a lawsuit initially filed on 12 November 1998.[184] This initial legislation was declared unconstitutional.[185] The British Columbia Government chose not to appeal, and instead revised legislation was adopted.[186] The new legislation was proclaimed into effect on 24 January 2001,[187] and on the same day the British Columbia Government filed a new Medicare cost-recovery lawsuit.[188] Ultimately, in 2005, a unanimous (9:0) Supreme Court of Canada upheld the British Columbia legislation as constitutional, concluding that the legislation was within provincial jurisdiction.[189] The legislation in the other eight common-law provinces is essentially identical to the British Columbia legislation. In Quebec, where aspects of the cost-recovery legislation[190] are different from that in British Columbia, a tobacco industry constitutional challenge is ongoing.[191]

In British Columbia, the tobacco industry named the federal government as a third-party defendant, arguing that the federal government should reimburse the tobacco industry for all or some of any eventual damages payable. In 2011, the Supreme Court of Canada unanimously (9:0) concluded that the federal government should not be a third-party defendant.[192]

Attempts by foreign parent companies such as British American Tobacco, Phillip Morris International and RJ Reynolds International to be removed as defendants have been dismissed in British Columbia,[193] New Brunswick,[194] Ontario,[195] and Quebec,[196] with motions filed in several other provinces.[197] The foreign companies have argued unsuccessfully that Canadian courts do not have jurisdiction to hear the claims against the foreign companies.

In 2000, Ontario had initially filed a US$40 billion Medicare cost-recovery lawsuit in US federal court under RICO. However, it was held that the US courts did not have jurisdiction to hear this type of claim by a foreign government such as Ontario.[198]

C Other Class Actions

One other class action has been certified in Canada, the *Knight* 'lights' class action in British Columbia for deception relating to 'light' and 'mild' cigarettes.[199] A trial date in this case has not been set.

VI FUTURE DIRECTIONS

Despite the progress made in Canada, an enormous amount of work remains to be done. Needed measures include:

- a successful public health outcome to the Medicare cost-recovery and class action lawsuits, which have the potential to fundamentally reform Canada's tobacco industry;
- a full comprehensive ban on tobacco advertising and promotion, including banning all promotional payments to tobacco retailers;
- plain packaging, including standardised package dimensions;
- reducing the number of tobacco retail locations;
- a ban on flavours for all tobacco products;
- a ban on 'slim' cigarettes, and standardising cigarette appearance;
- an appropriate response to the emergence of electronic cigarettes;
- further smoke-free measures, including for select outdoor areas and for multi-unit dwellings, and ensuring water pipes are covered by smoke-free laws;
- further tobacco tax increases and contraband prevention; and
- sustained funding for government tobacco control strategies, including prevention and cessation initiatives.

VII CONCLUSION

Canada has been able to achieve a significant level of tobacco control legislation, setting numerous world precedents along the way. Canada has been able to do so despite tobacco industry legal challenges, and despite claims that some proposed measures infringed international trade agreements.

Canada's Constitution includes a federal/provincial division of constitutional responsibilities, and an entrenched *Canadian Charter of Rights and Freedoms*. Most countries do not have a constitution that would prompt the type of legal challenges that Canada has seen. But for countries that may have similar legal issues, Canada provides an excellent example of how public health can nonetheless prevail.

Canada provides a case study that 'it can be done'. At the same time, it is essential that governments in Canada move aggressively to implement a long list of additional measures. The faster governments act, the faster will the tobacco epidemic and its devastating toll be curbed. Going forward, Canada has the opportunity to continue to be an example for other nations.

NOTES

1. Health Canada, *Canadian Tobacco Use Monitoring Survey – Historical Tables 1999–2011* (13 September 2012) <http://www.hc-sc.gc.ca/hc-ps/tobac-tabac/research-recherche/stat/_ctums-esutc_2011/ann-histo-eng.php>; Thomas Stephens, *A Critical Review of Canadian Survey Data on Tobacco Use, Attitudes and Knowledge* (Health and Welfare Canada, 1988). Another annual national survey (most recent year 2012), the Canadian Community Health Survey, reports smoking prevalence somewhat higher than CTUMS: Statistics Canada <http://www.statcan.gc.ca/tables-tableaux/sum-som/l01/cst01/health73b-eng.htm>.
2. Health Canada, above n 1; Stephens, above n 1.
3. World Health Organization, *The Tobacco Epidemic: A Global Public Health Emergency* (Tobacco Alert, Special Issue 1996).
4. From west to east, the provinces are British Columbia, Alberta, Saskatchewan, Manitoba, Ontario, Quebec, New Brunswick, Nova Scotia, Prince Edward Island, and Newfoundland and Labrador.
5. From west to east, the territories (all in northern Canada) are Yukon Territory, Northwest Territories and Nunavut.
6. *Constitution Act 1867* (Imp), 30 & 31 Vict, c 3.
7. *Canada Act 1982* (UK) c 11, sch B pt I.
8. Below the Supreme Court of Canada is the Court of Appeal in each province/territory, below which is the court of general jurisdiction in each province/territory, with names such as British Columbia Supreme Court, Alberta Court of Queen's Bench and Quebec Superior Court.
9. Rothmans, Benson & Hedges Inc was formed in 1986 with the merger of Benson & Hedges (Canada) Inc (a Philip Morris subsidiary) and Rothmans of Pall Mall Ltd (a Rothmans International subsidiary).
10. *Tobacco Act*, SC 1997, c 13.
11. Ibid pt IV. The *Tobacco Act*, pt IV, which deals with promotion, does not prohibit the package as advertising.
12. Ibid s 21.

13. Ibid ss 19, 22.
14. Ibid ss 24, 25.
15. Ibid s 29.
16. *Cigarette Advertising Code of Canadian Tobacco Manufacturers* (14 June 1964) Legacy Tobacco Documents Library <http://legacy.library.ucsf.edu/tid/zrc54e00>.
17. *Cigarette Advertising Code of the Canadian Tobacco Manufacturers' Council* (1 January 1972) Ministry of Health (British Columbia) <http://www.health.gov.bc.ca/guildford/pdf/074/00007511.pdf> (*Cigarette Advertising Code (1972)*).
18. Rob Cunningham, *Smoke & Mirrors: The Canadian Tobacco War* (International Development Research Centre, 1996) 95–9; Richard Pollay, 'Tobacco Promotion Spending Patterns in Canada' 2002, *JTI-Macdonald v Canada (Attorney General)*, Quebec Superior Court, Exhibit D-239, 1 (trial judgment reported at (2002), [2003] RJQ 181, 102 CRR (2d) 189 (Superior Court)).
19. SC 1988, c 20.
20. *RJR-Macdonald Inc v Canada (Procureur Général)*, Quebec Superior Court, file 500-05-009755-883; *Imperial Tobacco Ltd v Canada (Procureur Général)*, Quebec Superior Court, file 500-05-009760-883.
21. *RJR-MacDonald Inc v Canada (Attorney General)* [1995] 3 SCR 199 (*RJR-Macdonald*).
22. Ibid 240–67 [28]–[57], 326 [123], 351 [181].
23. Ibid 326–56 [124]–[192].
24. Ibid 355 [191], Iacobucci J speaking for two of the five justices comprising the majority: 'Perhaps proof exists for such a ban, but in my view the record does not establish it'.
25. Between 1989 and 2005, sponsorship advertising increased dramatically and substituted for much direct advertising.
26. *Tobacco Industry Voluntary Packaging and Advertising Code* (19 December 2005) Legacy Tobacco Documents Library <http://legacy.library.ucsf.edu/tid/jfk61d00; jsessionid=C369066820D1EFA517B1187A62EAD5EA.tobacco03>.
27. *RJR-Macdonald v Canada (Attorney General)*, Quebec Superior Court, file 500-05-031299-975, filed 18 April 1997; *Rothmans, Benson & Hedges Inc v Canada (Attorney General)*, Quebec Superior Court, file 500-05-031306-978, filed 19 April 1997; *Imperial Tobacco Ltd v Canada (Attorney General)*, Quebec Superior Court, file 500-05-031332-974, filed 21 April 1997. The trial judgment is reported at *JTI-Macdonald Corp v Canada (Attorney General)* (2002), [2003] RJQ 181, 102 CRR (2d) 189 (Superior Court).
28. *Canada (Attorney General) v JTI-Macdonald Corp* [2007] 2 SCR 610 (*JTI-Macdonald (2007)*).
29. Ibid 627–60 [32]–[129], 644 [141]–[142].
30. The Court stated that new evidence and context may lead to a different constitutional conclusion: ibid [11].
31. *Tobacco Act*, RSQ, c T-0.01, ss 21–8.
32. *Regulation Respecting the Warning Attributed to the Minister of Health and Social Services Concerning the Harmful Effects of Tobacco on Health*, RRQ, c T-0.01, r 2.
33. *An Act to Amend the Tobacco Act*, SC 2009, c 27, s 11.
34. *Tobacco Advertising Restraint Act*, SBC 1971, c 65, as repealed by *Tobacco Advertising Restraint Act Repeal Act*, SBC 1972 (2nd sess), c 12.
35. *Benson & Hedges (Canada) Ltd v Attorney General of British Columbia* (1972) 27 DLR (3d) 257 (British Columbia Supreme Court).
36. *Tobacco Products Act*, SBC 1972 (2nd Sess), c 13; *Tobacco Products Regulation*, BC Reg 258/72, amended by BC Reg 347/89, as repealed by BC Reg 216/94.
37. For example, in Ontario, signs can have only black text on a white background with no brand indications, have a maximum size of 968 cm^2 (about 31cm x 31cm), and

have a location not visible from outside the store: *General Regulation*, O Reg 48/06, s 7. Product catalogues are allowed for consumer consultation.

38. *The Tobacco Control Act*, SS 2001, c T-14.1, s 6.
39. *Tobacco Control Act*, No 6/2002, article 7, originally *Act No 74/1984 on Tobacco Prevention* as amended by Act No 95/2001.
40. *Rothmans, Benson & Hedges Inc v Government of Saskatchewan*, Saskatchewan Court of Queen's Bench, file 945 of 2002, filed 3 May 2002.
41. *Rothmans, Benson & Hedges Inc v Saskatchewan* [2005] 1 SCR 188, 193–8 [11]–[28].
42. *R v Mader's Tobacco Store Ltd* (2013) 329 NSR (2d) 349 (Nova Scotia Provincial Court); *R v Mader's Tobacco Store Ltd* (2010) 294 NSR 2(d) 180 (Nova Scotia Provincial Court).
43. *R v 712098 Alberta Ltd* [2012] ABPC 313 (Alberta Provincial Court).
44. *Tobacco Products Information Regulations*, SOR/2000-272, ss 1, 5.
45. *Tobacco Products Control Regulations*, SOR/89-21, ss 11, 15.
46. *Tobacco Products Control Regulations, amendment*, SOR/93-389, ss 4, 7, amending *Tobacco Products Control Regulations*, SOR/89-21, ss 11, 15.
47. *Tobacco Products Information Regulations*, SOR/2000-272, ss 1, 5.
48. *Tobacco Products Labelling Regulations (Cigarettes and Little Cigars)*, SOR/2011-177, ss 1, 12–14, sch 1.
49. Canadian Cancer Society, *Cigarette Package Health Warnings: International Status Report* (October 2012) Campaign for Tobacco Free Kids <http://global.tobacco freekids.org/files/pdfs/en/WL_status_report_en.pdf>.
50. *Cigarette Advertising Code (1972)*, above n 17.
51. *Tobacco Products Control Regulations*, SOR/89-21, ss 11, 15.
52. *Tobacco Products Control Regulations, amendment*, SOR/93-389, SOR/93-389, ss 4, 7, amending *Tobacco Products Control Regulations*, SOR/89-21, ss 11, 15.
53. *Tobacco Products Information Regulations*, SOR/2000-272, ss 1, 5.
54. *Tobacco Products Labelling Regulations (Cigarettes and Little Cigars)*, SOR/2011-177, ss 1, 12–14, 22–31, sch 1.
55. *Tobacco Products Information Regulations*, SOR/2000-272, ss 1, 5–6.
56. *Tobacco Products Labelling Regulations (Cigarettes and Little Cigars)*, SOR/2011-177, ss 17–21.
57. *Tobacco Products Control Regulations*, SOR/89-21, ss 1, 11, replaced by *Tobacco Products Information Regulations*, SOR/2000-272, ss 1, 9, sch 1, amended by *Regulations Amending the Tobacco Products Information Regulations*, SOR/2011-179, ss 8, 13. See also *Tobacco Products Labelling Regulations (Cigarettes and Little Cigars)*, SOR/2011-177, ss 1, 17–21.
58. *Promotion of Tobacco Products and Accessories Regulations (Prohibited Terms)*, SOR/2011-178, ss 1–7.
59. See, eg, *Agreement between Imperial Tobacco Canada Limited and the Commissioner of Competition*, signed 7 November 2006.
60. Department of Health (Canada), 'Tobacco Act: Proposed Tobacco Regulations' in Canada, *Canada Gazette, Part I*, Vol 135 No 48, 1 December 2001, 4299.
61. See, eg, Philip Morris International, Submission to National Center for Standards and Certification Information, *Foreign Trade Notification No G/TBT/N/CAN/22*, 2002.
62. Signed 12 December 1992, 32 ILM 289 (entered into force 1 January 1994).
63. *Marrakesh Agreement Establishing the World Trade Organization*, opened for signature 15 April 1994, 1867 UNTS 3 (entered into force 1 January 1995) annex 1A (*Agreement on Technical Barriers to Trade*).

64. *Marrakesh Agreement Establishing the World Trade Organization*, opened for signature 15 April 1994, 1867 UNTS 3 (entered into force 1 January 1995) annex 1C (*Agreement on Trade-Related Aspects of Intellectual Property Rights*).
65. *RJR-MacDonald* [1995] 3 SCR 199, 326–7 [124], 348–9 [172]–[174], 354–5 [190]–[191].
66. *Tobacco Act*, SC 1997, c 13, s 15(3); *Tobacco Products Information Regulations*, SOR/2000-272, s 4.
67. *JTI-Macdonald* [2007] 2 SCR 610, 660–63 [130]–[140].
68. Opened for signature 14 July 1967, 828 UNTS 306 (entered into force 26 April 1970).
69. See, eg, JTI-Macdonald, Submission to Health Canada, *Consultation on the Proposed Tobacco Products Labelling Regulations (Cigarettes and Little Cigars)*, 5 May 2011, 23–5.
70. *Tobacco Act*, SC 1997, c 13, ss 23, 33.
71. See, eg, *The Non-Smokers Health Protection Act*, CCSM c N92, s 9(1)(e); *Smoke-Free Ontario Act*, SO 1994 c 10, ss 19(1), 19(4).
72. House of Commons Standing Committee on Health, Parliament of Canada, *Towards Zero Consumption: Generic Packaging of Tobacco Products* (1994).
73. RJ Reynolds Tobacco Company, Submission to House of Commons Standing Committee on Health, 3 May 1994; Philip Morris International Inc, Submission to House of Commons Standing Committee on Health, 5 May 1994; Canadian Tobacco Manufacturers' Council, Submission to House of Commons Standing Committee on Health, 12 May 1994. For a discussion of the international trade issues, see Physicians for a Smoke-free Canada, *Packaging Phoney Intellectual Property Claims* (June 2009) <http://www.smoke-free.ca/plain-packaging/documents/2009/packagingphoneyipclaims-june2009-a4.pdf>.
74. *Non-smokers' Health Act*, SC 1988, c 21; *Non-smokers' Health Regulations*, SOR/90-21.
75. For a current municipal smoking bylaw database, see Non-Smokers' Rights Association, *NSRA's Smoke-Free Laws Database* (29 July 2013) <http://www.nsra-adnf.ca/cms/smoke-free-laws-database.html>.
76. See, eg, *Smoke-Free Ontario Act*, SO 1994 c 10, s 9.2; *Smoke-free Places Act*, SNS 2002, c 12, s 5(2A).
77. See, eg, *Tobacco Reduction Act*, SA 2005, c T-3.8, ss 1, 3(a); *Smoke-free Places Act*, SNS 2002, c 12, s 5(3); City of Ottawa, *Smoke-free – Public Places Bylaw*, No 2001-148, ss 1–3.
78. See, eg, Commissioner of the Correctional Service of Canada, *Commissioner's Directive 259: Exposure to Second-hand Smoke* (5 May 2008); Government of Saskatchewan, *Saskatchewan Government's Policy for a Smoke Free Workplace* (1 July 1994). (Quebec's smoking ban for prison outdoors has an implementation date in spring 2014: Ministry of Public Security, 'Le ministre de la Sécurité publique annonce une interdiction complète de fumer dans les établissements de détention au Québec' (Press Release, 19 April 2013) <http://communiques.gouv.qc.ca/gouvqc/communiques/GPQF/Avril2013/19/c6948.html>.)
79. See Non-Smokers' Rights Association, *Compendium of Smoke-free Workplace and Public Place Bylaws* (Spring 2012) <http://www.nsra-adnf.ca/cms/file/files/Compendium_Spring_2012.pdf>.
80. See, eg, *Tobacco Control Act*, RSBC 1996, c 451, s 2.2; *Smoke-free Places Act*, SNS 2002, c 12, ss 2(g), 5(2).
81. Non-Smokers' Rights Association, *The Evolution of Smoke-free Hospital Properties* (March 2013) <http://www.nsra-adnf.ca/cms/file/files/Evolution_of_S-F_hospitals_2013-FINAL(1).pdf>.

82. See, eg, University of Winnipeg, *Smoking on University Premises: Policy No 80.0005* (September 2008) <http://www.uwinnipeg.ca/index/cms-filesystem-action?file=pdfs/admin/policies/80.0005.pdf>; Dalhousie University, *Smoking Policy* (1 September 2003) <http://safety.dal.ca/programs_services/smokefree/>.

83. See, eg, Mount Royal University, *MRU Policy* (1 July 2006) <http://www.mtroyal.ca/CampusServices/WellnessServices/TobaccoFree/MRUPolicy/>.

84. *Air Regulations, Amendment*, SOR/87-554, sch, ss 1–2; *Non-smokers' Health Regulations*, SOR/90-21, ss 12–13; *Non-smokers' Health Regulations, Amendment*, SOR/90-70, sch s 1; *Non-smokers' Health Regulations, Amendment*, SOR/93-368, sch s 1; *Non-smokers' Health Regulations, Amendment*, SOR/94-487, sch s 1.

85. See, eg, *Pub and Bar Coalition of Ontario v Ottawa (City)* [2001] OJ No 3496 (Quicklaw) (Ontario Superior Court), affd [2002] OJ No 2240 (Quicklaw) (Ontario Court of Appeal); *Horton v Sudbury (City)* (2004) 70 OR (3d) 768 (Court of Appeal); *Cambridge Bingo Centre Inc v Waterloo (Regional Municipality)* [2000] OTC 695 (Ontario Superior Court); *Doll & Penny's Cafe Ltd. v Vancouver (City)* [2000] BCCA 382 (British Columbia Court of Appeal); *Ontario Restaurant Association v Toronto (City)* [1996] OJ No 5401 (Quicklaw) (Ontario Court, General Division); *Royal Canadian Horse Artillery Brigade Association v Kingston (City)* (2003) 39 MPLR (3d) 41 (Ontario Superior Court); *Dolan v Fredericton (City)* (2003) 264 NBR (2d) 59 (Queen's Bench); *Restaurant and Foodservices Association of British Columbia and the Yukon v Vancouver (City)* (1998) 155 DLR (4th) 587 (British Columbia Court of Appeal); *Rigg v Toronto (City)* (1989) 46 MPLR 113 (Ontario High Court of Justice); *R v Ample Annie's Itty Bitty Roadhouse Inc* [2001] OJ No 5968 (Quicklaw) (Ontario Court of Justice) (*Ample Annie's*).

86. See, eg, *Re Weir and The Queen* (1979) 26 OR (2d) 326 (Divisional Court); *Albertos Restaurant v Saskatoon (City)* (1999) 178 Sask R 219 (Queen's Bench), affd (2000) 199 Sask R 275 (Court of Appeal); *Fredericton (City) v Luna Pizza (1990) Inc* (2002) 252 NBR (2d) 1 (Queen's Bench).

87. *Boucher v Canada (Attorney General)* [2007] 325 FTR 122, 2007 FC 893 (Federal Court).

88. *Mercier v Correctional Service of Canada* [2010] FCA 167 (Federal Court of Appeal), leave to appeal refused 20 January 2011.

89. *Vaughn v Ontario* [2003] OJ No 5304 (Ontario Superior Court); *Regina Correctional Centre (Inmate Committee) v Saskatchewan (Department of Justice)* (1995) 133 Sask R 61 (Queen's Bench) (*Regina Correctional Centre*); *Saskatoon Correctional Centre (Inmate Committee) v Saskatchewan* (2000) 193 Sask R 248 (Queen's Bench) (*Saskatoon Correctional Centre*); *R v Denison* [1999] BCJ No 3280 (British Columbia Supreme Court).

90. Ibid. See also *McNeill v Ministry of Solicitor General & Correctional Services* (1998) 126 CCC (3d) 466 (Ontario Court, General Division) (*McNeill*).

91. *McNeill* (1998) 126 CCC (3d) 466. Constitutional claims of discrimination were also dismissed in *Regina Correctional Centre* (1995) 133 Sask R 61 (Queen's Bench); *Saskatoon Correctional Centre (Inmate Committee)* (2000) 193 Sask R 248 (Queen's Bench); *R v Denison* [1999] BCJ No 3280 (British Columbia Supreme Court).

92. *Club Pro Adult Entertainment Inc v Ontario* (2006) 150 CRR (2d) 1 (Ontario Superior Court) (*Club Pro*), affd 233 OAC 355 (Ontario Court of Appeal), leave to appeal refused 18 September 2008.

93. *Club Pro* (2006) 150 CRR (2d) 1; *Ample Annie's* [2001] OJ No 5968.

94. *An Act to Amend the Tobacco Act*, SC 2009, c 27 (also titled the *Cracking Down on Tobacco Marketing to Youth Act*).

95. Debra Steger (representing Philip Morris International), Submission to Standing Senate Committee on Social Affairs, Science and Technology, *Bill C-32: An Act to Amend Tobacco Act*, 28 September 2009.

96. See, eg, Doug Palmer, 'Tobacco Groups Ask Obama to Challenge Canadian Ban', *Reuters* (online), 29 October 2009 <http://www.reuters.com/article/2009/10/29/us-usa-canada-tobacco-idUSTRE59S4AO20091029>.

97. Bill C-32 was raised at Committee meetings held in November 2009, March 2010, June 2010, November 2010, and March 2011. See World Trade Organization, Committee on Technical Barriers to Trade, *Minutes of the Meeting of 5–6 November 2009*, WTO Doc G/TBT/M/49 (22 December 2009) [8]–[18]; *Minutes of the Meeting of 24–25 March 2010*, WTO Doc G/TBT/M/50 (28 May 2010) [182]–[210]; *Minutes of the Meeting of 23–24 June 2010*, WTO Doc G/TBT/M/51 (1 October 2010) [181]–[226]; *Minutes of the Meeting of 3–4 November 2010*, WTO Doc G/TBT/M/52 (10 March 2011) [203]–[228]; *Minutes of the Meeting of 24–25 March 2011*, WTO Doc G/TBT/M/53 (26 May 2011) [7], [11], [17], [215]–[227].

98. On the WTO challenge to the corresponding US law, see Chapter 6 of this volume.

99. *Tobacco Act*, SC 1997, c 13, s 1.

100. Propel Centre for Population Health Impact, 'National Youth Survey Reveals Cigarette, Cigarillo and Little Cigar Use Down but Susceptibility and Water-Pipe Use are Concerns' (News Release, 31 May 2012) <http://uwaterloo.ca/propel/news/national-youth-survey-reveals-cigarette-cigarillo-and-little>.

101. *Smoke-Free Ontario Act*, SO 1994 c 10, ss 1(1), 6.1; *General Regulation*, O Reg 48/06, ss 1.1, 11.1.

102. See, eg, *Smoke-Free Ontario Act*, SO 1994 c 10, s 4(2); *Tobacco Act*, RSQ, c T-0.01, s 18.

103. *Rosen v Ontario (Attorney General)* (1995) 27 CRR (2d) 162 (Ontario Court, General Division), affd (1996) 131 DLR (4th) 708 (Ontario Court of Appeal), leave to appeal refused 26 September 1996.

104. *Coutu v Ordre des pharmaciens du Québec* [1998] RJQ 2824 (Superior Court).

105. For a summary, see Ontario Tobacco Research Unit, *Prohibition of Tobacco Sales in Specific Places: Monitoring Update* (22 June 2012) <http://otru.org/wp-content/uploads/2012/10/sales2012.pdf>.

106. See, eg, *Tobacco Tax Act*, RSBC 1996, c 452, ss 5–6.

107. The New Brunswick fee is $100 for the initial year and $50 for subsequent years, while the Nova Scotia fee is $121 for three years. *General Regulation – Tobacco Tax Act*, NB Reg 84-250, s.3; *Revenue Act Regulations*, NS Reg 63/96, ss 3B(1)(m), 73(1A). In this chapter, currency is expressed in Canadian dollars, unless otherwise indicated.

108. St Albert, *Tobacco Retail Licensing Bylaw*, 20/96, as amended by Bylaw 29/2012.

109. *Tobacco Sales to Young Persons Act*, SC 1993, c 5, now replaced by *Tobacco Act*, SC 1997, c 13, s 8. A minimum federal age of 16 was established in 1908: *Tobacco Restraint Act*, SC 1908, c 73, with several provinces prior to 1908 already having legislation prohibiting tobacco sales to minors.

110. British Columbia, Ontario, New Brunswick, Nova Scotia, Prince Edward Island, Newfoundland and Labrador, Nunavut. See, eg, *Smoke-Free Ontario Act*, SO 1994 c 10, s 3.

111. Saskatchewan, Manitoba, Quebec, Northwest Territories. See, eg, *The Tobacco Control Act*, SS 2001, c T-14.1, s 4.

112. Alberta, Yukon Territory.

113. *Tobacco Act*, SC 1997, c 13, s 12.

114. See, eg, *Smoke-Free Ontario Act*, SO 1994 c 10, s 7.

115. *Tobacco Act*, SC 1997, c 13, s 11; and previously *Tobacco Sales to Young Persons Act*, SC 1993, c 5, s 5.

116. CRG Consulting, 'Evaluation of Retailers' Behaviour towards Certain Youth Access to Tobacco Restrictions. Final Report Findings: 2009' (Report prepared for Health Canada) (30 April 2010) <http://www.hc-sc.gc.ca/hc-ps/tobac-tabac/research-recherche/eval/index-eng.php>.

117. *R v Sobey's Inc* (1998) 172 NSR (2d) 165 (Court of Appeal) [6]–[11].

118. *R v Clothier* (2011) 330 DLR (4th) 125 (Ontario Court of Appeal) [27]–[50].

119. SOR/2000-273. Earlier reporting requirements, though less detailed, had been included in the *Tobacco Products Control Regulations*, SOR/89-21, ss 17–21.

120. *JTI-Macdonald Corp v Canada (Attorney General)* (2002), [2003] RJQ 181, 102 CRR (2d) 189 (Superior Court) [492]–[511], affd [2005] RJQ 2008, (2005) 260 DLR (4th) 224 (Court of Appeal), [174]–[192]. The tobacco manufacturers did not seek to appeal regarding the reporting regulations.

121. Ibid.

122. Nicotine replacement products are regulated under the federal *Food and Drugs Act*, RSC 1985, c F-27.

123. *Cigarette Ignition Propensity Regulations*, SOR/2005-178.

124. *Tobacco Fee Act*, SBC 1998, c 46 as repealed by *Deregulation Statutes Amendment Act*, SBC 2002, c 12, s 36.

125. Ibid.

126. It has been held that singling out tobacco for high taxation does not infringe tobacco farmers' right to life, liberty and security of the person, nor their equality rights: *Cosyns v Canada (Attorney General)* (1992) 7 OR (3d) 641 (Divisional Court). Also, having higher federal tobacco taxes in some provinces compared with other provinces does not infringe equality rights: *R v Estabrook* (1999) 154 Man R (2d) 235 (Queen's Bench), affd [2001] MJ No 170 (Quicklaw) (Court of Appeal).

127. Cunningham, above n 18, 125–35.

128. Ibid.

129. Canadian Cancer Society, Non-Smokers' Rights Association, Physicians for a Smoke-free Canada, Quebec Coalition for Tobacco Control, *Surveying the Damage: Cut-Rate Tobacco Products and Public Health in the 1990s* (October 1999) Physicians for a Smoke-Free Canada <http://www.smoke-free.ca/pdf_1/submission.PDF>.

130. *United States v Northern Brand International Inc* 268 F 3d 103 (2nd Cir, 2001).

131. 18 USC §§ 1961–8 (2013) (RICO).

132. *Attorney General of Canada v RJ Reynolds Tobacco Holdings, Inc*, 103 F Supp 2d 134 (ND NY, 2000), affd 268 F 3d 103 (2nd Cir 2001), cert denied United States Supreme Court 4 November 2002.

133. *Attorney General of Canada v RJ Reynolds Tobacco Holdings, Inc*, File No 03-CV-25385:CM1, Ontario Superior Court, filed 13 August 2003.

134. Royal Canadian Mounted Police, 'RCMP Lays Criminal Charges against Canadian Tobacco Company' (News Release, 28 February 2003). Overall, two executives from RJR-Macdonald (as it was then called), were convicted on guilty pleas: *R v Leslie Thompson* (unreported, 2 February 2000), (Ontario Court of Justice); *R v Stan Smith* (unreported, 5 January 2006), (Ontario Court of Justice). Leslie Thompson was also convicted in the US and sentenced to seven years' imprisonment: *United States v Leslie Thompson* (unreported, 25 March 1999), US District Court for the Northern District of New York, Criminal Action No 99-CR-93 (TJM).

135. Bankruptcy protection continued until 27 July 2010: see *Re JTI-Macdonald Corp* [2010] ONSC 4212 (Ontario Superior Court).

136. See, eg, *Imperial Tobacco Canada Ltd and Her Majesty the Queen in Right of Canada and the Provinces Listed on the Signature Pages Attached Hereto, Comprehensive Agreement*, signed 31 July 2008. The dates of the other settlements are:

Rothmans, Benson & Hedges Inc (31 July 2008); JTI-Macdonald (13 April 2010); and RJ Reynolds Tobacco Company (13 April 2010).

137. The Imperial Tobacco Canada Ltd and Rothmans, Benson & Hedges civil amounts were payable over multiple years, thus reducing the real value of the payments.

138. For a detailed critique, see Non-Smokers' Rights Association, *What Were They Smoking* (2012) (Report).

139. Eighth Report of the Monitor, *Re JTI-Macdonald Corp*, File No 04 CL 5530, 12 July 2005.

140. *Indian Act*, RSC 1985, c I-5, s 87.

141. Ibid.

142. Ibid.

143. Ibid; *Grand River Enterprises Six Nations Ltd v Canada*, 2012 FCA 239 (Federal Court of Appeal), leave to appeal refused 28 March 2013.

144. Aboriginal Affairs and Northern Development Canada, 'Registered Indian Population by Sex and Residence 2012' 2013 viii.

145. The number of cases in this area is too large for this chapter to include an appropriate summary.

146. *Excise Act, 2001*, SC 2002, c 22, ss 56–8, sch 3 ss 3–4.

147. *Tobacco Act*, SC 1997, c 13, s 13.

148. *Income Tax Act*, RSC 1985, c 1 (5th Supp), ss 182, 183.

149. *Excise Act 2001*, SC 2002, c 22, s 53, sch 3 s 1.

150. Prince Edward Island, however, requires the same markings as Nova Scotia. See *General Regulations*, PEI Reg EC147/08, s 4.

151. *JTI Macdonald Corp v Canada (Attorney General)* (2002), [2003] RJQ 181, 102 CRR (2d) 189 (Superior Court) [451]–[456], affd [2005] RJQ 2018, 260 DLR (4th) 224 (Court of Appeal) [166]–[169]. On the expropriation issue, the tobacco industry did not seek to appeal.

152. *Benson & Hedges (Canada) Ltd v Attorney General of British Columbia* (1972) 27 DLR (3d) 257 (British Columbia Supreme Court).

153. *Club Pro* (2006) 150 CRR (2d) 1.

154. *Pack MJ Inc v Canada* [1997] FCJ no 801 (Federal Court, Trial Division), affd [1998] FCJ no 1922 (Federal Court of Appeal), leave to appeal refused 23 September 1999.

155. *RJR-Macdonald Inc v Canada (Attorney General)* [1994] 1 SCR 311 (*RJR-Macdonald Inc (1994)*).

156. Ibid 347–9. The Court outlined three criteria to be met for the granting of a stay: (i) there is a serious issue to be determined; (ii) compliance with the new legislation will cause irreparable harm; and (iii) the balance of inconvenience, taking into account the public interest, favours retaining the status quo until the Court has disposed of the legal issues.

157. *Rosen v Ontario (Attorney General)* (1994) 27 CRR (2d) 159 (Ontario Court, General Division).

158. *Rothmans, Benson & Hedges Inc v Canada (Procureur Général)* [1997] JQ No 1261 (Quebec Superior Court).

159. *Rothmans, Benson & Hedges Inc v Attorney General of Canada* [2000] RJQ 257 (Quebec Superior Court).

160. *Dicaire v Québec (Procureur Général)* [2003] CanLII 9132 (Quebec Superior Court).

161. *Royal Canadian Horse Artillery Brigade Association v Kingston (City)* (2003) 39 MPLR (3d) 32 (Ontario Superior Court).

162. *Placements Sergakis Inc v Québec (Procureur Général)* [2006] QCCS 5242 (Quebec Superior Court).

163. Opened for signature 16 June 2003, 2302 UNTS 166 (entered into force 27 February 2005) (WHO FCTC).

164. *Décret 70-2006 concernant la déclaration du Québec de se lier à la Convention-cadre pour la lutte antitabac* (translation: *Decree 70-2006 Concerning the Declaration of Quebec to be Bound by the Framework Convention on Tobacco Control*), *Gazette Officielle du Québec*, Vol 138 No 10, 14 February 2006, 1288.

165. See, eg, Global Tobacco Control Forum, *Canada's Implementation of the Framework Convention on Tobacco Control: A Civil Society 'Shadow Report'* (November 2010) Physicians for a Smoke-Free Canada <http://www.smoke-free.ca/pdf_1/FCTC-Shadow-2010-Canada.pdf>.

166. [2007] 2 SCR 610–21 [10], 639 [66]–[67], 663 [138]. The Supreme Court cited WHO FCTC article 11 (packaging and labelling) and article 13 (advertising, promotion and sponsorship).

167. *R v Mader's Tobacco Store Ltd* (2013) 329 NSR (2d) 349 (Nova Scotia Provincial Court) [35]–[37].

168. *Conseil québécois sur le tabac et la santé v JTI-Macdonald Corp* [2005] CanLII 4070 (Quebec Superior Court). The class definitions were modified: *Conseil québécois sur le tabac et la santé v JTI-Macdonald Corp* [2013] QCCS 4904 (Quebec Superior Court).

169. Quebec Superior Court, file 500-06-000076-980, filed 19 November 1998.

170. *Conseil québécois sur le tabac et la santé v JTI-Macdonald Corp* [2013] QCCS 4904 (Quebec Superior Court), 15–16 [85]; *Conseil québécois sur le tabac et la santé and Blais v JTI-Macdonald Corp,* Plaintiffs' Amended Motion to Institute Proceedings, 31 March 2006, 42 [166].

171. Quebec Superior Court, file 500-06-000070-983, filed 10 September 1998.

172. *Conseil québécois sur le tabac et la santé v JTI-Macdonald Corp* [2013] QCCS 4904 (Quebec Superior Court), 16 [85]; *Létourneau v JTI-Macdonald,* Plaintiff's Motion to Institute Proceedings, 30 September 2005, 40–41 [185]–[188].

173. *Canada (Procureur Général) v Imperial Tobacco Ltd* [2012] RJQ 2046 (Quebec Court of Appeal), revg [2012] QCCS 474 (Quebec Superior Court).

174. Available at <https://tobacco.asp.visard.ca/Main.htm> (select 'Direct access to information').

175. The English blog is at: *Eye on the Trials* <http://tobaccotrial.blogspot.ca/>; the French blog is at: *Lumière sur les Procès du Tabac* <http://procesdutabac.blogspot.ca/>.

176. Yukon Territory has not yet adopted Medicare cost-recovery legislation.

177. See, eg, *Tobacco Damages and Health Care Costs Recovery Act*, SBC 2000, c 30; *Tobacco Damages and Health Care Costs Recovery Act*, 2009, SO 2009, c 13; *Tobacco-Related Damages and Health Care Costs Recovery Act*, RSQ, c R-2.2.0.0.1.

178. Canada has a universal health insurance system, primarily operated by provincial/territorial governments.

179. See, eg, *Her Majesty the Queen in Right of British Columbia v Imperial Tobacco Canada Ltd*, British Columbia Supreme Court, Vancouver Registry file S010421, Statement of Claim, filed 24 January 2001 (British Columbia Statement of Claim); *Her Majesty the Queen in Right of Ontario v. Rothmans Inc*, Ontario Superior Court, file CV-09-387984, Statement of Claim, filed 29 September 2009 (Ontario Statement of Claim); *Procureur Général du Québec v Imperial Tobacco Canada Limitée*, Quebec Superior Court, file 500-17-072363-123, Requête introductive d'instance, filed 8 June 2012 (Quebec Statement of Claim).

180. Nova Scotia Department of Justice, 'Nova Scotia Begins Process to Recover Health-care Costs from Tobacco Industry' (Press Release, 30 June 2011) <http://www.gov.ns.ca/news/details.asp?id=20110630006>; CBC News, *Nunavut to sue*

     tobacco companies, 5 August 2011, <http://www.cbc.ca/news/canada/north/story/2011/08/05/nunavut-tobacco-lawsuit.html>.

181. Ontario Statement of Claim, above n 179, 2 [1]; Quebec Statement of Claim, above n 179, 307.

182. The *Master Settlement Agreement* was signed by 46 states in November 1998: National Association of Attorneys General <http://www.naag.org/backpages/naag/tobacco/msa>. Mississippi, Florida, Texas and Minnesota previously had individual state settlements with the tobacco industry. See, eg, *State of Minnesota v Philip Morris Inc*, District Court of the State of Minnesota, County of Ramsey, Second Judicial District, Court File No C1-94-8565, Settlement Agreement and Stipulation for Entry of Consent Judgment, 19 May 1998, <http://publichealthlawcenter.org/sites/default/files/resources/mn-settlement-agreement.pdf>. See also Campaign for Tobacco-Free Kids, *Summary of the Master Settlement Agreement* (9 July 2003) <http://www.tobaccofreekids.org/research/factsheets/pdf/0057.pdf>; Campaign for Tobacco-Free Kids et al, *Broken Promises to Our Children: The 1998 State Tobacco Settlement Fourteen Years Later* (6 December 2012) i, <http://www.tobaccofreekids.org/content/what_we_do/state_local_issues/settlement/FY2013/1.%202012%20State%20Report%20-%20Full.pdf>.

183. *Tobacco Damages Recovery Act*, SBC 1997, c 41 (later renamed the *Tobacco Damages and Health Care Costs Recovery Act*), as amended by *Tobacco Damages Recovery Amendment Act*, SBC 1998, c 45, as repealed by SBC 2000, c 30, s 11.

184. *Her Majesty the Queen in Right of British Columbia v Imperial Tobacco Ltd*, British Columbia Supreme Court, Vancouver Registry file C985776, filed 12 November 1998.

185. *JTI-Macdonald Corp v British Columbia (Attorney General)* (2000) 184 DLR (4th) 335 (British Columbia Supreme Court).

186. *Tobacco Damages and Health Care Costs Recovery Act*, SBC 2000, c 30.

187. Ibid. The legislation was proclaimed into force by BC Reg 11/2001.

188. British Columbia Statement of Claim, above n 179.

189. *British Columbia v Imperial Tobacco Canada Limited* [2005] 2 SCR 473, 487–505 [26]–[78].

190. *Tobacco-Related Damages and Health Care Costs Recovery Act*, SQ 2009, c 34.

191. *Imperial Tobacco Canada Ltd v Quebec (Attorney General)*, Quebec Superior Court, file 500-17-052494-096, filed 25 August 2009.

192. *R v Imperial Tobacco Canada Ltd* [2011] 3 SCR 45, 66–166 [17]–[151].

193. *British Columbia v Imperial Tobacco Canada Ltd* (2005) 44 BCLR (4th) 125 (British Columbia Supreme Court), affd (2006) 273 DLR (4th) 711 (British Columbia Court of Appeal), leave to appeal refused 10 November 2006.

194. *New Brunswick v Rothmans Inc* (2010) 373 NBR (2d) 157 (New Brunswick Queen's Bench), leave to appeal refused [2011] NBJ No 116 (Quicklaw) (New Brunswick Court of Appeal), leave to appeal to Supreme Court of Canada refused 13 October 2011.

195. *Ontario (Attorney General) v Rothmans Inc* (2012) 28 CPC (7th) 68 (Ontario Superior Court), affd (2013) 305 OAC 261 (Ontario Court of Appeal), application for leave to appeal to Supreme Court of Canada filed 27 August 2013.

196. *Québec (Procureur Général) v Imperial Tobacco Canada Ltd* [2013] QCCS 2994 (Quebec Superior Court), leave to appeal refused 2013 QCCA 1702 (Quebec Court of Appeal).

197. See, eg, preliminary judgments/orders on such motions: *Manitoba v Rothmans, Benson & Hedges Inc* (2013) 293 Man R (2d) 313 (Queen's Bench); *Newfoundland and Labrador (Attorney General) v Rothmans Inc*, Newfoundland and Labrador Supreme Court Trial Division, file 2011 01G 0826, unreported, 26 March 2013.

198. *Ontario v Imperial Tobacco Ltd*, US District Court for the Southern District of New York, file 00 CIV. 1593, 7 August 2000.
199. *Knight v Imperial Tobacco Canada Ltd* (2005) 250 DLR (4th) 347 (British Columbia Supreme Court), affd in part (2006) 267 DLR (4th) 579 (British Columbia Court of Appeal). In this class action, the Supreme Court of Canada later held that the federal government could not be named as a third-party defendant: *R v Imperial Tobacco Canada Ltd* [2011] 3 SCR 45.

13. Tobacco control in Latin America

Oscar A Cabrera and Juan Carballo[*]

I INTRODUCTION

Latin America has experienced significant developments in tobacco control regulation in recent years. This includes legislation covering major tobacco control policies such as smoke-free environments, restrictions and regulations on packaging and labelling of tobacco products – including health warnings – and restrictions on tobacco advertisement, promotion and sponsorship, which includes countries moving towards comprehensive bans. The progress made in the region on tobacco control has certain unique characteristics. On the one hand, tobacco control laws and regulations in Latin America are closely connected with human rights. On the other hand, increasing importance is being placed on commercial–trade legal frameworks, and the lack of effective implementation, coupled with institutional weaknesses, in some cases allows the tobacco industry to interfere in the development of public policies to protect health.

The following section introduces the current situation of the tobacco epidemic in Latin America, which includes relatively high rates of tobacco consumption among women and poor people. In section III, we analyse the status of tobacco control laws and policies in the region. In section IV, we briefly analyse the relevant judicial decisions, addressing issues such as protection from the exposure to tobacco smoke, restrictions on packaging and labelling of tobacco products, and a comprehensive ban on tobacco advertising, promotion and sponsorship. Finally, in section V, we draw attention to some of the specific characteristics of tobacco control in the region.

It is important to clarify that for the purposes of this chapter our focus on Latin America will exclude the Caribbean countries. As many Latin American countries do not share the civil law system and other legal characteristics, we also decided to focus on those that can broadly be treated as a homogeneous group, namely: Argentina, Brazil, Chile,

Colombia, Costa Rica, Ecuador, El Salvador, Guatemala, Honduras, Mexico, Nicaragua, Panama, Paraguay, Peru, Uruguay and Venezuela.

II THE TOBACCO EPIDEMIC IN THE REGION

Worldwide, the regions with the highest proportion of deaths attributable to tobacco are the Americas and Europe (tobacco having been used in Europe for a longer period of time). Tobacco poses a major public health threat worldwide, although the tobacco industry is increasingly focusing on developing countries as a result of strong tobacco control laws and higher taxes imposed in the wealthier countries of North America and Europe. Tobacco kills 5 million people worldwide every year, including 1 million in the Americas. Worldwide, the mortality rates attributable to tobacco are higher among men than women. Notably, the Americas presents the smallest gap between males and females compared with any other region.[1]

There are more than 120 million smokers in Latin America, over half of whom will die from a tobacco-related disease.[2] Smoking rates are declining in the region,[3] but remain a concern, as comprehensive tobacco control policies are yet to be implemented in many countries. Recent data shows that 17 per cent of women in Latin America and the Caribbean smoke. However, there are wide variations across sub-regions, for example, the Southern Cone (Argentina, Chile, Paraguay and Uruguay) has the highest percentage of women smokers (30 per cent) and Central America the lowest (4 per cent). The overall regional prevalence of smoking among men is 31 per cent, with higher numbers of men smoking in the Southern Cone (44 per cent).[4]

Together with Africa, Asia and Eastern Europe, Latin America falls within the group of disadvantaged markets now receiving the focus of tobacco industry efforts.[5] Due to economic and institutional weaknesses, countries in these regions are often ill-equipped to counteract industry advertising and prevent tobacco consumption or to take on the resulting health and financial consequences. As a result, the major negative health and financial impacts caused by tobacco consumption are now becoming disproportionally concentrated among the poorest individuals,[6] who tend to have the highest tobacco consumption rates.[7] As we will show in this chapter, governments in Latin America are taking action to address these negative impacts by strengthening legal frameworks for tobacco control, a process that is also bringing about judicial discussion on different tobacco control policies.

III TOBACCO CONTROL LEGISLATION

A The WHO Framework Convention on Tobacco Control in Latin America – the Human Rights Connection

The *WHO Framework Convention on Tobacco Control* (WHO FCTC)[8] has been widely ratified in Latin America, and, with the exception of Argentina and El Salvador, all the countries in the region have ratified it. The Pan-American Health Organization (PAHO) has promoted its ratification, for instance, through the second resolution adopted by the 48th Directive Council,[9] which recognises that scientific evidence has unequivocally shown that tobacco use and exposure to tobacco smoke are causes of mortality, morbidity, and disability. Therefore, this resolution urges member states to consider ratification of the WHO FCTC, if they have not done so, and implement, when appropriate, its provisions.

It is important to point out that the WHO FCTC, similar to other international treaties in the region, is considered a binding instrument per se. It is not pertinent for this chapter to discuss the evolution of dualism and monism in Latin America, but it is worth mentioning that, in most cases, international treaties have mandatory effects for Latin American countries.[10] Moreover, some constitutions establish that international human rights treaties have constitutional hierarchy (eg, Argentina and Venezuela).[11] In this sense, some domestic high courts in Latin America have categorised the WHO FCTC as a human rights treaty, which may have significant implications.

For example, in a case before the Constitutional Tribunal of Peru, in upholding a tobacco control law as discussed further below, the Tribunal held that the WHO FCTC creates human rights obligations,[12] stating that 'the FCTC is a human rights treaty, since it seeks to clearly, expressly and directly protect the basic right to health protection recognized in Article 7 of the Constitution'.[13] Similarly, the Constitutional Chamber of the Costa Rican Supreme Court has also stated that the WHO FCTC is a human rights treaty.[14]

Considering that its structure differs from international human rights treaties, it could be said that the WHO FCTC is not technically a human rights treaty. However, it poses important implications for international human rights law. As argued before by one of the co-authors of this chapter:

> by ratifying the FCTC, member states acknowledge that the tobacco pandemic is a major threat to public health and that the FCTC is the minimum standard to protect the public's health. The FCTC creates a floor of a set of

minimum tobacco control measures state parties must implement. This requires states to develop laws and policies at the domestic level that meet these minimum international standards, and in doing so states protect the right to health.[15]

Thus, regardless of whether states consider the WHO FCTC a human rights treaty or a health law treaty, at a minimum the WHO FCTC functions as a legal standard that specifies the obligation to protect the right to health in the face of the tobacco epidemic.

This human rights connection has allowed United Nations treaty monitoring bodies to recommend that countries implement WHO FCTC's tobacco control policies, even to countries that have not yet ratified the WHO FCTC, such as Argentina. In its 2010 review of Argentina, for instance, the United Nations Committee on the Elimination of Discrimination against Women (CEDAW Committee) highlighted the relationship between the tobacco industry's current promotional strategies targeting women, and the state's international obligations under the *Convention on the Elimination of All Forms of Discrimination against Women* (CEDAW).[16] In order to fulfil CEDAW's obligations, the CEDAW Committee specifically urged Argentina to 'ratify and implement the World Health Organization's FCTC and put in place legislation aimed at restricting tobacco advertising and banning smoking in public spaces'.[17] Similarly, in its 2011 periodic review of Argentina, the United Nations Committee on Economic, Social and Cultural Rights (CESCR) recommended 'that the State party ratify and implement the [WHO FCTC] and develop effective public awareness and tax and pricing policies to reduce tobacco consumption, in particular targeting women and youth'.[18]

B Major Tobacco Control Policies in the Region

In this section we will briefly examine the status of the main tobacco control policies in the region, namely, exposure from tobacco smoke (WHO FCTC article 8), packaging and labelling of tobacco products (WHO FCTC article 11) and tobacco advertising, promotion and sponsorship (WHO FCTC article 13). In addition, we will examine other innovative policies that are being implemented in the region. These regulatory developments, as we will analyse later in this chapter, have triggered litigation, mainly challenging the constitutionality of these policies.

1 Protection from exposure to tobacco smoke (WHO FCTC article 8)

Currently, policies aimed at protecting individuals from exposure to tobacco smoke are present across the region, as shown in Table 13.1. Uruguay was the first country to lead the way in Latin America in enacting comprehensive smoke-free regulations (2008).[19] The most recent country added to this list is Chile, which recently adopted a tobacco control law (2013).[20]

Table 13.1   Latin American countries with comprehensive smoke-free provisions

Country	Year of law/ regulation	Law/regulation
Uruguay	2005	National Decree 268/05
Panama	2008	Law No 13, *Which Adopts Measures to Control Tobacco and its Harmful Effects on Health*
Guatemala	2008	Decree No 74-2008, *Law Creating Tobacco Smoke Free Environments*
Colombia	2009	Law No 1335, *Provisions by which Damages Caused to Minors and the Non-Smoking Population are Prevented and Public Policies Are Stipulated to Prevent Tobacco Consumption and the Cessation of the Smoker's Dependence on Tobacco and its Derivatives in the Colombian People*
Honduras	2010	Decree No 92-2010, *Special Tobacco Control Law (LECT)*
Peru	2010	Law No 29517, *Law Amending Law No 28705, General Law for the Prevention and Control of the Risks of Tobacco Use in Order to Adapt to the WHO Framework Convention on Tobacco Control*
Venezuela	2011	Res No 030, *Smoke-Free Environments*
Ecuador	2011	*Organic Law for the Regulation and Control of Tobacco*
Argentina	2011	Law 26687, *Advertising and Promotion and Tobacco Product Consumption*
Brazil	2011	Law No 12.546
Costa Rica	2012	Legislative Decree No 9028, *General Law for the Control of Tobacco and its Harmful Effects on Health*
Chile	2013	Law No 20.660, *Law Amending Law No 19.419 on Smoke-Free Environments*

Some of the countries listed in Table 13.1 have also approved restrictions on smoking in specific outdoor spaces, such as in the vicinity of educational or health institutions.[21]

In addition to these countries, others have passed some type of regulation for the protection against exposure to tobacco smoke, although some have implemented exceptions. Bolivia, for instance, currently accepts designated smoking rooms.[22] Also, it is important to note that federal countries (eg Brazil and Argentina) have also enacted comprehensive smoke-free provision at the sub-national level (states/provinces).[23]

2   Packaging and labelling of tobacco products (WHO FCTC article 11)

Since the WHO FCTC entered into force in 2005, many countries in Latin America have passed national legislation on packaging and labelling of tobacco products. In many cases, the new legislation is consistent with most of the provisions included in WHO FCTC's article 11 and the guidelines for implementation of that provision.[24] Twelve countries have promulgated laws specifying that warnings must cover between 50 per cent and 80 per cent of the main display areas of the pack and also must include images.[25] Colombia requires a warning covering only 30 per cent of the main display area, which is the minimum established by article 11.[26] Along the same lines, Mexico requires warnings to cover more than 50 per cent of the total surface, but the pictorial warning is mandatory for only 30 per cent of the reverse side.[27] In addition to that, for the most part countries in Latin America have banned the use of misleading terms on packaging and labelling, which may be rooted in consumer protection law.[28]

The case of Uruguay is worth noting. According to its current regulation, the government permits only one variety per brand (sub-brands, such as 'Marlboro Gold', 'Marlboro Green' etc are not allowed).[29] In addition, Uruguay requires one of the largest health warnings in the world (80 per cent on the front and back of tobacco packages).[30] Despite its clear positive impact,[31] these regulations have been challenged domestically before the Uruguayan Supreme Court,[32] and internationally before the World Bank's International Centre for Settlement of Investment Disputes (ICSID) alleging violations of property and brand rights.[33] These two cases will be briefly analysed later in this chapter.

Plain packaging is an issue that is attracting much attention from a legal standpoint given the current World Trade Organization (WTO) challenge to plain packaging in Australia.[34] Currently, no country in the Latin American region has moved towards this type of policy. There are initial discussions in countries such as Panama and Argentina,[35] although it is not likely that legislation on plain packaging could be approved without further discussions and local research backing its implementation.

3 Tobacco advertising, promotion and sponsorship (WHO FCTC article 13)

Panama, Colombia, Brazil and Ecuador are currently the only countries in Latin America that impose a comprehensive ban on tobacco advertising, promotion and sponsorship. Panama has developed the strongest policy by including product exhibition within the general ban.[36] Brazil amended its legislation to ban tobacco advertisement, promotion and sponsorship, with a sole exemption for point-of-sale product displays.[37] Colombia does not specifically regulate product exhibition, although it is a currently accepted marketing practice.[38] Ecuador has been the latest country in the region to introduce a total ban through its recently enacted *Communications Organic Law*.[39] Other countries, including Argentina, Costa Rica, Ecuador, El Salvador and Uruguay, also have strong bans with exceptions ranging from direct personal communication to point-of-sale advertisement.[40]

4 Other measures in the region

Latin America has managed to advance other tobacco control policies in areas in which there is little global experience. Two of these areas are tobacco content and protection from tobacco industry interference.

Brazil has passed regulations on the contents of tobacco products, including banning all additives except sugar starting in 2016 through Resolution 14, issued by the Brazilian Health Surveillance Agency in March 2012.[41] This regulation extends the prohibition to sweeteners, flavours, aromatisers, spices, seasonings, caffeine, and any other substance that imparts aroma or flavour to tobacco products. Some countries, including Chile, Costa Rica, Ecuador, and Uruguay, have granted authority to their national health authority to regulate tobacco products and impose some restrictions on additives.[42] Upcoming years are likely to see advancements in this area.

Latin America has also made progress on measures aimed at protecting health policies from commercial and other vested interests of the tobacco industry (WHO FCTC article 5.3). On 18 April 2012, the Brazilian Minister of Health issued a resolution establishing ethical guidelines for the members of the National Committee for FCTC Implementation (CONICQ).[43] The CONICQ is composed of representatives of 18 ministries and agencies at the federal level and is responsible for implementing policies to comply with the WHO FCTC.[44] The ethical guidelines state that the activities of the committee must be transparent and accountable, and highlight the fact that in accordance with article 5.3 of the WHO FCTC public health interests are irreconcilable with those of the tobacco industry.[45] In Panama, interactions between the Ministry of Health and the tobacco industry are undertaken by the National Commission for the Study of Smoking in Panama, and they are recorded.[46]

IV TOBACCO CONTROL LITIGATION

The tobacco industry, as well as other groups and actors with similar interests, has used litigation as a response to the advancement of tobacco control regulation in Latin America. In most cases, constitutional claims are used when trying to weaken effective tobacco control measures. This has happened in almost every country in Latin America after the passing of a tobacco control law or regulation.[47] In the following sections we will address some of the cases in detail.

On the flipside, tobacco control advocates have also used litigation as a tool for strengthening tobacco control laws and regulations, similarly to litigation used to advance health policies such as development of a specific vaccine[48] or access to water sanitation[49] in Argentina, or a general reform of the health care system in Colombia.[50] This type of litigation is not as common in the context of tobacco control, although there are examples with different results in India,[51] Belgium[52] and Mexico.[53]

In 2008, advocates in Mexico challenged that country's national tobacco control law as inadequately protecting the rights to health, information and life guaranteed by the *Mexican Constitution*.[54] Moreover, they argued that the law amended previous health laws in a way that stripped important powers that the Ministry of Health had previously used to regulate tobacco products. They argued that this reform was retrogressive, in violation of the principle of non-retrogression enshrined in the *International Covenant on Economic, Social and Cultural Rights*.[55] The Supreme Court ultimately dismissed the case on procedural grounds without considering the merits.[56] However, the case is noteworthy because, by granting the petitioner standing to bring the case, the Court affirmed the state's positive obligations to respect economic, social, and cultural rights such as the right to health.[57] This was a ground-breaking decision in Mexico, as the standing rules had traditionally posed a significant barrier to litigating economic, social and cultural rights. As has happened with other tobacco-control-related cases, the impact of this decision therefore extends beyond tobacco control, affecting justiciability more broadly.[58] In its 2011 decision on this case (*Balderas Woolrich*), the Supreme Court ruled that the petitioner had legal standing, clearly changing its position towards standing for right-to-health claims. The Court took a robust, substantive position on the right to health, explicitly linked it to the right to information, and affirmed the state's obligation to protect people from third parties – in this case the tobacco industry. Moreover, the Court stated that access to legal actions to claim proper protection of the right to health should be in place.[59] The Court concluded that rejecting 'a case such as the one under analysis ... due to the lack of legal standing would be based in a mistaken conception of the content and normative density of the right to health'.[60]

Even though this case did not achieve its ultimate goal, it brought about an important advancement in the justiciability of the right to health in Mexico. Given the heightened awareness of the importance of tobacco control policies, the growth of tobacco control civil society organisations and the constitutional frameworks in Latin America recognising health as a human right, it is likely that this type of litigation could be used more frequently in the region.

In the section below we will briefly analyse judicial cases connected to the main tobacco control policies described above: exposure from tobacco smoke (WHO FCTC article 8), packaging and labelling of tobacco products (WHO FCTC article 11) and tobacco advertising, promotion and sponsorship (WHO FCTC article 13).

A   Protection from Exposure to Tobacco Smoke: Cases before the Guatemalan Constitutional Court and Peruvian Constitutional Tribunal

The Guatemalan Chamber of Commerce challenged the constitutionality of certain provisions of Guatemala's smoke-free law that prohibit smoking in any enclosed space except for hotels and motels and establish pecuniary penalties for offenders.[61] The petitioner claimed that, among other things, the challenged provisions violate the freedom of industry and commerce. As summarised by the Court itself, the Guatemalan Chamber of Commerce understood that 'the application of the provisions of Article 3 of the *Law for the Creation of Tobacco Smoke Free Environments* shows a clear restriction of the exercise of the freedom of industry and commerce, beyond the margin of reasonability, and ultimately rendering the aforesaid freedom worthless'.[62] Referencing the WHO FCTC, stressing the importance of the existence of scientific evidence proving that exposure to tobacco smoke causes death, disease and disability, and emphasising that the *Guatemalan Constitution* recognises health as a fundamental right of every person, the Court upheld the challenged law.[63] The Court stated that:

> the establishing of limits on smoking in certain places does not imply, as alleged by the claimant in its brief, that the State has promoted a limitation of the freedom of industry and commerce of the entities manufacturing, producing, distributing and marketing tobacco products, as the purpose of the challenged norm is not to regulate such activities, but to regulate their consumption to protect the right to health of the consumers themselves, and that of non smokers.[64]

The court not only confirmed the constitutionality of the challenged regulation but also strengthened the executive's authority to fully implement the law. The Guatemalan Chamber of Commerce claim also argued that article 3(a) of the smoke-free environments law violates article 2 of the *Guatemalan Constitution*, establishing the principle of legal security, insofar as the language of article 3(a) does not define the term 'enclosed public space' and remains devoid of the certainty necessary for effective enforcement. The Court held that the absence of a definition of 'enclosed public spaces' in article 3(a) was not grounds for unconstitutionality. The 'very meaning of its words' satisfies the 'intellection' of the term, which here is related to 'the purpose of protecting non smokers exposed forcefully to second-hand smoke in places that, due to their enclosed structures, retain the smoke for a certain time forcing its inhalation'.[65] In this way, the Court gave regulatory authority to the executive branch, which then had more flexibility to implement the law.

In a similar case, 5000 Peruvians challenged the constitutionality of a tobacco control law[66] that prohibits smoking in certain public places, including outdoor areas of educational facilities.[67] They argued that these limits infringed their rights to personal autonomy and economic freedom and thus that the Peruvian Constitutional Tribunal should allow smoking in outdoor areas of institutions for higher learning for adults and in special smoking areas. The tribunal recognised that 'the act of smoking, while a demonstration of practiced freedom, is part of the constitutionally protected content of the basic right to free personal development, which is why any limitation on its performance will only become constitutional to the degree that it respects the principle of proportionality'.[68] The Tribunal dismissed the claimants' suit and confirmed the constitutionality and legality of the law.[69] The Tribunal held that the law satisfied a proportionality test, meaning that (a) it pursues a constitutionally valid end; (b) the law is suitable to achieve that end; (c) the law is necessary; and (d) the law is strictly proportional.[70] In performing this test, the

Tribunal considered that the protection of health through positive actions was not only a valid goal but also a mandatory one, according to the *Peruvian Constitution*.[71] Taking into account the available scientific evidence showing the effectiveness of the challenged tobacco control policies and the important negative consequences that the tobacco epidemic has in Peru, the Tribunal concluded that the measures were suitable and necessary to achieve the targeted health goals. It further ruled that the smoking ban was the ideal means to comply with WHO FCTC provisions requiring protection from exposure to tobacco smoke.[72]

As was raised earlier in this chapter, it is important to highlight the human rights perspective given by the Tribunal in this case. In upholding the constitutionality of the law, the Tribunal held that the WHO FCTC creates human rights obligations. Specifically, the Constitutional Tribunal of Peru stated 'the FCTC is a human rights treaty, since it seeks to clearly, expressly and directly protect the basic right to health protection recognized in Article 7 of the Constitution'.[73] The Tribunal further declared, 'the FCTC is a human rights treaty, because although it does not recognize the right to health protection as a "new right" ... it obliges State Parties clearly and directly to take steps that contribute to optimizing its effectiveness'.[74] From this perspective, the Court stated that establishing smoke-free environments 'is not just a constitutionally valid measure, but also required from the International Human Rights Law perspective and the obligation to protect the right to health'.[75]

B Packaging and Labelling of Tobacco Products: the Case before ICSID against the Government of Uruguay

As stated before, Uruguay has established one of the largest health warning requirements for tobacco products.[76] In addition, the law is complemented by a regulation allowing only one presentation per brand.[77] Not surprisingly, these regulations have been challenged by the tobacco industry at both domestic and international levels.

Domestically, the tobacco industry challenged the constitutionality of Law No 18256, arguing it breached the separation of powers by granting excessive power to the executive branch. The tobacco industry claimed that the tobacco control policies adopted by the executive within the frame of Law No 18256 illegitimately affected their rights. According to the tobacco industry, 'the rights of the individual may solely be limited by Parliament, by approving a formal law and for reasons of general interest, as it is the lawmaker and the lawmaker alone that has the right to affect the rights of the individual, having been authorized to do so by the Constitution'.[78] Without a substantial discussion of the tobacco control policies, the Supreme Court stated that Law No 18256 needs regulation for its effective enforcement, but the law does not provide for the necessary legislative delegation. The Court went further by stating:

> it is necessary to take into consideration the difference between legislative delegation and legal enhancement of the regulatory powers of the Executive Branch to matters beyond its normal jurisdiction. The former cannot be admitted under our constitutional framework, while the latter – ie, the authorization to regulate the details necessary for the enforcement of the law – is lawful.[79]

Thus the challenge was dismissed.[80] Even though it was not directly pertinent to the case, the Supreme Court also recognised the competency of the Ministry of Public Health to act pursuant to its authority to adopt all measures deemed necessary to maintain public health 'inasmuch as under Organic Public Health Law No 9202, such Ministry is charged with adopting all measures deemed necessary to maintain collective Health, issuing all regulations and provisions necessary for such main purpose'.[81]

In February 2010, three affiliate companies of Philip Morris International (PMI) – Philip Morris Products SA (PMI's Swiss affiliate); Abal Hermanos SA (a Uruguayan tobacco company); and FTR Holdings SA (a Swiss conglomerate that owns both co-plaintiffs) – filed an arbitration request before ICSID against the government of Uruguay.[82] The claim was presented under the umbrella of a 1991 bilateral investment treaty between Switzerland and Uruguay.[83] PMI claimed that Uruguay's restrictions on tobacco product packaging violated the bilateral investment treaty. Specifically, PMI objected to three provisions of the Uruguayan tobacco control legislation: (i) the requirement that 80 per cent of the front and back of tobacco packs must be covered with graphic health warnings; (ii) the specific content of the graphic images chosen for printing on tobacco packaging; and (iii) the restriction of brand usage to a single presentation. PMI argued that these were arbitrary and unreasonable measures that resulted in an indirect expropriation of their property rights, particularly trademarks, and that this amounted to an unfair and inequitable treatment. By the time of publication of this chapter, the case is still pending. The arbitration process started in May 2011 and is expected to last at least three to four years. Uruguay has unsuccessfully challenged the jurisdiction of the tribunal to hear the claim, arguing that health measures fall outside the scope of the bilateral investment treaty.[84]

The international community has provided support to the government of Uruguay. In September 2010, during the 50th Directing Council meeting of PAHO, ministers of health from PAHO's member states unanimously approved a resolution expressing:

> its support to the Eastern Republic of Uruguay for all the national measures it has adopted, pursuant to the provisions of the Framework Convention and its Guidelines, especially those on the packaging of tobacco products to inform the public about the risks of tobacco and prevent manufacturers from directly or indirectly suggesting that some products are less harmful to health.[85]

Furthermore, this resolution urged member states 'to oppose attempts by the tobacco industry or its allies to interfere with, delay, hinder, or impede the implementation of public health measures designed to protect the population from the consequences of tobacco consumption and exposure to second-hand smoke'.[86]

C Tobacco Advertising, Promotion and Sponsorship: the Case before the Constitutional Court of Colombia

In Colombia, plaintiff Corrales challenged the constitutionality of Law No 1335,[87] which established measures banning the advertisement and promotion of tobacco products, arguing that these measures violate commercial freedoms. The Colombian Constitutional Court emphasised the hazardous nature of tobacco, the necessity to protect the rights to life and health, and Colombia's obligations under the WHO FCTC. Concluding that commercial freedoms are not absolute, the court held that the imposed restrictions were reasonable considering tobacco's impact on public health.[88]

Responding to the argument that a ban on advertisement and promotion implicates the denial of freedom of enterprise, the Court stated:

> It is clear that the challenged norms merely impose prohibitions of behaviours directed to the promotion for the consumption of a group of given goods (tobacco products and their derivatives), without having the potential of affecting the manufacture of such products, or the possibility that they be placed at the disposal of the consumer. Therefore, it cannot be concluded that the measure of prohibition of the advertising of tobacco products and the sponsorship of cultural and sporting events by the tobacco companies in itself affects their freedom of enterprise.[89]

In its decision, the Court clearly stated that health goals are legitimate reasons to restrict commercial freedoms, even to a degree of restriction not seen before – such as a complete ban on tobacco advertisement and promotion. The Court started by connecting this measure with the protection of the right to health, arguing that 'imposing intense restrictions on such activities is a measure suitable for accomplishing the constitutionally-binding purpose of the State of guaranteeing the health of the inhabitants and the environment ... in this case by discouraging the consumption of tobacco products'.[90] The Court then explained that:

> the degree of restriction of commercial advertising admissible is directly proportional with the level of impact on goods of constitutional value. In the case under analysis, the full prohibition of advertising and promotion, and the broad restriction of sponsorship, are justified by the devastating effects – as characterized by the WHO – caused by the consumption of tobacco products.[91]

The Colombian Constitutional Court discussed in depth whether regulations restricting advertisement could imply a violation of freedom of speech. This analysis is extremely relevant, given that Colombia has one of the most advanced legal frameworks with regards to the regulation of tobacco advertisement, promotion and sponsorship. When addressing this issue, the Court started by analysing whether commercial speech was protected under the right to freedom of expression. In this sense, the Court noted that 'the advertising message is not only an instrument of information, but also is an expression of freedom of enterprise and an element of the guarantee of consumer rights'.[92] Thus, it stated that a systematic and teleological interpretation leads to the conclusion 'that commercial advertising does not receive the same constitutional protection as other contents covered by the freedom of speech. Therefore, the law may participate more intensely in publicity'.[93]

The WHO FCTC and World Health Organization played key roles in positioning the Court to justify restrictions of commercial rights in order to properly fulfil the right to health, linking the WHO FCTC with Colombian constitutional obligations. According to the Court:

> the purpose of the Convention, stated in its Article 3, lies in the protection of current and future generations with respect to the health, social, environmental and economic consequences of tobacco consumption and the exposure to smoke and, therefore, develops the principles contained in Articles 49, 78 and 79 of the Constitution. In fact, such norms state the obligation of the State to attend to health and environmental stewardship, in relation to the control of goods and services offered to the community, and the information that must be supplied to the public in their commercialization.[94]

It is pertinent to mention a pending case before the Argentinean Supreme Court in which Nobleza-Piccardo, a British American Tobacco subsidiary, presents similar arguments to those analysed in the Colombian case.[95] Nobleza-Piccardo challenges a sub-national law enacted in the province of Santa Fe, arguing that freedom of speech extends to its right to advertise its products through the mass media, and that restricting it would effect an illegitimate harm on the exercise of lawful economic activity. Even after the approval of a more protective national tobacco control law, the provincial law adopted in 2005[96] is still relevant in establishing more protective standards with regards to tobacco advertisement, promotion and sponsorship.

V REGIONAL CHARACTERISTICS OF THE LEGAL FRAMEWORK FOR TOBACCO CONTROL IN LATIN AMERICA

A Close Connection with Human Rights

As stated in the preceding sections, in Latin America, tobacco control policies and debates around them are starting to be linked with human rights. This connection might be more relevant in this region than in others, as human rights are often fundamental parts of Latin American constitutions, and human rights treaties are frequently considered to take primacy over other laws. Connecting tobacco control policies with human rights obligations strengthens arguments in favour of effective policies, which often entail restrictions on commercial freedoms, as seen in the judicial cases analysed above.

From a human rights perspective, the argument can be made that given the burden of tobacco-related diseases worldwide, states have an obligation to intervene to protect the right to health of their citizens.[97] This statement can be analysed in light of the three main obligations derived from human rights: to respect, protect and fulfil human rights.[98] Firstly, the obligation to respect human rights requires states to refrain from either directly or indirectly violating human rights or impeding their realisation.[99] In the realm of tobacco control, this means that, for example, states are prohibited from promoting, advertising or sponsoring the use of tobacco products,[100] something that is not relevant to Latin American countries as there are no state-owned tobacco companies. Secondly, the obligation to protect human rights requires that states take measures to prevent third parties from interfering with human rights.[101] In order to effectively protect the right to health, governments have a legal duty to regulate the tobacco industry to ensure that fewer individuals are subject to the negative health consequences of tobacco products. The economic power of transnational tobacco corporations has generated an unequal battle with the governments of countries that are ill-resourced to fully develop these policies, and the industry lobby has often prevailed over tobacco control initiatives.[102] Finally, the obligation to fulfil human rights requires governments to adopt all appropriate legislative, administrative, budgetary and other measures, which encompasses comprehensive tobacco controls.[103]

Human rights perspectives on tobacco control policies provide increased understanding of the impact of the tobacco epidemic on vulnerable populations: young people, women and poor people.[104]

B   Increasing Importance of Commercial–Trade International Legal Frameworks in Tobacco Control Discussions

The greater importance of commercial–trade international legal arguments on tobacco control discussions has been largely connected with packaging and labelling policies,[105] although it is likely to be connected in the future with product contents regulations, taxes and other tobacco control policies.

In the region, the first case where this growing relationship became clear was the Philip Morris challenge to Uruguay before ICSID, which was briefly described above. In response to this, the fourth session of the Conference of the Parties to the WHO FCTC voted unanimously in favour of the Punta del Este Declaration affirming the Parties' 'firm commitment to prioritize the implementation of health measures designed to control tobacco consumption in their respective jurisdictions' and their 'concern regarding actions taken by the tobacco industry that seek to subvert and undermine government policies on tobacco control'.[106] The declaration further states that 'Parties have the right to define and implement national public health policies pursuant to compliance with conventions and commitments under WHO, particularly with the WHO FCTC'.[107]

This is not the only case in the region in which international economic law arguments are used. Tobacco taxation debates in Argentina have also included considerations on their impact on commitments before the WTO.[108] Recently, Costa Rica's approval of tobacco health warnings regulations was suspended due to insistence from the Ministry of Economy that those regulations needed prior approval by the WTO. In addition, Latin American countries such as Honduras have challenged Australia's plain packaging legislation as a violation of the *Agreement on Trade-Related Aspects of Intellectual Property Rights*[109] (TRIPS) and the *Paris Convention for the Protection of Industrial Property*[110] under the WTO.[111]

These connections between tobacco control policies and trade, and international economic law more broadly, are likely to grow as attention turns to policies such as plain packaging or product regulation.

C   Lack of Effective Implementation: Cultural Patterns and Implementation Costs

After effective tobacco control measures are enacted, the main issue becomes implementation. In 2008, some argued that effective implementation of the WHO FCTC at a country level 'faces daunting economic, political and socio-cultural challenges in developing countries especially, despite their vocal support for the treaty during negotiations'.[112]

Latin America is not immune to this challenge. Moreover, Latin America must contend with a context whereby the gap between legal frameworks and practices is greater than in other regions. This has been widely studied, and it is mainly connected with the cultural perceptions of low respect for legal norms; scholars in Argentina,[113] Brazil,[114] Colombia[115] and Mexico,[116] among others, have addressed this. The fact that constitutional and legal frameworks of Latin American countries include direct protection of the right to health has facilitated the approval of tobacco control regulations.

Besides cultural issues, governments in the region need to deal with the problem of scarcity of public resources to advance economic, social and cultural rights. Although some tobacco control policies are not resource-intensive (such as smoke-free environments or bans on tobacco advertisement, promotion and sponsorship), their effective monitoring does require the allocation of scarce public resources, even if not as much as with other health policies. In a region in which there are strong public health care systems, it is important to point out that tobacco control policies lead to public savings in the long term, which can then be redirected to health needs. The Peruvian Constitutional Tribunal addressed this issue, noting that the state has the right to take all the necessary steps to significantly reduce the costs created by a behaviour that indirectly reduces the state's ability to meet its legal obligations to protect and guarantee the basic rights of all people. The Tribunal stated that 'it is constitutionally valid to seek to reduce the health costs incurred from treatments for tobacco-related diseases by significantly reducing its use through bans on smoking in enclosed public spaces and smoking in open areas located in or near adult educational centers'.[117]

In addition, the development of more advanced tobacco control policies similar to those dealing with the regulation of tobacco product contents or disclosures or those aimed at providing support for economically viable crop replacement alternatives will necessarily demand more public resources. In the Latin American region, this may become an important challenge to the advancement of tobacco control policies.

D   Institutional Weaknesses in the Region and Tobacco-industry Interference

In general, Latin American countries have been considered to have weak institutions with regards to accountability, control or transparency in general.[118] This general feature poses an important challenge in connection with tobacco control, as the tobacco industry could use those institutional weaknesses to undermine tobacco control policies.[119]

The WHO FCTC itself warns its parties of this danger in article 5.3, stating that 'in setting and implementing their public health policies with respect to tobacco control, Parties shall act to protect these policies from commercial and other vested interests of the tobacco industry in accordance with national law'.

Select examples of tobacco industry interference include reports of systematic efforts from the tobacco industry to influence the judiciary in Brazil,[120] clear conflicts of interest in public officers dealing with health-related policies in the executive branch in Chile,[121] and legislators in similarly compromising situations in Argentina.[122] In the Latin American context of weak or non-existent regulations on access to information, prevention of conflicts of interest, and control of lobbying activities, tobacco industry interference could become a major public health issue.

NOTES

*   All translations are unofficial translations from Campaign for Tobacco-Free Kids, *Tobacco Control Laws* <http://www.tobaccocontrollaws.org/>, except where otherwise indicated.

1.   WHO, *Global Report: Mortality Attributable to Tobacco* (WHO, 2012) <http://www.who.int/tobacco/publications/surveillance/rep_mortality_attributable/en/>.

2.   Fernando Muller and Luis Wehbe, 'Smoking and Smoking Cessation in Latin America: a Review of the Current Situation and Available Treatments' (2008) 3 *International Journal of Chronic Obstructive Pulmonary Disease* 285.

3.   Chile and Panama, for example, have been highlighted in WHO, *2012 Global Progress Report on Implementation of the WHO Framework Convention on Tobacco Control* (WHO, 2012).

4.   Sandhi Barreto et al, 'Epidemiology in Latin America and the Caribbean: Current Situation and Challenges' (2012) 41 *International Journal of Epidemiology* 557.

5. Thomas Bollyky and Lawrence Gostin, 'The United States' Engagement in Global Tobacco Control: Proposals for Comprehensive Funding and Strategies' (2010) 304(23) *Journal of the American Medical Association* 2637.

6. T Novotny and D Carlin, 'Ethical and Legal Aspects of Tobacco Control' (2005) 14 (supplement 2) *Tobacco Control* ii26.

7. 'It is the poorer and the poorest who tend to smoke the most. Currently, there are an estimated 1.3 billion smokers worldwide. Of these, 84% live in developing and transitional economy countries': WHO, *Tobacco and Poverty: A Vicious Circle* (WHO, 2004) 3 <http://www.who.int/tobacco/communications/events/wntd/2004/en/wntd2004_brochure_en.pdf>.

8. Opened for signature 16 June 2003, 2302 UNTS 166 (entered into force 27 February 2005).

9. Pan-American Health Organization, Directing Council, *WHO Framework Convention on Tobacco Control: Opportunities and Challenges for its Implementation in the Region of the Americas*, PAHO Doc CD50/26 (27 September 2010, original Spanish).

10. See, eg, Domingo Acevedo, 'Relación entre el Derecho Internacional y el Derecho Interno' (1992) 16 *Revista IIDH* 133.

11. See, eg, *Argentine National Constitution* article 75; *Chilean Constitution* article 5-II; *Nicaraguan Constitution* article 46; *Venezuelan Constitution* article 23.

12. *Jaime Barco Rodas contra el Artículo 3° de la ley N 28705 – Ley general para la prevención y control de los riesgos del consumo de tabaco*, unconstitutionality proceeding, July 2011 (Constitutional Tribunal, Peru) 67.

13. Ibid.

14. *Request on the Constitutionality of a Proposed Piece of Legislation*, Exp 12-002657-0007-CO, Res No 2012-003918, March 2012 (Constitutional Chamber of the Costa Rican Supreme Court).

15. Oscar Cabrera and Lawrence Gostin, 'Human Rights and the Framework Convention on Tobacco Control: Mutually Reinforcing Systems' (2011) 7(3) *International Journal of Law in Context* 285, 292.

16. Opened for signature 18 December 1979, 1249 UNTS 13 (entered into force 3 September 1981).

17. CEDAW Committee, *Concluding Observations of the Committee on the Elimination of Discrimination against Women: Argentina*, UN Doc CEDAW/C/ARG/CO/6 (13 July 2010) 39–40.

18. CESCR, *Concluding Observations of the Committee on Economic, Social and Cultural Rights: Argentina*, UN Doc E/C.12/ARG/CO/3 (2 December 2011) 7.

19. Law No 18.256 on Smoking Control Regulations (2008).

20. Law No 20.660 amending Law No 19.419 on Smoke-Free Environments (2013).

21. See, eg, Law No 29517 amending Law No 28705, *General Law for the Prevention and Control of the Risks of Tobacco Use in Order to Adapt to the WHO Framework Convention on Tobacco Control* (2010).

22. Supreme Decree No 29376/2007, regulations to Law No 3029 on the WHO FCTC (2007).

23. See, eg, Law No 9113 Córdoba Province (Argentina); Law 9220 Espirito Santo State (Brazil).

24. WHO FCTC Conference of the Parties, *Guidelines for Implementation of Article 11 of the WHO Framework Convention on Tobacco Control*, 3rd sess, WHO Doc FCTC/COP3(10) (17–22 November 2008).

25. Pan American Health Organization, *Manual for Developing Tobacco Control Legislation in the Region of the Americas* (PAHO, 2013).

26. Law No 1335, *Provisions by which Damages Caused to Minors and the Non-Smoking Population are Prevented and Public Policies are Stipulated to Prevent*

Tobacco Consumption and the Cessation of the Smoker's Dependence on Tobacco and its Derivatives in the Colombian People (2009) article 13.

27. *General Law on Tobacco Control (Mexico)* (2008).
28. Pan American Health Organization, *Manual for Developing Tobacco Control Legislation in the Region of the Americas* (PAHO, 2013).
29. That means, for example, that Marlboro may sell only one presentation per brand, eg Marlboro or Marlboro Red, or Gold, or Mint, etc: Ministry of Public Health Ordinance No 514 (Uruguay) article 3.
30. Ministry of Public Health Decree No 287/009 on Health Warnings (Uruguay) article 1.
31. Winston Abascal et al, 'Tobacco Control Campaign in Uruguay: a Population-based Trend Analysis' (2012) 380(9853) *The Lancet* 1575.
32. *Abal Hermanos, SA v Uruguay*, Sentencia No 1713, 2010 (Supreme Court, Uruguay).
33. *Philip Morris Brands Sàrl v Uruguay (Notice of Arbitration)* (ICSID Arbitral Tribunal, Case No ARB/10/7, 19 February 2010). See also Benn McGrady, 'Implications of Ongoing Trade and Investment Disputes: Philip Morris v Uruguay' in Andrew Mitchell, Tania Voon and Jonathan Liberman with Glyn Ayres (eds), *Public Health and Plain Packaging Of Cigarettes: Legal Issues* (Edward Elgar, 2012) 173.
34. See, eg, *Australia – Certain Measures Concerning Trademarks and Other Plain Packaging Requirements Applicable to Tobacco Products and Packaging: Request for the Establishment of a Panel by Ukraine*, WTO Doc WT/DS434/11 (17 August 2012); *Australia – Certain Measures Concerning Trademarks, Geographical Indications and Other Plain Packaging Requirements Applicable to Tobacco Products and Packaging: Request for Consultations by Indonesia*, WTO Doc WT/DS467/1 (25 September 2013). See also Chapter 14 of this volume and below n 111.
35. In both countries there are draft bills establishing plain packaging currently under discussion, although it is not likely that they will progress in the near future.
36. National Decree 611, 3 June 2010 (Panama).
37. National Law No 12546, 14 December 2011 (Brazil) article 49.
38. National Law No 1335, 21 July 2009 (Colombia) articles 14–16.
39. *Communications Organic Law 2013* (Ecuador), enacted on 24 June 2013, includes a general prohibition on any type of cigarette advertisement. It remains to be seen how this piece of legislation will operate alongside more specific tobacco control regulations regarding the applicability to other products or the scope of the definition of 'advertisement' in this law.
40. See, eg, Law 26687 (Argentina) article 6, which establishes exceptions for point-of-sale advertising, commercial publications aimed exclusively at persons or institutions involved in the business of tobacco, and direct communication to those over the age of 18, provided that their prior consent has been obtained and their age verified.
41. There is pending litigation with regards to this policy in Brazil.
42. See, eg, Law 19419 (Chile) article 9, which reads: 'The Ministry of Health can prohibit the use of additives and substances that are added to tobacco in the process of manufacture of the products addressed by this law that are intended to be sold in the national territory, when such additives and substances increase levels of addiction, harm or risk in the consumers of said products'.
43. Administrative Rule No 713, 17 April 2012 (Brazil).
44. The CONICQ was created through National Decree 3136, 1999 (Brazil).
45. Administrative Rule No 713, 17 April 2012 (Brazil).
46. *Panama: Third Implementation Report* (16 April 2012) <http://www.who.int/fctc/reporting/party_reports/pan>.

47. O'Neill Institute for National and Global Health Law, *Tobacco Industry Strategy in Latin American Courts – A Litigation Guide* (2012) 16.
48. Causa No 31.777/96, *Viceconte, Mariela Cecilia c/ Estado Nacional – Ministerio de Salud y Acción Social s/ amparo ley 16.986*, 2 June 1998 (Cámara Contenciosa Administrativa Federal, Sala V [National Administrative Chamber, House V]).
49. *Mendoza, Beatriz S c Estado Nacional*, 2006 (Supreme Court of Argentina).
50. Decision T-760, 2008 (Constitutional Court of Colombia).
51. *Murli Deora v Union of India*, WP No 316/1999, 11 February 2001 (Supreme Court of India).
52. *Vlaamse Liga tegen Kanker [Flemish Anti-Cancer League] v Belgium Council of Ministers*, Arrêt No 37/2011, 15 March 2011 (Constitutional Court of Belgium).
53. *Jorge Francisco Balderas Woolrich*, revised amparo 315/2010 against 1791/2008, 28 February 2011 (Supreme Court of Justice, Mexico).
54. *Complaint for Clínica de Interés Público del Centro de Investigación y Desarrollo de la Educación v Cámara de Senadores del Congreso de la Unión*, 2008 (Juzgado Primero de Distrito en Materia Administrativa en el Distrito Federal [Administrative Trial Court], Mexico).
55. United Nations Committee on Economic, Social and Cultural Rights, *General Comment No 3: The Nature of States Parties' Obligations (Article 2, Para 1, of the Covenant)*, 5th sess, UN Doc E/1991/23 (14 December 1990) [9].
56. *Jorge Francisco Balderas Woolrich*, revised amparo 315/2010 against 1791/2008, 28 February 2011 (Supreme Court of Justice, Mexico) 8.
57. Ibid.
58. Oscar Cabrera and Juan Carballo, 'Tobacco Control Litigation: Broader Impacts on Health Rights Adjudication' (2013) 41(1) *The Journal of Law, Medicine & Ethics, American Society of Law, Medicine & Ethics*, 157.
59. *Jorge Francisco Balderas Woolrich*, revised amparo 315/2010 against 1791/2008, 28 February 2011 (Supreme Court of Justice, Mexico) 43.
60. Ibid 33.
61. *Law Creating Tobacco Smoke Free Environment*, Decree No 74-2008 (Guatemala).
62. Docket No 2158, V, 11, 2009 (Constitutional Court of Guatemala) s III.
63. Ibid s IV.
64. Ibid s V.
65. Ibid s V.
66. Law No 29517, *Law Amending Law No 28705, General Law for the Prevention and Control of the Risks of Tobacco Use in Order to Adapt to the WHO Framework Convention on Tobacco Control* (Peru).
67. *Jaime Barco Rodas contra el Artículo 3° de la ley N 28705 – Ley general para la prevención y control de los riesgos del consumo de tabaco*, unconstitutionality proceeding, July 2011 (Constitutional Tribunal, Peru).
68. Ibid 24.
69. Ibid s V.
70. Ibid 30.
71. Ibid 63.
72. Ibid 92, 118, 141.
73. Ibid 67.
74. Ibid 69.
75. Ibid 81.
76. Ministry of Public Health Decree No 287/009 (Uruguay) on Health Warnings.
77. Ministry of Public Health Ordinance No 514 (Uruguay) article 3.
78. *Abal Hermanos, SA v Uruguay*, Sentencia No 1713, 2010 (Supreme Court, Uruguay).
79. Ibid III.

80. Ibid deciding section.
81. Ibid II.
82. *Request for Arbitration: FTA Holdings SA (Switzerland) v Uruguay* (19 February 2010).
83. *Agreement between the Swiss Confederation and the Oriental Republic of Uruguay on the Reciprocal Promotion and Protection of Investments*, dated 7 October 1988, 1976 UNTS 389 (entered into force 22 April 1991).
84. *Philip Morris Brands Sàrl v Uruguay (Decision on Jurisdiction)* (ICSID Arbitral Tribunal, Case No ARB/10/7 2 July 2013).
85. Pan American Health Organization, *Strengthening the Capacity of Member States to Implement the Provisions and Guidelines of the WHO Framework Convention on Tobacco Control*, PAHO Res CD 50.R6, 62nd sess, 6th plen mtg (29 September 2010) [1].
86. Ibid [2(a)].
87. Law No 1335, *Provisions by which Damages Caused to Minors and the Non-Smoking Population are Prevented and Public Policies are Stipulated to Prevent Tobacco Consumption and the Cessation of the Smoker's Dependence on Tobacco and its Derivatives in the Colombian People 2009* (Colombia) article 13.
88. Expediente D-8096 – Sentencia C-830/10, 2010 (Constitutional Court of Colombia).
89. Ibid 28.
90. Ibid.
91. Ibid 29.2.
92. Ibid 12.
93. Ibid 13.
94. Ibid 20.
95. *Nobleza Piccardo SAIC Y F v Provincia de Santa Fe*, 188/2006, 2006 (Supreme Court of Argentina).
96. Law No 12432, 2006 (Santa Fe Province, Argentina).
97. Cabrera and Gostin, above n 15, 286.
98. Ibid 288.
99. United Nations Committee on Economic, Social and Cultural Rights, *General Comment No 3: The Nature of States Parties' Obligations (Article 2, Para 1, of the Covenant)*, 5th sess, UN Doc E/1991/23 (14 December 1990) [9].
100. Oscar Cabrera and Alejandro Madrazo, 'Human Rights as a Tool for Tobacco Control in Latin America' (2010) 52 *Salud Pública de México* S288, S290-1.
101. United Nations Committee on Economic, Social and Cultural Rights, *General Comment No 14: The Right to the Highest Attainable Standard of Health*, 22nd sess, UN Doc E/C.12/2000/4 (11 August 2000) [33].
102. See, eg, WHO, *Tobacco Industry Interference with Tobacco Control* (WHO, 2009).
103. Cabrera and Madrazo, above n 100, S290.
104. World Health Organization, *Global Action Plan for the Prevention and Control of Non-communicable Diseases 2013–2020, Follow-up to the Political Declaration of the High-Level Meeting of the General Assembly on the Prevention and Control of Non-communicable Diseases*, WHO Res WHA66.10, 66th WHA, 9th plen mtg, Agenda Items 13.1 and 13.2 (27 May 2013) annex [25].
105. Tim Mackey, Bryan Liang and Thomas Novotny, 'Evolution of Tobacco Labeling and Packaging: International Legal Considerations and Health Governance' (2013) 103(4) *American Journal of Public Health* e39.
106. WHO FCTC Conference of the Parties, *Punta del Este Declaration on the Implementation of the WHO Framework Convention on Tobacco Control*, WHO Doc FCTC/COP4(5) (18 November 2010) [1]–[2].
107. Ibid [5].

108. Marcelo Rodríguez Faraldo and Hugo Zilocchi, *Historia del Cultivo del Tabaco en Salta* (Ministerio de Agricultura, 2012) 151.
109. *Marrakesh Agreement Establishing the World Trade Organization*, opened for signature 15 April 1994, 1867 UNTS 3 (entered into force 1 January 1995) annex 1C.
110. Opened for signature 14 July 1967, 828 UNTS 306 (entered into force 26 April 1970).
111. *Australia – Certain Measures Concerning Trademarks, Geographical Indications and Other Plain Packaging Requirements Applicable to Tobacco Products and Packaging: Request for the Establishment of a Panel by Honduras*, WTO Doc WT/DS435/16 (17 October 2012); *Australia – Certain Measures Concerning Trademarks, Geographical Indications and Other Plain Packaging Requirements Applicable to Tobacco Products and Packaging: Request for the Establishment of a Panel by the Dominican Republic*, WTO Doc WT/DS441/15 (14 November 2012); *Australia – Certain Measures Concerning Trademarks, Geographical Indications and Other Plain Packaging Requirements Applicable to Tobacco Products and Packaging: Request for Consultations by Cuba*, WTO Doc WT/DS458/1 (7 May 2013). See also above n 34.
112. Thomas Novotny and Hadii Mamudu, 'Progression of Tobacco Control Policies: Lessons from the United States and Implications for Global Action' (Discussion Paper, World Bank, May 2008) 35 <http://siteresources.worldbank.org/HEALTHNUTRITIONANDPOPULATION/Resources/281627-1095698140167/NovotnyPoliticalEconomy.pdf>.
113. Carlos Santiago Nino, *Un país al margen de la ley* (Emecé Editores, 1992).
114. Roberto DaMatta, *Carnivals, Rogues, and Heroes: An Interpretation of the Brazilian Dilemma* (John Drury, trans) (1991).
115. Mauricio García Villegas, *Normas de papel: La cultura del incumplimiento* (Siglo del Hombre Editores, 2010).
116. Claudio Lomnitz, 'La construcción de la ciudadanía en México' (2000) 4 *Metapolítica* 128.
117. *Jaime Barco Rodas contra el Artículo 3º de la ley N 28705 – Ley general para la prevención y control de los riesgos del consumo de tabaco*, unconstitutionality proceeding, July 2011 (Peru) 41–2.
118. Gretchen Helmke and Steven Levitsky, *Informal Institutions and Democracy: Lessons from Latin America* (Johns Hopkins University Press, 2006).
119. WHO, *Tobacco Industry Interference with Tobacco Control* (WHO, 2009).
120. Clarissa Homsi, *A indústria do tabaco e as tentativas de interferência junto ao Poder Judiciário* (18 April 2012) Aliança de Controle do Tabagismo <http://actbr.org.br/uploads/conteudo/707_artigo_Migalhas.pdf>.
121. García Giménez, Bernardita, 'El largo brazo del lobby de las tabacaleras, *El Mostrador* (online), 9 February 2012 <http://www.elmostrador.cl/noticias/pais/2012/02/09/el-largo-brazo-del-lobby-de-las-tabacaleras/>.
122. Ernesto Sebrie et al, 'Tobacco Industry Successfully Prevented Tobacco Control Legislation in Argentina' (2005) 14 *Tobacco Control* e2.

14. Tobacco control in Australia: the High Court challenge to plain packaging

Mark Davison

I INTRODUCTION

The unsuccessful challenge[1] to the tobacco plain packaging legislation[2] (the TPP) based on the *Australian Constitution* obviously demonstrates the compliance of the TPP with Australian domestic law. In that sense, the effects of the decision are confined to Australia. However, a further and related issue is the extent to which a number of issues addressed in the course of the constitutional case affect international legal challenges to Australia's plain packaging legislation. This chapter considers the decision of the High Court of Australia (Australia's highest court) and relevant pleadings and arguments put to the High Court. In doing so, it analyses the potential impact of various aspects of the litigation on the arbitration proceedings between Australia and Philip Morris Asia Limited (PMA).[3]

At the outset, it should be recognised that there are some difficulties associated with identifying the precise impact of the decision. The seven High Court justices wrote six different judgments, none of which referred directly to any of the other judgments. The six justices in the majority wrote five separate judgments, with only Hayne and Bell JJ writing a joint judgment. As the case turned on a very specific provision of the *Australian Constitution*, a number of justices unsurprisingly focused on that provision and did not address some tangential issues in any great detail. However, some important propositions can be distilled from the judgments with considerable certainty, and some but not total elucidation of other relevant propositions has been provided.

II THE EFFECT OF THE LEGISLATION

As the title of the *Tobacco Plain Packaging Act 2011* (Cth) suggests, the effect of the TPP on tobacco packaging is to make it 'plain' in the sense of greatly reducing the use of packaging to promote tobacco consumption. It does this by prohibiting the use of non-word trademarks or signs on retail tobacco packaging and heavily regulating the use of word trademarks for retail packaging.[4] The use of colours, logos and artistic devices of any sort are prohibited.[5] Packs are primarily 'drab brown' in colour.[6]

The only branding permitted on retail packets is the name of the brand and any variant of the brand.[7] Even that branding is subject to tight restrictions. The font size and the font face of the brand name and variant name are dictated by the TPP.[8] So too is the placement and the colour of the printing of the brand name and variant. There are other tight restrictions on the use of any signs to promote cigarettes. For example, the colour, design and shape of the cigarette sticks are prescribed, as too is the wrapping for the cigarettes so as to prevent those aspects of packaging being used to promote the cigarettes.[9] In another sense, the packaging is anything but plain. Text and confronting graphic warnings take up the majority of the space on packets.[10]

A summary of the legislation's effects on trademarks can then be stated as follows: word trademarks may continue to be used on retail packaging provided they are placed in a specified location and restricted to a specified font size, font and colour. Other trademarks are prohibited from appearing on retail packaging. In addition, much of the space on packaging is taken up with warnings which would, of themselves, severely restrict the opportunity to use trademarks on cigarette packaging.

Potentially, there were other consequences of the legislative prohibition for owners of registered trademarks. For example, a failure to use a trademark may eventually result in its removal for non-use under general trademark legislation.[11] The TPP provides that such non-use will not be a ground for removal of trademarks that have not been used because of the legislative prohibition on use at the retail level.[12] Consequently, registration of trademarks may be maintained, which carries with it the ongoing right to sue for infringement if a third party used the trademarks in Australia, even if that use also contravened the plain packaging legislation. In addition, registration of a trademark is usually dependent on an intention to use that trademark. Under the TPP, registration is permitted if there is no intention to use a trademark because of the effects of the TPP.

Other restrictions on property include the inability to exploit the goodwill associated with non-word trademarks, whether or not they are registered. In addition, the liberty to place signs on packaging as tobacco companies please is considerably reduced, although there were already significant restrictions on the design of tobacco packaging prior to the plain packaging legislation due to requirements to place both text and graphic warnings on tobacco packaging that took up 90 per cent of the back of a cigarette packet and 30 per cent of the front of a cigarette packet.

III   THE BASIS OF THE CONSTITUTIONAL CHALLENGE – AN ALLEGED ACQUISITION OF PROPERTY ON OTHER THAN JUST TERMS

The relevant constitutional provision provides that the Commonwealth government may acquire property on just terms.[13] In other words, it cannot acquire property on other than just terms. In order to establish their case, the plaintiffs had to identify the precise nature of the property of which they had been deprived, demonstrate how that property (or some corresponding property) had been acquired by the government, and demonstrate that the acquisition had not been on 'just terms'. Failure to satisfy any of those three requirements would have been fatal to the claim.

A   The Property and Alleged Deprivation of It

The pleadings referred to a number of different types of property, including one registered patent and a small number of designs. Obviously, there were references to registered trademarks and this was the main form of property discussed in the case. The pleadings also referred to even more difficult to define forms of property such as 'goodwill' and the amorphous concept of 'get-up'. In addition, the plaintiffs made much of their 'right' to place whatever labelling they wished on their packaging with the emphasis seemingly on the suggestion that they owned the 'plain', ie completely unmarked, packaging without any printing of any type on it at all and they had a right to place on it whatever they wished, including their trademarks and get-up. Consequently, the argument continued, their rights in respect of the packaging had been lost. This argument was rejected by the majority of the court. As Gummow J pointed out during the hearing, there is no right to put any printed material on any packaging.[14] For example, there is no right to put pornographic material on packaging and then to sell it in public. Hayne J stated that the argument started at too high a level of abstraction, with a theoretically blank piece of packaging, when the true position is that the tobacco industry, like other industries, needs to comply with government regulations concerning packaging for particular products if they wish to retail those products.[15]

The more complex issues related to the property of a registered trademark owner. The Australian trademark legislation specifically states that a trademark owner has the right to use a registered trademark, but the issue is more complicated than simply referring to that one provision in the trademark legislation. The nature of that 'right' was interrogated, as was the extent to which it was inherently subject to other legislation restricting the use of trademarks.

Submissions made by the Commonwealth and, in particular, the Solicitor-General for Queensland,[16] were based on an analysis of property and property rights pursuant to the well-known taxonomy of Hohfeld.[17] Consequently, they placed much emphasis on the view that the property rights of registered trademark owners are purely negative rights. Their arguments went that the relevant rights of registered trademark owners are the rights to exclude others from using their trademarks to the extent prescribed by the infringement provisions of the legislation. This perspective is based on the proposition that, in the absence of trademark legislation, everyone has a liberty to use a sign in any way that they see fit. Trademark legislation limits that liberty but retains the liberty for the registered owner of a sign that is a registered trademark. The liberty does not constitute a right, as there is no corresponding duty on the government to refrain from interfering with that liberty. Only the right to prevent others from exercising what would otherwise be their liberty to use the trademark is the relevant property right. Consequently, the argument went that no taking of property rights had occurred because tobacco trademark owners retain the right to prevent others from using their trademarks.

With regard to goodwill, a similar argument was employed. The tort of passing off protects goodwill only by excluding others from engaging in deceptive conduct, which suggests an association between the defendant and the owner of the goodwill generated, in part, by the use of trademarks, whether registered or not.

The responses in the judgments of the majority to this proposition were varied. French CJ accepted that the statutory rights in question are negative in character,[18] although he went on to say that 'rights to exclude others from using property have no substance if all use of the property is prohibited'.[19] He seemed to accept that property was taken in the sense that the plaintiffs were deprived of their ability to enjoy the fruits of their statutory monopolies but did not explicitly decide the issue.[20] In any event, the precise nature of the alleged 'taking' was not defined explicitly, other than as a restriction on the enjoyment of intellectual property rights.[21] As for the issue of goodwill, French CJ also acknowledged that goodwill is protected by a right of exclusion rather than use.[22] TPP was then considered to be legislation that restricted the enjoyment of the negative rights granted by the legislation.[23] Another way of expressing this, but not one stated in the Chief Justice's judgment, may be that the right of a trademark owner to exclude others is a pre-requisite to the trademark owner's liberty to exclusively use its trademarks. The real issue is that of the point at which a government's restriction on that liberty effectively constitutes a taking of property.

Gummow J also acknowledged the essentially negative nature of trademark rights.[24] He further acknowledged that registration does 'not confer a liberty to use a trademark free from what may be restraints found in other statutes or in the general law'.[25] However, he drew attention to other rights, namely the rights to assign trademarks and to license their use, and regarded them as proprietary in nature for the purposes of s 51(xxxi) of the *Constitution*.[26]

He was of the view that they had been 'denuded of their value and thus of their utility by the imposition of the regime under the Packaging Act'[27] and this was sufficient to constitute a 'taking' of these items of intellectual property. The references to the right to assign and to license are somewhat intriguing and curious in this context. The right of assignment is not lost due to the TPP. Owners of tobacco trademarks continue to be able to assign those trademarks. What is assigned are the rights owned by the assignor. If that is a right to prevent others from using the trademark, it is not clear how the right to assign that right has been lost. The assignment also effectively assigns the liberty to use the trademark that is created by the consequence of ownership of the right of exclusion but it is not apparent why the assignee is in any better position to resist government limitations on that liberty than the assignor was prior to the assignment. In addition, licensing would seem to be the selective exercise of the right to exclude others using one's trademark or the conferral on licensees of a liberty to use by relieving them of their duty not to use the owner's trademark. Again, the proposition does not address why the government does not have the power to restrict the liberty to use of either the owner or whoever has been licensed by the owner to use.

Hayne and Bell JJ simply indicated that it seemed that there had been a taking of property but the accuracy of that proposition need not be examined[28] and so they did not examine it. Instead, they focused on the lack of any acquisition of property and the absence of the Commonwealth's control over the packaging.[29]

Crennnan J appeared to reject the proposition that ownership of property had been taken away from the trademark owners. She found that:

> The complaint that the plaintiffs were deprived of the 'substance' and 'reality' of their proprietorship in their property because they could not use their registered trademarks as registered, or their associated product get-up, left out of account the significance of their ability to continue to use their brand names so as to distinguish their tobacco products, thereby continuing to generate custom and goodwill.[30]

Kiefel J acknowledged that 'some or much of the value of … [the plaintiffs'] intellectual property has been lost in Australia'.[31] Such comments do not directly address the proposition that property had been taken. Government regulation frequently affects the value of property, sometimes for the worse and sometimes for the better. Affecting value is not in itself a taking of property. Her Honour's focus was more on the issue of acquisition of any property. She noted that the TPP does not involve control in the sense of acquisition[32] and that the legislation was analogous to restrictions on land for town planning and other public purposes.[33] In his dissent, Heydon J was clearly of the view that there had been both a taking of property and an acquisition of it by the Commonwealth.

B   Acquisition of the Property

All six of the justices who formed the majority agreed that no acquisition of any property had occurred. The TPP was considered to be a form of regulation of packaging requirements, but it did not constitute an acquisition of property by the government. Tobacco companies still retain the liberty to sell cigarettes, but they can do so only in accordance with the regulatory requirements imposed by the government.

The government did not acquire the right of exclusion as only the trademark owner can bring civil proceedings for use by another of the trademarks in question via infringement action pursuant to the *Trade Marks Act 1995* (Cth). Nor did it acquire via the TPP the liberty to use the tobacco trademarks. Hence, even if that liberty were considered a key aspect of the trademark owner's property and its loss constituted the relevant taking, the property had not been acquired.

C 'Just Terms'

One of the unresolved issues from the decision was whether, if there had been an acquisition of property, the acquisition had been on 'just terms'. While no monetary compensation was paid or offered to the tobacco companies, the Commonwealth's argument in this respect was basically twofold. The first argument was that the constitutional provision was never intended to apply to the acquisition of some forms of property that were being used towards ends clearly harmful to the public interest and, in this case, public health. An extreme example would be the confiscation of a rifle used by a criminal while committing a robbery.

A related but separate argument was that, given the harm done to public health by tobacco, the legislation did constitute 'just terms' for the acquisition of any property and 'just terms' did not require monetary compensation. Few of the justices addressed the issue in any detail because six of them found that no acquisition of property had occurred and therefore the issue was moot. In a general sense, the issue may arise again in the context of the dispute between Australia and PMA, as discussed below.

IV POTENTIAL IMPLICATIONS OF THE DECISION FOR THE BILATERAL INVESTMENT TREATY DISPUTE BETWEEN PMA AND AUSTRALIA

There remain two more legal challenges to the TPP. One is the dispute initiated by PMA pursuant to the bilateral investment treaty (BIT) between Australian and Hong Kong (the *Australia–Hong Kong BIT*).[34] The BIT dispute between Australia and PMA is primarily a dispute about the nature of PMA's intellectual property rights and entitlements and the extent, if any, to which the treatment of that intellectual property by the TPP contravenes one or more of the obligations imposed on the Australian government by the *Australia–Hong Kong BIT*. While PMA does not directly hold any intellectual property in Australia, it owns companies that do. It owns 100 per cent of the shares in Philip Morris (Australia) Limited, which, in turn, owns 100 per cent of the shares in Philip Morris Limited (PML).[35] PML either owns, or holds licences to use in Australia, some key trademarks for cigarettes and other intellectual property. In particular, PML holds a licence from Philip Morris Brands Sàrl (a Swiss company) to use trademarks such as Alpine, Longbeach and Marlboro. PML also owns the registered trademark Peter Jackson.[36]

It is the impact of the TPP on that intellectual property that is the primary basis of the complaint by PMA. While it claims that its shareholdings will be affected, that effect is the direct consequence of the alleged impact on the intellectual property of its subsidiary, PML. There are multiple potential responses to the claims of PMA, and this chapter does not purport to deal with all of them. A few may be mentioned in passing. One is that PMA's investment in Australia purely constitutes shares as it does not directly hold any intellectual property. Its ownership and enjoyment of its shareholdings are unaffected by the TPP. The value of them may be affected – although even that has to be questioned if, as claimed by tobacco companies, plain packaging has no effect. In any event, it is difficult to envisage how an investment treaty guarantees that no government regulatory action will be taken that affects the value of shares, especially if the shares are held in a company that sells a product that is directly responsible for the deaths of many Australians and the product has few, if any, countervailing benefits.

An even greater stumbling block to PMA's claim is that it only acquired its shareholdings in Philip Morris (Australia) Limited about ten months after the Australian government publicly stated its intention to legislate for plain packaging.[37] On the surface, it appears that PMA knew full well what would happen to its investments before it made those investments, and that it may even have acquired those investments for the sole or primary purpose of attempting to artificially create grounds for a dispute under the *Australia–Hong Kong BIT*.

For present purposes, though, this chapter will focus on defining with some precision the nature of the intellectual property that PML actually holds in Australia and the legal effects of the TPP on that property. Essentially, when one drills down into the details of PMA's claim, its claim is that the Australian Government has directly or indirectly expropriated PML's intellectual property; its intellectual property has not been accorded fair and equitable treatment; or that its intellectual property has been impaired by unreasonable measures relating to the management, maintenance, use, enjoyment or disposal of the investments. Similar claims are made in respect of goodwill generated from the use of intellectual property. In order to assess these claims, especially that of expropriation, a starting point is identifying the nature of the rights associated with intellectual property and goodwill. The High Court decision and surrounding arguments and pleadings shed some light on that issue, as does well-recognised case law concerning intellectual property.

A   The Investments of Philip Morris Asia Limited

In its Notice of Arbitration, PMA claims that PML has 'rights with respect to certain intellectual property in Australia, including registered and unregistered trademarks; copyright works; registered and unregistered designs and overall get up of the product packaging ('intellectual property')'.[38] It also claims that PML has 'generated substantial goodwill from the use of the intellectual property on or in relation to Philip Morris' tobacco products and packaging'.[39]

A few points can be made in relation to this somewhat expansive view by PMA of its investments in light of both general law relating to intellectual property and some comments by the High Court justices. The first is that this part of PMA's claim clearly does not understate the nature of its investments. Indeed, the reverse would appear to be the case.

1   Unregistered trademarks

There are no significant rights in unregistered trademarks per se.[40] If an unregistered trademark has been used in Australia as a trademark, the user may be able to obtain registration of the trademark, subject to compliance with other requirements under the *Trade Marks Act 1995* (Cth). The first user in Australia is the owner of the trademark in that sense.[41] There may be some rights associated with the opportunity to seek registration of non-word trademarks that were used prior to the legislation coming into place, and these are unaffected by the legislation. Similarly, the opportunity to seek registration of inherently distinctive non-word trademarks, even though they have not yet been used, also remains intact.

However, until registration, the user has no rights in an unregistered trademark. It may have rights to bring an action in passing-off if it has acquired goodwill as a consequence of the use of the unregistered trademark. There is only a right to protect the goodwill generated in part as a consequence of the use of that unregistered trademark.[42] The form of protection of goodwill is by way of a negative right to prevent the exploitation of that goodwill by others engaging in deceptive conduct relating to the use of the trademarks that contribute to the generation of that goodwill. There is no common-law right to use a trademark, although the liberty to use it to the exclusion of others may have been generated by its use in such a way as to create the goodwill in question. One further point about the alleged goodwill of PML should also be mentioned. A significant number of the relevant tobacco trademarks are owned by companies other than PML. PML merely holds a licence to use the trademarks or the 'get-up' in question. The Marlboro trademark is an example. There is a real question as to whether the registered trademark owner, as opposed to PML, owns the goodwill associated with the trademark and therefore has the right to prevent others from passing off their products as those of the trademark owner. Most trademark licences would expressly provide that the registered owner retains the goodwill in the trademark at all times and, of course, most especially at the time of termination of the licence agreement.[43] The matter is almost certainly addressed in the licence agreements between PML and the trademark owners, but the wording of those agreements is obviously not publicly available. It might be the case that PMA's claim exaggerates the quantum of the goodwill held by PML in respect of the trademarks that PML uses pursuant to licences from trademark owners that are not, and could not be, a party to the BIT dispute because they are not Hong Kong investors.

2   'Overall get up of the product packaging'

The claim in this respect is really a claim in respect of unregistered trademarks or the goodwill from use of unregistered trademarks. Get-up, if used extensively, may be one source of goodwill. Goodwill is a form of intellectual property, as confirmed by the BIT itself, but get-up is not a form of intellectual property in itself, and suggestions to the contrary are simply untenable.[44]

3   Copyright

PML may possibly own copyright in some aspects of the previous packaging of tobacco products. Logos, pictures and other artistic devices would come within the definition of original artistic works. The exclusive rights of a copyright owner include a right to reproduce and to publish its works. What is not given is a right to reproduce the work and then attach it to, or place it on, any article of commerce that the owner pleases or to display it in public whenever or however the owner pleases. For example, copyright subsists in pornographic photographs, but there is no general right to place those photographs on any article of commerce and sell those articles at the retail level. While there may be a liberty to make such uses of the reproductions of the works, the liberty is subject to government power to reduce or even eliminate that liberty. While copyright was referred to in the pleadings in the High Court decision, the matter was not pursued in the hearing and oral argument for fairly obvious reasons.

In any event, PML may have some difficulty establishing ownership or its status as an Australian exclusive licensee in respect of artwork used in packaging for which it only has a licence, as that copyright ownership also may reside with the owners of those brands, which may well have initially commissioned the relevant artwork incorporated into the branding or employed the authors who created the artwork. Even for those brands of which it has ownership, given the lack of a registration process for copyright, PML would need to produce the relevant evidence of its ownership of the copyright, which would require evidence of a chain of title from the original author or authors of the artwork to PML.

4 Unregistered designs

There is no legal protection for unregistered designs in Australia per se. The claim may be referring to the possibility of subsequently registering currently unregistered designs owned by PML and the entitlement to obtain that registration. In any event, unregistered designs are unlikely to be a large part of the value of PML and therefore do not make a significant contribution to the value of PMA's shareholdings.

5 Registered designs

A few points can be made about any registered design rights that PMA may be alleging are affected by the TPP. First, any issues in relation to registered designs will almost certainly be equally applicable to the issues surrounding registered trademarks. Second, registered designs are protected for a maximum of ten years. The value of any registered designs will be significantly less than the value of any registered trademarks, which can be renewed forever.

6 Summary of the intellectual property in question

We are left, then, with a position in which PMA's claim comes down to registered trademarks and goodwill created by the use of registered and unregistered trademarks. Claims in respect of unregistered trademarks per se, unregistered designs, and get-up are effectively irrelevant. The claims in respect of copyright are easily addressed, and any claims in respect of registered designs stand or fall on similar grounds as those applicable to registered trademarks.

B 'Expropriation' or 'Deprivation' in the Context of the Australia–Hong Kong BIT

One of the issues that may arise in the BIT dispute is the extent to which the Australian law relating to taking and acquisition, or at least general concepts discussed in the Australian case law, is relevant to the interpretation and application of the *Australia-Hong Kong BIT*. One of PMA's claims is that the plain packaging legislation expropriates registered trademarks and goodwill. There is some ambiguity as to whether expropriation within the meaning of the *Australia–Hong Kong BIT* occurs whenever there is a deprivation of investments or whether expropriation also requires an acquisition of that property. The relevant clause in the *Australia–Hong Kong BIT* is headed 'Expropriation', but the words 'deprivation' and 'expropriation' are both used within the text of the clause.[45] The issue is discussed elsewhere, and it seems that a preponderance of arbitration decisions supports the latter view.[46] Clearly six of the High Court justices consider that there has been no acquisition within the meaning of the *Australian Constitution* and, in particular, no proprietary interest has been acquired by the Commonwealth.

On the other hand, it seems that a smaller majority of the High Court justices found that there has been a 'taking' of property although, within that majority, there is no clear agreement on precisely what has been taken. It would seem that the liberty to use has been substantially removed, and that may well be the taking to which the relevant justices were referring. It certainly seems that a majority of the justices accept the proposition that the rights of a trademark owner are primarily negative in nature and these have not been taken, although Gummow J seems to suggest that the rights to assign and license may be positive. Those views of Gummow J appear unusual, for reasons already explained above.

If, as it appears, the 'taking' is the liberty to use, the constitutional arguments about taking need to be considered in the context of a bedrock principle that no taking is contrary to the *Constitution* unless accompanied by an acquisition. Governments must have a general regulatory power to restrict and, if necessary, to remove liberties, but a broad view of what is and what is not the taking of property can be adopted and be consistent with that approach in a context where the complaining party must also demonstrate that the government[47] has also acquired that which was taken or some corresponding property. To adopt a narrow view of taking in that context would rob the constitutional guarantee of much of its intended force. The issue becomes significantly different in a different legal context.

Hence, even if the BIT is interpreted to mean that a taking or denial of pre-existing liberties *may* be sufficient to constitute 'deprivation' of property within the meaning of the BIT, the need for governments to retain regulatory powers to restrict liberties requires a narrower view of the concept of 'taking' or 'deprivation' for the purposes of the BIT than is the case in the context of the *Australian Constitution*. The constitutional issues tend more to a binary approach of either there has been a taking of property or there has not, which is then followed by consideration of the critical issue of whether there has been an acquisition. In a context where the emphasis is on the nature of the taking to determine whether it constitutes a deprivation, a more nuanced discussion is needed in order to accommodate the realities of and necessity for government regulatory conduct. Consequently, in BIT disputes, a number of factors are considered in making a final decision. The various factors that are relevant in the context of the BIT are discussed below.

In other words, it would be far too simplistic to assume that because a number of the judgments in the High Court suggested that a taking of property had occurred for the purposes of applying the *Australian Constitution*, the BIT's reference to 'deprivation' should adopt a similar meaning, even if the relevant clause in the BIT does not involve an acquisition. In any event, the terms used in bilateral investment treaties are not necessarily interpreted in a manner directly analogous to similar terms used in domestic law. In the context of expropriation clauses in investment treaties, Voon and Mitchell have identified other relevant factors to their interpretation.[48] However, some of the findings and views expressed by the High Court must surely be relevant to the application of those factors in the context of a bilateral agreement to which Australia is a party. The factors identified by Voon and Mitchell are discussed below with reference to the judgments in the constitutional challenge and the arguments made during it.

1   Degree and duration of interference with the investor's property
Clearly, there is considerable interference with the property of the trademark owners. There is some uncertainty within the High Court judgments about the nature and extent of that interference and the extent to which it involves a taking of property rights and property, as opposed to a diminution in their value as a consequence of government regulation. There is also some uncertainty as to which rights or property, if any, have been taken. For example, Gummow J seemed to focus almost exclusively on the rights to assign and license trademarks and Hayne and Bell JJ considered it unnecessary to consider the matter at all.

There has been a significant diminution in the liberty to use. The liberty to use non-word trademarks for retail purposes has been taken completely and the liberty to use word trademarks for retail purposes is seriously restricted. However, the key scaffolding of rights around the property remains in place and that scaffolding has certainly not been taken, even if one accepts the views of Gummow J. The registration of trademarks is retained, and they are immune from removal for non-use. The point is important, because the retention of rights and registration means that the regulatory position can be restored relatively quickly if the political will to do so via the Australian democratic process exists. There is a big difference between prohibiting someone from using their property on the one hand and totally destroying their property on the other.

2 Acquisition, taking or appropriation of 'control, use or enjoyment of property through the exercise of state powers'

On this point, it seems that all of the majority justices take the view that the Commonwealth has not appropriated control, use or enjoyment of property through the exercise of state powers. There has been no acquisition of property in any relevant sense.

3 The government's intention is a relevant but not necessary pre-requisite to establishing expropriation

Given the lack of expropriation in the sense of acquisition and the stated objectives of the legislation to pursue public health goals, it is difficult to characterise the government's actions as constituting an intention to expropriate PMA's investment. Kiefel J expressly rejected such a proposition.[49]

4 The existence of proportionality between the public interest pursued and the interference with the investor's property

This issue was raised in argument in the constitutional decision but not considered in any detail by any of the justices in the majority because it was unnecessary for them to do so. One aspect of the proportionality argument elucidated by the constitutional challenge is that only Heydon J, in dissent, unequivocally found that a wholesale taking of the plaintiff's property had occurred. Crennan and Kiefel JJ were quite circumspect on this point and focused more on the issue of acquisition. Hayne and Bell JJ did not address the issue in any detail relevant for current purposes and Gummow J appeared to restrict his approach to the rights of assignment and licensing only. As explained in dealing with factor one above, the essential elements of the property have been retained so that it can be used again with relative ease if the government process so decides. In addition, the retention of the liberty to use word trademarks is also a key part of the balancing act involved in assessing proportionality. The importance of the retention of the liberty to use word trademarks which are already the key means of distinguishing and promoting cigarettes was emphasised by Crennan J.

5 Legitimate expectations of investors

This issue has been addressed elsewhere.[50] However, given the nature of the regulatory environment in which tobacco has been sold in Australia, the fact that PMA only acquired its interest in PML some months after the public announcement of the government's intention to introduce the TPP and the consistency of the TPP with the *Australian Constitution*, it is difficult to imagine how PMA will mount a case based on its legitimate expectations. In addition, Crennan J noted that the primary objection of the plaintiffs was the effect on the promotional function of their trademarks[51] while also noting that the continuing use of word trademarks enables the core function of distinguishing one tobacco product from another.[52]

6 A further factor: general promotion of cigarettes

In addition to the factors identified by Voon and Mitchell, a further and closely related factor emerges from the pleadings of British American Tobacco Australasia Limited (BATA) and the judgment of Crennan J. One of the underlying assumptions of plain packaging is that tobacco packaging, in general, not only distinguishes one brand of cigarette from another but also promotes cigarette consumption generally. As this author has said elsewhere,[53] when the Marlboro Man was advertising Marlboro cigarettes, he was promoting cigarettes generally as well as distinguishing between Marlboro cigarettes and other cigarettes; and when Joe Camel was advertising Camel cigarettes, he was also performing the dual function of distinguishing Camel cigarettes from other cigarettes and promoting cigarettes generally. Jointly and severally, they were both promoting cigarettes.

All but one of the plaintiffs in the constitutional challenge denied that they used their packaging to promote the consumption of their cigarettes as opposed to distinguishing their cigarettes from other cigarettes. BATA is the one exception.[54] One of the High Court justices, Crennan J, addressed the issue and expressly held that trademarks (and presumably get-up generally) have a promotional function, as well as a function of distinguishing goods from other goods.[55]

While the proposition is denied by the other parties to the constitutional case, it does seem somewhat difficult to resist the proposition that if specific packaging for a particular brand of a product makes that brand more attractive to consumers, then all packaging for all brands of that product makes the product in general more attractive. The point has an impact on factors three, four and five above. With regard to factor three, the government's intention, the intention is not to directly affect the capacity to distinguish one brand of cigarettes from another but to significantly limit the promotion of cigarettes in general. The former function of cigarettes, to distinguish one brand from another, is reflected in the nature of the property rights conferred by ownership of trademarks, and the details of those property rights have been discussed already. The latter function, that of promoting a product, is not part of the property rights equation. It is a separate issue and a function not reflected in the nature of rights conferred on trademark owners. For that reason, the Australian Government's actions can be clearly categorised as focused on an intention unrelated to interference with PMA's investment.

The issue also affects the proportionality analysis. Proportionality necessarily implies a competition between competing factors. The competition here is between the capacity to distinguish between brands of cigarettes and the government's desire to prevent the promotion of cigarettes. With regard to the former, the TPP retains that capacity in two major respects. First, the use of word trademarks, the primary means by which cigarettes are identified and distinguished, is retained. Second, the opportunity to retain registration of non-word trademarks is provided by the TPP. If the legislation is ever repealed or fundamentally altered, tobacco companies could immediately resume distinguishing the goods by reference to those non-word trademarks. The other side of the proportionality equation is the desire to prevent the promotion of cigarettes. With regard to PMA's legitimate expectations, it might have some legitimate expectation that it will retain some capacity to distinguish its cigarettes from other cigarettes. As indicated in the previous paragraph, this capacity is retained by the TPP in two major respects. On the other hand, it is difficult to see how PMA would have any legitimate expectation that the government would not be seeking to prevent the promotion of cigarettes. The regulatory history of tobacco in Australia in the last 30 years is one of significant restriction of tobacco promotion.

C Just Terms, Proportionality and Legitimate Expectations

Finally, in terms of both proportionality and legitimate expectations, the general concept of 'just terms' that was raised in the constitutional challenge but not addressed in great detail also forms part of the discussion. In the context of the *Constitution*, the hurdle to clear in relation to acquisition may be so great that 'just terms' may be restricted to monetary compensation to the party whose property has been acquired. The issue was not resolved in the High Court.

However, if the relevant context in the BIT is that of 'taking' a liberty to use and a consideration of the extent of the regulatory power of the government to restrict that liberty, the issue certainly comes into play. The evidence about smoking that is accepted by public health bodies such as the Royal College of Physicians[56] and the United States Surgeon General[57] holds that nicotine is highly pharmacologically addictive: about as addictive as heroin and cocaine. In addition, there is no doubt that the vast majority of smokers become addicted while they are minors.[58] Today's addicted adult smokers were yesterday's addicted minors. The combination of those two facts is highly relevant to the concept of 'just terms' or, in the context of the BIT, 'legitimate expectations'. Whether by intention or otherwise, PMA's business model is dependent on the addiction of minors to a drug which, coupled with other chemicals in tobacco, will kill 50 per cent of long-term users.[59] It is difficult to see how those matters are not relevant to what might be a balancing act in relation to consideration of the extent of the regulatory powers of the Australian Government to limit the liberty of PMA to promote its products via the use of trademarks.

V   CONCLUSION

As indicated at the beginning of this chapter, the BIT dispute is based on a number of different grounds, and there are multiple potential responses to those claims. This chapter has endeavoured to provide some insight into the nature of the investment held by PMA. It has also endeavoured to elicit, from a diverse range of judicial opinions, some of the potential implications of the constitutional challenge for the claim of expropriation made in the BIT dispute. While the BIT is a different legal beast from the *Australian Constitution*, it is difficult to see how a conclusion could be reached that there has been expropriation if that term is interpreted, in essence, as involving an acquisition of property. Even if it is interpreted to be a 'taking', PMA cannot demonstrate that any of its property rights have been taken. At most, it has lost some of the liberty that it previously had but retained a liberty to use in respect of the key word trademarks used to distinguish its cigarettes from other cigarettes. It needs to make a case as to why the Australian Government cannot exercise its regulatory powers to limit that liberty in the manner that it has determined via its democratic processes.

NOTES

1. *JT International SA v Commonwealth* (2012) 291 ALR 669.
2. For the purposes of this chapter, 'TPP' refers to an act of parliament, the regulations to that act and information standards imposed pursuant to the *Competition and Consumer Act 2010* (Cth). The relevant act is the *Tobacco Plain Packaging Act 2011* (Cth) (*TPP Act*) and the regulations to that act are the *Tobacco Plain Packaging Regulations 2011* (Cth) (as amended by the *Tobacco Plain Packaging Amendment*

Regulations 2012 (Cth)) (*TPP Regulations*). The *TPP Act* and the *TPP Regulations* prescribe the nature of tobacco packaging and create the restrictions on the use of trademarks. The relevant information standard is the *Competition and Consumer (Tobacco) Information Standard 2011* (Cth), which imposes the requirements for text and graphic warnings on tobacco packaging.

3. Relevant documents relating to the dispute can be found at: Attorney-General's Department, *Investor–State Arbitration – Tobacco Plain Packaging* (2012) <http://www.ag.gov.au/Internationalrelations/InternationalLaw/Pages/Tobaccoplainpackaging.aspx>.
4. *TPP Act* s 20; *TPP Regulations* regs 2.3.1–2.3.9.
5. *TPP Act* ss 18–19.
6. Ibid s 19; *TPP Regulations* reg 2.2.1(2) requires that '[a]ll outer surfaces of primary packaging and secondary packaging must be the colour known as Pantone 448C'.
7. *TPP Act* s 20; *TPP Regulations* regs 2.3.1–2.3.9.
8. *TPP Act* s 21; *TPP Regulations* reg 2.3.2.
9. *TPP Act* s 22.
10. *Competition and Consumer (Tobacco) Information Standard 2011* (Cth) pt 2 sets out the location of health warnings on retail packaging of a tobacco product and pts 3–8 set out various warning statements and accompanying graphics.
11. *Trade Marks Act 1995* (Cth) pt 9.
12. *TPP Act* s 28.
13. *Australian Constitution* s 51(xxxi): 'The Parliament shall, subject to this Constitution, have power to make laws for the peace, order, and good government of the Commonwealth with respect to: … (xxxi.) The acquisition of property on just terms from any State or person for any purpose in respect of which the Parliament has power to make laws'.
14. See Transcript of Proceedings, *JT International SA v Commonwealth* [2012] HCATrans 92 (18 April 2012) 4210, 4230: Gummow J on the argument that rights in respect of the packaging had been lost: 'It could never be the case that you could put into trade a package with obscenities on it, for example … I cannot see any right that inheres at common law which sounds in any remedy which would be relevant in this present field of discourse you were trying to draw us into'.
15. Ibid 4315 (Hayne J): 'But you enter the debate at a level of abstraction where you have a notional manufacturer sitting there with a piece of cardboard saying, "How will I use this?" What is the utility of entering the debate at that point?'; *JT International SA v Commonwealth* (2012) 291 ALR 669, 713 [181].
16. Transcript of Proceedings, *JT International SA v Commonwealth* [2012] HCA Trans 92 (18 April 2012).
17. Wesley Newcomb Hohfeld, 'Some Fundamental Legal Conceptions as Applied in Judicial Reasoning' (1913) 23(1) *The Yale Law Journal* 16.
18. *JT International SA v Commonwealth* (2012) 291 ALR 669, 682 [36].
19. Ibid 683 [37].
20. Ibid 683 [38].
21. Ibid 685 [44].
22. Ibid 684 [40].
23. Ibid 685 [43]–[44].
24. Ibid 690–91 [76]–[77].
25. Ibid 691 [78].
26. Ibid 704 [137].
27. Ibid 704 [138].
28. Ibid 709 [164].
29. Ibid 713 [180]–[188].
30. Ibid 740 [294].

31. Ibid 757–8 [356].
32. Ibid 759 [362].
33. Ibid 759 [363].
34. *Agreement between the Government of Hong Kong and the Government of Australia for the Promotion and Protection of Investments*, signed 15 September 1993, 1748 UNTS 385 (entered into force 15 October 1993).
35. *Notice of Arbitration: Australia/Hong Kong Agreement for the Promotion and Protection of Investments* (21 November 2011) Attorney-General's Department <http://www.ag.gov.au/Internationalrelations/InternationalLaw/Documents/Philip%20 Morris%20Asia%20Limited%20Notice%20of%20Arbitration%2021%20November% 202011.pdf> [1.3].
36. Ibid [1.4]; Philip Morris Limited, *PETER JACKSON*, Australian Registered Trademark No 612770 (30 September 1993).
37. Australian Government Solicitor, *Australia's Response to the Notice of Arbitration* (21 December 2011) Attorney-General's Department <http://www.ag.gov.au/ Internationalrelations/InternationalLaw/Documents/Australias%20Response%20to% 20the%20Notice%20of%20Arbitration%2021%20December%202011.pdf> 9 [30].
38. *Notice of Arbitration*, above n 35, [1.3].
39. Ibid [4.6].
40. It might be possible to assign or license an unregistered trademark without goodwill. See, Gummow J in *JT International SA v Commonwealth* (2012) 291 ALR 669, 705 [142]:

> At common law the goodwill would be assignable only in conjunction with the goodwill of the business in respect of which the get-up was used. The underlying reason for the common law taking this attitude to assignments of goodwill is the loss of distinctiveness leading to the likelihood of deception of consumers as to the origin of goods. This reasoning may also apply to licensing of common law marks' (footnotes omitted).

41. Mark Davison and Ian Horak, *Shanahan's Australian Law of Trade Marks and Passing Off* (Thomson Reuters, 5th ed, 2012) ch 3, 61.
42. See, eg, *AG Spalding v AW Gamage Ltd* (1918) 35 RPC 101.
43. See Davison and Horak, above n 41, ch 17, 583.
44. See, eg, French CJ in *JT International SA v Commonwealth* (2012) 291 ALR 669, 684 [40]: 'It has rightly been said that "[t]here is no 'property' in the accepted sense of the word in a get-up".'
45. *Australia–Hong Kong BIT* article 6(1):

> Investors of either Contracting Party shall not be deprived of their investments nor subjected to measures having effect equivalent to such deprivation in the area of the other Contracting Party except under due process of law, for a public purpose related to the internal needs of that Party, on a non-discriminatory basis, and against compensation. Such compensation shall amount to the real value of the investment immediately before the deprivation or before the impending deprivation became public knowledge whichever is the earlier. Where that value cannot be readily ascertained, the compensation shall be determined in accordance with generally recognised principles of valuation and equitable principles taking into account the capital invested, depreciation, capital already repatriated, replacement value, currency exchange rate movements and other relevant factors. Compensation shall include interest at a normal commercial rate from the date the measures were taken until the date of payment, shall be made without undue delay, be effectively realisable, freely transferable and payable in either the original currency of the investment or, if requested by the investor, in any other freely convertible currency. The investor affected shall have a right, under the law of the

Contracting Party making the deprivation, to prompt review by a judicial or other independent authority of that Party, of the investor's case and of the valuation of the investment in accordance with the principles set out in this paragraph.

Australia–Hong Kong BIT article 6(2):

Where a Contracting Party expropriates the assets of a company which is incorporated or constituted under the law in force in any part of its area, and in which investors of the other Contracting Party own shares, it shall ensure that the provisions of paragraph (1) of this Article are applied to the extent necessary to guarantee compensation referred to in paragraph (1) in respect of their investment to such investors of the other Contracting Party who are owners of those shares.

46. See Tania Voon and Andrew Mitchell, 'Implications of International Investment Law for Plain Tobacco Packaging: Lessons from the Hong Kong–Australia BIT' in Tania Voon, Andrew Mitchell and Jonathan Liberman with Glyn Ayres (eds), *Public Health and Plain Packaging of Cigarettes: Legal Issues* (Edward Elgar, 2012), 137; Benn McGrady, 'Implications of Ongoing Trade and Investment Disputes Concerning Tobacco: Philip Morris v Uruguay' in Tania Voon, Andrew Mitchell and Jonathan Liberman with Glyn Ayres (eds), *Public Health and Plain Packaging of Cigarettes: Legal Issues* (Edward Elgar, 2012), 173.

47. The relevant acquisition may also be by a third party but, for present purposes, this possibility is not relevant.

48. Tania Voon and Andrew Mitchell, 'Time to Quit? Assessing International Investment Claims Against Plain Tobacco Packaging in Australia' (2011) 14(3) *14 Journal of International Economic Law* 515.

49. *JT International SA v Commonwealth* (2012) 291 ALR 669, 761 [372].

50. See Voon and Mitchell, above n 46.

51. *JT International SA v Commonwealth* (2012) 291 ALR 669, 738 [287].

52. Ibid 740 [293].

53. Mark Davison, 'Plain Packaging and the TRIPS Agreement: A Response to Professor Gervais' (2013) 23 *Australian Intellectual Property Journal* 160.

54. Commonwealth of Australia, 'Submissions of the Commonwealth of Australia', Submission in *British American Tobacco Australasia Limited v Commonwealth*, S389 of 2011, 5 April 2012, 11 [29]:

the packaging and appearance of tobacco products has become the principal means available to be used, and in fact used, by tobacco companies to promote their respective tobacco products to members of the public. In the case of BATA, that is both agreed to be fact and acknowledged to be a logical step in establishing the reputation and goodwill it claims will be acquired under the TPP Act. In the case of other tobacco companies, the use of packaging and the appearance of tobacco products to promote their respective tobacco products to members of the public (although formally denied) must similarly be a logical step in establishing the reputation and goodwill each claims will be acquired under the TPP Act (footnotes omitted).

55. *JT International SA v Commonwealth* (2012) 291 ALR 669, 738 [286].

56. Royal College of Physicians of London, *Nicotine Addiction in Britain: A Report of the Tobacco Advisory Group of The Royal College of Physicians* (2000), xiv, 77, 98–9.

57. See, eg, United States Department of Health and Human Services, *The Health Consequences of Smoking: Nicotine Addiction: a Report of the Surgeon General* (1988), 25. More recently, see, eg, United States Department of Health and Human Services, *Preventing Tobacco Use among Youth and Young Adults* (2012).

58. United States Department of Health and Human Services, *Preventing Tobacco Use among Youth and Young Adults* (2012), 111: '[t]he evidence is sufficient to conclude that there is a causal relationship between smoking and addiction to nicotine, beginning in adolescence and young adulthood'.

59. Richard Doll et al, 'Mortality in Relation to Smoking: 40 Years' Observations on Male British Doctors' (1994) 309 *British Medical Journal* 901; Richard Doll et al, 'Mortality in Relation to Smoking: 50 Years' Observations on Male British Doctors' (2004) 328 *British Medical Journal* 1519.

15. Tobacco control in Taiwan

Chuan-Feng Wu

I BACKGROUND

Scientific evidence demonstrates that smoke and the inhalation of second-hand smoke causes serious illnesses, from lung cancer, emphysema and cardiovascular disease to early death.[1] Taiwan is facing a public health crisis due to smoking[2] and spends an estimated US$1.5 billion annually via National Health Insurance (NHI) expenditures to treat smoking-related illnesses.[3] In 2009, 20 per cent of Taiwanese adults used tobacco regularly (35.4 per cent of males; 4.2 per cent of females)[4] as did 14.8 per cent of teenagers (19.6 per cent of males; 9.1 per cent of females).[5] Additionally, in one survey, 20.8 per cent of respondents reported daily exposure to second-hand smoke in their households,[6] 14 per cent in the workplace or office,[7] and 7.8 per cent in indoor public places.[8] Besides its impact on public health, tobacco consumption also causes serious economic losses, such as increasing health care costs and job productivity losses.[9] Studies also show that smoking greatly impacts the mortality and death rates in Taiwan.[10] From 1982 to 1986, Taiwan's smokers had a 140 per cent increase in risk of death from all cancer sites combined, and 730 per cent increase from lung cancer.[11]

To respond to the tobacco epidemic, Taiwan passed the *Tobacco Hazards Prevention Act 1997* (Taiwan) (1997 THPA).[12] However, the Act failed to incorporate effective tobacco control initiatives, such as tobacco advertising bans, graphic health warnings, cigarette tax increases, bans on smoking in public places, and tobacco cessation subsidisations. Therefore, the THPA was regarded as inept in preventing or retarding the 'tobacco epidemic'.[13]

In 2009, inspired by the first worldwide public health convention, the *WHO Framework Convention on Tobacco Control* (WHO FCTC),[14] Taiwan amended the THPA after ten years of enforcement.[15] The amendment adopts most of the WHO FCTC's tobacco control strategies and addresses major issues such as protecting the public from second-hand smoke, increasing the size of health warnings (including graphic warnings) on tobacco packaging, banning written content or pictures that could lure people into smoking or that downplay tobacco's hazardous effects, limiting point-of-sale tobacco product displays, banning pregnant woman from smoking, banning tobacco product sales to teenagers, and increasing the tobacco tax (health and welfare surcharge). After the THPA amendment took effect in 2009, Taiwan increased its efforts to promote comprehensive tobacco control, and the general population's smoking rate dropped by 2.8 per cent to 19.1 per cent over the following three years.[16] Additionally, the percentage of smokers who tried to quit smoking increased by 6.8 per cent to 43.4 per cent over the following year.[17] The proportion of smoke-free workplaces increased from 55.8 per cent in 2008 to 80.5 per cent in 2009.[18] Based upon these statistics, Taiwan's THPA appears to have helped reduce smoking and protect public health.

II AN OVERVIEW OF TAIWAN'S TOBACCO HAZARDS PREVENTION ACT

This section outlines the basic elements of the 2009 THPA amendment (THPA). The THPA contains two types of measure: (i) measures relating to tobacco demand reduction, including health and welfare surcharges, tobacco products administration (regulations on tobacco product contents, disclosures, packaging, labelling, and advertising and promotion), places where tobacco use is restricted (providing protection from exposure to tobacco smoke), and education campaigns on tobacco hazards (education and public awareness, and tobacco cessation services); and (ii) measures relating to tobacco supply reduction, including the prohibition of tobacco sales to minors and pregnant women.

A Price and Tax Measures

Article 6 of the WHO FCTC indicates that price and tax measures are an effective and important means of reducing tobacco consumption. Numerous studies have shown that higher tobacco taxes, which raise tobacco product prices, are highly effective in reducing cigarette demand.[19] Thus, tax-based measures to promote tobacco control have been implemented worldwide.[20] Further, in 2012, the WHO FCTC's Fifth Conference of the Parties (COP 5) passed the *Set of Guiding Principles and Recommendations for Implementation of Article 6 of the WHO FCTC (Article 6 Guidelines)* and confirmed that tobacco taxes benefit not only tobacco control[21] but also state revenue[22] and health promotion.[23]

Before the 1990s, the price of tobacco products in Taiwan was relatively low compared with international standards.[24] Therefore, Taiwan decided to levy a health and welfare surcharge on tobacco products in 1997.[25] Laws were subsequently passed to raise the health and welfare surcharge on cigarettes from zero to NT$5 (US$0.17) in 2002, with another NT$5 surcharge in 2006, and NT$10 (US$0.33) in 2009[26] (a total surcharge increase of NT$20 (US$0.66) in 8 years), bringing cigarette prices to roughly NT$50–NT$90 (US$1.66–US$2.99) per package. These surcharge increases significantly lowered tobacco use among low-income and young consumers.[27]

In comparison with the relevant WHO FCTC provisions, Taiwan developed a comprehensive and effective tobacco taxation mechanism. Due to the complex nature of taxation, WHO FCTC parties had conflicting views on how to develop tobacco taxation. Debates regarding how to use the collected revenues, how to decide the tax amount, and the relationship between taxation and illicit trade[28] have substantially prevented the parties from reaching consensus on the *Article 6 Guidelines*.[29] For example, para 11 of the *Article 6 Guidelines* asserts that parties could consider 'dedicating revenue to tobacco-control programmes, such as those covering awareness raising, health promotion and disease prevention, cessation services, economically viable alternative activities, and financing of appropriate structures for tobacco control'. However, the parties had strong opinions regarding earmarking tobacco tax revenues for problems caused by tobacco products. During the discussion at COP 5, the European Union (EU), Japan, and China argued that the earmark requirement is an infringement of a state's sovereign right to determine tobacco taxation policies.[30] Brazil also argued that article 26.2 of the WHO FCTC does not restrict the use of revenues.[31]

Studies show that tobacco tax proposals can obtain strong citizen support if tax revenues are clearly earmarked for tobacco control uses[32] and are aimed at reducing tobacco consumption rather than generating general state revenue. Without these stipulations, some states might improperly impose tobacco taxes for the primary purpose of generating revenue and place smoking reduction as a secondary benefit.[33] If this is the case, states might face conflicts between dependence on tobacco revenues and tobacco control obligations.[34] To avoid this possible conflict of interest, article 4(IV) of Taiwan's THPA states that the surcharges shall be used exclusively to support specific NHI, anti-tobacco and health measures. Most of these tobacco-tax-funded programmes are related to treating tobacco-related illness, combating tobacco smuggling and reducing tobacco growing.[35]

As another example, article 2 of the *Article 6 Guidelines* recommends that, when establishing national levels of tobacco taxation, parties 'should take into account ... both price elasticity and income elasticity of demand, as well as inflation and changes in household income' and 'should consider having regular adjustment processes or procedures for periodic revaluation of tobacco tax levels'. However, article 2 uses a vague formula to calculate tax levels and fails to oblige the state to conduct periodic tobacco tax adjustments. The provision therefore falls short for two reasons. First, without regular mandatory evaluation of tobacco taxation and its influences, the core strategies of tobacco control cannot be effective.[36] Second, even though price elasticity of demand for tobacco products is considered an important factor for revenue-generating potential,[37] it should not be connected directly to taxation levels. Article 2 of the *Article 6 Guidelines* reflects the tobacco industry's argument that tobacco taxes might fall disproportionately and unfairly on the poor because they spend a larger percentage of income on tobacco products.[38] But this objection overlooks the fact that tobacco taxes that shift intake from tobacco products to other goods would benefit the poor both by improving health and by lowering expenditures on tobacco products.[39] In other words, since the goal justifying a substantial increase in tobacco taxes is helping to deter individuals from smoking, different price elasticities for tobacco products between the rich and poor (typically with higher price elasticity among lower-income smokers) should not be the primary factor for consideration when developing tobacco price and tax measures. The price elasticity of tobacco demand can be used to evaluate tobacco tax measures but should not be the basis for tobacco tax levels.

Unlike the *Article 6 Guidelines*, article 4(II) of Taiwan's THPA proposes that the amounts of the health and welfare surcharge should be evaluated every two years on the basis of: the medical costs of treating smoke-related diseases; tobacco consumption and smoking rates; the ratio of tobacco taxes to retail prices; national income; and other relevant factors affecting tobacco control. Therefore, price elasticity is only one of many factors to be taken into consideration when deciding tobacco tax levels. In other words, policymakers in Taiwan are required to consider the effects of tobacco taxes on public health grounds.

But two major problems remain with Taiwan's tobacco tax measures. First, besides the health and welfare surcharge, the tobacco tax has not been raised since 1987,[40] and the current prices of tobacco products are still lower than the World Bank's recommended standard.[41] Therefore, on 9 May 2013, Taiwan's Executive Yuan approved a draft bill to raise the tobacco tax by NT$5 (US$0.17, from NT$11.80 to NT$16.80) and the health and welfare surcharge by NT$20 (US$0.66, from NT$20 to

NT$40),[42] which together cost individuals an extra NT$56.80 (US$1.89) for purchasing a packet of cigarettes. But anti-smoking groups suggested that the tobacco tax alone should be raised by NT$30 (US$1.00, about 60 per cent of the average cigarette packet retail price).[43] Second, article 12 of the *Article 6 Guidelines* proposes that 'Parties should consider prohibiting or restricting the sale ... of tax-free or duty-free tobacco products'. This brings us to the second problem with Taiwan's current laws: duty-free sales of tobacco products are still legal in Taiwan. Therefore, anti-smoking groups suggested that, even if it is difficult to prohibit or restrict sales or importation of duty-free tobacco products, those products should still be subject to the health and welfare surcharge.[44]

B   Tobacco Advertising and Promotion

Countries around the world have learned that the tobacco industry employs not only advertising to increase tobacco use but also charitable activities as a covert tactic to convey tobacco product information.[45] Therefore, WHO FCTC article 13 emphasises that countries should take action to comprehensively ban tobacco advertisements, promotion and sponsorship activities. The WHO FCTC's recommendations were heeded in THPA article 9, which rigorously restricts advertising, promotion and sponsorship not only by tobacco manufacturers/importers but also by advertising and media outlets, with the former liable to fines between NT$5 000 000 and NT$25 000 000 (US$165 761–US$397 826) for violation (article 26(I)) and the latter liable to fines between NT$200 000 and NT$1 000 000 (US$6630–US$33 152) (article 26(II)).

Furthermore, THPA article 10(I) requires that retailers' displays of tobacco products 'shall be limited to the necessary extent in allowing consumers to acquire information on brand names and prices of the tobacco products'. Article 4 of the *Regulations for Governing Labelling and Displaying at Point of Sale of Tobacco Product 2008* (Taiwan)[46] (*Regulations*) requires tobacco product display areas to not exceed two square metres, and be placed at least two metres from the cashier's counter. Additionally, article 8 of the *Regulations* bans the display of tobacco products via using digital screens, motion pictures, movable settings, sound, scent, or light.

However, the comprehensive ban on tobacco advertising and promotion has sparked much debate over the impact on the freedom of speech (especially commercial speech). This issue is discussed fully in section III(A) below.

C Packaging and Labelling

According to WHO FCTC article 11, tobacco packing and labelling cannot promote a tobacco product with false or misleading impressions, must carry health warnings, and must contain information on relevant tobacco product ingredients and emissions. WHO FCTC article 11(1)(b)(iv) further requires tobacco health warnings and messages to cover 30–50 per cent of the principal display areas. However, before 2009, Taiwan's THPA required tobacco companies to place only written warnings on tobacco packaging, which have been declared sub-optimal on their own in conveying tobacco hazards.[47]

To correspond with the WHO FCTC requirements, the 2009 THPA amendment expanded the size of required tobacco warnings to 35 per cent of the principal display area (front and back) on unit tobacco packaging (article 6(II)). The THPA also requires that the health warning include not only written messages but also pictures/graphics and information to help smokers quit.[48] To align with WHO FCTC article 11(1)(a), THPA article 6(I) further bans packaging descriptions (including brand names) such as 'light, low tar, or any other misleading words or marks' that imply that smoking has no or minor harmful health effects.

Although the THPA authorised six pictorial health warnings with accompanying text, one of which was required to be displayed on cigarette packs, the size of health warnings was relatively small, ranking 35th worldwide in terms of size.[49] Therefore, anti-smoking groups have proposed increasing the health warning size to 50 per cent of the package.[50] Additionally, even though article 5(I) of the *Regulations for Testing of Yields of Nicotine and Tar Contained in Tobacco Products and Cigarette Container Labelling 2009* (Taiwan)[51] require health warnings to be printed on cigarette containers, the regulations do not prevent warnings from being concealed by tax stamps or other required markings. In contrast, according to article 10 of the *Guidelines for Implementation of Article 11 of the WHO FCTC*,[52] parties should ensure that health warnings are not obstructed by other required packaging and labelling markings or by commercial inserts.

Another problem with Taiwan's tobacco packaging and labelling regulations is that, although THPA article 7(I) states that 'the level of nicotine and tar contained in the tobacco products shall be indicated … on the tobacco product containers', the information disclosure requirements fail to fulfil individuals' rights to access health-related information regarding tobacco.[53] According to WHO FCTC article 11(2), the state should require outside packaging and labelling of tobacco products, in addition to health warnings, to contain information on relevant constituents and emissions of tobacco products. However, instead of tobacco product constituents, THPA article 7(I) requires only the display of nicotine and tar levels on tobacco packaging, which is problematic because nicotine and tar levels should not be the only material information that the public receives. For example, studies have shown that tobacco manufacturers use numerous ingredients in their products,[54] some of which are associated with adverse effects (eg, those that enhance or quicken nicotine delivery). Therefore, in addition to nicotine and tar levels, information about other ingredients pertinent to an individual's health care decisions (smoking or quitting smoking) should be mandated on tobacco product labels.[55] Furthermore, even though harmful health effects of both mainstream smoke (inhaled by smokers) and side-stream smoke (environmental tobacco smoke exposure) are broadly documented and understood,[56] THPA article 7(I) fails to require tobacco manufacturers and distributors to place information regarding tobacco emissions on packaging.

Some might argue that the THPA does not restrict an individual's right to access health-related information because THPA articles 8(I) and (II) require tobacco companies to report information regarding tobacco contents, additives, and emissions to the competent authority, and such information should be periodically and voluntarily disclosed to the public. But package labelling (described in THPA article 7 and WHO FCTC article 11) and disclosures (THPA article 8 and WHO FCTC article 10) provide different accessibility levels, as individuals might have difficulty accessing relevant government information. For example, even though information regarding tobacco content and emissions is available online,[57] it is not clear whether Taiwanese citizens know the website address or that such information exists. Therefore, by failing to mandate tobacco contents and emissions information on tobacco packaging, the THPA might be preventing consumers from accessing essential health-related tobacco information. Thus, to align with WHO FCTC article 11, and to guarantee citizens the right to access health-related tobacco information, the THPA should be modified to require the display of descriptive tobacco constituents and emissions content on all packaging.

The strict regulations on tobacco packaging and labelling (especially mandatory health warnings) also raised a constitutional question based upon freedom of speech. The tobacco industry argued that the THPA regulations restrict their freedom of speech and, in particular, their freedom to passively express their opinion on tobacco hazards. This issue is discussed fully in section III(A) below.

D Sales to and by Minors

Similarly to WHO FCTC article 16, Taiwan's THPA bans individuals under the age of 18 from smoking (article 12(I)) and prohibits the sale of tobacco products to those under 18 (article 13(I)). Teenage violators must attend a smoking-cessation health class (article 28(I)); failing to attend without justifiable cause can result in fines of between NT$2000 and NT$10 000 (US$66.30–US$331.52) (article 28(II)). Individuals and businesses selling tobacco products to minors can be fined between NT$10 000 and NT$50 000 (US$331.52–US$1657.61) (article 29). Additionally, to deter underage tobacco use, THPA article 11, following WHO FCTC article 16(1)(c), states that 'no person shall manufacture, import or sell tobacco products in the form of candies, snacks, toys or any other objects'.

Furthermore, Taiwan's THPA is the first tobacco control law in the world that prohibits smoking during pregnancy (article 12(II)).[58] But unlike the prohibition of smoking by minors, this violation carries no punishment.[59] Scholars generally agree that this unique regulation concerning a woman's body has its own social meaning.[60] For example, anti-smoking advocates and medical scholars who support foetal-protection policies support the smoking prohibition during pregnancy because significant evidence shows that smoking can cause foetal harm such as low birth weight and stillbirth.[61] Nonetheless, some legal scholars query this regulation because 'targeting only pregnant smokers while ignoring other harmful factors (unrelated to smoking) to the fetus does not protect fetal rights'[62] and 'merely reinforces gender discrimination and increases the unreasonable costs of motherhood'.[63] In addition, some argue that THPA article 12(II) discriminates against pregnant women and might violate women's right to non-discrimination. However, I do not propose that THPA article 12(II) is morally unjustified. The state can justify unequal treatment in this case for tobacco control if a compelling interest exists.[64] But the trade-off between unequal treatment and proposed social benefits must be carefully evaluated. Unfortunately, the Taiwanese Government has failed to prove whether the right of a fetus to develop in a womb free of tobacco effects exists, and whether this imposes an unreasonable and discriminatory burden on women as a class.[65]

E Smoke-free Public Places

Scientific evidence confirms that the inhalation of second-hand smoke causes tobacco-related illnesses that can lead to disease, disability and death.[66] Therefore, WHO FCTC article 8(II) urges each party to provide protection from exposure to tobacco smoke in indoor workplaces, public transport, indoor public places and other public places. Aligned with the WHO FCTC, THPA article 15(I) extends the number of smoke-free places to communities, schools, military bases and workplaces. THPA article 31 also specifies fines of between NT$2000 and NT$10 000 (US$66.30–US$331.52) for violations.[67]

However, the THPA fails to provide definitions of key terms (eg, indoor, workplace, public transportation), and the lack of definition might hinder implementation of the THPA. In other words, the THPA's list of smoke-free areas might be interpreted as excluding potentially relevant 'indoor' areas and would thus be contrary to WHO FCTC article 8.

First, the THPA defines 'indoor workplaces' as 'places jointly used by three or more persons'. But the definition of indoor workplaces ignores para 20 of the *Guidelines for Implementation of Article 8 of the WHO FCTC*[68] (*Article 8 Guidelines*), which broadly defines workplaces as 'any place' used by 'any workers'. The THPA definition also appears contrary to para 7 of the *Article 8 Guidelines*, which clearly states that 'all people should be protected from exposure to tobacco smoke'. Additionally, it is unclear whether the THPA bans smoking in places commonly used by workers in the course of their employment, such as stairwells, toilets, outbuildings or commercial/business vehicles.

Second, without a proper definition of 'indoor', the THPA excludes semi-outdoor restaurants from its indoor smoke-free places list (article 15(I)(11)). However, according to para 19 of the *Article 8 Guidelines*, 'indoor areas' should be defined as 'any space covered by a roof or enclosed by one or more walls or sides'. Thus, the THPA erroneously concludes that semi-outdoor restaurants meet the exemption criteria. Even though Taiwan's Department of Health later passed the *Regulations for Establishment of Indoor Smoking Rooms 2008* (Taiwan),[69] defining 'semi-outdoor' as having 'no walls or its total open areas directly facing outside are more than one-fourth of its total wall areas' (article 3), the conflict between the different laws (the THPA and Department of Health regulations) remains.

Third, the THPA lists exemptions for indoor smoke-free places, such as businesses that open only after 9:00 pm and serve only persons older than age 18 (article 15(I)(11)), and social centres for the elderly with separate partitions equipped with independent air-conditioning or ventilation systems (article 15(I)(3)). But according to the *Article 8 Guidelines*, these public places should be smoke-free. Thus, the THPA's exemptions might breach a basic principle of WHO FCTC article 8: that all indoor workplaces and indoor public places should be smoke-free without exception (para 7 of the *Article 8 Guidelines*).

F   Tobacco Cessation

The state's responsibility to provide appropriate and effective measures for tobacco cessation is linked to an individual's right to access health-care.[70] A lack of easy access to smoking cessation services reflects a state's lack of appreciation for tobacco's serious health hazards and is a serious violation of the right to health.[71] Aligned with WHO FCTC article 14, THPA article 21 states that 'medical institutions, mental health counseling institutions and public interest groups may provide smoking cessation services'. In practice, Taiwanese smokers can go to clinics and receive medication (eg, nicotine patches and selective serotonin reuptake inhibitors (SSRIs)) to help them quit smoking, and they can call a toll-free helpline that offers professional psychological counselling to help them quit.[72]

However, compared with the amount of money spent on smoking prevention programmes, its focus on advertising bans, and efforts to expand smoke-free areas, the Taiwanese Government seems to overlook smoking cessation as a viable tobacco control policy.[73] For example, studies show that less than 1 per cent of Taiwan's smokers have quit annually with the help of medically assisted cessation programmes.[74] This dismal number may be explained in part by the fact that Taiwan's NHI excludes treatment of drug addiction (including clinical smoking cessation) from its coverage.[75] Instead of a national health insurance scheme, medication subsidies for smoking cessation are provided by the Bureau of Health Promotion,[76] and only partial reimbursement for limited smoking cessation programmes is provided.

In addition, similar to the WHO FCTC, Taiwan's THPA does not mandate the state to offer smoking cessation services.[77] Even though Taiwan's Bureau of Health Promotion provides subsidies for some smoking cessation programmes and medication,[78] without firm mandates in the THPA for the state to offer clinical smoking cessation programmes, subsidies for such health care series are regarded as voluntary and philanthropic rather than a legal obligation. In other words, the Taiwanese Government maintains substantial authority to offer whatever services it wishes, to make arbitrary decisions and broad claims as to how, when and how much resources to devote towards treating tobacco dependence,[79] and to restrict individuals' rights to access health care (in the form of tobacco cessation services) without justification.[80] For example, the 2006 THPA amendment decreased the proportion of the health and welfare surcharge allocated for tobacco control programmes from 10 per cent to 3 per cent with no clear explanation.

Frustrated with the government's failure to adequately fund and promote smoking cessation programmes, anti-smoking groups have urged the Taiwanese Government to extend its efforts based on the right to health[81] and the right to life.[82] For example, instead of moral obligations, the THPA and *National Health Insurance Act 2011* (Taiwan) (NHIA)[83] should impose legal obligations on the government to provide medical programmes to diagnose and treat tobacco dependence and also to provide counselling and preventative programmes for addicted tobacco users.[84] In addition, a sustainable source of funding for cessation treatment should be established (eg, by requiring the tobacco industry to pay for it through designated tobacco taxes and tobacco manufacturing licensing fees).[85]

III HUMAN RIGHTS AND TOBACCO CONTROL IN TAIWAN: FREEDOM OF SPEECH

The 1997 THPA and the 2009 THPA amendment provided strong governance against the tobacco threat to the population's health, but it also granted the government substantial power to intervene in the lives of individuals in the name of public health protection.[86] More specifically, after the enactment of the 2009 THPA amendment, some human rights concerns were raised. On the one hand, the THPA grants the government authority to adopt legislative and other coercive measures to protect individuals from tobacco-related health hazards. On the other hand, smokers and tobacco manufacturers have argued that the THPA's harsh provisions and penalties violate their liberties, such as autonomy, freedom of speech and expression, and property rights. A recent wave of litigation challenging the constitutionality of the THPA's ban on tobacco advertising and mandatory health warnings under the freedom of speech doctrine provides a prime example of this tension in tobacco control.

To improve and protect public health, 1997 THPA article 8(I) (which is the same as 2009 THPA amendment article 7(I)) requires tobacco manufacturers/importers to ensure that all tobacco product packages contain labels with the amount of nicotine and tar (see section II(C) above). Tobacco companies consequently alleged in several cases before Taiwan's Constitutional Court that article 8(I) unconstitutionally violated their freedom of speech (that is, their freedom not to reveal information/ freedom of passive omission). In 2004, the Court issued Judicial Yuan Interpretation No 577 (Shizi No 577),[87] in which the Court ruled that the tobacco labelling requirement in 1997 THPA article 8(I) is not unconstitutional because the freedom of speech restriction is justified as a means to promote social welfare and improve national health. In this section I explain the reasons for the Court's decision.

A   Identifying Human Rights Burdens

To balance conflicting freedoms in tobacco control policies, Taiwan's Constitutional Court first identified the freedoms that are affected by the THPA programme and the potential human rights burdens. One issue regarding the constitutionality of tobacco labelling requirements for tar and nicotine content is bound up with the scope of the right to freedom of speech.[88] Based upon Judicial Yuan Interpretation No 414 (Shizi No 414),[89] which deals with the constitutionality of censorship on drug commercials and defines the scope of the freedom of speech, the Court in Shizi No 577 argued that tobacco product labelling law should be regarded as a human rights burden on the freedom of speech.[90] More specifically, in Shizi No 414 the Court recognised that the freedom of speech protected in article 11 of the *Constitution of the Republic of China (Constitution)*[91] should not only include political speech but also academic speech and commercial speech.[92] Based upon Shizi No 414, the Court in Shizi No 577 found that tobacco product labelling 'constitutes a type of commercial speech and shall fall within the scope of protection to freedom of speech provided by the Constitution'.[93] In other words, because the aim of tobacco product labelling is to promote lawful trading and prevent false or misleading speech, this type of commercial speech 'has the same function of promoting self-realization as other types of speech by providing information and helping people to form opinions'[94] and is consistent with the values that underlie freedom of speech.

Another issue then raised is whether tobacco companies' silence on tobacco contents and emissions constitutes expression, and whether requiring them to disclose such information (compelled speech) violates their rights to freedom of speech. According to the Court in Shizi No 577, since freedom of speech includes both the freedom of active expression and passive omission, the tobacco companies' freedom to refuse to put certain information on product labels should be respected too. Taking this into consideration, requiring that tobacco companies label the amount of nicotine and tar contained in tobacco products then 'constitutes a restriction on the freedom of passive omission by compelling [tobacco companies] to provide material product information'[95] and should be regarded as a coercive programme that substantially regulates the tobacco companies' freedom of speech.

B Examining Justifications of Tobacco Labelling Requirement

According to article 23 of the *Constitution*, the restriction on freedom of speech imposed by 1997 THAP article 8(I) can be justified if and only if it is 'necessary to prevent infringement upon the freedoms of other persons, to avert an imminent crisis, to maintain social order or to advance public welfare'. Scholars universally interpret 'necessary' to be equivalent to the proportionality principle,[96] which consists of three sub-principles:[97] (i) the coercive policy is reasonably likely to achieve proposed objectives; (ii) the coercive policy is the least restrictive alternative that burdens individual rights/freedoms to a lesser extent, while still having a good likelihood of achieving proposed objectives (the 'least infringement' principle); and (iii) there is a proper trade-off between restricted rights/freedoms and public interests served by the coercive policy.

Applying the proportionality principle to examine the constitutionality of tobacco labelling requirement, the Court in Shizi No 577 first examined the public purpose of 1997 THPA article 8(I). On an individual level, the Court found that, because consumers cannot make a rational and informed choice about tobacco use without health-related tobacco information (eg, nicotine and tar levels), the labelling requirement should be regarded as a necessary means 'to provide consumers with truthful and complete information and to prevent any misleading information or deception caused by the content of product labelling'[98] and 'to help consumers to realize and to be alert to the potential danger caused by smoking'.[99] On the societal level, the Court argued that, since health-related tobacco information strongly and positively correlates with public health protection, article 8(I) can help to 'advance … substantial public interests'[100] and is consistent with article 157 of the *Constitution* and the *Constitution Amendments* article 10(VII) (relating to improving the health of nationals).

The Court then evaluated whether the tobacco labelling requirement is the least restrictive alternative to achieve the proposed purpose. In general, the tobacco industry argued that instead of requiring tobacco companies to provide certain information, government agencies or schools should be responsible for providing anti-smoking education, as this would be a less restrictive means to enhance the accessibility of information about tobacco products' toxic contents and emissions.[101] Thus, article 8(I) violated the least infringement principle. However, the Court found that 'such compulsory education is less effective to achieve the government objective in comparison with the duty to disclose

material product information imposed upon the tobacco product sup-
pliers'.[102] Empirical evidence also shows that individuals have limited
access to complete information about tobacco contents,[103] and that
smokers in low- and middle-income groups are unaware of the health
risks.[104] Therefore, the Court argued that, without imposing a legal duty
on tobacco manufacturers to disclose such information, individuals'
rights to access health-related tobacco information could not be guaranteed. Furthermore, because other less intrusive alternatives cannot
achieve similar purposes as well as the tobacco labelling requirement, the
imposition of 'duty to disclose' upon tobacco companies (restricting the
freedom of passive omission) cannot be found to violate the least
infringement principle.[105]

Finally, the Court examined whether, in the 1997 THPA's tobacco
labelling regulations, the burden imposed on the freedom of speech is
disproportionate to the public order objective or social benefits. Generally, freedom of speech is not an absolute right and can be regulated in
the interests of other liberties or rights, or for greater economic or social
benefits. In addition, commercial speech should not be subject to similar
protection of political or social speech[106] because commercial speech is
relevant neither to individuals' free use of public reason to judge and
regulate the basic justice structure nor to their capability to form
conceptions of the good.[107] Therefore, the tobacco industry's claims for
freedom of (commercial) speech called for careful reflection. As commercial speech is less protected than political and social speech, the
Court in Shizi No 577 ruled that the interests of freedom of commercial
speech are weaker, and the case for state restraints stronger than in other
areas of speech.[108] Thus, unlike the protection of political and social
speech, which can be regulated only when such speech injures a very
narrow class of the state's compelling interests, the Court reasoned that it
is justified to regulate commercial speech (tobacco labelling) to pursue a
'substantial governmental interest'[109] (eg, public benefits or economic
interests). In other words, since tobacco labelling requirements provide
necessary information on tobacco product content and protect public
health, and because the restriction on tobacco companies' freedom of
speech is minor and tolerable, the Court ruled that the weight of the
restricted commercial speech is not disproportionate to the weight of
pursued public order and that 1997 THPA article 8(I) is constitutionally
justified.

Based upon the reasoning in Shizi No 577, the mandatory health
warnings requirement in 2009 THPA amendment article 6 and the ban on
tobacco advertising and promotion in article 9, which could also be

viewed as an infringement of tobacco companies' freedom of commercial speech, are generally regarded as constitutionally justified.[110]

IV FUTURE CHALLENGES

Taiwan has been implementing a range of tobacco control strategies for many years. Based upon the government's effective implementation of the THPA and anti-smoking groups' efforts, the Taiwanese public has been increasingly making healthy lifestyle choices of quitting smoking and not taking up tobacco use.[111] However, several tobacco control policy problems remain unresolved. For example, tobacco product packages should have more detailed health warnings and larger pictorial warnings; the tobacco tax should be raised; the state's responsibility to provide smoking cessation services remains ambiguous and needs to be clarified and consistently enforced; and definitions of 'smoke-free public places' need to be established. In addition, the tobacco industry and 'smoking rights advocacy groups'[112] have started to deploy arguments based upon certain purported rights (such as right to freedom of speech, right to economic freedom, right to property, right to non-discrimination, and right to work)[113] in courts, trying to dilute or weaken tobacco control laws.[114] But Taiwan's Constitutional Court in Shizi No 577 dealt only with the conflict between freedom of speech and THPA's ban on tobacco advertising and mandatory labelling/health warnings. Therefore, regarding the relationship between human rights protection and tobacco control, the Court still needs to decide: (i) whether the THPA's strict tobacco control measures (eg, comprehensive bans on smoking in public places) unjustifiably restrict the freedom to smoke;[115] (ii) whether banning smoking in leisure entertainment businesses interferes with business owners' freedom of business and economic rights; (iii) whether the prohibition of smoking by pregnant women violates their right to non-discrimination; and (iv) whether tobacco labelling constitutes a restriction on tobacco companies' property rights.

In addition, the growing consumption of smokeless tobacco products (SLTPs) and e-cigarettes (electronic nicotine delivery systems) raises new challenges. Briefly, THPA article 2(I)(1) defines tobacco products as 'cigarettes, cut tobacco, cigars and other products entirely or partly made of the leaf tobacco or its substitute as raw material manufactured to be used for smoking, chewing, sucking, snuffing or other methods of consuming'. Given such a broad definition, SLTPs are included and considered as general tobacco products, subject to the same level of regulation in regard to smoked tobacco. However, some tobacco control measures cannot be directly applied to SLTP regulations. For example, the contents of health warnings and the disclosure of SLTP constituents should be re-evaluated because of the huge diversity of SLTPs. Banning SLTP use in public places might be difficult, but the Taiwanese Government should consider prohibiting SLTP use on campus.

Unlike SLTPs, e-cigarettes are likely excluded from the THPA's scope since the definition of tobacco products under THPA is limited to those made of 'leaf tobacco', while most e-cigarettes are designed as an 'electronic nicotine delivery system' and not made of leaf tobacco.[116] To fill the gap in tobacco control regulations, Taiwan's Department of Health used the pharmaceutical regulatory framework to regulate e-cigarette marketing. According to the *Pharmaceutical Affairs Act* (Taiwan), article 6, the term 'drugs' refer to materials that 'are sufficient to affect the body structure and physiological functions of human beings'. As e-cigarettes deliver nicotine and other substances to a user and can potentially influence an individual's physical functions and health, they fall within the scope of 'drugs' in Taiwan. Even though the pharmaceutical regulatory framework is stricter than the tobacco control regulatory framework (eg, e-cigarette manufacturers need to submit advertisements to the Department of Health for approval and cannot claim that e-cigarettes have therapeutic effects without the Department of Health's approval), treating e-cigarettes as drugs might give people the false impression that e-cigarettes have a therapeutic benefit, such as smoking cessation and minimising nicotine addiction. Therefore, for regulatory purposes, separate regulations specifically designed for e-cigarettes should be developed.

In closing, this chapter has highlighted the fact that the tobacco industry has employed various legal strategies to dilute or weaken tobacco control regulations. Therefore, it is essential for us to continually reassess current tobacco control laws and strategies and to diligently work to reduce tobacco hazards, strengthen public awareness, and explore and implement more efficient tobacco control measures to reduce the tobacco epidemic in Taiwan and globally.

NOTES

1. Chuan-Feng Wu, 'State Responsibility for Tobacco Control: The Right to Health Perspective' (2008) 3(2) *Asian Journal of WTO & International Health Law and Policy* 379, 381.
2. See, eg, Chi-pang Wen et al, 'Smoking Attributable Mortality for Taiwan and Its Projection to 2020 under Different Smoking Scenarios' (2005) 14 *Tobacco Control* i76, i76–i80.

3. Bureau of Health Promotion (Taiwan), *Taiwan Tobacco Control Annual Report 2010* (October 2010) 5 <http://tobacco.bhp.doh.gov.tw/Upload/FTB/UpFiles/2010 en.pdf>.

4. Bureau of Health Promotion (Taiwan), *Adult Smoking Behaviour Survey 2009* (2009) <http://tobacco.hpa.gov.tw/Show.aspx?MenuId=581>.

5. Bureau of Health Promotion (Taiwan), *Global Youth Tobacco Survey 2009* (2009) <http://tobacco.hpa.gov.tw/Show.aspx?MenuId=582>.

6. Bureau of Health Promotion (Taiwan), *Adult Smoking Behavior Survey 2009*, above n 4.

7. Bureau of Health Promotion (Taiwan), *National Occupational Health Workplace Environment Investigation 2009* (2009) <http://www.hpa.gov.tw/Bhpnet/Web/News/News.aspx?No=200712250342>.

8. Bureau of Health Promotion (Taiwan), *Adult Smoking Behavior Survey 2009*, above n 4.

9. Shu-Fang Shih et al, 'An Investigation of the Smoking Behaviours of Parents Before, During and After the Birth of Their Children in Taiwan' (2008) 8 *BMC Public Health* 67, 68.

10. Wu, above n 1, 381.

11. Kuo-Meng Liaw and C Chen, 'Mortality Attributable to Cigarette Smoking in Taiwan: A 12-Year-Follow-Up Study' (1998) 7 *Tobacco Control* 141, 144–6.

12. YanHe FangZhi Fa.

13. Bureau of Health Promotion (Taiwan), *Taiwan Tobacco Control Annual Report 2008* (July 2008) 8. <http://tobacco.hpa.gov.tw/Upload/Documents/63028ef072d 24b19b42d.pdf>; Chien-Hung Liu, 'The Analysis of Tobacco Hazards Prevention Act 2007' (2007) 150 *Taiwan Law Review* 186, 186–93.

14. Opened for signature 16 June 2003, 2302 UNTS 166 (entered into force 27 February 2005) (WHO FCTC).

15. Bureau of Health Promotion (Taiwan), *Taiwan Tobacco Control Annual Report 2010*, above n 3, 5.

16. Bureau of Health Promotion (Taiwan), *Adult Smoking Behavior Survey 2009*, above n 4.

17. Bureau of Health Promotion (Taiwan), *Taiwan Tobacco Control Annual Report 2010*, above n 3, 10.

18. Ibid 4.

19. See, eg, Frank Chaloupka et al, 'The Economics of Tobacco Control' (2005) 63 *Briefing Notes in Economics* 1, 5; Prabhat Jha and Frank Chaloupka (eds), *Tobacco Control in Developing Countries* (Oxford University, 2000); Kenneth Warner et al, 'Determining an Optimal Cigarette Tax: The Economist's Perspective' (1995) 4 *Tobacco Control* 380; Frank Chaloupka et al, 'Prices, Policies and Youth Smoking' (2003) 98 *Addiction* 105.

20. World Health Organization, *WHO Report on the Global Tobacco Epidemic 2011: Warning about the Dangers of Tobacco* (2011) 7 <http:// whqlibdoc.who.int/ publications/2011/9789240687813_eng.pdf>.

21. Conference of the Parties to the WHO Framework Convention on Tobacco Control, *Set of Guiding Principles and Recommendations for Implementation of Article 6 of the WHO Framework Convention on Tobacco Control (Price and Tax Measures to Reduce the Demand for Tobacco)*, 5th sess, WHO Doc FCTC/COP5(7) (17 November 2012) article 1.2 (*Article 6 Guidelines*).

22. Ibid article 1.3.

23. Ibid article 1.4.

24. Chi-pang Wen, 'Facilitating the Critical Process in Tobacco Control' (2005) 14 (Suppl I) *Tobacco Control* i1, i1.

25. Bureau of Health Promotion (Taiwan), *Taiwan Tobacco Control Annual Report 2010*, above n 3, 75; THPA article 4(I).
26. Bureau of Health Promotion (Taiwan), *Taiwan Tobacco Control Annual Report 2010*, above n 3, 74.
27. Ibid; Fung-Mey Huang and Yu-Ning Chien, 'Short-run or Long-run Impacts of Tobacco Tax on Teenager's Smoking? A Ten-year Longitudinal Study' (Working Paper No 2012–1, Chung-Hua Institution for Economic Research, February 2012) 1 <http://www.cier.edu.tw/public/Data/2012-1.pdf>.
28. Framework Convention Alliance, 'The Road to Article 6 Guidelines' (2012) 118 *Bulletin* 1.
29. Framework Convention Alliance, '176 Parties to the FCTC, Not 27' (2012) 120 *Bulletin* 1, 6; Ulysses Dorotheo, 'A Ray of Sunshine for Use of Revenues for Tobacco Control: Dedicating Revenues to Tobacco Control Programmes' (2012) 122 *Bulletin* 3.
30. Framework Convention Alliance, 'Last Chance in Seoul' (2012) 121 *Bulletin* 1. Discussion on this topic is also based on author's personal observations during the course of COP 5 proceedings.
31. Comment from the author's personal observations of COP 5.
32. Constantine Vardavas et al, 'Tobacco Taxation: The Importance of Earmarking the Revenue to Health Care and Tobacco Control' (2012) 10 *Tobacco-Induced Diseases* 21, 54–5; William Hamilton et al, 'Who Supports Tobacco Excise Taxes? Factors Associated with Towns' and Individuals' Support in Massachusetts' (2005) 11(4) *Journal of Public Health Management Practice* 333, 333–40.
33. Brian Dean Abramson, 'Let Them Eat Smoke: The Case for Exempting the Tobacco Industry from Antitrust' (2008) 6 *Cardozo Public Law, Policy and Ethics Journal* 345, 392; Margaret Clark, 'Cigar, Cigarette, and Loose Tobacco Taxes: Increase Excise Tax Rate on Little Cigars, C Cigars, and Cigarettes and Impose Excise Tax on Loose Tobacco' (2003) 20 *Georgia State University Law Review* 233, 234.
34. Andrew Haile, 'Sin Taxes: When the State Becomes the Sinner' (2009) 82 *Temple Law Review* 1041, 1053.
35. *Regulation of the Tobacco Health and Welfare Surcharge Distribution and Utilization 2000* (Taiwan) article 3.
36. Christopher Banthin and Richard Daynard, 'Room for Two in Tobacco Control: Limits on the Preemptive Scope of the Proposed Legislation Granting FDA Oversight of Tobacco' (2008) 11 *Journal of Health Care Law & Policy* 57, 80–81.
37. Conference of the Parties to the WHO Framework Convention on Tobacco Control, *Price and Tax Policies (in Relation to Article 6 of the Convention): Technical Report by WHO's Tobacco-Free Initiative*, 4th sess, WHO Doc FCTC/COP/4/11 (15 August 2010) [20].
38. Lawrence Gostin, 'Conceptualizing the Field after September 11th: Foreword to a Symposium on Public Health Law' (2002) 90 *Kentucky Law Journal* 791, 806–7.
39. Lauren Kaplin, 'A National Strategy to Combat the Childhood Obesity Epidemic' (2011) 15 *UC Davis Journal of Juvenile Law & Policy* 347, 390–91.
40. Hsun-hsieh Chen and Ann Chen, 'Taiwan Mulling Higher Tobacco Tax, Surcharge', *Focus Taiwan News Channel* (online), 19 March 2013 <http://focustaiwan.tw/news/aeco/201303190039.aspx>.
41. Wendy Zeldin, *Taiwan: Proposals to Increase Taxation of and Health Surcharge on Tobacco Products* (13 May 2013) The Law Library of Congress <http://www.loc.gov/lawweb/servlet/lloc_news?disp3_l205403590_text>.
42. Chia-chen Hsieh, Ching-fang Chen and Liu Kay, 'Cabinet Approves Proposed Hikes in Tobacco Tax, Surcharge', *Focus Taiwan News Channel* (online), 9 May 2013 <http://focustaiwan.tw/news/aall/201305090026.aspx>.
43. Ibid.

44. According to article 8(5) of *Regulations Governing the Establishment and Management of Duty-Free Shops 2008* (Taiwan) and articles 5(2) and 22-1 of the *Tobacco and Alcohol Tax Law 2010* (Taiwan), duty-free purchases of departing or arriving passengers are not subject to the tobacco health and welfare surcharge.

45. Bureau of Health Promotion (Taiwan), *Taiwan Tobacco Control Annual Report 2010*, above n 3, 56, 70.

46. FanMai YanPin ChangSuo BiaoQi Ji ZhanQi BanFa.

47. Fong-ching Chang et al, 'The Impact of Graphic Cigarette Warning Labels and Smoke-free Law on Health Awareness and Thoughts of Quitting in Taiwan' (2011) 26 *Health Education Research* 179, 185.

48. Bureau of Health Promotion (Taiwan), *Taiwan Tobacco Control Annual Report 2010*, above n 3, 56, 70.

49. Twenty-seven countries require the size of the health warnings to cover at least 50 per cent of tobacco packaging, see Geoffrey Fong, David Hammond and Sara Hitchman, 'The Impact of Pictures on the Effectiveness of Tobacco Warnings' (2009) 87 *Bulletin of the World Health Organization* 640.

50. Cecilia Fanchiang, 'DOH Not Just Blowing Smoke over Tobacco Plan', *Taiwan Today* (online), 16 January 2004 <http://www.taiwantoday.tw/ct.asp?xItem=20465&CtNode=451>.

51. YanPing NiGuDing JaioYou HanLiang JianCe Ji RongGi BiaoQi BanFa.

52. Conference of the Parties to the WHO Framework Convention on Tobacco Control, *Guidelines for Implementation of Article 11 of the WHO Framework Convention on Tobacco Control*, 3rd sess, WHO Doc FCTC/COP3(10) (17–22 November 2008).

53. According to articles 2 and 3 of the *Act to Implement the International Covenant on Civil and Political Rights and the International Covenant on Economic, Social and Cultural Rights 2009* (Taiwan) (Two Covenants Implementation Act), human rights protection provisions in ICCPR and ICESCR (including their legislative purposes and interpretations by the Human Rights Committee) have domestic legal status. Since para 11 of the *Committee of Economic, Social, and Cultural Rights General Comment No 14* (CESCR General Comment No 14) has confirmed that 'the right to health [should be interpreted] as an inclusive right extending not only to timely and appropriate health care but also to … access to health-related education and information', in accordance with the *Two Covenants Implementation Act* the Taiwanese Government has the human rights obligation to positively promote the realisation of individuals' right to access and receive health-related information (including health risks of smoking and constituents of tobacco products and their emissions).

54. Andrew Nix, 'Statutory Disclosure of Tobacco Ingredients: Secrets Up in Smoke?' (2003) 54 *Alabama Law Review* 1413, 1415.

55. Wu, above n 1, 409.

56. Patricia Davidson, 'Tobacco Ingredients and Smoke Constituent Reporting and Disclosure Law: The Case for Expansion' (1999) 77 *Denver University Law Review* 1, 1–2.

57. See Bureau of Health Promotion (Taiwan), *Tobacco Product Ingredients Website* (28 November 2012) <http://tobacco-information.bhp.doh.gov.tw>.

58. 'Tobacco Ban to Be Extended to Protect Pregnancy', *China Post* (online), 15 March 2005 <http://www.chinapost.com.tw/taiwan/detail.asp?ID=59659&GRP=B>.

59. Hsiao-Wei Kuan, 'The Unbearable Heaviness of Reproductive Duty: The Social Meaning of the Smoking Ban on Pregnant Women in Taiwan's Tobacco Control Law' in Chuan-Feng (ed), *Biennial Review of Law, Science and Technology: Health, Science and Human Rights 2011* (Academia Sinica, 2012) 518–36.

60. Ibid 503.

61. Hui-ling Shi, 'Fetal and Children's Protection under the Tobacco Hazard Control Act – An Opinion from the Expert' (2004) 294 *Taipei Bar Journal* 15, 15–27; Yu-Bing Kan, 'A Study on Protection of Fetus and Young Children's Health Rights – Focusing on the Proposal for Suppression Legislation of Tobacco Hazards' (2003) 4 *Journal of Children Welfare* 43, 43–62.

62. Chih-Chieh Lin, 'Regulating Pregnancy in Taiwan: An Analysis from an Asian Legal Feminist Using Feminist Legal Theories' (2009) 39 *University of Baltimore Law Forum* 204, 221.

63. Ibid.

64. For example, it is justified to trade individual tobacco users' autonomy or freedom to smoke in enclosed public places for the safety and well-being of the public: see, Taiwo Oriola, 'Ethical and Legal Analyses of Policy Tobacco Smoking in Enclosed Public Spaces' (2009) 37 *Journal of Law, Medicine & Ethics* 828, 828.

65. Lin, above n 62, 221.

66. See, eg, Eugene Rogot and James Murray, 'Smoking and Causes of Death among U.S. Veterans: 16 Years of Observation' (1980) 95 *Public Health Reports* 213, 213–22; E Cuyler Hammond and Herbert Seidmen, 'Smoking and Cancer in the United States' (1980) 9 *Preventive Medicine* 169, 169–73; Richard Doll and Richard Peto, 'Mortality in Relation to Smoking: 20 Years' Observation on Male British Doctors' (1976) 2 *British Medical Journal* 1525, 1525–36.

67. However, unlike [33] and [34] of the *Article 8 Guidelines*, Taiwan's THPA has no administrative sanctions (eg, suspension of business licences) or criminal penalties for violations.

68. Conference of the Parties to the WHO Framework Convention on Tobacco Control, *Guidelines for Implementation of Article 8 of the WHO FCTC*, 2nd sess, WHO Doc FCTC/COP2(7) (July 2007).

69. ShiNa XiYanShi SheZhi BanFa.

70. Wu, above n 1, 398. The right to access health (including the right to access health care) can be derived from article 22 of the *Constitution*, which states that '[a]ll other freedoms and rights of the people that are not detrimental to social order or public welfare shall be guaranteed under the Constitution'. More specifically, even though the right to health is a 'non-enumerated right' under the *Constitution*, Grand Justices and scholars generally agree that this right could still be recognised as a legally enforceable fundamental constitutional right under article 22 of the *Constitution* because it shares characteristics relevant to identification of fundamental rights and relates to intimate and important decisions about one's life or relationships. See Grand Justices Shin-min Chen's and Chang-fa Lo's concurring opinions in Shizi No 701: Constitutional Court Interpretation No 701, The Republic of China Constitutional Court (Grand Justices Council) Reporter, Shizi (Judicial Yuan Interpretation) No 701 (6 July 2012) (Taiwan). See also Ming-hsin Lin, 'The Right to Health: Based on the Protective Obligation of the State' (2005) 32 *Law Forum* 26, 26–36; Chen-shan Li, 'The Multiple Dimensions of Non-Enumerated Constitutional Rights: Focusing on the Article 22 of the ROC Constitution' in Chen-Shan Li (ed), *Plurality, Tolerance, and the Protection of Human Rights: Focusing on the Protection of Non-Enumerated Rights* (Angle, 2005) 33–40.

71. Robin Appleberry, 'Breaking the Camel's Back: Bringing Women's Human Rights to Bear on Tobacco Control' (2001) 13 *Yale Journal of Law & Feminism* 71, 86.

72. Bureau of Health Promotion (Taiwan), *Taiwan Tobacco Control Annual Report 2010*, above n 3, 56, 60.

73. Chi-pang Wen et al, 'The Framework Convention on Tobacco Control – Article 14 "Demand Reduction" (Smoking Cessation) – The Weakest Link of FCTC in Asia' (2010) 5(2) *Asian Journal of WTO & International Health Law and Policy* 381, 388.

74. Ibid.
75. *National Health Insurance Act* (Taiwan) (NHIA) article 51(1).
76. Fong-ching Chang et al, 'Effects of Financing Smoking Cessation Outpatient Services in Taiwan' (2008) 17 *Tobacco Control* 183, 183.
77. Wu, above n 1, 384. See also Chang-fa Lo, 'Establishing Global Governance in the Implementation of FCTC: Some Reflections on the Current Two-Pillar and One-Roof Framework' (2006) 1 *Asian Journal of WTO & International Health Law and Policy* 569, 583.
78. Bureau of Health Promotion (Taiwan), *Taiwan Tobacco Control Annual Report 2010*, above n 3, 57.
79. Wu, above n 1, 400.
80. Ibid 384.
81. See more discussion below, n 71.
82. *Constitution of the Republic of China 1946* article 15.
83. Quanmin JianKang BaoXian Fa.
84. Wu, above n 1, 402.
85. Wu, above n 1, 389.
86. Lin, above n 62, 221.
87. *Constitutional Court Interpretation No 577*, The Republic of China Constitutional Court (Grand Justices Council) Reporter, Shizi (Judicial Yuan Interpretation) No 577 (7 May 2004) (Taiwan).
88. Oscar Cabrera also identified the scope of freedom of speech scope as an important issue in several tobacco cases in South America: O'Neill Institute for National and Global Health Law, *Tobacco Industry Strategy in Latin American Courts* (February 2012) 19 <http://www.law.georgetown.edu/oneillinstitute/documents/2012_Oneill TobaccoLitGuide_ENG.PDF>.
89. *Constitutional Court Interpretation No 414*, The Republic of China Constitutional Court (Grand Justices Council) Reporter, Shizi (Judicial Yuan Interpretation) No 414 (8 November 1996) (Taiwan).
90. *Constitutional Court Interpretation No 577*, The Republic of China Constitutional Court (Grand Justices Council) Reporter, Shizi (Judicial Yuan Interpretation) No 577 (7 May 2004) (Taiwan).
91. *Constitution of the Republic of China 1946* article 11.
92. *Constitutional Court Interpretation No 414*, The Republic of China Constitutional Court (Grand Justices Council) Reporter, Shizi (Judicial Yuan Interpretation) No 414 (8 November 1996) (Taiwan).
93. *Constitutional Court Interpretation No 577*, The Republic of China Constitutional Court (Grand Justices Council) Reporter, Shizi (Judicial Yuan Interpretation) No 577 (7 May 2004) (Taiwan).
94. Ibid.
95. Ibid.
96. Chung-Lin Chen, 'In Search of a New Approach of Information Privacy Judicial Review: Interpretation No 603 of Taiwan's Constitutional Court as a Guide' (2010) 20 *Indiana International & Comparative Law Review* 21, 26–7.
97. The three sub-principles of the proportionality principle can also be found in *Administrative Procedure Act 1999* article 7.
98. *Constitutional Court Interpretation No 577*, The Republic of China Constitutional Court (Grand Justices Council) Reporter, Shizi (Judicial Yuan Interpretation) No 577 (7 May 2004) (Taiwan).
99. Ibid.
100. Ibid.
101. Ibid.

102. Ibid.
103. Nix, above n 54, 1415.
104. Working Group of the WHO Framework Convention on Tobacco Control, *Economics of Tobacco Control*, 1st mtg, WHO Doc A/FCTC/WG1/2 (20 August 1999).
105. The Court in different cases (eg, Shizi Nos 414, 577, 617 and 623) consistently argued that, even though commercial speech is 'inextricably intertwined' with other protected speech, it does no more than propose a commercial transaction and should not be regarded as fully protected speech (such as political or social speech). Therefore, some legal scholars debate how to apply the least infringement principle to commercial speech. For example, in Grand Justice Syueming Yu's concurring opinion in Shizi No 577, he challenged the necessity to require either an absolute least severe alternative or a reasonable 'fit' between the state's ends and the means chosen to accomplish when examining the constitutionality of tobacco labelling requirements. This issue is beyond the scope of this chapter. See further Constitutional Court Interpretation No 577, The Republic of China Constitutional Court (Grand Justices Council) Reporter, Shizi (Judicial Yuan Interpretation) No 577 (7 May 2004) (Taiwan); see also Wen-zheng Xie, *Tobacco Product Advertisement* and *Freedom of Commercial Speech* (National Taiwan University, 2004) 91.
106. O'Neill Institute for National and Global Health Law, above n 88, 18–19.
107. John Rawls, *Justice as Fairness: A Restatement* (Harvard University, 2001) 113–14; Lawrence Gostin, *Public Health Law: Power, Duty, Restraint* (University of California, 2008) 379.
108. *Constitutional Court Interpretation No 577*, The Republic of China Constitutional Court (Grand Justices Council) Reporter, Shizi (Judicial Yuan Interpretation) No 577 (7 May 1996) (Taiwan).
109. See Grand Justice Syue-ming Yu's concurring opinion in Shizi No 577: Ibid; see also John Zelezny, *Communication Law: Liberties, Restraints, and the Modern Media* (Cengage Learning, 1993) 379.
110. Tse-jung Chen, *Review of Mandatory Tobacco Health Warnings and Tobacco Advertising Bans from the Constitutional Protection of Commercial Speech Freedom Perspective* (National Cheng Kung University, 2003) 117–28.
111. Chang, above n 47, 179–91. Shu-hui Chuang and Song-Lih Huang, 'Changes in Smoking Behavior among College Students Following Implementation of a Strict Campus Smoking Policy in Taiwan' (2012) 57 *International Journal of Public Health* 199, 199–205. Fong-ching Chang et al, 'Impact of the 2009 Taiwan Tobacco Hazards Prevention Act on Smoking Cessation' (2013) *Addiction* 1–7, doi: 10.1111/add.12344 <http://onlinelibrary.wiley.com/doi/10.1111/add.12344/pdf>.
112. After the enactment of the *Two Covenants Implementation Act*, smokers began to organise groups (eg, the Smokers' Rights Advocacy Association) through Internet networks and used human rights language to challenge tobacco control initiatives. See, eg, Gui-xiang Wen, 'Smokers' Rights Advocacy Association: Stop: Stop Health and Welfare Surcharge', *Focus Taiwan Today* (online), 24 October 2013 <http://www.cna.com.tw/news/aIPL/201310240293-1.aspx>.
113. O'Neill Institute for National and Global Health Law, above n 88, 18–43.
114. Ibid 11.
115. Even though it is debatable whether the concepts of freedom can be so broad as to cover any interest (such as smoking interests) without rigorous reasoning, some scholars still assert the existence of the freedom to smoke. Taiwo Oriola, 'Ethical and Legal Analyses of Policy Tobacco Smoking in Enclosed Public Spaces' (2009) 37 *Journal of Law, Medicine and Ethics* 828, 828; Michele Tyler, 'Blowing Smoke: Do Smokers Have a Right? Limiting the Privacy Rights of Cigarette Smokers' (1998) 86 *Georgetown Law Journal 783*, 801; Zhiyong Xie, 'A Fiction: The Right

or Freedom of Smoking' (2013) 8(1) *Asian Journal of WTO & International Health Law and Policy*, 149, 152–3.

116. However, e-cigarettes made of leaf tobacco are still subject to THPA's regulations.

16. Tobacco control in India

Amit Yadav and Deepti Singh

I INTRODUCTION

Historically, India was introduced to tobacco by the Portuguese through barter trade in the sixteenth century and later became a cash crop in the late eighteenth century in the British Raj. Commercial manufacturing of cigarettes started in the early twentieth century with the incorporation of the Imperial Tobacco Company of India Limited in 1910. The production of bidi, the Indian version of cigarettes (tobacco wrapped in tendu leaves), started in the late nineteenth century. The commercial production of smokeless tobacco, although used for centuries in chewing form, peaked in the late twentieth century with the advent of gutkha in the 1990s.[1]

What was initially introduced in the royal courts soon found favour with the masses. Although some people, including physicians, suspected that it could be harmful, tobacco soon came to be widely used and cultivated in India. Today, nearly 275 million Indians use tobacco in some form (48 per cent male and more than 20 per cent female), and this number is increasing at an alarming rate, especially among vulnerable populations including women and youth.[2] According to the *Global Youth Tobacco Survey Fact Sheet: 2009*, 14.6 per cent of youth (13–15-year-olds) use tobacco in some form.[3] Sixth grade students are two to four times more likely to consume tobacco than eighth grade students.[4] The gender gap is narrowing, with more young girls starting to use tobacco.[5] In India, more than 1 million deaths annually are attributed to smoking alone.[6]

Tobacco use contributes to approximately 60 per cent of all cardio-vascular disease deaths in India,[7] and 42 per cent and 18 per cent of cancer deaths among men and women respectively are due to tobacco use.[8] Tobacco use is not only a health burden; huge economic losses are incurred due to massive expenditures on the treatment of diseases caused by tobacco use.[9] It is estimated that direct expenditures on tobacco use and out-of-pocket expenditures on health care costs, which otherwise could be spent on food or education for children, impoverishes roughly 15 million people in India.[10]

In the seventeenth century, Emperor Jahangir passed orders prohibiting smoking, but these were not effective for long.[11] Subsequently, no significant legislation was passed until the second half of the nineteenth century, although article 47 of the *Constitution of India* directed the state to endeavour to prohibit the consumption, except for medicinal purposes, of intoxicating drinks and drugs that are injurious to health.[12] During Constituent Assembly debates in parliament, Sardar Bhopinder Singh Mann proposed inserting the word 'tobacco' between the words 'drinks' and 'drugs' in this constitutional provision, but the Constituent Assembly rejected his motion, leaving the provision open to interpretation.[13]

The very first pan-Indian legislative efforts in tobacco control began with the *Cigarettes (Regulations of Production, Supply and Distribution) Act 1975* (India) under the aegis of the Ministry of Commerce. This legislation required the 'text only' statutory warning 'cigarette smoking is injurious to health' to be included on all cigarette packages and cigarette advertisements in India. In 1991, the Ministry of Health and Family Welfare convened a National Conference on Tobacco or Health, which recommended national tobacco control legislation.[14] In 1995, the Parliamentary Committee Report on Subordinate Legislation of the 10th Lok Sabha suggested stronger tobacco control provisions.[15] During 1996–2002, the governments of Delhi, Tamil Nadu, Goa, Assam, West Bengal and others enacted laws against smoking in public places.[16] Considering the health hazards of second-hand tobacco smoke and the rights of individuals to breathe in a pollution-free environment, in 2001 the Supreme Court of India mandated all public places to be smoke-free and called upon the legislature to enact a comprehensive tobacco control law.[17]

In 2001, the National Human Rights Commission recognised tobacco control as integral to human rights.[18] During 2000–04, several states, including Maharashtra, Tamil Nadu, Madhya Pradesh, Goa and Bihar, banned production and sale of gutkha and paan masala under the *Prevention of Food Adulteration Act 1954* (India). Later, in 2003, the Parliament of India adopted the *Cigarettes and Other Tobacco Products (Prohibition of Advertisement and Regulation of Trade and Commerce, Production, Supply and Distribution) Act 2003* (India) (COTPA). The law received assent of the President of India on 18 May 2003 and came into force on 1 May 2004.

In parallel developments, the 56th World Health Assembly of the World Health Organization (WHO) adopted the *WHO Framework Convention on Tobacco Control* (WHO FCTC)[19] in May 2003. India ratified soon after, in February 2004, to become the eighth and largest party to the treaty. The WHO FCTC requires that nations develop action plans for public health policy, *inter alia*, to prohibit direct and indirect tobacco advertising, institute pro-tobacco control tax regimes, promote smoke-free public places, and include pictorial warnings and health messages on tobacco packages.[20]

The key provisions of COTPA include prohibitions on direct and indirect advertising of tobacco products, sale of tobacco products to and by minors, and smoking in public places. COTPA also mandates textual and pictorial health warnings.[21] However, the WHO FCTC encourages nations to take advanced steps, even beyond those recommended in the Treaty, and implement measures with stricter requirements in agreement with national and international laws and best practices.[22]

Taking the tobacco control efforts a step forward, during the 11th Five-Year Plan, the Ministry of Health and Family Welfare launched the National Tobacco Control Programme (NTCP) in 2007 as a pilot project. The programme currently covers 42 districts in 21 states in the country. The primary objective of the programme is to create awareness about the hazards of tobacco use, reduce tobacco consumption, and minimise tobacco-related deaths.[23] The programme envisions building human and institutional capacities at the national, state and district levels to:

- advance tobacco control and effectively implement all tobacco control initiatives;
- train health and social workers;
- take up appropriate information, education and communication and mass awareness campaigns including a school health programme; and
- ensure effective monitoring of tobacco control implementation, including under a global tobacco surveillance system.[24]

COTPA regulates all types of tobacco products, but the increasing burden of smokeless tobacco in India remains of great public health concern. Several measures have been undertaken to curb the use of smokeless tobacco, including statutory health warnings on all tobacco products,[25] and prohibition on the use of tobacco as an ingredient in toothpaste and, under the *Food Safety and Standards Act 2006* (India) (FSSA), in any food item.[26] The manufacturing and sale of gutkha, paan masala, and other chewable forms of tobacco that come under the category of 'food' have been prohibited since August 2011 by FSSA. Regulation 2.3.4 of the *Food Safety and Standards (Prohibition and Restriction on Sales) Regulations 2011* (India) is being implemented by all the states and union territories in the country by prohibiting the sale of gutkha and certain categories of smokeless tobacco and paan masala.[27] Smokeless tobacco manufacturing units were granted licences and registrations under the FSSA,[28] but pursuant to reg 2.3.4 new licences and licence renewals for products containing tobacco and nicotine are precluded.

Tobacco control efforts in India have been galvanised by active civil society advocacy along with the supportive Indian judiciary, which played an important role in the enactment and later in the enforcement of tobacco control laws. This chapter aims to capture all the legislative, administrative and judicial developments pertaining to the discourse of tobacco control in India. It presents a review of existing laws and regulations, including judicial and administrative steps, that have resulted in an effective tobacco control policy framework in compliance with and beyond the requirements of the WHO FCTC. Taking into account the constitutional obligation of the state to improve public health, the chapter highlights recent developments such as regulations prohibiting the depiction of tobacco use in films and television programmes, strict regulation of point-of-sale advertising, and the introduction of a private member's bill in the parliament to amend COTPA by requiring the 'plain' packaging of tobacco products.

II KEY LEGISLATION IMPACTING TOBACCO CONTROL

A Constitution-based Protections: The Right to Life and Liberty

The *Constitution of India* guarantees every individual the right to life and personal liberty.[29] The ambit of this right extends to living in a pollution-free environment, which has provided the premise for prohibiting smoking in public places. The highest standards of public health and wellbeing are emphasised in the *Constitution*, with article 39(e) requiring the state to direct policy towards securing the health and strength of workers, men, women and children.

The constitutional directive contained in article 47 of the *Constitution of India* obliges the state to ensure the creation and maintenance of conditions congenial to good health. This provision imposes a primary duty on the government to prohibit consumption of products injurious to health.[30]

Further, entry six of the state list contained in the 7th schedule to the *Constitution* empowers state legislatures to make laws with respect to public health. Several states including Maharashtra,[31] Goa,[32] Delhi,[33]

West Bengal,[34] Tamil Nadu[35] and Assam[36] have enacted laws to prohibit smoking in public places and public service vehicles[37] to protect public health.[38] In addition, these state laws prohibit: advertisements that may promote smoking or sale of cigarettes, cigar and bidis in any public place or any public service vehicle; sale of the smoking form of tobacco products to a person below the age of 18 years; and storage, sale and distribution of the smoking form of tobacco products within 100 metres of educational institutions and, in some cases, places of worship.

B   Criminal Laws: Second-hand Smoke as a Public Nuisance

Before the enactment of specific tobacco control laws, judicial statements made clear that second-hand smoke is a public nuisance punishable under s 290 of the *Indian Penal Code 1860* (India) (IPC). Several states have used this provision of the IPC to prevent smoking in public places and have directed enforcement officers to take action on complaints of smoking in public places under the IPC.[39] A person who continues to engage in such public nuisance, after an instruction from the enforcement authority to discontinue, is liable to imprisonment for up to six months or a fine under s 291 of the IPC. Section 133 of the *Criminal Procedure Code 1973* (India) empowers a magistrate to order a person causing nuisance injurious to the health or physical comfort of the community to desist within a given period.

C   Other Legislation Affecting Tobacco Control

Several other statutes give indirect effect to the above-mentioned constitutional directives. The *Poisons Act 1919* (India)[40] and the *Insecticide Act 1968* (India)[41] preclude nicotine from use as an additive, declaring it poisonous and providing for its regulation in smokeless tobacco. Other legislation such as the *Cinematograph Act 1952* (India) prohibits scenes tending to encourage, justify or glamourise the consumption of tobacco or smoking.[42] The *Consumer Protection Act 1986* (India) addresses consumer complaints against defective products and deficient services,[43] and this provision may be used to complain against restaurants or hotels for the sale and serving of food contaminated with tobacco smoke, seeking compensation towards health costs. Section 167 of the *Indian Railways Act 1989* (India) prohibits smoking in any compartment of a train if objected to by any person.

In 1975, India passed specific legislation imposing certain restrictions regarding cigarette production, supply, distribution and trade.[44] This law introduced the first mandatory 'text only' health warning – 'cigarette smoking is injurious to health' – for all cigarettes and cigarette advertisements in India.[45] However, the law covered only cigarettes and no other tobacco products. Nevertheless, the *Prevention of Food Adulteration Act 1954* (India) was subsequently amended to mandate health warnings on such products including gutkha and paan masala.[46]

D Comprehensive Law on Tobacco Control: COTPA

The Indian tobacco control law, COTPA, is designed to protect people from the hazards that tobacco poses to the health of both users and non-users, and to address other indirect social, environmental and economic costs. Enacted in 2003 and in force since May 2004, the law addresses second-hand smoke by prohibiting smoking in public places[47] and prevents minors' access to tobacco products by prohibiting sale of tobacco products to any person below the age of 18 years and within 100 yards of any educational institution.[48] Violation of these provisions is punishable with a fine of up to 200 rupees.[49] The law also prohibits tobacco advertisements, promotion and sponsorships including restrictions on point-of-sale advertising and display.[50] Any violation of the provision or regulations made therein is punishable with up to two years' imprisonment, a fine of up to 1000 rupees, or both. Subsequent offences attract up to five years' imprisonment and a fine of up to 5000 rupees.[51] In line with the WHO FCTC, the law prescribes mandatory depiction of pictorial health warnings on all tobacco products[52] and its violation is punishable with, for producers and manufacturers, up to two years' imprisonment, or a fine of up to 5000 rupees, or both. For a second or subsequent conviction, penalties are imprisonment of up to five years and a fine of up to 10 000 rupees. Retailers face up to one year of imprisonment, a fine of up to 1000 rupees, or both, and for second or subsequent convictions up to two years' imprisonment and a fine of up to 3000 rupees.[53]

Implementation of the provisions of COTPA began in May 2004. However, subsequently passed rules and regulations increased and clarified the ambit of the law by redefining its terms. In particular, smoke-free areas were extended to certain open spaces and the meaning of 'smoking area or space' was redefined to ensure smoke-free public places.[54] The prohibition on sale to minors was extended to prohibit sale by minors.[55] The ban on tobacco advertisements, promotion and sponsorship was also extended to indirect advertisements, which now prohibits:[56]

- the use of a name or brand of tobacco products for marketing, promoting or advertising other goods, services and events;

- the marketing of tobacco products with the aid of a brand name or trademark which is known as, or in use as, a name or brand for other goods and services;
- the use of particular colours and layout and or presentation that are associated with particular tobacco products; and
- the use of tobacco products and smoking scenes when advertising other goods and services.

With regard to pictorial warnings, COTPA mandated the depiction of a skull and crossbones on all tobacco product packages, along with textual and additional graphic health warnings.[57] Although these warnings were notified in July 2006,[58] the skull and crossbones and chosen graphics were removed through an amendment of COTPA in 2007,[59] due to opposition from the tobacco industry (particularly the bidi industry). A milder set of pictorial health warnings came into force in India on 31 May 2009[60] and were later revised in 2011.[61]

Strengthening the implementation of the ban on tobacco advertisements, promotion and sponsorship, the Ministry of Health and Family Welfare has subsequently restricted advertisements at the point of sale. The amended regulations prescribe that only the tobacco products available may be listed at the point of sale, along with a health warning message.[62]

The likelihood of using tobacco among students who are highly exposed to the use of tobacco in Bollywood films is more than twice that among students with low exposure.[63] Considering the influence of films and television on Indian youth, the Ministry of Health and Family Welfare introduced a strict regulation against depiction of tobacco use on screen.[64]

III LITIGATION AS A STRATEGY OF TOBACCO PROMOTION AND TOBACCO CONTROL

Indian courts are known for their judicial activism. Allowing public interest litigation (courts in India relax the rule of *locus standi* and accept petitions filed in public interest by a member of the public or an organisation interested in a public cause) on matters of public importance is one such mode of judicial intervention. More specifically, the Indian judiciary has played an important role in India's tobacco control movement, as shown by examples below. Judicial pronouncements have resulted in enforcement of tobacco control laws at both national and sub-national levels. Court cases have opened new fronts in the public critique of tobacco industry behaviour and in countering misleading advertisements and prohibiting the distribution of tobacco products to children. Public scrutiny and media reporting about the law and associated litigation have also increased general awareness about the addictive and adverse effects of tobacco products as well as the misleading nature of tobacco promotions.

The Kerala High Court declared smoking in public places illegal, considering it a public nuisance, and observed that smoking in public places causes non-smokers to involuntarily inhale smoke from smokers nearby.[65]

The Supreme Court of India read 'right to health' as part of the 'right to life' under article 21 of the *Constitution* and banned smoking in public places until the relevant statutory provision was made and implemented. The Supreme Court directed the central and state governments to take effective steps to ensure a ban on smoking in public places, including necessary and effective steps to give wide publicity to the order of the Court.[66] The relevant legislation was introduced in 2001.[67]

The Bombay High Court, in public interest litigation, directed the government to ensure a prohibition on the sale of tobacco products within 100 yards of educational institutions. As a result s 6(b) of the COTPA was notified and came into force on 18 September 2009.[68]

Challenging the ban on the sale of tobacco products within 100 yards of educational institutions, an association of wholesalers of tobacco products sought an exemption from s 6(b) of the COTPA, on the pretext that they do not sell their products to end users. However, the Delhi High Court not only dismissed the petition, but also imposed costs on the association to be paid to central and state governments for anti-tobacco initiatives.[69]

The tobacco industry challenged the comprehensive smoke-free regulations notified on 31 May 2008 and to be implemented from 2 October 2008. However, the Supreme Court of India directed that the ban on smoking in public places should be implemented without exemption. Denying a stay on implementation of the smoke-free rules, the Court also prevented other Indian courts from passing adverse orders against the rules.[70]

The idea of including pictorial warnings on all tobacco packages was initiated through public interest litigation in the High Court of Himachal Pradesh in December 2004.[71] The petitioner insisted that India follow best practices of other countries in tobacco control. On repeated requests from the Shimla High Court,[72] the Ministry of Health and Family Welfare devised rules on packaging and labelling including four strong pictorial warnings covering 50 per cent of the principal display area of all tobacco product packages, to be implemented from 1 February 2007.[73] However, the pictorial warnings came into force only in 2009 when the Supreme Court directed that the government must undertake to implement the *Cigarettes and Other Tobacco Products (Packaging and Labelling) Rules 2008* (India) (the '*Rule*'), with effect from 31 May 2009.[74]

The High Court of Gujarat issued directions to the Gujarat State Road Transport Corporation and the Ahmedabad Municipal Transport Services for removal of advertisements of gutkha or paan masala displayed on public transport.[75] The Karnataka High Court directed the government of India to withdraw sponsorship extended by the Tobacco Board of India (an organisation under the Department of Commerce) to an industry-sponsored event in October 2010, in compliance with s 5 of COTPA.[76] Further, on 8 February 2011 the government undertook to adhere strictly to and fully implement the provisions of COTPA.[77] The government also assured the High Court of Karnataka that it would consider the petitioner's proposal for a code of conduct for public officials to prevent the tobacco industry interference in developing and implementing public health policies and programmes related to tobacco control. Article 5(3) of the WHO FCTC, significantly, requires tobacco control policies to be protected from commercial and vested interests. The Delhi High Court quashed a notification whereby executive authorities had restored subsidies and exemptions to manufacturers of gutkha and chewing tobacco products.[78] The government subsequently withdrew the notification.

A film director and producer challenged the prohibition on indirect advertisements of tobacco products in films and television programmes. The Delhi High Court struck down the ban on smoking scenes in films, indicating that onscreen smoking is part of an artist's creative licence. The Court also allowed indirect advertising in print media, on the grounds that film and print media cannot be classified differently.[79] The government appealed to the Supreme Court of India, which stayed implementation of the order of the Delhi High Court.[80] After modifying the relevant rules, the government re-introduced them with effect from 14 November 2011.[81] Due to subsequent litigation and a series of discussions between the Ministry of Health and Family Welfare, the Ministry of Information and Broadcasting, and the Ministry of Law and Justice, the regulations were amended and notified again on 21 September 2012 and have now been in force since 2 October 2012.[82]

Distributors of tobacco products challenged the regulation of point-of-sale advertisements, alleging violation of the right to freedom of speech and expression under article 19(1)(a) and the right to trade under article 19(1)(g) of the *Constitution*. Enforcement of these regulations was stayed in an *ex parte* proceeding by the Bombay High Court in 2005.[83] Through civil society intervention via public interest litigation, the Supreme Court of India revoked the stay in 2013.[84]

IV ADMINISTRATIVE EFFORTS

Not only legislative and judicial efforts, but also administrative orders and decisions have supported tobacco control initiatives in India. Various government departments have contributed to the establishment of administrative mechanisms to advance tobacco control policies within their jurisdictions. Some of the key efforts at national and state levels are:

- Under a cancer control programme, the Bombay police prohibited smoking and spitting in government premises in Maharashtra in 1987.[85]
- The use of tobacco within school premises by students, teachers, parents and visitors was banned from 1995 for all Central Board of Seconday Education (CBSE) schools.[86] All national schools and Navodaya schools were told by the national government to ban sales of tobacco and tobacco products within a distance of 100 metres.[87] In 2011, all Kendriya Vidyalayas in the country were declared tobacco-free to prevent youth access and exposure to tobacco use.[88] The order prevented the use of tobacco by students, teachers and non-teaching staff in school premises during and after school hours.
- Railway authorities banned the sale of gutkha and other tobacco products including bidi and cigarettes on trains and platforms.[89]
- The Ministry of Environment and Forest prohibited the use of plastic materials in sachets for storing, packing or selling gutkha, tobacco and paan masala.[90]
- As part of the NTCP, the Ministry of Health and Family Welfare established a national toll-free number (1800 110 456) to help in recording and monitoring violations of COTPA provisions across the country.[91]
- An Inter-Ministerial Task Force on Tobacco Control has been constituted at the national level, and a National Steering Committee to take cognisance of violations of s 5 of COTPA operates under the chairmanship of the Secretary of Health.[92]
- Several administrative guidelines have been issued, including on the implementation of various provisions of COTPA and the NTCP.[93]
- Directives for state authorities have been issued from time to time to: increase taxation (value added tax) on tobacco products;[94]

undertake a monthly review of COTPA violations;[95] enforce the prohibition on direct and indirect advertising of tobacco products;[96] and impose a ban on all smokeless tobacco products[97] in line with the regulations under the FSSA and judgment of the Supreme Court of India.

- At the state level, governments have been implementing various laws and policies relating to tobacco control, including (as noted above) the prohibtion on the sale of gutkha and certain other smokeless tobacco products in 30 Indian states. Some of the other state-level initiatives include: implementation of the NTCP in 42 districts in 21 states; formation of state tobacco control cells; directives for compliance with provisions of COTPA at a district level; integration of tobacco control and prevention of non-communicable diseases (NCDs) in Andhra Pradesh; formation of a raiding squad at the district and sub-district levels in Bihar; and all districts, and collectively the state of Himachal Pradesh, declared smoke-free.

All of this has been possible with active support from the national-, state- and local-level adminstrators.[98]

V CHALLENGES: THE WAY FORWARD

Tobacco control efforts in India have leapt ahead in the last decade, but at the same time the tobacco industry has intensified its efforts to derail, dilute and delay the implementation and enforcement of tobacco control initiatives. Several key issues need to be addressed to ensure a robust and comprehensive tobacco control regime in India.

COTPA needs to be amended to include:

- provisions concerning retail licensing;
- well-framed definitions for technical terms in accordance with international standards;
- a prohibition on sale of cigarettes singly or in small packages;
- powerful enforcement mechanisms to track sale to and by minors;
- stronger pictorial warnings to appear on all main faces or principal display areas of tobacco product packages;
- removal of designated smoking areas or spaces;
- a ban on the manufacture of smokeless tobacco products; and
- the establishment of a National Tobacco Regulatory Authority with responsibility to ensure implementation of COTPA, the WHO FCTC, and other innovative tobacco control initiatives.

Apparent contradictions in trademark laws and tobacco control laws that aid indirect tobacco advertising must be resolved in favour of public health. Similar contradictions prevail under the FSSA and COTPA with regard to surrogate advertisements and brand extension of smokeless tobacco products.

All government agencies must work in tandem to thwart tobacco industry tactics to derail tobacco control initiatives. The lack of coordination in the past between the Ministry of Health and Family Welfare, the Ministry of Information and Broadcasting, and the Ministry of Law and Justice contributed to delays in implementation of regulations restricting depiction of tobacco use in films and television programmes. Coordination mechanisms must be established at all levels of governance.

Effective enforcement of laws, regulations and judicial pronouncements is a precondition to the realisation of underlying objectives. Enforcement agencies must implement the laws in spirit and to the letter.

Compliance with existing laws strengthens the overall tobacco control environment and paves the way for stronger measures. The progress achieved by the 30 states and union territories banning the sale of gutkha and paan masala containing tobacco or nicotine has given several states the impetus to ban other kinds of smokeless tobacco products as well. Taking it a step further, India is also at a stage where it is cautiously moving ahead to follow the best practices pursued by Australia and Ireland. Building on civil society efforts to support plain packaging of tobacco products in India, a member of parliament has introduced a private member's bill to amend COTPA to mandate the plain packaging of tobacco products in India.[99]

VI CONCLUSION

Legal and policy developments in tobacco control in India point to the need for a comprehensive national tobacco control policy framework with multi-sectoral involvement specifying targets, time frames and responsibilities of governmental and non-governmental stakeholders.

With the coming into effect of the *Food Safety and Standards Regulation 2011* (India), 30 states and union territories have made a concerted effort towards ending the tobacco epidemic by prohibiting the sale of gutkha (as well as paan masala and zarda in some states) – a great leap towards effective tobacco control in this country. These nationwide tobacco control efforts go a long way in shaping the global debate on the prevention and control of NCDs and present an opportune time to assess and evaluate current national and global strategies to fight NCDs and tobacco in particular.

Successful court cases for tobacco control have pointed to the hazards of tobacco and the tactics used by tobacco companies, compelled governmental action, and lent strength and support to effective compliance with tobacco control laws. Article 19 of the WHO FCTC encourages parties to strengthen legal procedures to deal with criminal and civil liability, including compensation where appropriate, to advance tobacco control. A holistic understanding of judicial pronouncements must be achieved in order to implement stronger and more effective tobacco control policies, holding the tobacco industry liable for the loss of life and property caused by tobacco use.

Lastly, governmental actions and policies must be focused to improve the health and well-being of the people of India. The government needs to plan and implement a comprehensive tobacco control policy covering all forms of tobacco products.

NOTES

1. K Srinath Reddy and Prakash Gupta (eds), *Report on Tobacco Control in India* (Ministry of Health and Family Welfare, Government of India, 2004) 6.
2. Ministry of Health and Family Welfare, Government of India, *Global Adult Tobacco Survey: India 2009–2010* (World Health Organization, 2010).
3. Ministry of Health and Family Welfare, Government of India, *Global Youth Tobacco Survey Fact Sheet: 2009* (Fact Sheet, World Health Organization, 2009).
4. K Srinath Reddy et al, 'Differences in Tobacco Use Among Young People in Urban India by Sex, Socioeconomic Status, Age, and School Grade: Assessment of Baseline Survey Data' (2006) 367 *The Lancet* 589.
5. Amenah Babar et al, 'Tobacco-Use Psychosocial Risk Profiles of Girls and Boys in Urban India: Implications for Gender-Specific Tobacco Intervention Development' (2010) 12 *Nicotine & Tobacco Research* 29.
6. Prabhat Jha et al, 'A Nationally Representative Case-Control Study of Smoking and Death in India' (2008) 358 *New England Journal of Medicine* 1137, 1146.
7. Sailesh Mohan, K Srinath Reddy and D Prabhakaran, *Chronic Non-Communicable Diseases in India: Reversing the Tide* (Public Health Foundation of India, 2011).
8. Rajesh Dikshit et al, 'Cancer Mortality in India: A Nationally Representative Survey' (2012) 379 *The Lancet* 1807.
9. Riti Shimkhada and John Peabody, 'Tobacco Control in India' (2003) 81 *Bulletin of the World Health Organization* 48.
10. Rijo John et al, 'Counting 15 Million More Poor in India, Thanks to Tobacco' (2011) 20 *Tobacco Control* 349.
11. Reddy and Gupta, above n 1, 15.
12. *Constitution of India* article 47: 'The State shall regard the raising of the level of nutrition and the standard of living of its people and the improvement of public health as among its primary duties and, in particular, the State shall endeavour to

bring about prohibition of the consumption except for medicinal purposes of intoxicating drinks and of drugs which are injurious to health'.

13. See the statement by Sardar Bhopinder Singh Man (East Punjab: Sikh) while moving his amendment motion in the Constituent Assembly on 24 November 1948: India, *Parliamentary Debates*, Constituent Assembly of India, 24 November 1948, Vol VII, 12.

14. Reddy and Gupta, above n 1, 216.

15. Ibid 236.

16. See, eg, *The Delhi Prohibition of Smokers and Non-Smokers Health Protection Act 1996* (Delhi). See also Reddy and Gupta, above n 1.

17. *Murli S Deora v Union of India* (2001) 8 SCC 765. See also Reddy and Gupta, above n 1, 180.

18. National Human Rights Commission (India), *Regional Consultation on Public Health & Human Rights: Report & Recommendations* (2001).

19. Opened for signature 16 June 2003, 2302 UNTS 166 (entered into force 27 February 2005).

20. WHO FCTC articles 6, 8, 11, 13.

21. COTPA s 7.

22. WHO FCTC article 2(1).

23. Ministry of Health and Family Welfare, Government of India, *National Tobacco Control Programme* (6 August 2012) <http://www.mohfw.nic.in/index1.php?lang=1&level=2&sublinkid=671&lid=662>.

24. Centers for Disease Control and Prevention, Global Tobacco Surveillance System Data (27 May 2011) <www.cdc.gov/features/dsglobaltobaccouse/index.html>.

25. *The Cigarettes and Other Tobacco Products (Prohibition of Advertisement and Regulation of Trade and Commerce, Production, Supply and Distribution) Act 2003* (India).

26. *Food Safety and Standards Act 2006* (India) (FSSA).

27. *Food Safety and Standards (Prohibition and Restrictions on Sales) Regulations 2011* (India) reg 2.3.4.

28. FSSA s 31.

29. *Constitution of India* article 21: 'No person shall be deprived of his life or personal liberty except according to procedure established by law'.

30. *Constitution of India* article 47: 'The State shall regard the raising of the level of nutrition and the standard of living of its people and the improvement of public health as among its primary duties and, in particular, the State shall endeavour to bring about prohibition of the consumption except for medicinal purposes of intoxicating drinks and of drugs which are injurious to health'.

31. *Bombay Police Act 1951* (Maharashtra) implemented from 1987 onwards.

32. *The Goa Prohibition of Smoking and Spitting Act 1997* (Goa).

33. *The Delhi Prohibition of Smoking and Non-Smokers Health Protection Act 1996* (Delhi).

34. *The West Bengal Prohibition of Smoking and Spitting and Protection of Health of Non-Smokers and Minors Act 2001* (West Bengal).

35. *The Tamil Nadu Prohibition of Smoking and Spitting Act 2003* (Tamil Nadu).

36. *The Assam Prohibition of Smoking and Non Smokers Health Protection Act 1999* (Assam).

37. Public service vehicle means any motor vehicle used or adapted to be used for the carriage of passengers for hire or reward, and includes a maxicab, a motorcab, contract carriage and stage carriage: *Motor Vehicles Act 1988* (India) s 2(35) (definition of 'public service vehicle').

38. See also *The Andhra Pradesh Prohibition of Smoking and Health Protection Act 2002* (Andhra Pradesh); *The Meghalaya Prohibition of Smoking and Non-Smokers*

Health Protection Act 1998 (Meghalaya); *The Sikkim Prohibition of Smoking and Non-Smokers Health Protection Act 1997* (Sikkim); *The Himachal Pradesh Prohibition of Smoking and Non-Smokers Health Protection Act* 1997 (Himachal Pradesh); *The Karnataka Prohibition of Smoking and Protection of Health of Non-Smokers Act 2001* (Karnataka).

39. Health Related Information Dissemination Amongst Youth, *Tobacco Control Laws: A Resource Manual* (3rd ed, 2010).
40. *The Poisons Act 1919* (India).
41. *The Insecticides Act 1968* (India).
42. *The Cinematograph Act 1952* (India).
43. *The Consumer Protection Act 1986* (India).
44. *The Cigarettes (Regulations of Production, Supply and Distribution) Act 1975* (India) Preamble.
45. *The Cigarettes (Regulations of Production, Supply and Distribution) Act 1975* (India) s 2(m).
46. The amendments occurred in 1990 and 2006 respectively.
47. COTPA s 4.
48. COTPA s 6.
49. COTPA ss 21, 24.
50. COTPA s 5.
51. COTPA s 22.
52. COTPA s 7.
53. COTPA s 20.
54. *Prohibition of Smoking in Public Places Rules 2008* (India) rr 2(d) (definition of 'public place'), (e) (definition of 'smoking area or space'), 4.
55. COTPA s 6.
56. COTPA s 5.
57. COTPA ss 7–11.
58. *Cigarettes and Other Tobacco Products (Packaging and Labelling) Rules 2006* (India).
59. *Cigarettes and Other Tobacco Products (Packaging and Labelling) Amendment Rules 2007* (India).
60. *Cigarettes and Other Tobacco Products (Packaging and Labelling) Amendment Rules 2009* (India).
61. *Cigarettes and Other Tobacco Products (Packaging and Labelling) Amendment Rules 2011* (India).
62. *Cigarettes and Other Tobacco Products (Prohibition of Advertisement and Regulation of Trade and Commerce, Production, Supply and Distribution) Amendment Rules 2005* (India). See also *Cigarettes and Other Tobacco Products (Prohibition of Advertisement and Regulation of Trade and Commerce, Production, Supply and Distribution) Amendment Rules 2011* (India).
63. Monika Arora et al, 'Tobacco Use in Bollywood Movies, Tobacco Promotional Activities and Their Association with Tobacco Use among Indian Adolescents' (2012) 21 *Tobacco Control* 482.
64. *Cigarettes and other Tobacco Products (Prohibition of Advertisement and Regulation of Trade and Commerce, Production, Supply and Distribution) Amendment Rules 2012* (India).
65. *Ramakrishnan v State of Kerala* AIR 1999 Ker 385 (High Court of Kerala).
66. *Murli S Deora v Union of India* (2001) 8 SCC 765.
67. COTPA.
68. *Sumaira Abdulali v Union of India*, PIL/182/2007 (High Court of Bombay).
69. *Naya Bans Sarv Vyapar Association v Union of India*, WP No 7292/2011 (High Court of Delhi).

70. *Union of India v ITC Ltd*, Diary No 28322/2008 (Supreme Court of India).
71. *Ruma Kaushik v Health Secretary*, CWP No 1223/2004 (High Court of Himachal Pradesh).
72. *Ruma Kaushik v Union of India*, CWP No 1259/2007 (High Court of Himachal Pradesh).
73. *Cigarettes and Other Tobacco Products (Packaging and Labelling) Rules 2006* (India).
74. *Health for Millions v Union of India*, CC No 22186–22187/2012 (Supreme Court of India).
75. *Amarsinh Z Choudhari v State of Gujarat*, Special Civil Application No 4848/2009 (High Court of Gujarat).
76. *Institute of Public Health v State Government of Karnataka*, WP No 27692/2010 (High Court of Karnataka).
77. Ibid.
78. *Bejon Mishra v Union of India* (2006) (High Court of Delhi).
79. *Mahesh Bhatt v Union of India*, WP No 18761/2005 (High Court of Delhi).
80. *Union of India v Mahesh Bhatt*, CC No 3709–3711/2009 (Supreme Court of India).
81. *Cigarettes and Other Tobacco Products (Prohibition of Advertisement and Regulation of Trade and Commerce, Production, Supply and Distribution) (Second Amendment) Rules 2011* (India).
82. *Cigarettes and Other Tobacco Products (Prohibition of Advertisement and Regulation of Trade and Commerce, Production, Supply and Distribution) Amendment Rules 2012* (India).
83. *Namdeo Kamathe v Union of India*, WP No 8763/2005 (High Court of Bombay); *Sridhar Kulkarni v Union of India*, WP No 6151/2005 (High Court of Bombay).
84. *Health for Millions v Union of India*, CC No 22186–22187/2012 (Supreme Court of India).
85. *Bombay Police Act 1951* (India) s 116.
86. Letter from Central Board of Secondary Education to Heads of Independent Schools Affiliated to the CBSE, *Observation of International Day against Drug Abuse and Illicit Trafficking on 26th June, 2009*, 19 June 2009 <cbse.nic.in/circulars/cir18-2009.doc>.
87. Ibid.
88. Letter from Joint Commissioner (Acad) Kendriya Vidyalaya to all the Deputy Commissioners, 13 September 2011.
89. *Indian Railways Executive Order 2011* (India).
90. *Plastic Waste (Management and Handling) Rules 2011* (India).
91. National Tobacco Control Cell, Ministry of Health and Family Welfare, Government of India, *Operational Guidelines: National Tobacco Control Programme* (2012) 27.
92. Ibid 11.
93. Ibid.
94. Letter from Additional Secretary, Ministry of Health and Family Welfare, Government of India, to the Chief Secretaries of all states, 14 March 2012.
95. Letter from Additional Secretary, Ministry of Health and Family Welfare, Government of India, to the Director General of Police of all states, 9 December 2011.
96. Letter from Special Secretary, Ministry of Health and Family Welfare, Government of India, to the Chief Secretaries of all the states and union territories of India, January 2013.
97. Letter from Special Secretary, Ministry of Health and Family Welfare, Government of India, to the Chief Secretaries of all the states and union territories of India, 21 November 2013.

98. World Health Organization Regional Office for South-East Asia, *Winners of the 2013 World No Tobacco Day Awards in the South-East Asia Region* (Media Release, 2013) <http://www.searo.who.int/entity/tobacco/wntd/wntd2013_winners/en/index.html>.
99. *Cigarettes and Other Tobacco Products (Prohibition of Advertisement and Regulation of Trade and Commerce, Production, Supply and Distribution) Amendment Bill 2012* (India).

Bibliography

BOOKS

Aaken, Anne van, *Begrenzte Rationalität und Paternalismusgefahr: Das Prinzip des schonenden Paternalismus* (Max Planck Society, 2006).

Barnett, Michael and Duvall, Raymond (eds), *Power in Global Governance* (Cambridge University Press, 2005).

Beyer, Joy de and Brigden, Linda Waverley (eds), *Tobacco Control Policy: Strategies, Successes and Setbacks* (World Bank and Research for International Tobacco Control, 2003).

Brandt, Allan, *The Cigarette Century: The Rise, Fall and Deadly Persistence of the Product that Defined America* (Basic Books, 2007).

Brown, Chester and Miles, Kate (eds), *Evolution in Investment Treaty Law and Arbitration* (Cambridge University Press, 2011).

Buckley, Christopher, *Thank You for Smoking* (Allison & Busby, 2003).

Callies, Christian and Ruffert, Matthias (eds), *EUV/AEUV: Das Verfassungsrecht der Europäischen Union mit Europäischer Grundrechtecharta – Kommentar* (CH Beck, 4th ed, 2011).

Carpenter, Daniel and Moss, David (eds), *Preventing Capture: Special Interest Influence in Regulation and How to Limit it* (Tobin Project, 2013).

Cremona, Marise (ed), *Developments in EU External Relations Law* (Oxford University Press, 2008).

Cunningham, Rob, *Smoke & Mirrors: The Canadian Tobacco War* (International Development Research Centre, 1996).

DaMatta, Roberto, *Carnivals, Rogues, and Heroes: An Interpretation of the Brazilian Dilemma* (John Drury, trans, 1991).

Davison, Mark and Horak, Ian, *Shanahan's Australian Law of Trade Marks and Passing Off* (Thomson Reuters, 2012).

Ehlers, Dirk, *European Fundamental Rights and Freedoms* (Walter de Gruyter, 2007).

Ehlers, Dirk (ed), *Europäische Grundrechte und Grundfreiheiten* (Walter de Gruyter, 3rd ed, 2009).

Faraldo, Marcelo Rodríguez and Zilocchi, Hugo, *Historia del Cultivo del Tabaco en Salta* (Ministerio de Agricultura, 2012).

Fauchald, Ole Kristian and Nollkaemper, André (eds), *The Practice of International and National Courts and the (De-)Fragmentation of International Law* (Hart Publishing, 2012).

Fenton Cooper, Andrew and Kirton, John J (eds), *Innovation in Global Health Governance: Critical Cases* (Ashgate, 2009).

Fitzmaurice, Malgosia and Sarooshi, Dan, *Issues of State Responsibility before International Judicial Institutions* (Hart, 2004).

Frenz, Walter, *Handbuch Europarecht Vol 1 – Europäische Grundfreiheiten* (Springer, 2004).

Goldsmith, Jack and Posner, Eric, *The Limits of International Law* (Oxford University Press, 2005).

Gostin, Lawrence, *Public Health Law: Power, Duty, Restraint* (University of California, 2008).

Gruszczynski, Lukasz, *Regulating Health and Environmental Risks under WTO Law. A Critical Analysis of the SPS Agreement* (Oxford University Press, 2010).

Gugler, Philippe and Chaisse, Julien (eds) *Competitiveness of the ASEAN Countries, Corporate and Regulatory Drivers* (Edward Elgar Publishing, 2010).

Helmke, Gretchen and Levitsky, Steven, *Informal Institutions and Democracy: Lessons from Latin America* (Johns Hopkins University Press, 2006).

Heselhaus, Sebastian and Nowak, Carsten (eds), *Handbuch der Europäischen Grundrechte* (CH Beck, 2006).

Hilf, Eberhard Grabitz Meinhard and Nettesheim, Martin (eds), *Das Recht der Europäischen Union* (CH Beck, 46th ed, 2011).

Hilgers, Simone Susanne, *Plain Packaging, Vereinbarkeit mit deutschen, unionsrechtlichen und völkerrechtlichen Vorgaben* (Dr Kovac, 2013).

Hirschhorn, Norbert, *Evolution of the Tobacco Industry Positions on Addiction to Nicotine* (World Health Organization, 2008).

Huerta-Goldman, Jorge, Romanetti, Antoine and Stirnimann Fuentes, Franz (eds), *WTO Litigation, Investment and Commercial Arbitration: Cross-fertilization and Reciprocal Opportunities* (Kluwer, 2013).

Inghelram, Jan, *Legal and Institutional Aspects of the European Anti-Fraud Office (OLAF): An Analysis with a Look Forward to a European Public Prosecutor's Office* (Europa, 2011).

Jarass, Hans, *EU-Grundrechte* (CH Beck, 2005).

Jarass, Hans, *New Dimensions of Tobacco Regulation and Fundamental Rights and Freedoms: Basic Questions of Brand Packaging, Product Display and Product Ingredients* (lexxion, 2012).

Jha, Prabhat and Chaloupka, Frank, *Curbing the Epidemic: Governments and the Economics of Tobacco Control* (World Bank, 1999).

Jha, Prabhat and Chaloupka, Frank (eds), *Tobacco Control in Developing Countries* (Oxford University, 2000).

Kawachi, Ichiro and Wamala, Sarah (eds), *Globalization and Health* (Oxford University Press, 2006).

Kelsey, Jane, *Serving Whose Interests? The Political Economy of Trade in Services Agreements* (Routledge, 2008).

Kelsey, Jane (ed), *No Ordinary Deal: Unmasking the Trans-Pacific Partnership Free Trade Agreement* (Allen & Unwin, 2010).

Li, Chen-Shan (ed), *Plurality, Tolerance, and the Protection of Human Rights: Focusing on the Protection of Non-Enumerated Rights* (Angle, 2005).

Lim, CL, Elms, Deborah and Low, Patrick (eds), *The Trans-Pacific Partnership: A Quest for a Twenty-first Century Trade Agreement* (Cambridge University Press, 2012).

Mackay, Judith and Eriksen, Michael, *The Tobacco Atlas* (World Health Organization, 1st ed, 2002).

McGrady, Benn, *Confronting the Tobacco Epidemic in a New Era of Trade and Investment Liberalization* (World Health Organization, 2012).

Mistelis, Loukas (ed), *Concise International Arbitration* (Kluwer Law International, 2010).

Mohan, Sailesh, Reddy, K Srinath and Prabhakaran, D, *Chronic Non-Communicable Diseases in India: Reversing the Tide* (Public Health Foundation of India, 2011).

Montt, Santiago, *State Liability in Investment Treaty Arbitration: Global Constitutional and Administrative Law in the BIT Generation* (Hart, 2009).

Nino, Carlos Santiago, *Un país al margen de la ley* (Emecé Editores, 1992).

Nowak, Celina (ed), *Fight against EU Fraud: Administrative and Criminal Law Issues* (LEX, 2011).

Öberg, Mattias et al, *Global Estimate of the Burden of Disease from Second-hand Smoke* (World Health Organization, 2010).

Proctor, Robert, *Golden Holocaust: Origins of the Cigarette Catastrophe and the Case for Abolition* (University of California Press, 2011).

Rawls, John, *Justice as Fairness: A Restatement* (Harvard University, 2001).

Reed, Lucy, Paulsson, Jan and Blackaby, Nigel, *Guide to ICSID Arbitration* (Kluwer Law International, 2011).

Rengeling, Hans-Werner and Szczekalla, Peter, *Grundrechte in der Europäischen Union – Charta der Grundrechte und Allgemeine Rechtsgrundsätze* (Carl Heymanns Verlag, 2004).

Roemer, Ruth, *Legislative Action to Combat the World Smoking Epidemic* (World Health Organization, 1982).

Roemer, Ruth, *Legislative Action to Combat the World Tobacco Epidemic* (World Health Organization, 2nd ed, 1993).

Schweitzer, Michael, Bock, Yves and Schroeder, Werner, *EG-Binnenmarkt und Gesundheitsschutz – Am Beispiel der neuen Tabakrichtlinie der Europäischen Gemeinschaft* (Verlag Recht und Wirtschaft, 2002).

Shafey, Omar, Dolwick, Suzanne and Guindon, G Emmanuel (eds), *Tobacco Control Country Profiles* (American Cancer Society, 2nd ed, 2003).

Stefanou, Constantin, White, Simone and Xanthaki, Helen, *OLAF at the Crossroads: Action against EU Fraud* (Hart Publishing, 2011).

Sunstein, Cass, *Worst-case Scenarios* (Harvard University Press, 2009).

Villegas, Mauricio García, *Normas de papel: La cultura del incumplimiento* (Siglo del Hombre Editores, 2010).

Voon, Tania (ed), *Trade Liberalisation and International Co-operation: A Legal Analysis of the Trans-Pacific Partnership Agreement* (Edward Elgar, 2013).

Voon, Tania, Mitchell, Andrew and Jonathan Liberman with Ayres, Glyn (eds), *Public Health and Plain Packaging of Cigarettes: Legal Issues* (Edward Elgar, 2012).

Waibel, Michael et al (eds), *The Backlash against Investment Arbitration: Perceptions and Reality* (Kluwer Law International, 2010).

Wu, Chuan-Feng (ed), *Biennial Review of Law, Science and Technology: Health, Science and Human Rights 2011* (Academia Sinica, 2012).

JOURNAL ARTICLES

Abascal, Winston et al, 'Tobacco Control Campaign in Uruguay: a Population-based Trend Analysis' (2012) 380(9853) *The Lancet* 1575.

Abbott, Kenneth et al, 'The Concept of Legalization' (2000) 54 *International Organization* 401.

Abramson, Brian Dean, 'Let Them Eat Smoke: The Case for Exempting the Tobacco Industry from Antitrust' (2008) 6 *Cardozo Public Law, Policy and Ethics Journal* 345.

Acevedo, Domingo, 'Relación entre el Derecho Internacional y el Derecho Interno' (1992) 16 *Revista IIDH* 133.

Agius, Maria, 'Strategies and Success in Litigation and Negotiation in the WTO' (2012) 17 *International Negotiation* 139.

Alemanno, Alberto, 'Out of Sight, Out of Mind – Towards a New EU Tobacco Products Directive' (2012) 18 *Columbia Journal of European Law* 197.

Alemanno, Alberto and Bonadio, Enrico, 'Do You Mind My Smoking? Plain Packaging of Cigarettes under the TRIPS Agreement' (2011) 10(3) *The John Marshall Review of Intellectual Property Law* 451.

Appleberry, Robin, 'Breaking the Camel's Back: Bringing Women's Human Rights to Bear on Tobacco Control' (2001) 13 *Yale Journal of Law & Feminism* 71.

Arora, Monika et al, 'Tobacco Use in Bollywood Movies, Tobacco Promotional Activities and Their Association with Tobacco Use among Indian Adolescents' (2012) 21 *Tobacco Control* 482.

Babar, Amenah et al, 'Tobacco-use Psychosocial Risk Profiles of Girls and Boys in Urban India: Implications for Gender-specific Tobacco Intervention Development' (2010) 12 *Nicotine & Tobacco Research* 29.

Banthin, Christopher and Daynard, Richard, 'Room for Two in Tobacco Control: Limits on the Preemptive Scope of the Proposed Legislation Granting FDA Oversight of Tobacco' (2008) 11 *Journal of Health Care Law & Policy* 57.

Barker, Kevin Gauntt, 'Thank You for Regulating: Why Philip Morris's Embrace of FDA Regulation Helps the Company but Harms the Agency' (2009) 61 *Administrative Law Review* 197.

Barreto, Sandhi, et al, 'Epidemiology in Latin America and the Caribbean: Current Situation and Challenges' (2012) 41 *International Journal of Epidemiology* 557.

Bates, Clive, 'Developing Countries Take the Lead on WHO Convention' (2001) 10 *Tobacco Control* 204.

Bélanger, Louis and Fontaine-Skronski, Kim, '"Legalization" in International Relations: A Conceptual Analysis' (2012) 51 *Social Science Information* 238.

Bettcher, Douglas W et al, 'International Law and Health, Two Approaches: The World Health Organization's Tobacco Initiative and International Drug Controls' (2000) 94 *Proceedings of the Annual Meeting of the American Society of International Law* 193.

Bollyky, Thomas and Gostin, Lawrence, 'The United States' Engagement in Global Tobacco Control: Proposals for Comprehensive Funding and Strategies' (2010) 304(23) *Journal of the American Medical Association* 2637.

Boyle, Peter et al, 'Measuring Progress against Cancer in Europe: Has the 15% Decline Targeted for 2000 Come About?' (2003) 14 *Annals of Oncology* 1312.

Buchanan, Mark, 'Public Policy and International Commercial Arbitration' (1998) 26 *American Business Law Journal* 514.

Bump, Christine, 'Close but no Cigar: The WHO Framework Convention on Tobacco Control's Futile Ban on Tobacco Advertising' (2003) 17 *Emory International Law Review* 1251.

Burci, Gian Luca, 'Introductory Note to WHO: Framework Convention on Tobacco Control' (2003) 42 *International Legal Materials* 515.

Cabrera, Oscar and Carballo, Juan, 'Tobacco Control Litigation: Broader Impacts on Health Rights Adjudication' (2013) 41(1) *The Journal of Law, Medicine & Ethics, American Society of Law, Medicine & Ethics* 157.

Cabrera, Oscar and Gostin, Lawrence, 'Human Rights and the Framework Convention on Tobacco Control: Mutually Reinforcing Systems' (2011) 7(3) *International Journal of Law in Context* 285.

Cabrera, Oscar and Madrazo, Alejandro, 'Human Rights as a Tool for Tobacco Control in Latin America' (2010) 52 *Salud Pública de México* S288.

Carrubba, Clifford and Gabel, Matthew, 'Courts, Compliance, and the Quest for Legitimacy in International Law' (2013) 14 *Theoretical Inquiries in Law* 505.

Chaloupka, Frank et al, 'Prices, Policies and Youth Smoking' (2003) 98 *Addiction* 105.

Chaloupka, Frank et al, 'The Economics of Tobacco Control' (2005) 63 *Briefing Notes in Economics* 1.

Chang, Fong-ching et al, 'Effects of Financing Smoking Cessation Outpatient Services in Taiwan' (2008) 17 *Tobacco Control* 183.

Chang, Fong-ching et al, 'The Impact of Graphic Cigarette Warning Labels and Smoke-free Law on Health Awareness and Thoughts of Quitting in Taiwan' (2011) 26 *Health Education Research* 179.

Charoenca, Naowarut et al, 'Success Counteracting Tobacco Company Interference in Thailand: An Example of FCTC Implementation for Low- and Middle-income Countries' (2012) 9 *International Journal of Environmental Research and Public Health* 1111.

Chen, Chung-Lin, 'In Search of a New Approach of Information Privacy Judicial Review: Interpretation No 603 of Taiwan's Constitutional Court as a Guide' (2010) 20 *Indiana International & Comparative Law Review* 21.

Chuang, Shu-hui and Huang, Song-Lih, 'Changes in Smoking Behavior among College Students Following Implementation of a Strict Campus Smoking Policy in Taiwan' (2012) 57 *International Journal of Public Health* 199.

Clark, Margaret, 'Cigar, Cigarette, and Loose Tobacco Taxes: Increase Excise Tax Rate on Little Cigars, C Cigars, and Cigarettes and Impose Excise Tax on Loose Tobacco' (2003) 20 *Georgia State University Law Review* 233.

Collin, Jeff, 'Tobacco Politics' (2004) 47(2) *Development* 91.

Crescenti, Marcelo, 'The New Tobacco World' (1998) 3 *Tobacco Journal International* 51.

Cunningham, Rob and Kyle, Ken, 'The Case for Plain Packaging' (1995) 4 *Tobacco Control* 80.

Davidson, Patricia, 'Tobacco Ingredients and Smoke Constituent Reporting and Disclosure Law: The Case for Expansion' (1999) 77 *Denver University Law Review* 1.

Davison, Mark, 'Plain Packaging and the TRIPS Agreement: A Response to Professor Gervais' (2013) 23 *Australian Intellectual Property Journal* 160.

Di Franza, Joseph et al, 'RJR Nabisco's Cartoon Camel Promotes Camel Cigarettes to Children' (1991) 22 *The Journal of the American Medical Association* 3149.

Dikshit, Rajesh et al, 'Cancer Mortality in India: A Nationally Representative Survey' (2012) 379 *The Lancet* 1807.

Doll, Richard and Peto, Richard, 'Mortality in Relation to Smoking: 20 Years' Observation on Male British Doctors' (1976) 2 *British Medical Journal* 1525.

Doll, Richard et al, 'Mortality in Relation to Smoking: 40 Years' Observations on Male British Doctors' (1994) 309 *British Medical Journal* 901.

Doll, Richard et al, 'Mortality in Relation to Smoking: 50 Years' Observations on Male British Doctors' (2004) 328 *British Medical Journal* 1519.

Dorotheo, Ulysses, 'A Ray of Sunshine for Use of Revenues for Tobacco Control: Dedicating Revenues to Tobacco Control Programmes' (2012) 122 *Bulletin* 3.

Efroymson, Debra et al, 'Hungry for Tobacco: An Analysis of the Economic Impact of Tobacco Consumption on the Poor in Bangladesh' (2001) 10 *Tobacco Control* 212.

Fong, Geoffrey, Hammond, David and Hitchman, Sara, 'The Impact of Pictures on the Effectiveness of Tobacco Warnings' (2009) 87 *Bulletin of the World Health Organization* 640.

Gau, Michael Sheng-ti, 'The Legal Controversies between China and Taiwan in the WHO from the Perspectives of an International Law Scholar in Taiwan' (2008) 1 *Journal of East Asia & International Law* 159.

Germain, Daniella, Wakefield, Melanie and Durkin, Sarah, 'Adolescents' Perceptions of Cigarette Brand Image: Does Plain Packaging Make a Difference?' (2010) 46 *Journal of Adolescent Health* 385.

Gleeson, Deborah and Friel, Sharon, 'Emerging Threats to Public Health from Regional Trade Agreements' (2013) 381 *The Lancet* 1507.

Global Youth Tobacco Survey Collaborating Group, 'Differences in Worldwide Tobacco Use by Gender: Findings from the Global Youth Tobacco Survey' (2003) 73 *Journal of School Health* 207.

Goldstein, Judith and Martin, Lisa, 'Legalization, Trade Liberalization, and Domestic Politics: A Cautionary Note' (2000) 54 *International Organization* 603.

Gostin, Lawrence, 'Conceptualizing the Field after September 11th: Foreword to a Symposium on Public Health Law' (2002) 90 *Kentucky Law Journal* 791.

Hacker, Jacob, 'The Road to Somewhere: Why Health Reform Happened' (2010) 8 *Perspectives on Politics* 861.

Haile, Andrew, 'Sin Taxes: When the State Becomes the Sinner' (2009) 82 *Temple Law Review* 1041.

Hamilton, William et al, 'Who Supports Tobacco Excise Taxes? Factors Associated with Towns' and Individuals' Support in Massachusetts' (2005) 11(4) *Journal of Public Health Management Practice* 333.

Hammond, E Cuyler and Seidmen, Herbert, 'Smoking and Cancer in the United States' (1980) 9 *Preventive Medicine* 169.

Hammond, Ross, 'Consolidation in the Tobacco Industry' (1998) 7 *Tobacco Control* 426.

Hardach, Felix and Ludwigs, Markus, 'Die Novellierung der Warnhinweispflicht für Tabakerzeugnisse im Lichte der negative Meinungsfreiheit – Eine grundrechtliche Neubewertung' (2007) 7 *Die Öffentliche Verwaltung* 288.

Helfer, Laurence and Slaughter, Anne-Marie, 'Why States Create International Tribunals: A Response to Professors Posner and Yoo' (2005) 93 *California Law Review* 899.

Hodge, James and Eber, Gabriel, 'Tobacco Control Legislation: Tools for Public Health Improvement' (2004) 32 *Journal of Law, Medicine & Ethics* 516.

Hohfeld, Wesley Newcomb, 'Some Fundamental Legal Conceptions as Applied in Judicial Reasoning' (1913) 23(1) *The Yale Law Journal* 16.

Horst, Matthias and Bergmann, Joachim, 'Erklärung des Rechtsausschusses des Bundes für Lebensmittelrecht eV (BLL) zu Einheitspackung als Instrument des Vebraucherschutzes' (2012) 4 *Zeitschrift für das gesamte Lebensmittelrecht* 405.

Jacob, Gregory, 'Without Reservation' (2004) 5 *Chicago Journal of International Law* 287.

Janušauskaitė, Kristina, 'Litauen – A Proposal to Introduce "Plain Packaging Requirement" in the Law on Tobacco Control Fails in Parliament' (2010) 10 *Gerwerblicher Rechtsschutz und Urheberrecht Internationaler Teil* 908.

Jha, Prabhat et al, 'A Nationally Representative Case-control Study of Smoking and Death in India' (2008) 358 *New England Journal of Medicine* 1137.

John, Rijo et al, 'Counting 15 Million More Poor in India, Thanks to Tobacco' (2011) 20 *Tobacco Control* 349.

Kan, Yu-Bing, 'A Study on Protection of Fetus and Young Children's Health Rights – Focusing on the Proposal for Suppression Legislation of Tobacco Hazards' (2003) 4 *Journal of Children Welfare* 43.

Kaplin, Lauren, 'A National Strategy to Combat the Childhood Obesity Epidemic' (2011) 15 *UC Davis Journal of Juvenile Law & Policy* 347.

Keller, L Robin, Simon, Jay and Wang, Yitong, 'Multiple Objective Decision Analysis Involving Multiple Stakeholders' (2009) *Tutorials in Operations Research* 139.

Kelsey, Jane, 'The Trans-Pacific Partnership Agreement: A Gold-Plated Gift to the Global Tobacco Industry?' (2013) 39 *American Journal of Law & Medicine* 237.

Koh, Harold Hongu, 'The 1998 Frankel Lecture: Bringing International Law Home' (1998) 35 *Houston Law Review* 623.

Lester, Simon, 'Free Trade and Tobacco: Thank You for Not Smoking (Foreign) Cigarettes' (15 August 2012) 49 *Free Trade Bulletin* 1.

Levy, David et al, 'Smoking-related Deaths Averted Due to Three Years of Policy Progress' (2013) 91 *Bulletin of the World Health Organization* 509.

Liaw, Kuo-Meng and Chen, C, 'Mortality Attributable to Cigarette Smoking in Taiwan: A 12-Year-Follow-Up Study' (1998) 7 *Tobacco Control* 141.

Liberman, Jonathan et al, 'Opportunities and Risks of the Proposed FCTC Protocol on Illicit Trade' (2011) 20 *Tobacco Control* 436.

Liberman, Jonathan, 'Combating Counterfeit Medicines and Illicit Trade in Tobacco Products: Minefields in Global Health Governance' (2012) *Journal of Law, Medicine and Ethics* 326.

Liberman, Jonathan, 'Four COPs and Counting: Achievements, Under-achievements and Looming Challenges in the Early Life of the WHO FCTC Conference of the Parties' (2012) 21 *Tobacco Control* 215.

Lin, Chih-Chieh, 'Regulating Pregnancy in Taiwan: An Analysis from an Asian Legal Feminist Using Feminist Legal Theories' (2009) 39 *University of Baltimore Law Forum* 204.

Lin, Ming-hsin, 'The Right to Health: Based on the Protective Obligation of the State' (2005) 32 *Law Forum* 26.

Lin, Tsai-yu, 'Compulsory License for Access to Medicines, Expropriation and Investor-State Arbitration under Bilateral Investment

Agreements: Are There Issues beyond the TRIPS Agreement?' (2009) 40 *IIC-International Review of Intellectual Property and Competition Law* 167.

Lin, Tsai-yu, 'Systemic Reflections on Argentina's Non-compliance with ICSID Arbitral Awards: A New Role of the Annulment Committee at Enforcement?' (2012) 5 *Contemporary Asia Arbitration Journal* 1.

Liu, Chien-Hung, 'The Analysis of Tobacco Hazards Prevention Act 2007' (2007) 150 *Taiwan Law Review* 186.

Lo, Chang-fa, 'Establishing Global Governance in the Implementation of FCTC: Some Reflections on the Current Two-pillar and One-roof Framework' (2006) 1 *Asian Journal of WTO & International Health Law and Policy* 569.

Lo, Chang-fa, 'Principles and Criteria for International and Transnational Public Policies in Commercial Arbitration' (2008) 1 *Contemporary Asia Arbitration Journal* 82.

Lo, Chang-fa, 'External Regime Coherence: WTO/BIT and Public Health Tension as an Illustration' (2012) *Asian Journal of WTO and International Health Law and Policy* 263.

Lo, Chang-fa, 'Plain Packaging and Indirect Expropriation of Trademark Rights under BITs' (2012) 32 *Medicine and Law Journal* 521.

Lomnitz, Claudio, 'La construcción de la ciudadanía en México' (2000) 4 *Metapolítica* 128.

MacKay, Judith, Rithhiphakdee, Bungon and Reddy, K Srinath, 'Tobacco Control in Asia' (2013) 381(9877) *The Lancet* 1581.

Mackey, Tim, Liang, Bryan and Novotny, Thomas, 'Evolution of Tobacco Labeling and Packaging: International Legal Considerations and Health Governance' (2013) 103(4) *American Journal of Public Health* e39.

Mamudu, Hadii and Glantz, Stanton, 'Civil Society and the Negotiation of the Framework Convention on Tobacco Control' (2004) 4(2) *Global Public Health* 150.

Mamudu, Hadii, Hammond, Ross and Glantz, Stanton, 'International Trade versus Public Health during the FCTC Negotiations, 1999-2003' (2011) 20(1) *Tobacco Control* e3.

Matz-Lück, Nele, 'Framework Conventions as Regulatory Tools' (2009) 1 *Goettingen Journal of International Law* 439.

Mitchell, Andrew and Wurzberger, Sebastian, 'Boxed in? Australia's Plain Tobacco Packaging Initiative and International Investment Law' (2011) 27(4) *Arbitration International* 623.

Moodie, Crawford et al, 'Young People's Perceptions of Cigarette Packaging and Plain Packaging: An Online Survey' (2012) 1 *Nicotine & Tobacco Research* 98.

Muller, Fernando and Wehbe, Luis, 'Smoking and Smoking Cessation in Latin America: A Review of the Current Situation and Available Treatments' (2008) 3 *International Journal of Chronic Obstructive Pulmonary Disease* 285.

Nix, Andrew, 'Statutory Disclosure of Tobacco Ingredients: Secrets Up in Smoke?' (2003) 54 *Alabama Law Review* 1413.

Novotny, T and Carlin, D, 'Ethical and Legal Aspects of Tobacco Control' (2005) 14 (supplement 2) *Tobacco Control* ii26.

O'Connor, Richard et al, 'What Would Menthol Smokers Do If Menthol in Cigarettes Were Banned? Behavioral Intentions and Simulated Demand' (2012) 107 *Addiction* 1330.

Onzivu, William, 'The Public Health Implications of the Association of Southeast Asian Nations (ASEAN) Legal Regime on Tobacco Control' (2002) 4(2) *Australian Journal of Asian Law* 160.

Oriola, Taiwo, 'Ethical and Legal Analyses of Policy Tobacco Smoking in Enclosed Public Spaces' (2009) 37 *Journal of Law, Medicine & Ethics* 828.

Pasche, Eckhard and Roesch, Franziska, 'Europäischer Grundrechtsschutz nach Lissabon – die Rolle der EMRK und der Grundrechtecharta in der EU' (2008) *Europäische Zeitschrift für Wirtschaftsrecht* 519.

Pauling, Reinhard, 'Nichtraucherschutz in der EU soll verbessert werden' (2010) 2 *Europäische Zeitschrift für Wirtschaftsrecht* 42.

Picco, Louisa et al, 'Smoking and Nicotine Dependence in Singapore: Findings from a Cross-sectional Epidemiological Study' (2012) 41 *Annals Academy of Medicine* 325.

Posner, Eric and Yoo, John, 'Judicial Independence in International Tribunals' (2005) *California Law Review* 1.

Prindle, David, 'Importing Concepts from Biology into Political Science: The Case of Punctuated Equilibrium' (2012) 40 *Policy Studies Journal* 21.

Reddy, K Srinath et al, 'Differences in Tobacco Use Among Young People in Urban India by Sex, Socioeconomic Status, Age, and School Grade: Assessment of Baseline Survey Data' (2006) 367 *The Lancet* 589.

Roberts, Anthea, 'Power and Persuasion in Investment Treaty Interpretation: The Dual Role of States' (2010) 104 *American Journal of International Law* 179.

Roemer, Ruth, Taylor, Allyn and Lariviere, Jean, 'Origins of the WHO Framework Convention on Tobacco Control' (2005) 95 *American Journal of Public Health* 936.

Rogot, Eugene and Murray, James, 'Smoking and Causes of Death among U.S. Veterans: 16 Years of Observation' (1980) 95 *Public Health Reports* 213.

Sadeleer, Nicolas de, 'Procedures for Derogation from the Principle of Approximation of Laws under Article 95 EC' (2003) 40 *Common Market Law Review* 889.

Scheffels, Janne and Sæbø, Gunnar, 'Perceptions of Plain and Branded Cigarette Packaging among Norwegian Youth and Adults: A Focus Group Study' (2012) 2 *Nicotine & Tobacco Research* 450.

Sebrie, Ernesto et al, 'Tobacco Industry Successfully Prevented Tobacco Control Legislation in Argentina' (2005) 14 *Tobacco Control* e2.

Shi, Hui-ling, 'Fetal and Children's Protection under the Tobacco Hazard Control Act – An Opinion from the Expert' (2004) 294 *Taipei Bar Journal* 15.

Shih, Shu-Fang et al, 'An Investigation of the Smoking Behaviours of Parents Before, During and After the Birth of Their Children in Taiwan' (2008) 8 *BMC Public Health* 67.

Shimkhada, Riti and Peabody, John, 'Tobacco Control in India' (2003) 81 *Bulletin of the World Health Organization* 48.

Shmatenko, Leonid, 'Verfassungsmäßigkeit von Einheitsverpackungen (*Plain Packaging*) bei Zigaretten' (2013) 35 *Jura* 74.

Siekmann, Helmut, 'Verfassungsmäßigkeit eines umfassenden Verbots der Werbung für Tabakprodukte' (2003) 16 *Die Öffentliche Verwaltung* 662.

Tauras, John et al, 'Menthol and Non-menthol Smoking: The Impact of Prices and Smoke-free Air Laws' (2010) 105 *Addiction* 115.

Taylor, Allyn, 'Making the World Health Organization Work: A Legal Framework for Universal Access to the Conditions for Health' (1992) 18 *American Journal of Law & Medicine* 301.

Taylor, Allyn, 'An International Regulatory Strategy for Global Tobacco Control' (1996) 21 *Yale Journal of International Law* 257.

Tyler, Michele, 'Blowing Smoke: Do Smokers Have a Right? Limiting the Privacy Rights of Cigarette Smokers' (1998) 86 *Georgetown Law Journal* 783.

Vardavas, Constantine et al, 'Tobacco Taxation: The Importance of Earmarking the Revenue to Health Care and Tobacco Control' (2012) 10 *Tobacco-Induced Diseases* 21.

Volden, Craig and Wiseman, Alan, 'Breaking Gridlock: The Determinants of Health Policy Change in Congress' (2011) 36 *Journal of Health Politics, Policy and Law* 227.

Voon, Tania, 'International Decision: *United States – Measures Affecting the Production and Sale of Clove Cigarettes*' (2012) 106(4) *American Journal of International Law* 824.

Voon, Tania, 'Flexibilities in WTO Law to Support Tobacco Control Regulation' (2013) 39 *American Journal of Law & Medicine* 199.

Voon, Tania and Mitchell, Andrew, 'Face Off: Assessing WTO Challenges to Australia's Scheme for Plain Tobacco Packaging' (2011) 22(3) *Public Law Review* 218.

Voon, Tania and Mitchell, Andrew, 'Time to Quit? Assessing International Investment Claims against Plain Tobacco Packaging in Australia' (2011) 14(3) *Journal of International Economic Law* 515.

Warner, Kenneth et al, 'Determining an Optimal Cigarette Tax: The Economist's Perspective' (1995) 4 *Tobacco Control* 380.

Weiss, Andrew and Woodhouse, Edward, 'Reframing Incrementalism: A Constructive Response to the Critics' (1992) 25 *Policy Sciences* 255.

Wen, Chi-pang, 'Facilitating the Critical Process in Tobacco Control' (2005) 14 *Tobacco Control* i1.

Wen, Chi-pang et al, 'Smoking Attributable Mortality for Taiwan and Its Projection to 2020 under Different Smoking Scenarios' (2005) 14 *Tobacco Control* i76.

Wen, Chi-pang et al, 'The Framework Convention on Tobacco Control – Article 14 "Demand Reduction" (Smoking Cessation) – The Weakest Link of FCTC in Asia' (2010) 5(2) *Asian Journal of WTO & International Health Law and Policy* 381.

White, Anna, 'Controlling Big Tobacco: The Winning Campaign for a Global Tobacco Control Treaty' (2004) 25(1/2) *Multinational Monitor* 13.

Wu, Chuan-Feng, 'State Responsibility for Tobacco Control: The Right to Health Perspective' (2008) 3(2) *Asian Journal of WTO & International Health Law and Policy* 379.

Yerger, VB and Malone, RE, 'African American Leadership Groups: Smoking with the Enemy' (2002) 11 *Tobacco Control* 336.

Zhiyong, Xie, 'A Fiction: The Right or Freedom of Smoking' (2013) 8(1) *Asian Journal of WTO & International Health Law and Policy* 149.

Ziegenaus, Fabian, 'No Logo? Pläne der EU-Kommission zu Zigaretten in Einheitsverpackungen auf dem Prüfstand' (2010) 21 *Gewerblicher Rechtsschutz und Urheberrecht. Praxis im Immaterialgüter- und Wettbewerbsrecht* 475.

Index